MORALITIES OF DRONE VIOLENCE

For Bree and Henry

MORALITIES OF DRONE VIOLENCE

Christian Enemark

EDINBURGH
University Press

Edinburgh University Press is one of the leading university
presses in the UK. We publish academic books and journals
in our selected subject areas across the humanities and social
sciences, combining cutting-edge scholarship with high
editorial and production values to produce academic works
of lasting importance. For more information visit our website:
edinburghuniversitypress.com

We are committed to making research available to a wide
audience and are pleased to be publishing an Open Access
ebook edition of this title.

Edinburgh University Press Ltd
13 Infirmary Street
Edinburgh EH1 1LT

First published in hardback by Edinburgh University Press 2023

Typeset in 11/13 Adobe Sabon by
IDSUK (DataConnection) Ltd

A CIP record for this book is available from the British Library

ISBN 978 1 4744 9008 5 (hardback)
ISBN 978 1 4744 9009 2 (paperback)
ISBN 978 1 4744 9010 8 (webready PDF)
ISBN 978 1 4744 9011 5 (epub)

CONTENTS

Acknowledgements   vi

List of Abbreviations   vii

1   Introduction: Armed Drones and Drone Violence   1

2   Warfare   26

3   Violent Law Enforcement   53

4   The Problem of 'Grey' Drone Violence   93

5   Tele-intimate Violence   123

6   Devolved Violence   161

7   Conclusion: Drone Violence and the Scope for Future Restraint   200

Bibliography   204

Index   247

ACKNOWLEDGEMENTS

Research for this book was supported by funding from the European Research Council, under the European Union's Horizon 2020 research and innovation programme, for the 'Emergent Ethics of Drone Violence: Toward a Comprehensive Governance Framework' (DRONETHICS) project (ERC-CoG-2017 grant no. 771082).

While writing this book, I was often inspired by ideas advanced by the two postdoctoral research fellows who joined me on the DRONETHICS project: Thompson Chengeta and Lindsay Clark. I am grateful also for the advice and encouragement I received in conversation or correspondence with Nilza Amaral, Daniele Amoroso, Russell Bentley, Christian Braun, Max Brookman-Byrne, Dan Brunstetter, Peter Burt, Toni Cerkez, Chris Cole, Jen Daly, Dan Devine, Ben Donaldson, Jessica Dorsey, Alex Edney-Browne, John Emery, Jeanne Frebault, Chris Fuller, Roger Gardner, Tom Gregory, Caroline Holmqvist, Gerry Hughes, Jesse Kirkpatrick, Nina Kollars, Sarah Kreps, Shaun Lamb, Peter Lee, Brian McElwee, Denis McManus, Elizabeth Minor, Iain Overton, David Owen, Doug Pryer, Gopal Ramchurn, Regina Rauxloh, Malte Riemann, Cristina Rotaru, Matt Ryan, Jim Scanlan, Eileen Schell, Elisabeth Schröder-Butterfill, Elke Schwarz, Rob Sparrow, Tracy Strong, Adrian Viens and Alan Wong.

Most of all, I thank my wife and son for their constant patience and support.

LIST OF ABBREVIATIONS

AI	artificial intelligence
CCW	Convention on Certain Conventional Weapons
CIA	Central Intelligence Agency
FATA	Federally Administered Tribal Areas
HMI	human–machine interaction
IACP	International Association of Chiefs of Police
IHL	international humanitarian law
IHRL	international human rights law
LAWS	lethal autonomous weapon system
MHC	meaningful human control
PTSD	post-traumatic stress disorder
RAF	Royal Air Force
UN	United Nations
USAF	United States Air Force

Chapter 1

INTRODUCTION: ARMED DRONES AND DRONE VIOLENCE

Qasem Soleimani died in Iraq on 3 January 2020 when the Iranian general's vehicle was struck by two missiles on a quiet road near Baghdad International Airport. With authorisation from the then-president of the United States, Donald Trump, the missiles had been launched by the remote operators of a MQ-9 Reaper drone aircraft flying overhead. Nine other people were killed in the attack: four Iranian officers and five members of the Iraqi Popular Mobilisation Forces.[1] US intelligence officials had earlier managed to obtain secret details of Soleimani's visit to Iraq,[2] enabling the timely positioning of the Reaper. Then, for the first time, an armed drone was used by one state against a high-level official of another state on the territory of a third state. An international killing had occurred without any need for the killers to leave the United States, and without any immediate risk of their being discovered, captured and questioned by foreign authorities. Consequently, it has remained unclear what those US-based drone operators understood about what they were doing and what kind of violence they were perpetrating on this occasion. Was this drone strike against a foreign general from an unfriendly country an act of war, or was it an instance of 'use of force below the threshold of war'?[3] Was it intended, in the manner of an intervention by armed police officers, to prevent an imminent and violent threat to public safety inside Iraq? Was the strike rather a means of punishing someone who was guilty of committing crimes against Americans? Or was it none, or somehow all, of those things?

The rationale offered by the US government at the time was a mixed one.[4] An initial Defense Department statement described its drone-based killing as a 'defensive action to protect U.S. personnel abroad' whom Soleimani was 'actively developing plans to attack'.[5] Such language suggests that the strike was driven by military concerns and had a warlike quality. Yet the statement also claimed that Soleimani was 'responsible

1

for the deaths of hundreds of American and coalition service members and the wounding of thousands more',[6] suggesting that the strike might also have been an act of punishment for past wrongdoing. Later, President Trump characterised the drone strike as being both preventive and punitive: a 'bold and decisive action to save American lives and deliver American justice'.[7] Regarding the need to act preventively, there was some official disagreement about whether Soleimani had been about to order an attack. US Defense Secretary Mark Esper acknowledged that he had not seen specific evidence that American embassies were in jeopardy immediately prior to the drone strike.[8] But Secretary of State Mike Pompeo insisted that Soleimani really had posed an 'imminent' threat, such that the president's 'decision to remove Qasem Soleimani from the battlefield saved American lives'.[9] Even so, the punitive rationale for the drone strike remained a consistent feature in the US government's explanations. Attorney General William Barr opined that 'this concept of imminence is something of a red herring' anyway, and Trump tweeted likewise that 'it doesn't really matter because of [Soleimani's] horrible past!'.[10]

Some US allies publicly supported the killing of Soleimani as an exercise in 'self-defence',[11] although Iraq's prime minister condemned it as an 'assassination'.[12] Then, in August 2020, this drone strike became the centrepiece of a report by Agnès Callamard, the United Nations (UN) Special Rapporteur on extrajudicial, summary or arbitrary executions. Callamard found it difficult to frame the strike as an action in war such as would attract the application of international humanitarian law (IHL). At the relevant time, neither the United States nor Iran appeared to consider that a condition of war existed between them,[13] and Callamard questioned whether 'IHL standards' were the best 'fit' for the purpose of legally assessing the known circumstances surrounding Soleimani's death outside of an active conflict zone.[14] The better view, she argued, was that international human rights law (IHRL) remained applicable to this instance of non-war killing.[15] In which case, the US government was responsible for arbitrarily violating Soleimani's right to life when it sought to obtain 'justice' in an improper way.[16] Critically, though, Callamard also acknowledged that this was an example of how '[s]ome drone strikes' raise 'genuine uncertainty' about the basis for their justification.[17]

Moral uncertainty surrounding the use of armed drones more generally has been a persistent problem during the last two decades. This is partly attributable to the technological novelty of uninhabited aircraft equipped with video cameras and weapons, but ethical controversies mainly arise from the way in which some drone-using states have chosen to exploit and apply this emergent technology. In the associated debate among ethicists, lawyers and policy practitioners, the moral rectitude of particular drone strikes and of drone strikes in general has often been fiercely contested. However, these debaters have sometimes talked past each other, ethically speaking, because they have brought different conceptual understandings to bear upon the violence that is under consideration. In response, *Moralities of Drone Violence* aims to provide greater clarity, for debate purposes, by exploring and ordering a variety of ways in which the violent use of an armed drone can be judged as just or unjust. Accordingly, this introductory chapter outlines the book's organisation of moral ideas around a series of concepts of 'drone violence': warfare, violent law enforcement, tele-intimate violence, and violence devolved from humans to artificial intelligence (AI) technologies. At the outset, though, it is important to establish what 'armed drones' are, how they are used, and who uses them.

ARMED DRONES: USES AND USERS

To begin, it is worth emphasising that the term 'drone' is employed here only for the sake of linguistic simplicity and because it is in common usage. The term is sometimes criticised (mainly by individuals with a military background) for being imprecise or carrying 'negative connotations'.[18] However, in a discussion of ethics that proceeds without prejudice, it is not clear that any analytical benefit would accrue from routinely replacing 'drone' with a more cumbersome term (such as 'uninhabited aerial vehicle' or 'remotely piloted aircraft').[19] Arguably, then, it is better to employ simpler language and to assume that the ethical significance of drones lies less in what they are called and more in how they are used.

With the advent and advancement of drone technology, some tasks that could previously be performed only by the on-board pilots of aircraft can now be performed more easily by the remote controller of a drone. Moreover, the availability of drones has made possible the performance of new kinds of tasks. This is because, when an aircraft operates without a human on board, there is more scope for that aircraft to vary in size, and it can fly higher, faster and for longer periods than the human body can normally tolerate.[20] Throughout the world, these technical advantages are mostly applied for benign purposes, and most drones are not armed. For example, remotely controlled and camera-equipped aircraft (sometimes with additional load-bearing capacity) have been useful in the provision of emergency healthcare,[21] the delivery of medical supplies,[22] the monitoring of endangered wildlife,[23] and the rescuing of pets.[24] Nevertheless, 'drones' in general can still seem fearsome and untrustworthy, even to people in need of drone-based assistance, because of the notorious association of *some* drones with violence.[25] This is mainly attributable to sustained media coverage of long-range strikes conducted by the US government since late 2001 (when the Afghanistan War began), although public attention has more recently turned also towards other uses of armed drones by numerous other governments.

For present purposes, an 'armed drone' is defined narrowly: it is a reusable aircraft that does not carry a human operator, carries at least one weapon, and incorporates on-board sensor and communication technologies for directing that weapon. This book is therefore not directly concerned with non-aerial (land-based or maritime) vehicles, unarmed drones that provide targeting assistance for other weapon platforms,[26] or with non-recoverable aerial devices (including missiles and so-called 'kamikaze drones') that crash into a target.[27] Each of these technologies is worthy of attention from an ethical perspective,[28] but they are excluded here in the cause of pursuing a focused and coherent inquiry into the moralities of drone violence.

Uses for armed drones

An armed drone collects information from the environment where it is flying and delivers a weapon towards a target (on the ground or in the air) within that environment. For the most part, based on existing technology, such violence manifests in ground attack mode (involving air-to-surface weapons). When operating in this mode, a drone might be useful for protecting or supporting friendly or allied ground troops in armed conflicts. This could involve, for example, coordinating missile strikes with troop attacks and providing air cover to facilitate tactical troop withdrawals.[29] Alternatively, a drone that launches air-to-surface weapons might be used for killing a particular individual located within or outside a conflict zone, or perhaps for the domestic policing purpose of neutralising a criminally violent threat to public safety.

Two types of drone aircraft, controlled over a satellite radio communication link, have been used most extensively by the US government for striking targets on the ground in distant foreign territories: the MQ-1 Predator and the newer MQ-9 Reaper. The Predator is a 27-foot-long aircraft that can operate on 24-hour missions, up to 770 miles away from its base, at an altitude of up to 25,000 feet. The US Air Force (USAF) started using it for surveillance and reconnaissance in 1996, and in 2002 this type of drone was armed with two AGM-114 Hellfire missiles. These could be guided towards ground-based targets by the Predator's on-board 'Multi-Spectral Targeting System' which integrates an infrared sensor, high-definition video cameras, and, for targeting purposes, a laser designator and laser illuminator.[30] The USAF eventually retired the Predator and transitioned to using mainly the MQ-9 Reaper,[31] which was designed from the start to carry weapons. The Reaper carries a similar set of sensor and munition-guidance technologies as the Predator, but it can fly farther and higher than its predecessor and is large enough (at 36 feet long) to be more heavily armed (with up to eight Hellfire missiles or with a variety of larger bombs).[32]

The salient feature of these large and long-range drones (as the US government has used them) is that they enable the killing, in near-real time, of another person made visible at a precise location in another part of the world. Indeed, in using the satellite-linked Reaper to project power abroad, the US has arguably been able to transcend limits of time and space to an unprecedented degree. However, smaller drones can be useful too, when operating in ground attack mode at short range, even though their payload capacity and flying time are much less than a Reaper's.[33] In general, a small drone is operated by a single person within 'line of sight' range, which is the distance (actually extending beyond visual range) a control signal can travel between the airborne aircraft and a ground controller's radio.[34] Examples of small-sized armed drones include the Tikad (equipped with a machine gun),[35] the Cerberus GL (for carrying a single bomb, a 12-gauge shotgun or a launcher for three grenades),[36] and the Smash Dragon (which can fire assault or sniper rifles as it hovers over a target).[37] Or, for the dispersal of 'less-lethal' munitions such as pepper spray balls (perhaps as a law enforcement tactic), the Skunk Riot Control Copter is available.[38]

The ability to use weapons in air-to-surface mode is largely dependent on dominating the airspace. To this end, some drone manufacturers and governments are interested in armed drones that can use air-to-air weapons and prevail in aerial combat with other aircraft. The propeller-powered Reaper (made by General Atomics) used by the US and UK governments has been useful for conducting strikes against technologically weak adversaries on the ground in places where airspace is largely uncontested. However, this drone is not as fast and agile as modern fighter jets (like the F-22 and F-35),[39] so its utility is limited against the sophisticated airpower assets of more powerful adversaries like Russia and China.[40] Drones designed to operate only in ground attack mode could be modified, for greater 'survivability', to carry air-to-air missiles (like the short-range AIM-9 Sidewinder), but this might not be enough.[41] In which case, according to some drone-using states, there is a mounting need for drones that are designed afresh to be swifter, stealthier and more heavily armed than their predecessors. Prototypes of drones that are thus more suitable for aerial combat include General Atomics' jet-powered MQ-20 Avenger,

Northrop Grumman's X-47B, BAE's Taranis, and Dassault Aviation's nEUROn.[42]

In the design and experimental development of such drones, there is a capacity for some of their system functions (such as navigation and mid-air refuelling) to be performed 'autonomously' (by an AI technology rather than a human).[43] Such a capacity is especially advantageous for a drone flying at extreme distances from its ground control station. This is because it can otherwise take several seconds for data and control signals to transmit via satellite between a drone aircraft and its remote human controller. This 'latency' has required the US government, for example, to reduce the risk of crashes by arranging for take-offs and landings to be handled by operators deployed close to the drone's runway on a base abroad.[44] In general, reducing human involvement and reliance upon long-distance communication would accelerate function-performance processes, making some elements of a drone's operation more efficient. However, it remains to be seen whether or how future drone-users will be able and willing also to incorporate AI into the process of controlling a drone's weapons.

Users of armed drones

In the short history of armed drones, they have predominately been used by states. Violent non-state actors have occasionally equipped drones with air-to-surface weapons. In 2016, for example, members of the Islamic State group modified small, short-range, commercially available drones to drop grenades on enemy personnel, equipment and buildings in Syria and Iraq.[45] Some other incidents, though, have been misreported as 'drone' attacks by non-state actors when, in fact, the attacks involved a remote-controlled and explosive-laden aircraft being crashed into a target.[46] State actors, by contrast, have tended to be much more serious and successful as users of armed drones, because they are far more likely to possess the technology, resources and infrastructure necessary to sustain this method of violence. Granted, most states are incapable of sustaining drone use on the same scale as the United States has done.[47] Even so, the very idea of engaging with enemies on a remote-control basis remains powerfully attractive to some political leaders, and this adds impetus to the international proliferation of armed drones. The desire for these weapon systems might in some cases be attributable to a perceived need to project power in a new way. Or, as some authors have argued, acquiring armed drones might also be a response to domestic political pressure and a 'post-heroic' aversion to casualties among national personnel.[48] In any event, around the world, drone technology has continued to attract government interest and investment, either as a means of supporting personnel deployed to dangerous places or as an alternative to such deployment.

In retrospect, it is now possible to identify a 'first drone age', beginning in late 2001, during which armed drones were used only by Israel, the United Kingdom and the United States. For the Israeli government, armed drones (built in Israel) have mainly been used for conducting short-range airstrikes in nearby territories.[49] The UK government, using US-made drones, has conducted strikes inside Afghanistan, Iraq and Syria.[50] And the US government, with its global network of military bases and intelligence resources, has been able to deploy its drones in those places too, as well as in Libya, Pakistan, Somalia and Yemen.[51] For about fourteen years, this tiny group of drone-using states retained exclusive access to armed drones. Then, in 2015, there began what has since been described as a 'second drone age', characterised by the emergence of new drone manufacturers and the widespread proliferation of weaponised drone technology.[52]

In September of that year, the Pakistani army announced that it had used one of its Burraq aircraft to conduct its first drone strike, killing three 'high-profile terrorists' inside North Waziristan (a region in north-western Pakistan).[53] Then, in early 2016, a Nigerian military crew operating a Chinese-made Cai Hong drone conducted a strike, against members of the insurgent Boko Haram group, in a remote forest in north-eastern Nigeria.[54] Soon afterwards, Iran began using its armed Shahed 129 drones to strike targets in Syria.[55] And, in the same year, the Turkish government began using a new type of armed drone (designed and built in Turkey), the TB2 Bayraktar.[56] Turkish drones have since been used extensively within the country's borders against the separatist Kurdistan Workers' Party, and also against Islamic State and Kurdish groups in northern Iraq and Syria.[57] Moreover, Turkey (like China) has become a major exporter of armed drones for wartime use by foreign governments.[58]

In 2017 a Syrian government drone fired at US-led coalition forces operating inside Syria,[59] and two years later both sides in Libya's ongoing civil war began deploying foreign allies' drones against each other. While the UN-recognised Government of National Accord (GNA) in Tripoli used Turkish-supplied Bayraktars, the rival Libyan National Army was supported by the United Arab Emirates' use of Chinese-made Wing Loong drones against GNA targets.[60] France carried out its first-ever drone strike in late 2019, using an armed Reaper in support of French commandos under attack by 'a group of terrorists on motorbikes' in central Mali.[61] In 2020, during fighting over the Nagorno-Karabakh territory (claimed by both Armenia and Azerbaijan), the Azeri military reportedly used imported Bayraktars to conduct missile strikes.[62] In 2021, Ethiopia's national government purchased armed drones from Turkey and Iran for use against the rebellious Tigray People's Liberation Front.[63] And, in 2022, the Ukrainian government's defence against invading Russian forces included the use of small drones carrying small bombs as well as, again, missile-armed Turkish Bayraktars.[64]

At the time of writing, according to a database maintained by the UK-based organisation Drone Wars, fourteen states have conducted drone strikes, five states are involved in exporting armed drones, and fourteen states have imported them. In addition, fifteen other states are 'near' to operating armed drones.[65] For example, Italy has received approval from the US government to arm its two Reapers with Hellfire missiles and laser-guided bombs.[66] India has ordered ten armed Heron TP drones from an Israeli manufacturer.[67] And Germany's parliamentary defence committee has reportedly approved the purchase of 140 Herons as part of a boost to the country's military capabilities following Russia's invasion of Ukraine.[68] Thus, it is clear that drone proliferation is real and ongoing, and that many lives will be at stake if this leads to a worldwide increase in the violent use of drones. However, the future extent and effect of this violence are arguably not determined by technological advancements and political factors alone. Rather, that future might yet be shaped also by concerns about justice and by associated commitments to exercise principled restraint. Accordingly, the remainder of this chapter turns to the making of moral judgements about 'drone violence', which is open to be conceptualised in various ways.

DRONE VIOLENCE: CONCEPTS AND MORALITIES

The academic literature addressing the use of armed drones has grown to incorporate a wide variety of disciplinary perspectives, but it also exhibits a common tendency among authors to refer to such activity as 'drone warfare'.[69] Much of the time, 'warfare' is indeed what is going on when a drone is used. In some circumstances, though, it is impossible, implausible or insufficiently helpful to conceptualise drone use in that way. For example, one drone-user might rather engage in what is essentially a law enforcement action. Another instance of violent drone use might be difficult to recognise as being either warfare or law enforcement,[70] or it might appear somehow to bear the characteristics of both.[71] In addition, the concept of 'drone warfare' arguably does not fully capture the essence of an individual's hands-on experience of using an armed drone, and nor does this concept account well for the future possibility of such use being controlled to some extent by AI technologies. For these reasons, the task of conceptualising the use of armed drones needs to begin, instead, with a more general term: 'drone violence'. This then makes available a range of approaches to thinking ethically about violent drone use (extending beyond the Just War morality traditionally applicable to war violence), which in turn affords greater scope to discern and address its potential to generate injustice.

With these objectives in mind, it is firstly worth noting that the word 'violence' has the analytical advantage of not being a euphemism for something else. Also, it is important to emphasise that that word is employed here in a morally neutral fashion (without carrying a negative connotation). That is, *Moralities of Drone Violence* necessarily rejects a 'legitimist' definition of violence that 'incorporates a reference to an illegal or illegitimate use of force'.[72] No assumption is made that violence per se is, by default, 'something we should disapprove of',[73] so the act of referring to 'violence' should not be understood here as one of condemnation. Rather, in this book, 'drone violence' serves as a basic term upon which a number of more specific concepts (to be introduced later in this chapter) can be overlaid. Thus, the discussion of multiple moralities can proceed based on drone violence being conceptualised *as* 'warfare', 'violent law enforcement', 'tele-intimate violence' or 'devolved (to AI) violence'.

Conceptualising violence, then judging it

For present purposes, conceptualisation is understood as something that logically precedes ethical assessment. That is, prior to considering whether and why a given instance of violence is just or unjust, it is necessary to establish what kind of violence this is. It is sometimes the case in practice, though, that value judgements are smuggled into the conceptualisation process, causing 'the conceptual and the ethical' to be 'muddled together'.[74] And, typically, such muddling originates in a person's preformed desire ultimately to render a justification or a condemnation. The moral judgement (for or against) that they would prefer to reach about an instance of violence is what then drives and prejudices a choice about framing it conceptually. However, this judgemental 'conceptualisation' is clearly not intended to reveal the pre-ethical nature of whatever violence is under consideration. Instead, it is a technique for enabling that violence to escape, or to be captured by, certain moral expectations (and any associated rules and governance measures).

On the one hand, for example, to label a killing an 'assassination' is not to conceptualise violence but to condemn it. This is because, around the world, there is general agreement that assassination is (and should be) illegal;[75] there cannot be 'good assassinations'. On the other hand, referring to violence as 'war' can be part of an attempt to afford it some (potential) legitimacy, for there *can* be 'just wars'. As Ian Clark has observed, the war concept thus often 'serves as a residual . . . normative source in its own right'.[76] And, according to Emily Kalah Gade, 'war' can be a political term used by state actors attempting to 'legitimize and formalize the violence in which they engage'.[77] Conversely, the condemnation of violence sometimes consists in describing it as 'not war', such as when circumstances of extreme asymmetry are perceived as morally wrong. This is the moral judgement that appears to drive Jean Baudrillard's claim that the 1991 Gulf War, involving overwhelming US airpower and few American casualties, 'did not take place'.[78] And, similarly, the huge imbalance in casualties among Israelis and Palestinians caused during Israel's Operation Cast Lead in Gaza (launched in December 2008) is what prompted Avi Shlaim to describe this violence as 'not a war . . . but a one-sided massacre'.[79] In both cases, an alternative approach would have been to conceptualise the relevant violence (as 'war', for example) and then to judge it (as *unjust* war).

This approach, arguably, is also the better one when it comes to ethical assessment, because it is less vulnerable to prejudice and more conducive to meaningful debate. As different ways of thinking about violence 'profoundly shape the possibilities and limits of the ethical debate that can take place',[80] settling on a concept first is important if debaters are to avoid talking past each other. If it is accepted that war is going on, a debate in the language of military ethics can proceed. But if the violence under consideration is essentially a practice of law enforcement, the ethical debate about this is necessarily restricted to the moral vocabulary of criminal justice (qua policing or punishment). A prior debate can still be had about whether a condition of war or law enforcement exists in the first place, but this is a conceptual debate not an ethical one. So, for example, the answer to Michael Gross's question of whether 'targeted killings' are '[permissible] acts of self-defence or [impermissible] extra-judicial execution' depends upon 'which of the two paradigms that justify lethal force – war or law enforcement – we choose to analyze targeted killing'.[81] The same approach, applied to the use of armed drones, means that expectations about what conduct is appropriate 'are dependent upon the particular concept of the use of force in which [drones] are initially located'.[82]

The conceptual location of state violence within either of two paradigms – war or law enforcement – is critically significant,[83] because the morality that attends the latter (a peacetime activity) is traditionally much less tolerant of killing than is war's morality. It is generally understood that many of the violent actions which warriors may commit in war may *not* be committed by other state agents (police and executioners) when violently enforcing the criminal law. The difference, then, between abiding by the more permissive 'ethos of warfare' or the more restrictive 'ethos of policing' can be measured in terms of who may be killed and in what circumstances.[84] And, as between these different pathways of departure from every human's presumptive right to life, the humanitarian outcomes (measured in injuries and deaths) are likely also to differ accordingly. In matters of law enforcement, the ethical expectation is that state violence is directed towards a person based only on wrongful behaviour (what they are doing or have done). By contrast, wartime targeting is permitted also according to a person's generally threatening status (as a combatant or direct participant in hostilities).[85] Consequently, there tends to be far more moral scope for killing enemies in war than there is for killing criminals in peacetime.[86]

This traditional notion of distinct moralities of violence is rejected by some moral philosophers who insist, instead, that there is only 'one morality'.[87] According to Jeff McMahan, for example, the justifications for killing people in war are no different from those that apply in other contexts. So, rather than focusing on the supposed moral difference between war and peace as overarching conditions, his 'individualist' approach to the assessment of violence emphasises the moral inequality among participants in a violent encounter. Ethical assessment then comes down to distinguishing between, on the one hand, 'those who are in the right' who are 'permitted to use force' and, on the other hand, 'those who are in the wrong' who have no such permission.[88] According to this reasoning, a robber is clearly 'in the wrong' when they mug a pedestrian on the street. And, whereas the robber is not morally permitted to use violence for this unjust purpose, the pedestrian does have permission (as a matter of self-defence) to violently resist the violence being wrongly visited upon them. Moreover, a passing police officer who intervenes to protect the attacked pedestrian is morally entitled to act violently too (as a matter of other-defence).

In seeking to apply this one (individualist) morality to *all* violence, however, there is a practical difficulty: it is often much harder to establish who is 'in the right' in the politically messier reality of violent encounters that are called 'war'. Notoriously, each side in a war tends to proclaim that they alone have justice on their side, so comparisons to righteous police and culpable robbers must struggle to achieve relevance. Also, as Michael Walzer has argued, war as 'a coercively *collectivizing* enterprise' makes it impossible to pay attention to 'each person's moral standing' when inquiring into the overall justification for this kind of violence.[89] Thus, it is generally considered more useful to follow the orthodox 'collectivist' approach: to regard war and peace as morally distinct paradigms, and to hold war-wagers and law-enforcers to differing standards of violent conduct.

Four moralities of drone violence

In this book, the idea of multiple moralities is critical because it enables a widening of the scope for normative inquiry into the use of armed drones. By conceptualising drone violence in various ways, different and novel approaches to moral judgement are made available, and this has the potential overall to reveal more about what it means for this violence to be just or unjust. To conceptualise drone violence more narrowly, though, is to run a greater risk of failing to capture the full range of potential injustices. On the matter of justification, there is no shortage of scholarship that examines the use of armed drones from a legal perspective.[90] And it is indeed possible to criticise or defend such use purely by reference to the international law on resorting to force, to IHL, and/or to IHRL.[91] By contrast, in *Moralities of Drone Violence*, the meaning of 'morality' is understood to extend beyond points of legality.

Specific laws are occasionally mentioned herein as reflections of underlying moral principles, but sometimes the discussion of an ethical concept or a type of injustice needs to proceed in the absence of any corresponding legal rule. Also, for present purposes, any invoking of legality is not intended to truncate what it means to behave morally or to be affected by others' immoral behaviour.[92] As Elke Schwarz has suggested, it would be short-sighted to conflate 'thinking ethically' about drones with merely 'adhering to existing laws'.[93] And it is worth recalling that law tends to work 'externally' in the sense that people obey it mainly because they believe 'the law reflects some *collectively* held judgment of the right'.[94] Yet, as Valerie Morkevičius has observed, morality has a broader and deeper meaning and influence: it occasions individuals also to be 'inward-looking', thus shaping behaviour based on 'how we see ourselves' and 'even if no one is looking'.[95]

A discussion of the rights *and* wrongs of drone violence is premised also on an understanding that armed drones, as weapons systems, are not *mala in se* ('inherently evil').[96] As several other authors have observed, related moral concerns are generally not technology-specific but rather they arise from how drones are used.[97] Even so, the practice of drone violence is morally interesting in the way it can uniquely exacerbate or illuminate broader problems. These are explored in later chapters, and they include the moral problems of: unjustly resorting to war; conduct-ing war unjustly; excessively forceful policing; extrajudicial punishment of criminal wrongdoing; assertions of the existence of an unbounded battlefield; incurring moral injury from the experience of killing; and inadequate human control over the operation of weapon systems. To bring a drone-specific perspective to bear upon each of these problems, this book's discussion of ethics is structured around four concept-based themes: (1) drone violence as warfare; (2) drone violence as violent law enforcement; (3) drone violence as the 'tele-intimate' violence wielded by drone operators; and (4) drone violence devolved from humans to AI.

Chapter 2 addresses the morality of drone violence conceptualised as warfare. It begins with consideration of what essentially defines 'war' between contending belligerents, focusing especially on the conceptual significance of mutual exposure to physical risk. This informs a subse-quent discussion of the kinds of circumstances in which the use of armed drones can plausibly be characterised as warlike. Violence that counts as warfare can be subjected to ethical judgement by reference to principles of Just War morality, so the chapter goes on to consider how drone war-fare can relate to the justice of resorting to war (*jus ad bellum*) and the just conduct of war (*jus in bello*). Potential concerns include, for exam-ple, the temptation for drone-using states to act violently too often, and whether armed drone systems adequately enable discrimination between combatants and civilians. In response, Chapter 2 then offers some sug-gestions for raising moral standards in the practice of drone warfare.

If an instance of drone violence is different in nature from warfare, Just War morality is not available as a source of permission. So, in Chapter 3, attention turns to the morality of an alternative concept of drone violence: violent law enforcement. Here, the discussion of ethics is divided according to two sub-concepts of that violence: the punish-ment of criminal wrongdoing, and domestic policing for the protection of public safety. The first part of the chapter focuses on drone violence conceptualised as lethal, punitive law enforcement (capital punishment). It explores the notion that, sometimes, the user of armed drones appears to act in the manner of a 'lawman' delivering 'wild justice' to outlaws. Focusing on the US government's conduct of so-called 'personality strikes' against alleged terrorists located in remote parts of the world, an argument is presented for characterising such violence as 'administrative execution'. This punitive application of drone violence is 'wild' because it merely mimics (and thereby rejects) the legalism of proper criminal justice practice. And the ethical problem arising from this is that, when drone-based killings are sanctioned by non-judicial agents of a govern-ment, there is too much potential for unjust violation of the human right to life. A potential response to this problem is to require judicial authorisation for drone executions. However, as the chapter explains, attempting to tame such violence in that way would itself be morally risky.

Further to the theme of law enforcement, governments around the world are already making unarmed drones available to police for various purposes. Equipped with cameras, these aircraft provide a powerful and mobile surveillance capacity that can be highly effective in detecting suspicious activity and guiding police operations. In addition, however, for situations where criminal violence presents a danger to public safety, some governments might in future elect to empower their police to neutralise threats using drones that are equipped also with weapons. In anticipation of this, the second part of Chapter 3 discusses whether or how police should use armed drones. Established ethical principles on police use of force (necessity, proportionality and precaution) are relevant here, and the discussion explores some of the challenges a 'tele-present' police drone-user could face in seeking to adhere to those principles.

Chapter 4 addresses instances of drone violence that are 'grey' in the sense of being hard to categorise as either warfare or violent law enforcement. Here, conceptual uncertainty is a problem because it can generate confusion over applicable moralities, and this in turn can generate difficulties from a governance perspective.[98] Various international organisations have passed resolutions calling upon states to use armed drones in compliance with 'international law'.[99] However, these resolutions have not themselves resolved the critical uncertainty that sometimes exists about what kind of law is applicable to drone violence. For this very reason, moreover, conceptual 'greyness' can work to the advantage of a drone-using state that wishes to proceed with violence by giving itself (rather than prospective victims) the benefit of the doubt. The chapter focuses on circumstances, such as existed for a period of years inside Pakistan, in which a foreign government's armed drones are a constant presence. A lesson from US experience there is that the persistent threat of drone strikes is intended to suppress 'terrorist' activities that endanger the drone-using state's security. But this threat also and inevitably affects innocent people living within potential strike zones. To judge such drone use by reference to military ethics principles is to assume that 'war' is going on, but indefinite drone deployments are arguably difficult to conceptualise as war, so traditional Just War thinking does not suffice as a basis for moral judgement. In assessing the US government's commitment to drone-based containment of security risks emerging in faraway territories, the chapter considers three alternative conceptualisations of such violence – *vim* (force short of war), terrorism and imperialism – and explains why these are unsuitable. It then suggests a concept of 'quasi-imperialistic' drone violence and explores the ethical implications of this by reference to the right to life.

In much of the ethical debate surrounding the use of armed drones, attention usually focuses on the agency of a drone-using state and on the victimhood of targeted individuals (as well as any other people nearby). By contrast, in Chapter 5 the focus shifts towards the individual agency of drone operators who are employed to kill and the potential for these perpetrators of state-sanctioned violence to be included among its victims. When an armed and remote-controlled aircraft is equipped with a powerful camera providing real-time video footage, this gives rise to another concept of drone violence: 'tele-intimate' violence. Here, arguably, the direct *experience* of using an armed drone is ethically significant because the operator who kills, after closely observing another (targeted) person, thereby runs the risk of incurring moral injury. This might especially be the case in circumstances where it is hard to conceptualise such killing as being, also, essentially either warfare or law enforcement. A remote and ground-based operator who uses a drone to kill is likely often to experience no physical endangerment. However, a *moral* injury might still be incurred if that person judges themselves so harshly as to be undone by their own sense of virtue, becoming victim to a debilitating conviction that they have done wrong. In response, Chapter 5 goes on to explore how the state employers of drone operators might better care for their moral well-being in the workplace.

Short of avoiding the perpetration of drone violence altogether, sparing drone operators from the risk of moral injury might, in future, entail radically reducing the extent of their involvement in the functioning of armed drone systems. In this scenario, AI technologies would be used as alternative (non-human) performers of system functions, and so Chapter 6 turns to this book's fourth concept of drone violence: violence devolved from humans to AI. The incorporation of AI into the operation of weapon systems appears to have the potential both to improve or to degrade the protection of human life in the practice of state violence. Thus, as more governments worldwide plan to develop and apply AI for military or law enforcement purposes, a fierce debate is ongoing among scholars and policymakers about the ethics and governance of so-called 'lethal autonomous weapon systems'. A critical issue in this debate is whether any system can or should incorporate ethical decision-making by AI (effectively functioning as a moral agent). However, progress has arguably been inhibited by excessive attention to 'lethal' weapons and by confusion over the meaning of 'autonomous'. Chapter 6 responds by outlining an alternative, differentiated approach to the task of ethically assessing the incorporation of AI technologies into weapon systems, focusing on one kind of system deployed in the air domain: the armed drone. This differentiated approach rejects the notion of artificial moral agency and is based instead upon the emergent principle of 'meaningful human control' (MHC). After introducing the concept of 'devolved violence', the chapter emphasises the performance (by humans or AI) of 'critical' functions within drone systems that operate in different modes of human–machine interaction (HMI) to satisfy different MHC standards. Then, the moral permissibility of devolving function-performance to AI is assessed according to whether drone violence involving HMI is directed against human or non-human targets, whether it serves an offensive or defensive purpose, and whether it occurs in a warfare or law enforcement environment.

Overall, in assessing the use of armed drones by reference to these four concepts of violence (warfare, law enforcement, tele-intimate and devolved), *Moralities of Drone Violence* aims to provide a broadened framework for ethical thinking on this issue. This is important in enabling and encouraging a wide range of potential injustices to be discerned, debated and addressed. As international proliferation and violent applications of drone technology continue, there will be a deepening need for principled restraint. And, to maximise the benefit of this throughout the world, it is arguably necessary for future approaches to the governance of drones to be underpinned by multiple moralities. Accordingly, this book maps out a succession of pathways towards the making of moral judgements about instances of drone violence. The journey begins, in the next chapter, with the concept and morality of warfare.

NOTES

1. BBC, 'Qasem Soleimani: US kills top Iranian general in Baghdad air strike', *BBC News*, 3 January 2020, <https://www.bbc.co.uk/news/world-middle-east-50979463>; Peter Beaumont, 'Making of a martyr: how Qassem Suleimani was hunted down', *The Guardian*, 5 January 2020, <https://www.theguardian.com/world/2020/jan/05/making-of-a-martyr-how-qassem-suleimani-was-hunted-down>.
2. Patrick Wintour, 'Iran to execute "CIA agent" over Gen Suleimani intelligence', *The Guardian*, 9 June 2020, <https://www.theguardian.com/world/2020/jun/09/iran-to-execute-cia-agent-over-gen-suleimanis-death>.
3. C. Anthony Pfaff, 'Military Ethics below the Threshold of War', *Parameters*, 50 (2) (2020): 69–77, at 69.
4. Zachary B. Wolf and Veronica Stracqualursi, 'The evolving US justification for killing Iran's top general', *CNN*, 8 January 2020, <https://edition.cnn.com/2020/01/07/politics/qasem-soleimani-reasons-justifications/index.html>.

5. US Department of Defense, 'Statement by the Department of Defense', *US Department of Defense*, 2 January 2020, <https://www.defense.gov/Newsroom/Releases/Release/Article/2049534/statement-by-the-department-of-defense/>.

6. Ibid.

7. Reuters, 'Killing Iran general delivered "American justice", Trump tells rally', *The Guardian*, 10 January 2020, <https://www.theguardian.com/us-news/2020/jan/10/killing-iran-general-suleimani-american-justice-donald-trump-ohio-rally>.

8. Laura King, Nabih Bulos and Sarah Parvini, 'Defense secretary "didn't see" intelligence backing Trump's claim of Iran plot against U.S. embassies', *Los Angeles Times*, 12 January 2020, <https://www.latimes.com/world-nation/story/2020-01-12/iran-leaders-protests-ukrainian-plane>.

9. Louisa Loveluck, 'Iran vows revenge after U.S. drone strike kills elite force commander', *Washington Post*, 3 January 2020, <https://www.washingtonpost.com/world/middle_east/iran-vows-revenge-after-us-drone-strike-kills-elite-force-commander/2020/01/03/345127d6-2df4-11ea-bffe-020c88b3f120_story.html>.

10. Philip Rucker, John Hudson, Shane Harris and Josh Dawsey, '"Four embassies": the anatomy of Trump's unfounded claim about Iran', *Washington Post*, 13 January 2020, <https://www.washingtonpost.com/politics/four-embassies-the-anatomy-of-trumps-unfounded-claim-about-iran/2020/01/13/2dcd6df0-3620-11ea-bf30-ad313e4ec754_story.html>.

11. Patrick Wintour, 'European leaders call for de-escalation of crisis after Suleimani killing', *The Guardian*, 3 January 2020, <https://www.theguardian.com/world/2020/jan/03/qassem-suleimani-killing-may-spell-end-iran-nuclear-deal-europe-fears>; Heather Stewart, 'Britain "on same page" as US over Suleimani killing, says Raab', *The Guardian*, 5 January 2020, <https://www.theguardian.com/politics/2020/jan/05/britain-sympathetic-to-us-over-killing-of-qassem-suleimani>.

12. BBC, 'Qasem Soleimani: US kills top Iranian general in Baghdad air strike', *BBC News*, 3 January 2020, <https://www.bbc.co.uk/news/world-middle-east-50979463>.

13. Agnès Callamard, *Use of Armed Drones for Targeted Killings*. Report of the Special Rapporteur on extrajudicial, summary or arbitrary executions (A/HRC/44/38), Human Rights Council, United Nations General Assembly, 15 August 2020: Annex, para. 24.

14. Ibid. para. 36.

15. Ibid. para. 39.

16. Ibid. paras 33, 82.

17. Ibid. para. 11.

18. Wayne Phelps, *On Killing Remotely: The Psychology of Killing with Drones*, New York: Little, Brown and Company, 2021: 36. See also: Peter Lee, 'Rights, Wrongs and Drones: Remote Warfare, Ethics and the Challenge of Just War Reasoning', *Air Power Review*, 16 (3) (2013): 30–49, at 46 (note 8); and Joseph O. Chapa, 'Remotely Piloted Aircraft, Risk, and

Killing as Sacrifice: The Cost of Remote Warfare', *Journal of Military Ethics*, 16 (3–4) (2017): 256–71, at 268 (note 2).

19. See: Gregory S. McNeal, 'Just Call It a Drone', *Forbes*, 2 March 2013, <http://www.forbes.com/sites/gregorymcneal/2013/03/02/just-call-it-a-drone/>.

20. Arash Heydarian Pashakhanlou, 'AI, Autonomy, and Airpower: the End of Pilots?', *Defence Studies*, 19 (4) (2019): 337–52, at 339 and 340.

21. BBC, 'Drone helps save cardiac arrest patient in Sweden', *BBC News*, 6 January 2022, <https://www.bbc.co.uk/news/technology-59885656>.

22. Ali Mitib, 'Drones fly to the rescue of patients in remote areas of Scotland', *The Times*, 27 December 2021, <https://www.thetimes.co.uk/article/drones-fly-to-the-rescue-of-patients-in-remote-areas-of-scotland-dmkv0p-5bl>; Samuel Okiror, '"Gamechanger": Uganda launches drone delivering HIV drugs to remote islands', *The Guardian*, 4 May 2021, <https://www.theguardian.com/global-development/2021/may/04/gamechanger-uganda-launches-drone-delivering-hiv-drugs-to-remote-islands>.

23. Anthea Lipsett, 'Drones and big data: the next frontier in the fight against wildlife extinction', *The Guardian*, 18 February 2019, <https://www.theguardian.com/education/2019/feb/18/drones-and-big-data-the-next-frontier-in-the-fight-against-wildlife-extinction>.

24. Katie Gibbons, 'Drones with sausages lure missing dog out of danger', *The Times*, 20 January 2022, <https://www.thetimes.co.uk/article/drones-with-sausages-lure-missing-dog-out-of-danger-xf9fn8xdj>.

25. See: Faine Greenwood, 'Drones and distrust in humanitarian aid', *Humanitarian Law & Policy*, 22 July 2021, <https://blogs.icrc.org/law-and-policy/2021/07/22/drones-distrust-humanitarian/>.

26. See: George Grylls, 'German drone to direct Ukrainian fire from the skies', *The Times*, 18 April 2022, <https://www.thetimes.co.uk/article/german-drone-to-direct-ukrainian-fire-from-the-skies-kmsxvd7tj>.

27. See: Michael C. Horowitz, 'Drones aren't missiles, so don't regulate them like they are', *Bulletin of the Atomic Scientists*, 26 June 2017, <https://thebulletin.org/2017/06/drones-arent-missiles-so-dont-regulate-them-like-they-are/>; Will Knight, 'Russia's killer drone in Ukraine raises fears about AI in warfare', *Wired*, 17 March 2022, <https://www.wired.com/story/ai-drones-russia-ukraine/>.

28. See, for example: Arthur Holland Michel, *Unarmed and Dangerous: The Lethal Applications of Non-Weaponized Drones*, Annandale-on-Hudson, NY: Center for the Study of the Drone at Bard College, 2020.

29. See: Brian Everstine, 'Inside the Air Force's drone operations', *Air Force Times*, 22 June 2015, <https://www.airforcetimes.com/news/your-air-force/2015/06/22/inside-the-air-force-s-drone-operations/>; Joe Ritter, 'Hellfires wanted: it's time to start tasking armed drones as combat aircraft', *War on the Rocks*, 24 June 2021, <https://warontherocks.com/2021/06/hellfires-wanted-its-time-to-start-tasking-armed-drones-as-combat-aircraft/>.

30. USAF, 'MQ-1B Predator', *US Air Force*, September 2015, <https://www.af.mil/About-Us/Fact-Sheets/Display/Article/104469/mq-1b-predator/> (accessed 4 February 2022).

31. Christian Clausen, 'Air Force to retire MQ-1 Predator drone, transition to MQ-9 Reaper', *US Defense Department*, 27 February 2017, <https://www.defense.gov/News/News-Stories/Article/Article/1095612/air-force-to-retire-mq-1-predator-drone-transition-to-mq-9-reaper/>.

32. USAF, 'MQ-9 Reaper', *US Air Force*, March 2021, <https://www.af.mil/About-Us/Fact-Sheets/Display/Article/104470/mq-9-reaper/> (accessed 5 February 2022).

33. See: Jack Watling and Nicholas Waters, 'Achieving Lethal Effects by Small Unmanned Aerial Vehicles', *The RUSI Journal*, 164 (1) (2019): 40–51, at 40.

34. Wayne Phelps, *On Killing Remotely: The Psychology of Killing with Drones*, New York: Little, Brown and Company, 2021: 104.

35. Mary-Ann Russon, 'US firm reveals gun-toting drone that can fire in mid-air', *BBC News*, 11 August 2017, <https://www.bbc.co.uk/news/technology-40901393>.

36. Kelsey D. Atherton, 'Grenade launching drone will be part of Army exercise in 2020', *C4ISRNET*, 19 November 2019, <https://www.c4isrnet.com/unmanned/2019/11/19/grenade-launcher-drone-is-backpackable-air-support/>.

37. Michael Evans, 'Israeli firm develops Smash Dragon, the drone that fires a rifle as it flies', *The Times*, 11 January 2022, <https://www.thetimes.co.uk/article/israeli-firm-develops-smash-dragon-the-drone-that-fires-a-rifle-as-it-flies-5778j52bd>.

38. Desert Wolf, 'Skunk riot control opter', *Desert Wolf*, no date, <http://www.desert-wolf.com/dw/products/unmanned-aerial-systems/skunk-riot-control-copter.html> (accessed 7 February 2022).

39. Dave Blair, 'A Categorical error: rethinking "drones" as an analytical category for security policy', *Lawfare*, 24 April 2016, <https://www.lawfareblog.com/categorical-error-rethinking-drones-analytical-category-security-policy>.

40. Michael Mayer, 'The New Killer Drones: Understanding the Strategic Implications of Next-Generation Unmanned Combat Aerial Vehicles', *International Affairs*, 91 (4) (2015): 765–80, at 769; Valerie Insinna, 'Could a commercial drone replace the MQ-9 Reaper? The Air Force is considering it', *Defense News*, 12 March 2020, <https://www.defensenews.com/air/2020/03/12/could-a-commercial-drone-replace-the-mq-9-reaper-the-air-force-is-considering-it/>.

41. Rachel S. Cohen, 'MQ-9 air-to-air missiles postponed for higher priorities', *Air Force Magazine*, 21 June 2019, <https://www.airforcemag.com/MQ-9-Air-to-Air-Missiles-Postponed-for-Higher-Priorities/>; John A. Tirpak, 'Air force to upgrade MQ-9's mission and capabilities for near-peer fight', *Air Force Magazine*, 21 April 2021, <https://www.airforcemag.com/air-force-to-upgrade-mq-9s-mission-and-capabilities-for-near-peer-fight/>.

42. General Atomics, 'Predator C Avenger', *General Atomics*, no date, <https://www.ga-asi.com/remotely-piloted-aircraft/predator-c-avenger> (accessed 7 February 2022); Northrop Grumman, 'X-47B UCAS', Northrop Grumman,

no date, <https://www.northropgrumman.com/what-we-do/air/x-47b-ucas/> (accessed 8 February 2022); BAE, 'Taranis', *BAE Systems*, no date, <https://www.baesystems.com/en-uk/product/taranis1> (accessed 7 February 2022); Dassault Aviation, 'nEUROn', *Dassault Aviation*, no date, <https://www.dassault-aviation.com/en/defense/neuron/> (accessed 7 February 2022).

43. See, for example: Anonymous, 'USAF's Skyborg ACS flies onboard MQ-20 Avenger tactical UAV', *Air Force Technology*, 30 June 2021, <https://www.airforce-technology.com/news/usafs-skyborg-acs-flies-onboard-mq-20-avenger-tactical-uav/>.

44. Andrew Cockburn, *Kill Chain: Drones and the Rise of High-Tech Assassins*, London: Verso, 2016: 5.

45. Wayne Phelps, *On Killing Remotely: The Psychology of Killing with Drones*, New York: Little, Brown and Company, 2021: 38. See also: Nicholas Grossman, *Drones and Terrorism: Asymmetric Warfare and the Threat to Global Security*, London: I. B. Tauris, 2018: 1.

46. See: Geoff Brumfiel, 'In Yemen conflict, some see a new age of drone warfare', *NPR*, 29 May 2019, <https://text.npr.org/726760128>; Nabih Bulos, 'Carnage escalates, options for U.S. diminish in new round of Yemeni civil war attacks', *Los Angeles Times*, 21 January 2022, <https://www.latimes.com/world-nation/story/2022-01-21/houthis-yemen>.

47. See: Shashank Joshi and Aaron Stein, 'Emerging Drone Nations', *Survival*, 55 (5) (2013): 53–78, at 69; Andrea Gilli and Mauro Gilli, 'The Diffusion of Drone Warfare? Industrial, Organizational, and Infrastructural Constraints', *Security Studies*, 25 (1) (2016): 50–84.

48. David Dunn, 'Drones: Disembodied Aerial Warfare and the Unarticulated Threat', *International Affairs*, 89 (5) (2013): 1237–46, at 1238; Christian Enemark, *Armed Drones and the Ethics of War: Military Virtue in a Post-Heroic Age*, London: Routledge, 2014: 9–21; Sebastian Kaempf, *Saving Soldiers or Civilians? Casualty-Aversion versus Civilian Protection in Asymmetric Conflicts*, Cambridge: Cambridge University Press, 2018: 244.

49. See: Human Rights Watch, 'Precisely wrong: Gaza civilians killed by Israeli drone-launched missiles', *Human Rights Watch*, June 2009, <https://www.hrw.org/report/2009/06/30/precisely-wrong/gaza-civilians-killed-israeli-drone-launched-missiles>; Stefan Borg, 'Assembling Israeli Drone Warfare: Loitering Surveillance and Operational Sustainability', *Security Dialogue*, 52 (5) (2021): 401–17.

50. BBC, 'UK drone carries out first strike in Iraq', *BBC News*, 10 November 2014, <https://www.bbc.co.uk/news/world-middle-east-29992686>; Chris Cole, 'Finally revealed: UK drone strikes in Afghanistan by province', *Drone Wars*, 2 April 2015, <https://dronewars.net/2015/04/02/finally-revealed-uk-drone-strikes-in-afghanistan-by-province/>; UK Parliament, 'UK Lethal Drone Strikes in Syria' (HC 1152), Intelligence and Security Committee of Parliament, London: House of Commons, 2017.

51. Christopher J. Fuller, *See It / Shoot It: The Secret History of the CIA's Lethal Drone Program*, Yale University Press, 2017: 10.

52. See: Umar Farooq, 'The Second Drone Age', *The Intercept*, 14 May 2019, <https://theintercept.com/2019/05/14/turkey-second-drone-age/>; Ruth Pollard, 'The Second Drone Age is here and it's a free-for-all', *Bloomberg*, 2 January 2022, <https://www.bloomberg.com/opinion/articles/2022-01-02/the-second-drone-age-is-a-weaponized-free-for-all-energized-by-global-commerce>.

53. W. J. Hennigan, 'A fast growing club: countries that use drones for killing by remote control', *Los Angeles Times*, 22 February 2016, <https://www.latimes.com/world/africa/la-fg-drone-proliferation-2-20160222-story.html>.

54. Ibid.

55. Paul McLeary, 'Iranian drones now hitting rebel targets in Syria', *Foreign Policy*, 29 February 2016, <https://foreignpolicy.com/2016/02/29/iranian-drones-now-hitting-rebel-targets-in-syria/>.

56. Umar Farooq, 'The Second Drone Age', *The Intercept*, 14 May 2019, <https://theintercept.com/2019/05/14/turkey-second-drone-age/>.

57. Dan Sabbagh, 'Killer drones: how many are there and who do they target?', *The Guardian*, 18 November 2019, <https://www.theguardian.com/news/2019/nov/18/killer-drones-how-many-uav-predator-reaper>; BBC, 'Syria war: Turkish drone strikes "kill 19 Syrian soldiers"', *BBC News*, 2 March 2020, <https://www.bbc.co.uk/news/world-middle-east-51701069>.

58. Aaron Stein, 'From Ankara with implications: Turkish drones and alliance entrapment', *War on the Rocks*, 15 December 2021, <https://warontherocks.com/2021/12/from-ankara-with-implications-turkish-drones-and-alliance-entrapment/>.

59. BBC, 'Syrian pro-government drone shot down by US military', *BBC News*, 8 June 2017, <https://www.bbc.co.uk/news/world-middle-east-40206957>.

60. Arnaud Delalande, 'How Libya's skies became battleground for UAE-Turkey proxy war', *Middle East Eye*, 27 August 2019, <https://www.middleeasteye.net/news/how-libyas-skies-became-battleground-uae-turkey-proxy-war>; Dan Sabbagh, Jason Burke and Bethan McKernan, '"Libya is ground zero": drones on frontline in bloody civil war', *The Guardian*, 27 November 2019, <https://www.theguardian.com/news/2019/nov/27/libya-is-ground-zero-drones-on-frontline-in-bloody-civil-war>.

61. AFP, French army carries out first-ever drone strike during Mali op', *France 24*, 23 December 2019, <https://www.france24.com/en/20191223-french-army-carries-out-first-ever-drone-strike-during-mali-op>.

62. Bethan McKernan, 'Trench warfare, drones and cowering civilians: on the ground in Nagorno-Karabakh', *The Guardian*, 13 October 2020, <https://www.theguardian.com/artanddesign/2020/oct/13/trench-warfare-drones-and-cowering-civilians-on-the-ground-in-nagorno-karabakh>.

63. Michael Evans and Jane Flanagan, 'Ethiopia's war turns into a testing ground for the deadliest drones', *The Times*, 31 December 2021, <https://www.thetimes.co.uk/article/civilians-are-drone-warfare-guinea-pigs-in-ethiopia-r5x50b230>; Jonathan Marcus, 'Combat drones: we are in a new

era of warfare – here's why', *BBC News*, 4 February 2022, <https://www.bbc.co.uk/news/world-60047328>.

64. Julian Borger, 'The drone operators who halted Russian convoy headed for Kyiv', *The Guardian*, 28 March 2022, <https://www.theguardian.com/world/2022/mar/28/the-drone-operators-who-halted-the-russian-armoured-vehicles-heading-for-kyiv>; Kirsten Fontenrose and Andy Dreby, 'Turkish drones won't give Ukraine the edge it needs', *Defense News*, 1 April 2022, <https://www.defensenews.com/opinion/commentary/2022/04/01/turkish-drones-wont-give-ukraine-the-edge-it-needs/>.

65. Drone Wars, 'Who has armed drones?', *Drone Wars*, July 2021, <https://dronewars.net/who-has-armed-drones/> (accessed 25 April 2022).

66. W. J. Hennigan, 'A fast-growing club: countries that use drones for killing by remote control', *Los Angeles Times*, 22 February 2016, <https://www.latimes.com/world/africa/la-fg-drone-proliferation-2-20160222-story.html>.

67. Many Pubby, 'India all set to get missile armed drones from Israel', *Economic Times*, 14 July 2018, <https://economictimes.indiatimes.com/news/defence/india-all-set-to-get-missile-armed-drones-from-israel/articleshow/57980098.cms>.

68. AFP, 'Turning to Israel, Germany to get weaponized drones for the first time', *Times of Israel*, 6 April 2022, <https://www.timesofisrael.com/turning-to-israel-germany-to-get-weaponized-drones-for-the-first-time>.

69. See, for example: Hasain Marouf, *Drone Warfare and Lawfare in a Post-Heroic Age*, Tuscaloosa: University of Alabama Press, 2016; Ian G. R. Shaw, *Predator Empire: Drone Warfare and Full Spectrum Dominance*, Minneapolis: University of Minnesota Press, 2016; Marcus Schulzke, *The Morality of Drone Warfare and the Politics of Regulation*, Palgrave Macmillan, 2017; Lindsay C. Clark, *Gender and Drone Warfare: A Hauntological Perspective*, Abingdon: Routledge, 2019; Katherine Chandler, *Unmanning: How Humans, Machines and Media Perform Drone Warfare*, New Brunswick: Rutgers University Press, 2020.

70. See: Paul Kahn, 'Imagining Warfare', *European Journal of International Law*, 24 (1) (2013): 199–226, at 224.

71. See: Hugh Gusterson, *Drone: Remote Control Warfare*, London: MIT Press, 2016: 8; Grégoire Chamayou, *Drone Theory*, trans. Janet Lloyd, London: Penguin, 2015: 32.

72. C. A. J. Coady, *Morality and Political Violence*, New York: Cambridge University Press, 2008: 23. See also: Claire Thomas, 'Why Don't We Talk about "Violence" in International Relations?', *Review of International Studies*, 37 (4) (2011): 1815–36, at 1817. A legitimist definition of 'violence' is used in: Leslie Macfarlane, *Violence and the State*, London: Nelson, 1974.

73. Christopher J. Finlay, 'The Concept of Violence in International Theory: A Double-Intent Account', *International Theory*, 9 (1) (2017): 67–100, at 70.

74. Ian Clark, *Waging War: A New Philosophical Introduction*, 2nd edn, Oxford: Oxford University Press, 2015: 69.

75. See: Chris Downes, '"Targeted Killings" in an Age of Terror: The Legality of the Yemen Strike', *Journal of Conflict & Security Law*, 9 (2) (2004): 277–94, at 279; Markus Gunneflo, *Targeted Killing: A Legal and Political History*, Cambridge: Cambridge University Press, 2016: 1.

76. Ian Clark, *Waging War: A New Philosophical Introduction*, 2nd edn, Oxford: Oxford University Press, 2015: 16.

77. Emily Kalah Gade, 'Defining the Non-Combatant: How Do We Determine Who is Worthy of Protection in Violent Conflict?', *Journal of Military Ethics*, 9 (3) (2010): 219–42, at 221.

78. Jean Baudrillard, *The Gulf War Did Not Take Place*, trans. Paul Patton, Indianapolis: Indiana University Press, 1995.

79. Avi Shlaim, 'Ten years after the first war on Gaza, Israel still plans endless brute force', *The Guardian*, 7 January 2019, <https://www.theguardian.com/commentisfree/2019/jan/07/ten-years-first-war-gaza-operation-cast-lead-israel-brute-force>.

80. Ian Clark, *Waging War: A New Philosophical Introduction*, 2nd edn, Oxford: Oxford University Press, 2015: 4.

81. Michael L. Gross, 'Assassination and Targeted Killing: Law Enforcement, Execution or Self-Defence?', *Journal of Applied Philosophy*, 23 (3) (2006): 323–35, at 323.

82. Ian Clark, *Waging War: A New Philosophical Introduction*, 2nd edn, Oxford: Oxford University Press, 2015: 129.

83. Some authors reject the distinction between warfare and violent law enforcement. For example, Mark Neocleous has advocated 'a critical theory of state power that assumes that war and police are *always already* together': Mark Neocleous, 'Air Power as Police Power', *Environment and Planning D: Society and Space*, 31 (2013): 578–93, at 587 (original emphasis). See also: Caroline Holmqvist-Jonsäter, 'War as Perpetual Policing', in *The Character of War in the 21st Century*, ed. Caroline Holmqvist-Jonsäter and Christopher Coker, London: Routledge, 2010: 103–18.

84. Paul W. Kahn, 'Imagining Warfare', *European Journal of International Law*, 24 (1) (2013): 199–226, at 221.

85. Paul Kahn, 'The Paradox of Riskless Warfare', *Philosophy and Public Policy Quarterly*, 22 (3) (2002): 2–8 at 4; Steven P. Lee, 'The Ethics of Current Drone Policy', *International Journal of Applied Philosophy*, 30 (1) (2016): 115–32, at 117.

86. Some authors have argued that, through the 'individualisation of war', some violent state actors appear to diminish the conceptual difference between killing enemies and killing criminals. See, for example: Gabriella Blum, 'The Individualization of War: From War to Policing in the Regulation of Armed Conflicts', in *Law and War*, ed. Austin Sarat, Lawrence Douglas and Martha Merrill Umphrey, Stanford: Stanford University Press, 2013: 48–82; Derek Gregory, 'Drone Geographies', *Radical Philosophy*, 183 (2014): 7–19, at 12.

87. Christian Nikolaus Braun, '*Jus ad Vim* and Drone Warfare: A Classical Just War Perspective', in *Ethics of Drone Strikes: Restraining Remote-Control*

Killing, ed. Christian Enemark, Edinburgh: Edinburgh University Press, 2021: 31–49, at 34.

88. Jeff McMahan, *Killing in War*, Oxford: Oxford University Press, 2009: 35.

89. Michael Walzer, 'Response to McMahan's Paper', *Philosophia*, 34 (2006): 43–5, at 43 (emphasis added).

90. See, for example: Ryan J. Vogel, 'Drone Warfare and the Law of Armed Conflict', *Denver Journal of International Law and Policy*, 39 (1) (2010): 101–38; Alan Backstrom and Ian Henderson, 'New Capabilities in Warfare: An Overview of Contemporary Technological Developments and the Associated Legal and Engineering Issues in Article 36 Weapons Reviews', *International Review of the Red Cross*, 94 (2012): 483–514; Klem Ryan, 'What's Wrong with Drones? The Battlefield in International Humanitarian Law', in *The American Way of Bombing: Changing Ethical Norms from Flying Fortresses to Drones*, ed. Matthew Evangelista and Henry Shue, Ithaca, NY: Cornell University Press, 2014: 207–23; Vivek Sehrawat, 'Legal Status of Drones under LOAC and International Law', *Penn State Journal of Law and International Affairs*, 5 (1) (2017): 165–206.

91. See: Christof Heyns, Dapo Akande, Lawrence Hill-Cawthorne and Thompson Chengeta, 'The International Law Framework Regulating the Use of Armed Drones', *International and Comparative Law Quarterly*, 65 (2016): 791–827.

92. See: Thomas Gregory, 'Drones, Targeted Killings, and the Limitations of International Law', *International Political Sociology*, 9 (2015): 197–212, at 206.

93. Elke Schwarz, *Death Machines: The Ethics of Violent Technologies*, Manchester: Manchester University Press, 2018: 122.

94. Valerie Morkevičius, 'Looking Inward Together: Just War Thinking and Our Shared Moral Emotions', *Ethics and International Affairs*, 31 (4) (2017): 441–51, at 441 (emphasis added).

95. Ibid. 441.

96. Christof Heyns, Dapo Akande, Lawrence Hill-Cawthorne and Thompson Chengeta, 'The International Law Framework Regulating the Use of Armed Drones', *International and Comparative Law Quarterly*, 65 (2016): 791–827, at 793. An armed drone system controlled entirely by AI might be described as *mala in se* if the notion of 'artificial moral agency' is rejected (see Chapter 6).

97. See: Alan Backstrom and Ian Henderson, 'New Capabilities in Warfare: An Overview of Contemporary Technological Developments and the Associated Legal and Engineering Issues in Article 36 Weapons Reviews', *International Review of the Red Cross*, 94 (2012): 483–514, at 487; Ryan J. Vogel, 'Droning On: Controversy Surrounding Drone Warfare is Not Really about Drones', *The Brown Journal of World Affairs*, 19 (2) (2013): 111–21; Michael J. Boyle, 'The Legal and Ethical Implications of Drone Warfare', *The International Journal of Human Rights*, 19 (2) (2015): 105–26, at 105; Jean-Baptiste Jeangène Vilmer, 'France and the American Drone Precedent', in *The Ethics of War and Peace Revisited*, ed. Daniel R. Brunstetter and Jean-Vincent Holeindre, Washington, DC: Georgetown

University Press, 2018: 97–116, at 99; Brianna Rosen, 'To end the forever wars, rein in the drones', *Just Security*, 16 February 2021, <https://www.justsecurity.org/74690/to-end-the-forever-wars-rein-in-the-drones/>.

98. See: Hugh Gusterson, *Drone: Remote Control Warfare*, London: MIT Press, 2016: 8; UNIDIR, *Increasing Transparency, Oversight and Accountability of Armed Unmanned Aerial Vehicles*, United Nations Institute for Disarmament Research, 2017: 1.

99. UN General Assembly, 'Protection of human rights and fundamental freedoms while countering terrorism' (A/RES/68/178), New York, United Nations, 18 December 2013; European Parliament resolution of 27 February 2014 on the use of armed drones (2014/2567(RSP)); UN Human Rights Council, 'Ensuring use of remotely piloted aircraft or armed drones in counterterrorism and military operations in accordance with international law, including international human rights and humanitarian law' (A/HRC/RES/25/22), New York: UN General Assembly, 15 April 2014; Parliamentary Assembly of the Council of Europe, 'Drones and targeted killings: the need to uphold human rights and international law' (Resolution 2051(2015)), 23 April 2015.

Chapter 2

WARFARE

When the violent use of armed drones is described as 'drone warfare', this is usually done without consideration of what makes violence count as 'war'. All war is violent, but not all violence is war, so not all drone violence will be drone warfare. It is important to be confident, in conceptual terms, about the true nature of violence, because its essence determines the kind of morality that can be brought to bear. That determination then affects what moral permissions are available to the perpetrators of violence and what restraints should be exercised for the benefit of prospective victims. Warfare is the only kind of violence that is subject to moral judgement according to traditional Just War principles. But if war is not what is going on, there is no opportunity to make claims about 'just war' or 'unjust war'. Rather, non-war violence must be justified or condemned in some other way.

Once the conceptual gateway to Just War morality is open, there are principles of *jus ad bellum* (the justice of resorting to war) and *jus in bello* (the just conduct of war) to be applied. *Jus ad bellum* includes ethical requirements that the resort to war should be: based upon a just cause; a proportionate response to the injustice to be remedied; properly authorised; assessed as having a reasonable prospect of success; and a problem-solving measure of last resort.[1] Then, if war commences, *jus in bello* requires that the practice of warfare should: discriminate between combatants (who may legitimately be targeted) and non-combatants (who may not); and be anticipated to generate a degree of harm (including unintended harm to civilians) that is proportional (not excessive) in relation to the expected military benefit.[2] All these Just War principles have been developed and recognised over many centuries,[3] and their enduring influence is today reflected in international laws for restraining armed conflict, such as the 1945 UN Charter (*jus ad bellum*) and the 1949 Geneva Conventions (*jus in bello*).

Gaining access to the special morality applicable within the war paradigm can be politically attractive because this morality is relatively permissive of harm to people and things. By contrast, as will be shown in Chapter 3, there is generally less tolerance of killing during peacetime when, for example, a state authority is violently enforcing its domestic criminal law. For this reason, a state might sometimes prefer its violence to be judged according to the morality of war instead of law enforcement. And, to this end, it might conspicuously commit to adhere to Just War principles when acting violently. However, the invoking of these principles does not itself establish the existence of a condition of war,[4] and to think it does would amount to putting the moral 'cart' before the conceptual 'horse'. What is rather required, to render the morality of war applicable, is a prior and plausible conceptualisation of the relevant violence as warfare. Without that in place, there is a risk that excessive violence and unjust harm will occur if, for example, an instance of essentially non-war violence is mistakenly conceptualised as warfare or is deliberately mis-conceptualised as such.

When it comes to the use of armed drones, and before such violence can be subjected to ethical assessment, an important conceptual distinction must be drawn between uses that are warlike (drone warfare) and uses that are unwarlike. Accordingly, this chapter begins with a discussion of when and why drone violence can plausibly be conceptualised as warfare. Here, the mutual experiencing of physical risk is arguably a critical factor because war is by nature a contest between contending belligerents. The discussion of ethics then proceeds by reference to *ad bellum* and *in bello* principles of Just War, and the chapter lastly outlines some reasons why standards of moral conduct can and should be raised in the practice of drone warfare.

CONCEPTUALISING DRONE VIOLENCE AS WARFARE

During the years of debate among scholars and policymakers about the use of armed drones, a critical point of contention has been whether a user (for example, the US government) is 'actually at war' when it wields drone violence.[5] Establishing this is important because only in a condition of war can a violent actor avail themselves of a morality (and an associated legal regime) that affords them greater permission to cause harm. Beyond that condition, the human right to life is generally considered to be the paramount moral value, so violence against persons is only rarely permitted as a matter of ethics and law.[6] Given this difference in moral expectations, it is easy enough to claim that injuries and deaths arising from drone *warfare* will generally be more easily justified than those arising from unwarlike instances of drone violence. However, to draw that distinction is to assume that any drone violence at all can be conceptualised as warfare. This might be difficult, in the eyes of some observers, because armed drones that are controlled remotely seem to disrupt traditional ideas about the relationship between war, warriors and physical risk.

In seeking to determine when (if ever) drone violence counts as drone warfare, a useful starting point is to think more generally about the essence of 'war'. Once the idea of allowing governments to determine war's existence subjectively and self-interestedly is rejected,[7] conceptualising an instance of violence as warfare becomes a matter of referring to 'objective criteria'.[8] In the most basic sense, war can be differentiated from other forms of violence by identifying it as being public and political in nature. Violence wielded exclusively for private pleasure and/or for a criminal purpose can thus be deemed unwarlike.[9] Beyond that, though, war's political essence is rooted in the idea of *contending* political communities, which means war necessarily involves a struggle *between* opposing belligerents. If, instead, violent effects were arranged to flow entirely in one direction (from one side to another), that physically uncontested practice would not count as warfare. Rather, it would stand alone as merely 'naked' violence,[10] exhibiting none of the togetherness implied by the 'with' prefixes ('con' and 'com') in words like 'conflict', 'combat' and 'contest'.

The war-as-contest concept was originally advanced by the Prussian general Carl von Clausewitz in his nineteenth-century book *On War*.[11] It continues to influence more recent thinkers who insist, for example, that war is essentially 'interactive',[12] an 'exchange of violence' rather than 'unilateral force',[13] and something that is distinguishable from 'killing people who do not or cannot resist'.[14] Clausewitz argued that it is 'the element of the thing itself' that war is 'nothing but a duel on an extensive scale', and he likened it to a match between 'two wrestlers' each of whom 'strives by physical force to compel the other to submit to his will'.[15] In this way, he placed dynamic interaction at the heart of his concept of war, and he went on to explain what kind of violence would fall outside of that concept: 'War is always the shock of two hostile bodies in collision, not the action of a living power upon an inanimate mass, because *an absolute state of endurance* would not be making War'.[16] Later, a similar idea was evident in the German philosopher Carl Schmitt's observation that '[t]o war on both sides belongs a certain *chance*, a minimum of possibility for victory'.[17] When that is no longer the case, he argued, 'the opponent becomes nothing more than an object of violent measures'.[18]

The notion of both opposing sides necessarily experiencing 'chance' during war could also be described, in conceptual terms, as a condition of mutual *risk*. In the absence of this condition, according to Paul Kahn, any so-called warfare 'is not war at all', and the idea of 'riskless warfare' is nonsense (or a 'paradox').[19] In his conceptualisation of war, the reflected personal experience of killers and victims is of central significance, which is why Kahn has advocated thinking of warfare as 'reciprocal acts of self-sacrifice'.[20] Similarly, Henry Shue has argued that 'war . . . is about killing people who may otherwise kill you'.[21] However, a conceptual requirement that opposing warriors must *directly* reciprocate threats towards each other is probably setting the bar of 'mutual risk' too high (and it would certainly render unwarlike a great many modern military practices). Such a requirement seems more appropriate in the context of a private duel between individual antagonists, but it is not well matched to the idea that warfare is also an essentially *public* form of violence that is engaged in by members of a political collective.

Perhaps, then, a better approach to thinking about risk within a war-as-contest concept is to set a minimum conceptual requirement of mutuality rather than reciprocity. Accordingly, a condition of warfare would be understood to exist if, on both sides, some degree of physical risk (large or small) is experienced *while* violence is wielded. The idea of 'warfare' could thus extend to encompassing some highly asymmetric instances of violence, such as the actions of a bomber flying at high altitude or a missile-launcher on a submarine at sea. Conceivably, it might sometimes be the case that neither of these violent actors is within easy reach of enemy retaliation. And yet, by virtue of being airborne or underwater, their violence could still be described as warlike because it occurs while the respective physical risk of crashing or drowning is endured. By contrast, an armed drone's operator, if they are on the ground and far away from a targeted enemy, appears to endure no physical risk at all. In which case, it is reasonable to ask: how could their violence possibly count as warfare? The question cannot be sidestepped by asserting that drone operators are morally *liable* (as warriors) to be attacked,[22] because that is to presume the applicability of Just War morality. What rather matters, conceptually, is 'whether drone operators are really at war at all'.[23] And, for present purposes, the critical issue is: do the operators of armed drones experience mutual risk when they kill?

In answer, it is important first to acknowledge that a drone operator in a ground control station has the potential to be exposed to physical risk. In practice, to date, armed drones have mainly and notoriously been used, by the US government, against relatively weak enemies located in extremely distant places. However, not every armed drone can or will be used across vast distances, so not every drone operator will ever be beyond the reach of enemy violence. The operators of small, short-range drones deployed to areas where fighting is going on are more likely to be at risk of enemy attack. And, in a future confrontation between powerful and well-armed states, geographical distancing might afford little protection to each side's drone operators once their bases were targeted by long-range aircraft or missiles. For now, though, the use of armed drones from beyond the reach of enemy violence seems likely to remain the preferred method for drone-using states that are casualty-averse, so it is this kind of drone violence that most warrants conceptual and moral assessment.

When the spectacle of drone operators killing without experiencing physical risk has caused observers to feel confusion and unease, one common response has been to highlight the numerous other participants in drone violence who do face danger.[24] While that violence (targeting and striking) is directly controlled by individuals in, say, the United States or the United Kingdom – far from where a drone strike occurs in, say, the Middle East – the drone aircraft itself is typically armed, fuelled, launched, landed and maintained by forward-deployed personnel located at air bases abroad. Moreover, to gather the intelligence upon which many drone strike decisions are based, a drone-using state might deploy spies on dangerous missions inside foreign territories.[25] Thus, it could be said, the *entirety* of the enterprise of using armed drones is neither uniformly remote nor wholly devoid of physical risk. Even so, this assertion misses the point that support staff and spies are, in truth, not the ones doing the killing. That task remains solely and literally in the hands of those faraway operators who aim and fire a drone's weapons, so the conceptualising of drone violence as 'warfare' requires that mutual risk be somehow an element of *their* experience.

Satisfying this condition can understandably seem difficult when a drone-using state deliberately arranges for its drone operators to be physically safe. However, it is made possible by applying a broad understanding of mutuality. Arguably, then, drone violence can count as 'drone warfare' if it involves a *vicarious* experience of being at risk. Here, what matters conceptually is: firstly, that there are at-risk people on the ground (friendly or allied personnel, or local civilians) in whose experience a drone operator can sympathetically 'participate' (albeit from afar);[26] and, secondly, that his or her violence functions to alleviate an immediate danger to others. Conversely, where not even this is the case, drone violence is in no sense mutual risky and must therefore fall outside the concept of warfare.

Such an approach to the war-as-contest concept resonates with the distinction that some authors have drawn between, on the one hand, the use of drones in conflict zones to provide air support to ground troops and, on the other hand, their use against individuals who are far from any fighting and thus not immediately threatening to anyone.[27] The argument that usually accompanies the drawing of this distinction is that, whereas the first kind of drone violence is more readily classified as warfare (for ethical or legal purposes), the second kind is less likely to warrant that status. Indeed, once the point is reached where, for one side, there is nobody available for violent interaction, the other side's use of armed drones ceases to be mutually risky even in a minimal (vicarious) sense. That drone violence then cannot count as warfare, and it must instead be judged morally in non-war terms. An example of such judgement is provided in Chapter 3 (which addresses violent law enforcement), but for now it remains to explore the morality of that which *is* drone warfare by reference to Just War principles.

DRONE WARFARE AND *JUS AD BELLUM*

The ethics of drone warfare can begin to be assessed by inquiring into how the availability of armed drones affects the justness of decisions to resort to war. From a *jus ad bellum* perspective, and even when there is mutual risk, much moral concern has centred on the idea that drone warfare is 'easy' warfare. This concern is reflected, for example, in arguments that extreme geographical distancing reduces risk to such an extent as to make states 'more willing to go to war',[28] or that armed drones are conducive to the waging of aggressive 'wars of choice'.[29] Here, the moral objection appears to be that states' commitment to self-restraint according to *jus ad bellum* principles is effectively weakened because drones make war itself seem less dangerous and the avoidance of war less important. It is not necessarily the case, however, that an ability to resort to war *more* easily than before is morally problematic. Indeed, swift action could be considered a virtue if a just cause for war needed to be urgently pursued. Rather, the key moral issue is whether the use of armed drones makes it *excessively* easy for states to act violently in world affairs. For the purpose of exploring this issue, there are five *jus ad bellum* principles worth considering in turn: just cause, right authority, proportionality, reasonable prospect of success, and war as a last resort.

A cause for resorting to war is just if it is based on self-defence or the defence of others (sometimes called 'humanitarian intervention'), but base motivations like revenge, greed, mischief-making or aggression do not amount to having a just cause. It is a moral problem, then, if warfare does not tend somehow to be 'essentially defensive' in its strategic purpose.[30] When it comes to the use of armed drones, and to the extent that they make it easy 'to get at our enemies',[31] one concern is that this capability might tempt drone-users to act violently without a just cause. For example, more and more 'enemies' might end up being subjected to drone strikes because they *can* be struck (just in case), rather than because they truly pose a threat that warrants a defence. Also, as long-range drones especially are well suited to clandestine operation, the resort to drone warfare can sometimes be hard to attribute to a specific drone-user and therefore easy for that user to mendaciously deny.[32] Thus, secrecy and deniability could combine to increase the likelihood of states getting away with drone strikes that have nothing to do with national self-defence, which is worrying from a *jus ad bellum* perspective. Whereas, as a matter of principle, states ought to arrange for their violence to serve only a just cause, some states with armed drones at their disposal might instead feel encouraged merely to 'meddle in conflicts' in which they do not have a vital stake.[33] On the other hand, when the just cause for war is other-defence, the availability of armed drones might sometimes be morally advantageous. As some authors have argued, these aircraft have the potential to facilitate and improve the practice of armed intervention to prevent or stop large-scale atrocities.[34] If indeed it is easy to dispatch armed drones swiftly to places where civilians are immediately threatened by genocidal violence and in need of aerial protection, this rapid-response capacity might make a morally desirable intervention more likely to occur.

In 2011 the US government deployed armed Predator drones to Libya, in support of allied forces (local and foreign), for the purpose of protecting civilians from attack by their own government.[35] But in that instance of pursuing an other-defence cause, there potentially arose a problem of adherence to another *jus ad bellum* principle: right authority. This principle requires that, as the resort to war is a grave and potentially high-risk decision, it must be properly authorised. On the international plane of decision-making, the US resort to drone warfare was duly covered by UN Security Council Resolution 1973, which authorised UN member states 'to take all necessary measures . . . to protect civilians and civilian populated areas under threat of attack'.[36] As a matter of domestic decision-making, however, the then-president Barack Obama determined that his executive authorisation for using armed drones did not require approval from the US Congress. The reasoning behind this determination was that, as no personnel and only drones were deployed to Libya at the time, the chance of escalation to the point of harming US interests was so low that congressional authorisation was not required.[37] And yet, in this way, Congress was arguably denied the opportunity to consent, on behalf of the American people, to assuming the risk that Obama's optimism might later be proven wrong. Moreover, two years later, Obama acknowledged that the secrecy often involved in drone strikes more generally 'can end up shielding our government from the public scrutiny that a troop deployment invites'.[38] In a democracy, such scrutiny is important in adhering to the right-authority principle, because it underpins the granting of citizens' *informed* consent to hazard the potential 'blowback' from a state's outward acts of violence.[39] For this reason, as several authors have warned, a democratic deficit in the way drone warfare is authorised has the potential to weaken its *ad bellum* legitimacy.[40]

Another relevant principle is *ad bellum* proportionality, which requires prospective users of warlike violence to engage in a weighing of its costs and benefits. Even if war is initially resorted to and then continued for a just cause (for example, self-defence), that war is or becomes morally wrong if the outward damage expected to be caused is excessive in relation to the injury to be remedied.[41] In other words, if the geographical scope, timescale and/or human quantity of harm exceeds what is reasonably necessary for one side to achieve its defensive purpose, that side becomes more sinning than sinned against from a *jus ad bellum* perspective. Thus, for instance, the US-led expulsion of Iraqi forces from Kuwait in 1991 was proportionate to the injury (invasion) suffered by that country. But had Kuwait's defenders gone on to invade and occupy Iraq in return, that would have been disproportionate. Today, when armed drones are available to be used in war, one potential proportionality problem is strategic overreach (or 'mission creep'). Here, the moral concern is that a drone-using state, which can easily strike targets remotely, might 'lose sight of its goals and drift into a growing number of conflicts worldwide'.[42] Alternatively, it could be argued, the deployment of drones instead of inhabited aircraft might reduce the pressure towards waging a disproportionate war. In terms of its potential to induce escalation, losing a drone to anti-aircraft fire seems less serious than losing an airborne pilot.[43] And, apparently for this reason, in 2019 the former US president Donald Trump called off a retaliatory strike (which might have killed an estimated 150 people) against Iran after it shot down a US drone.[44] As he explained at the time: 'We didn't have a man or woman in the drone. It would have made a big, big difference'.[45] Even so, as Michael Boyle has argued, the option to use airpower in a way that does not endanger a pilot might be exactly what encourages a drone-using state to run the risk of provoking enemy attacks and escalatory responses.[46] In which case, drone warfare could still be morally disadvantageous from the perspective of *ad bellum* proportionality.

Turning to the principle of 'reasonable prospect of success', this is the requirement that war should not be resorted to if the damage thus caused is likely to be in vain.[47] Given that death and human suffering are wrong by default, they can carry no moral weight in *ad bellum* terms if their occurrence is reasonably expected to be futile. Drone warfare is potentially problematic in this regard if decision-makers are occasioned to rush into war without adequately considering how the meaning of 'success' could change. That is, after initially being seduced by the apparently low cost of engaging with an enemy by using armed drones, there is a risk that those decision-makers might later find themselves facing a crisis situation that cannot be resolved without their side incurring heavier costs (measured in lives lost).[48] If that eventuality ought reasonably to have been anticipated and planned for, but an 'escalation to success' does not occur,[49] that planning failure when resorting to drone warfare would be a *jus ad bellum* failure too. On the other hand, it could also be argued that armed drones are more conducive to avoiding futile loss of life because their use makes military endeavours more likely to endure for as long as is necessary to achieve success. In war, 'staying the course' can be difficult, from a domestic politics perspective, when a perceived excess of casualties sparks public demands to stop fighting and abandon a war's just cause.[50] However, to the extent that drone warfare reduces the loathed endangerment of national personnel, it arguably carries the moral advantage (in *ad bellum* terms) of sometimes making strategic success more likely in a war of long duration.

The final (but not least important) principle to be considered is that, even when there is a just cause, resorting to war should be a last resort. This principle requires that there be genuine reluctance rather than eagerness on the part of decision-makers to choose violence (with all the human harm that that entails) as a way of resolving political disputes in the world. Such reluctance is usually highly likely to be felt when troops would need to be deployed to places within easy reach of armed enemies. And it could also be felt, albeit to a lesser degree, at the prospect of deploying airborne pilots into enemy territory where they are exposed to the physical risks of crashing or being captured. In that scenario, the distressing possibility of losing national personnel and causing grief to their families at home might well have a restraining influence upon conscientious political leaders who are otherwise keen to wage war.[51] But if armed drones were instead available to be deployed to dangerous places, and the perceived risk of losing lives was thereby reduced, it could become more difficult in practice to resist temptation and adhere to the principle of war as a last resort.[52] In *ad bellum* terms, the resulting moral risk would be one of violence (drone strikes) being wielded too quickly and too often, to the undue detriment of people living in targeted territories.

DRONE WARFARE AND *JUS IN BELLO*

Once a war has commenced, and regardless of its *jus ad bellum* status, the protecting of people from unjust harm is mainly achieved through adherence to *jus in bello* principles for conducting warfare. The strict separation of these two sets of 'logically independent' principles represents the orthodox understanding of Just War morality,[53] and it is reflected in the way international law is likewise divided into distinct *ad bellum* and *in bello* branches of law. The rationale for keeping the two separate is to avoid any attempt to justify violations of *jus in bello* rules by reference to adherence to *jus ad bellum* rules, and vice versa.[54] Accordingly, it is understood that warriors on both sides can and should fight justly, even in an unjust cause, and that pursuing a just cause does not afford warriors any moral permission to fight unjustly. Some moral philosophers take a different ('revisionist') view: that the justness of resorting to war and of conducting it are interdependent. Consequently, they argue, nothing just (as a matter of war's conduct) can be done in furtherance of a war effort that is unjust (as a matter of cause).[55] However, this approach has been criticised for placing too much importance upon *jus ad bellum*. According to Michael Schmitt, for example, it encourages a harmful '"good guys" versus "bad guys" dichotomy', whereby the latter (as participants in war) are denied the benefits of their enemies' *in bello* restraint.[56] And, in any event, a more general problem with applying the 'revisionist' approach is that it is historically and notoriously difficult to establish which side in war is truly the champion of a just cause.[57] Both sides often claim that theirs is the just war, but they cannot both be right, and there is usually too little time to determine this matter definitively while a war is ongoing and *in bello* risks are immediate. For this reason, and for present purposes, the better approach is to consider *ad bellum* and *in bello* principles separately.

When used in war, armed drones undoubtedly can cause harm to civilians. In 2016, for example, the UN reported that a drone strike in Afghanistan (probably conducted by the US military) had killed at least fifteen civilians.[58] In 2019 another US strike there killed at least thirty people who, it turned out, were civilian workers harvesting nuts.[59] And, just as the War in Afghanistan was ending in late August 2021, a US drone killed a misidentified aid worker and nine members of his family as he arrived at his home in Kabul.[60] The fact of civilian deaths occurring has been widely cited as a concern by observers who oppose either drone use in war or violence in general. However, in terms of Just War morality, the causing of civilian harm per se is not enough to warrant condemnation. Rather, drone warfare is understood to be morally unacceptable only if, under the circumstances, the injury or death of one or more civilians is *too much* harm.

To determine whether this is so, *jus in bello* ethics generally requires the application of two principles – discrimination and proportionality – which also underpin certain rules of international humanitarian law. The first principle rests upon the drawing of a status-based distinction between combatants (who may legitimately be targeted) and non-combatants (who may not).[61] Or, if status-based differentiation is difficult (because, for example, military uniforms are not worn), 'discrimination' involves the targeting only of people whose observed behaviour reasonably indicates their 'direct participation in hostilities'.[62] The second principle (proportionality) requires that the practice of warfare should be anticipated to generate a degree of harm (including unintended harm to civilians) that is proportional (not excessive) in relation to the military benefit expected to be achieved.[63] Moreover, in practice, adherence to this principle is enhanced when war's practitioners are pro-active in attempting to reduce the likelihood of civilian harm,[64] for example by exercising 'all feasible precautions' when planning attacks.[65]

It is in the nature of some weapons that their use in war simply cannot be restrained according to *in bello* principles, so these weapons are considered *mala in se* (inherently bad) as a matter of Just War morality. For example, nuclear weapons, biological weapons (involving a contagious microorganism) and anti-personnel landmines are not designed to enable discrimination between combatant and civilian victims. Also, their largely uncontrollable and unpredictable effects make it impossible to assess proportionality with any accuracy. And the only available 'method' of using such weapons precautiously, therefore, is not to use them at all. By contrast, in the case of armed drones, there is arguably no characteristic of this weapon technology that makes unjust effects inevitable or that makes compliance with Just War principles impossible.[66] On the contrary, drone warfare is in some ways well suited to adhering to war's rules and 'limiting the violence inflicted on civilians',[67] although this form of wartime violence still carries a degree of moral risk in terms of discrimination and proportionality.

From a *jus in bello* perspective, the principal advantage of using an armed and camera-equipped drone is that, compared to many other weapon platforms, it affords a powerful capacity to identify targets correctly.[68] Under the favourable condition of air superiority, and if the military need for an airstrike is not urgent, a drone can hover undetected over an area for long periods of time while relaying video imagery back to base. This enables the drone's operator to obtain a clear and continuous picture of what usually happens (and of any unusual activity) in that area. Then, by watching and waiting until 'the ideal moment to strike',[69] or by delaying or aborting the launch of a weapon, the operator can better avoid striking the wrong person or harming any nearby civilians. This harm-avoidance capacity is well illustrated by a scenario described by a member of a UK drone crew:[70]

We saw, before sunrise, a man leave a compound and go to an area behind a building. He started digging, interacting with the ground. The controller [a friendly soldier on the ground] saw that and immediately suggested that it was an IED [improvised explosive device], and started trying to arrange permission for us to strike under the 'hostile act' ROE [rule of engagement]. . . . My crew disagreed, and as we watched longer and more closely, we could pick out some of the tools he was using and started to assess them as regular farming tools. Eventually with the first fringes of sunrise, we could tell he was just seeding a small patch of ground. Watching him for an hour let us see that he had none of the hallmarks of a traditional IED emplacer.

When a drone strike is planned and an individual target is identified in advance, the risk of unjust outcomes is indeed reduced by timing the strike for when that individual is away from civilians.[71] However, that risk is likely to be higher in instances of 'dynamic targeting' where there is less scope to choose when and where to strike. And it might be higher still if an armed drone is used in support of friendly or allied troops who are under enemy fire yet close to local civilians.[72] It is important to note, also, that the careful timing of a drone strike is more difficult when the aircraft is controlled via satellite at extremely long range. The transmission of image data and control signals can be delayed by several seconds in this circumstance,[73] and that delay might sometimes be enough to prevent the correction of targeting mistakes. This is probably why, for example, a UK drone strike in 2018 'unintentionally' killed a civilian on a speeding motorbike when he suddenly rode across the target area.[74] In that instance, arguably, using a non-remote method of violence would (if feasible) have been more precautious than using an armed drone.

Another moral risk arises in the conduct of so-called 'signature strikes' (to be discussed further in Chapter 4), and here the main concern is adherence to the principle of discrimination. In the practice of drone warfare, killing someone whose behaviour matches predesignated signs of dangerousness is not necessarily discriminate killing, especially if there is a problem with the signatures themselves.[75] For example, the targeting of people in certain locations who are both male and military-aged does not equate to targeting members of an armed group or direct participants in hostilities,[76] and it therefore carries a high risk that the wrong people (civilians) will be killed. Worse still, from this perspective, is the idea that people who immediately come to the aid of drone strike victims are in that way behaving in the manner of targetable enemies. In the 'double-tap' version of a signature strike, an armed drone continues flying over the site of an initial strike and then launches a second attack upon the original targets' rescuers.[77] But, in this circumstance, the discrimination principle is arguably not respected, because the logic of neutralising violent threats appears to be replaced by that of merely and intentionally punishing sympathy with an injured enemy.

Where the use of an armed drone might (foreseeably), by contrast, cause some unintended harm to one or more civilians, the *jus in bello* principle of proportionality requires the anticipated harm to be out-weighed in value by the military benefit to be achieved. Regardless of the method of attack, the moral worth of engaging in such a weighing exer-cise is open to doubt if, as is sometimes argued, civilian harms and mili-tary benefits are fundamentally incommensurable values.[78] However, in the practice of drone warfare, there is some scope at least to respect the spirit of the proportionality principle by taking positive steps to reduce the potential for civilian exposure to a strike's harmful effects. And, if 'harm' is understood narrowly to mean injuries and deaths, the choosing of a weapon to be fired from a drone is especially relevant here.

The Hellfire air-to-ground missile used on many US drones, for exam-ple, has a much smaller explosive charge than other available missiles,[79] but it still generates a blast that often far exceeds what is necessary to kill one individual. Thus, it is inherently dangerous also to other (innocent) people who might happen to be in the vicinity of a strike. To address this concern, the US military has sometimes reportedly used non-explosive warheads when, in urban areas especially, the risk of 'collateral damage' from an explosion is normally high. Its R9X 'flying Ginsu' version of the Hellfire contains long metal blades for lethally slicing through (rather than blasting) a vehicle carrying a targeted individual.[80] Assuming, then, that the military value of killing that individual is high, the reasonable anticipa-tion of a lesser degree of incidental civilian harm can make drone warfare of this kind appear morally superior from a proportionality perspective. And yet, from an intelligence-based targeting perspective, it can also be immensely challenging to accurately identify and track a person as they move quickly through a crowded city. So, for *jus in bello* purposes, the risk remains that even the 'precise' use of a non-explosive missile could still end up killing precisely the wrong person. Moreover, if the moral advan-tage of such a weapon were nevertheless overestimated, this would carry the additional risk of drone strikes occurring more often inside cities, to the overall detriment of the many civilians who live in them.[81]

Further to the issue of proportionality, the use of armed drones in gen-eral is sometimes praised not only for being 'good' (as a matter of *jus in bello*) but also for being morally better than other methods of violence. Drones, as the argument goes, are 'the least lethal means of conduct-ing the fight',[82] they 'do better at . . . avoiding collateral damage than anything else we have',[83] and as Barack Obama once professed 'with great certainty': the rate of civilian casualties 'in any drone operation' is 'far lower than the rate of civilian casualties that occur in conventional war'.[84] One problem with such claims is their implication that 'other' (non-drone) weapons can only be less discriminate and proportionate in their effects. Yet there are some weapons, such as bayonets and pistols, that can more easily be used in a way that minimises civilian victimhood, provided that the associated risk to their users (of close-range warfighting) is tolerated. Also, in the advancing of a drones-are-better claim from a proportionality standpoint, the drawing of a favourable comparison with non-drone methods of warfare is necessarily a conditional one. That is, it presumes that the latter would certainly be used if armed drones were not available. But where there is not a serious prospect of instead engaging an enemy by, say, firing artillery shells or dropping bombs from inhabited aircraft, it is not possible to justify drone warfare by presenting it as 'better' than those methods. Rather, in that circumstance, there is really no comparison to be made, so the use of armed drones in war must be ethically assessed only on its own merits.

WAGING DRONE WARFARE AND RAISING MORAL STANDARDS

In one important sense, from an ethical perspective, an armed drone equipped with video-cameras really is beyond compare in the way it enables users to watch and record the circumstances surrounding a strike. This capacity for real-time tactical observation and detailed review – unmatched by other weapon technologies – also then enables and requires a raising of moral expectations when it comes to discrimination and proportionality in the practice of drone warfare. This is so for two reasons. First, as a greater degree of care *can* be taken in that practice, it follows that armed drones *should* be used according to a higher standard of adherence to *in bello* principles, to the overall benefit of war's potential victims. Second, as so many of the decisions, actions and consequences of a drone strike can be recorded and subsequently analysed, this facility affords a high potential for drone-users constantly to learn lessons from past practice and accordingly to make constant improvements. Thus, overall, the expectation of meeting a higher standard of moral conduct in *drone* warfare is a corollary of 'the relative ease with which [morally relevant] information can be acquired'.[85] In addition, as Bradley Strawser has argued, when an armed drone is used at extremely long range, a drone operator's consequent lack of concern for individual self-defence ought to make them 'more capable, not less, of behaving justly'.[86] Or, as Marcus Schulzke has explained it, when that operator need not weigh their own safety against that of at-risk civilians in a targeted territory abroad, he or she is well positioned to 'exercise a higher degree of restraint when faced with ambiguous potential threats than a human soldier who could be injured or killed because of a miscalculation'.[87]

In response to the idea that drone warfare's distinguishing features are morally significant, Christof Heyns has argued that 'specifically rigorous' governance is required,[88] and Janina Dill has suggested that 'positing informal norms [of drone use] that reframe or exceed legal obligations might be sensible'.[89] To this end, one worthwhile approach is to focus on raising moral standards in relation to two key question that frequently arise in debates about drones: who is (not) targetable as an 'enemy', and how much civilian harm is disproportionate? Accordingly, in future, the just conduct of drone warfare could require the adoption of a narrow concept of enemy targetability and a broad concept of civilian harm. In practice, then, it would rightly be more challenging to adhere to the *jus in bello* principles of discrimination and proportionality, respectively.

When armed drones make it operationally easier to spot and strike a wide range of 'targetable' persons, this carries the risk that a drone-user will feel tempted to interpret too liberally the moral limits on who may be killed and under what circumstances. To counteract this temptation, the point could be emphasised that the answers to those questions 'do not differ based on the choice of weapon'.[90] However, this argument would be an encouragement only to wage drone warfare in a manner *not worse*, ethically speaking, than any other form of wartime violence. What rather matters is that armed drones *are* different in morally significant ways and, for that reason, should be held to a higher standard of civilian protection. This, in effect, involves taking a broad view of who counts as a 'civilian' in the first place and, consequently, a narrow view of who may legitimately be targeted.

An accusation levelled against the US and UK governments during recent years has been that their drone strikes sometimes kill people who have not been 'properly counted as civilians'.[91] Here, the underlying ethical concern is not that outright indiscriminate killing has occurred, but rather that some strikes have proceeded upon too broad a view of a person's status as a 'combatant' or of their behaviour as constituting 'direct participation in hostilities'. One way of raising the *jus in bello* standard of drone warfare could therefore be to adhere voluntarily and more closely to non-binding 'guidance' on targeting issued by the International Committee of the Red Cross. Accordingly, drone strikes would not be permitted against anyone who can clearly be seen (via video-camera) performing 'exclusively political, administrative or other non-combat functions'.[92] This would rule out, for example, the violent neutralisation of any 'threat' perceived to be posed by individuals who raise funds for the enemy side (perhaps by criminal means) but who do not themselves ever take up arms in its cause.[93] In refraining from killing such individuals, the potential operational disadvantage is that an enemy's overall capacity to wage war is possibly left undiminished, making it harder eventually to bring about their defeat. However, there is a countervailing moral advantage of exercising this much *in bello* restraint when applying the principle of discrimination: by narrowing the scope for targetability, fewer civilians are placed at risk of being mistakenly identified as 'threatening' and of subsequently being killed in a drone strike.

Enhancing civilian protection could also be achieved by conducting drone warfare according to an augmented standard of proportionality. This would involve a narrowing of the range of circumstances in which strikes are permissible, because the expected civilian risks and military benefits would need to be weighed differently. That is, if a broad concept of civilian harm were adopted when using armed drones, the expectation of that harm would carry more moral weight, so the value of military benefits to be achieved would generally need to be higher. Such a change is arguably warranted because, in contrast to many other methods of wartime violence, the highly vision-based practice of drone warfare enables drones' operators sometimes to acquire a richer understanding of what victimhood actually means. This then puts them (or their commanders) on notice, morally, to account for that richness when deciding whether or how to proceed with a strike.

In the traditional application of the proportionality principle, and regardless of what weapon is used, 'harm' tends to be understood exclusively in terms of immediate physical 'casualties' (injuries and deaths).[94] Thus, if the lethal blast range of an exploding weapon is known to be roughly a 20-metre radius from the point of impact, a civilian standing 200 metres away from a precisely targeted individual is liable to be assessed as unlikely to be harmed. In the longer term, however, that civilian could yet suffer harm of a non-physical nature, but which is directly attributable to the targeted person's death. Beyond killing and maiming, as Tony Coady has observed, '[w]ar . . . injures [people] in many complex and enduring ways . . . and radically alters the normal conditions of their existence'.[95] Such alteration can include, for example, a descent into debilitating grief or mental torment, and for this reason several authors have advocated routinely including psychological injuries in calculations of *in bello* proportionality.[96] In principle, this is a sound suggestion, although in practice it would probably be impossible to anticipate with any accuracy how much psychological harm is likely to be experienced by any given civilian survivor of a drone strike. By contrast, non-physical harm is more readily understood and anticipated in relation to what drone operators are themselves made to feel about the killing they do, and this issue is explored in Chapter 5. Even so, when it comes to the victimhood that is experienced at the receiving-end of drone warfare (and witnessed at the delivery-end), there may yet be scope to apply the proportionality principle in a way that accounts for another kind of harm: depriving a civilian of their caregiver.

In some parts of the world, when drone strikes occur, this can have a devastating effect on families.[97] Although the same could be said about wartime killings in general, one morally significant difference arises when a camera-equipped drone is used to kill: a targeted individual's family relationships can sometimes be observed in detail beforehand. This will not usually be the case at other times, such as when drones provide support for troops under fire, because pre-strike observations of enemies tend then to be only fleeting. But when a particular enemy is targeted while they are temporarily away from the fighting, much of that prospective victim's humanity can be revealed while drone operators wait for a suitable moment to strike.

If, for example, an individual fighting in an insurgency is observed regularly returning home to be with family, their role as a provider of care for other people (for example, children) can quickly become obvious. This then makes it difficult, arguably, for a drone-user to insist upon a narrow concept of civilian harm when making a proportionality assessment. In anticipating the effects of a missile strike, it could well be projected that the targeted individual's family members would likely be left physically unharmed. However, the likely non-physical harm of depriving them of a caregiver would be undeniable under the circumstances. A wife who survives will have lost a husband (or vice versa), and a child who survives will have lost a parent. To spare those civilians that fate, a higher standard of *in bello* proportionality would need sometimes to be applied, and the military benefit of a planned killing would accordingly need to be worthy of more moral weight. This higher standard of drone warfare would rest upon a broadened notion of harm, and it would account for the clarity with which an armed drone's camera can show how widely harmful a strike could be.

CONCLUSION

Only war attracts the application of Just War morality. So, before applying it to an instance of political violence, it is important to be confident that that violence counts as war. As this chapter has shown, the experiencing of physical risk while posing a physical threat to others is a key conceptual element when thinking about what warfare is and what warriors do. Drone-based violence, although it appears often to be an exercise in risk-avoidance, can nevertheless amount to drone warfare if it is wielded against enemies in circumstances of mutual risk. At a minimum, this conceptualisation encompasses the vicariously risky experience of using armed drones to support others (friendly or allied troops, and local civilians) who are immediately at risk of enemy attack. But without even that minimal level of mutuality in place, drone violence is not warfare and so must be judged according to non-war morality.

Once the conceptual path towards applying Just War principles is open, it is possible to identify several potential problems with the use of armed drones from a *jus ad bellum* perspective. These relate mainly to the idea that drone warfare might be or become 'too easy' to wage, especially when a state does not also place some of its own personnel at physical risk (by land, sea or air) while using drones violently in a conflict. From a *jus in bello* perspective, armed drones have the potential to afford some moral advantage in the sense that warfare could be conducted according to more exacting standards of discrimination and proportionality. However, it is arguably important, as a matter of Just War morality, to keep any such advantage separate from the process of making *jus ad bellum* assessments. That is, if adherence to an augmented *in bello* standard when conducting drone warfare is itself a morally worthwhile end, this should have no bearing upon the issue of whether resorting to war is justified. A drone-using state that has a greater ability to 'kill well' does not, on that basis, acquire a greater permission to wage war. And, more generally, there could be a humanitarian danger in linking *ad bellum* and *in bello* ethics if, in different circumstances, the importance of the latter was downgraded. That is, where one side in war asserted a strong *ad bellum* case, it could purport to claim a corresponding right to be less careful in adhering to *in bello* principles, to the overall detriment of the war's potential victims.

Alternatively, when a state uses armed drones with a strong sense of being in the right and of opposing those who are in the wrong, there is scope for threatening 'enemies' to be politically transformed into guilty 'criminals'.[98] This, though, could contribute to a departure from the war paradigm, whereupon Just War morality would no longer be available to the drone-user. In the past, airpower has sometimes been accompanied by a narrative of earthly villains being punished from on high by righteous actors. For example, Carl Schmitt once compared pilots dropping bombs on foreign populations to the way 'St George used his lance against the dragon', and he warned of a condition in which war becomes 'a police action against troublemakers, criminals, and pests'.[99] In today's use of armed drones, by contrast, one accompanying narrative draws a comparison to the cutting actions of a surgeon.[100] And yet, in the very exercise of extreme care when deciding whether or when to kill a targeted person, drone violence too is sometimes apt to be conceptualised as something other than warfare: violent law enforcement. When the practice of drone 'warfare' is highly individualised, for example, it might be hard to distinguish from a punitive process of criminal justice.[101] And, as will also be discussed in the next chapter, some drone violence might soon need to be judged according to the moral principles that govern violent action by police.

NOTES

1. For a comparison of different accounts of *jus ad bellum*, see: Christopher Toner, 'The Logical Structure of Just War Theory', *The Journal of Ethics*, 14 (2) (2010): 81–102.

2. See: Helen Frowe, *The Ethics of War and Peace: An Introduction*, 2nd edn, London: Routledge, 2016: 99–122.

3. James Turner Johnson, *Ethics and the Use of Force: Just War in Historical Perspective*, Farnham: Ashgate, 2011.

4. Likewise, from a legal perspective, a commitment to act violently in accordance with the law of war does not itself settle the issue of whether that kind of law is applicable. See: Stuart Casey-Maslen, 'Pandora's Box? Drone Strikes under *Jus ad Bellum*, *Jus in Bello*, and International Human Rights Law', *International Review of the Red Cross*, 94 (886) (2012): 597–625, at 615.

5. Thomas Gregory, 'Drones, Targeted Killings, and the Limitations of International Law', *International Political Sociology*, 9 (2015), 197–212, at 202.

6. See: Christof Heyns, Dapo Akande, Lawrence Hill-Cawthorne and Thompson Chengeta, 'The International Law Framework Regulating the Use of Armed Drones', *International and Comparative Law Quarterly*, 65 (2016): 791–827, at 805.

7. See: Rosa Brooks, *How Everything Became War and the Military Became Everything: Tales from the Pentagon*, New York: Simon & Schuster, 2016.

8. Philip Alston, 'Report of the Special Rapporteur on Extrajudicial, Summary or Arbitrary Executions. Addendum: Study on Targeted Killings' (A/HRC/14/24/Add.6), Human Rights Council, United Nations General Assembly, 28 May 2010: para. 46.

9. Ian Clark, *Waging War: A New Philosophical Introduction*, 2nd edn, Oxford: Oxford University Press, 2015: 79.

10. Ian G. R. Shaw, *Predator Empire: Drone Warfare and Full Spectrum Dominance*, Minneapolis and London: University of Minnesota Press, 2016: 44.

11. Carl von Clausewitz, *On War*, London: Penguin, 1982 [1832].

12. Christopher Mewett, 'Understanding war's enduring nature alongside its changing character', *War on the Rocks*, 21 January 2014, <https://warontherocks.com/2014/01/understanding-wars-enduring-nature-alongside-its-changing-character/>.

13. Gloria Gaggioli and Pavle Kilibarda, 'Counterterrorism and the Risk of Over-Classification of Situations of Violence', *International Review of the Red Cross*, 103 (916–17) (2021): 203–36, at 221 and 223.

14. Martin van Creveld, *The Transformation of War*, New York: The Free Press, 1991: 159.

15. Carl von Clausewitz, *On War*, London: Penguin, 1982: 101.

16. Ibid. 104 (emphasis added).

17. Carl Schmitt, *The* Nomos *of the Earth: In the International Law of the* Jus Publicum Europaeum, trans. G. L. Ulmen, New York: Telos Press, 2003: 320 (emphasis added).

18. Ibid. 320.

19. Paul Kahn, 'The Paradox of Riskless Warfare', *Philosophy and Public Policy Quarterly*, 22 (3) (2002): 2–8, at 4.

20. Paul Kahn, 'Imagining Warfare', *European Journal of International Law*, 24 (1) (2013): 199–226, at 218.

21. Henry Shue, 'Do We Need a "Morality of War"?', in *Just and Unjust Warriors: The Moral and Legal Status of Soldiers*, ed. David Rodin and Henry Shue, Oxford: Oxford University Press, 2008: 87–111, at 100.

22. Martin L. Cook, 'Drone Warfare and Military Ethics', in *Drones and the Future of Armed Conflict*, ed. David Cortright, Rachel Fairhurst and Kirsten Wall, Chicago and London: University of Chicago Press, 2015: 46–62, at 58. See also: Richard Norton-Taylor and Alice Ross, 'RAF base may be legitimate target for Isis, says ex-Nato commander', *The Guardian*, 25 November 2015, <https://www.theguardian.com/uk-news/2015/nov/25/raf-base-may-be-legitimate-target-isis-ex-nato-commander>.

23. David Whetham, 'Killer Drones: The Moral Ups and Downs', *RUSI Journal*, 158 (3) (2013): 22–32, at 26.

24. See, for example: Peter Lee, 'Remoteness, Risk and Aircrew Ethos', *Air Power Review*, 15 (1) (2012): 1–19, at 12; Christopher Jones, 'Risky Business: How Remote Operations Shift the Risks of Combat', *Global Affairs*, 3 (4–5) (2017): 431–40, at 435; Wayne Phelps, *On Killing Remotely: The Psychology of Killing with Drones*, New York: Little, Brown and Company, 2021: 85.

25. In late 2009, in apparent retaliation for a drone strike, seven US agents were killed when a suicide bomber attacked a CIA base in south-east Afghanistan: BBC, 'US drone strike in Pakistan "killed key al-Qaeda man"', *BBC News*, 18 March 2010, <http://news.bbc.co.uk/2/hi/americas/8573652.stm>.

26. See: W. J. Hennigan, 'The U.S. is now routinely launching "danger-close" drone strikes so risky they require Syrian militia approval', *Los Angeles Times*, 15 August 2017, <https://www.latimes.com/world/la-fg-raqqah-drones-20170808-story.html>.

27. See: Noam Lubell and Nathan Derejko, 'A Global Battlefield: Drones and the Geographical Scope of Armed Conflict', *Journal of International Criminal Justice*, 11 (2013): 65–88, at 77; Hugh Gusterson, *Drone: Remote Control Warfare*, London: MIT Press, 2016: 157; Agnès Callamard, *Use of Armed Drones for Targeted Killings*. Report of the Special Rapporteur

on extrajudicial, summary or arbitrary executions (A/HRC/44/38), Human Rights Council, United Nations General Assembly, 15 August 2020: para. 41.

28. John Williams, 'Distant Intimacy: Space, Drones, and Just War', *Ethics and International Affairs*, 29 (1) (2015): 93–110, at 95.

29. Laurie Calhoun, *We Kill Because We Can: From Soldiering to Assassination in the Drone Age*, London: Zed Books, 2015: xii.

30. C. A. J. Coady, 'The Morality of Terrorism', *Philosophy*, 60 (231) (1985): 47–69, at 59.

31. Michael Walzer, 'Just and Unjust Targeted Killing and Drone Warfare', *Daedalus*, 145 (4) (2016): 12–24, at 18.

32. See: Agnès Callamard, *Use of Armed Drones for Targeted Killings*. Report of the Special Rapporteur on extrajudicial, summary or arbitrary executions (A/HRC/44/38). New York: Human Rights Council, United Nations General Assembly, 15 August 2020: para 13.

33. Wolfram Lacher, 'Drones, deniability, and disinformation: warfare in Libya and the new international disorder', *War on the Rocks*, 3 March 2020, <https://warontherocks.com/2020/03/drones-deniability-and-disinformation-warfare-in-libya-and-the-new-international-disorder/>.

34. Zack Beauchamp and Julian Savulescu, 'Robot Guardians: Teleoperated Combat Vehicles in Humanitarian Military Intervention', in *Killing by Remote Control: The Ethics of an Unmanned Military*, ed. Bradley Jay Strawser, New York: Oxford University Press, 2013: 106–25; Arash Heydarian Pashakhanlou, 'Air Power in Humanitarian Intervention: Kosovo and Libya in Comparative Perspective', *Defence Studies*, 18 (1) (2018): 39–57, at 52.

35. Jane Cowan, 'US launches Predator drones in Libya conflict', *ABC News*, 22 April 2011, <http://www.abc.net.au/news/stories/2011/04/22/3198588.htm>.

36. Department of Public Information, 'Security Council approves "no-fly zone: over Libya, authorizing "all necessary measures" to protect civilians, by vote of 10 in favour with 5 abstentions', *United Nations*, 17 March 2011, <http://www.un.org/press/en/2011/sc10200.doc.htm>.

37. See: Barack Obama, 'Letter from the President on the War Powers Resolution', *The White House*, 15 June 2011, <https://obamawhitehouse.archives.gov/the-press-office/2011/06/15/letter-president-war-powers-resolution>.

38. Barack Obama, 'Remarks by the President at the National Defense University', *The White House*, 23 May 2013, <https://obamawhitehouse.archives.gov/the-press-office/2013/05/23/remarks-president-national-defense-university>.

39. See: Chalmers Johnson, *Blowback: The Costs and Consequences of American Empire*, New York: Time Warner, 2002.

40. Peter W. Singer, 'Do drones undermine democracy?', *New York Times*, 22 January 2012: SR5; Jesse Kirkpatrick, 'State Responsibility and Drone Operators', in *Drones and Responsibility: Legal, Philosophical, and Sociotechnical Perspectives on Remotely Controlled Weapons*, ed. Ezio Di Nucci and Filippo Santoni de Sio, London: Routledge, 2016: 101–16, at 104–5;

Steven P. Lee, 'The Ethics of Current Drone Policy', *International Journal of Applied Philosophy*, 30 (1) (2016): 115–32, at 123.

41. See: Nicholas Fotion, *War and Ethics: A New Just War Theory*, London: Continuum, 2007: 19; Thomas Hurka, 'Proportionality in the Morality of War', *Philosophy and Public Affairs*, 33 (1) (2005): 34–66, at 35.

42. Michael J. Boyle, *The Drone Age: How Drone Technology Will Change War and Peace*, New York: Oxford University Press, 2020: 77.

43. See: Erik Lin-Greenberg, 'Game of drones: what experimental wargames reveal about drones and escalation', *War on the Rocks*, 10 January 2019, <https://warontherocks.com/2019/01/game-of-drones-what-experimental-wargames-reveal-about-drones-and-escalation/>.

44. Patrick Wintour and Julian Borger, 'Trump says he stopped airstrike on Iran because 150 would have died', *The Guardian*, 21 June 2019, <https://www.theguardian.com/world/2019/jun/21/donald-trump-retaliatory-iran-airstrike-cancelled-10-minutes-before>.

45. Patrick Wintour, 'Donald Trump "cancelled Iran strikes with planes in the air"', *The Guardian*, 21 June 2019, <https://www.theguardian.com/world/2019/jun/21/united-airlines-halts-some-flights-mumbai-to-avoid-iran-after-drone-attack>.

46. Michael J. Boyle, *The Drone Age: How Drone Technology Will Change War and Peace*, New York: Oxford University Press, 2020: 237. See also: Kelsey D. Atherton, 'One drone down and the new nuance of escalation', *Defense News*, 20 June 2019, <https://www.defensenews.com/unmanned/2019/06/20/one-drone-down-and-the-new-nuance-of-escalation/>.

47. See: Frances V. Harbour, 'Reasonable Probability of Success as a Moral Criterion in the Western Just War Tradition', *Journal of Military Ethics*, 10 (3) (2010): 230–41.

48. David Whetham, 'Killer Drones: The Moral Ups and Downs', *RUSI Journal*, 158 (3) (2013): 22–32, at 29.

49. The British general Rupert Smith evoked the idea of 'escalation to success' in 1995 in the context of UN-sponsored military efforts to protect civilians in Bosnia from attacks by Serbian forces: Mark Danner, 'Bosnia: Breaking the Machine', *The New York Review*, 19 February 1998, <https://www.nybooks.com/articles/1998/02/19/bosnia-breaking-the-machine/>.

50. Amitai Etzioni, 'Unmanned Aircraft Systems: The Moral and Legal Case', *Joint Force Quarterly*, issue 57, 2nd quarter (2010): 66–71, at 71.

51. Alan Dowd, 'Moral Hazard: Drones & the Risks of Risk-Free War', *Providence*, 15 December 2016, <https://providencemag.com/2016/12/moral-hazard-drones-risks-risk-free-war/>.

52. See: Ministry of Defence, *Future Operating Environment 2035*. First Edition. UK Government, 14 December 2015, <https://www.gov.uk/government/publications/future-operating-environment-2035>: 31–2.

53. Michael Walzer, *Just and Unjust Wars: A Moral Argument with Historical Illustrations*, 4th edn, New York: Basic Books, 2006: 21.

54. Kinga Tibori-Szabó, 'Self-Defence and the United States Policy on Drone Strikes', *Journal of Conflict & Security Law*, 20 (3) (2015): 381–413, at

388–9. See also: Max Brookman-Byrne, 'Drone Use "Outside Areas of Active Hostilities": An Examination of the Legal Paradigms Governing US Covert Remote Strikes', *Netherlands International Law Review*, 64 (2017): 3–41, at 5.

55. See, for example: Seumas Miller, *Shooting to Kill: The Ethics of Police and Military Use of Lethal Force*, New York: Oxford University Press, 2016: 169; Thomas Hurka, 'Proportionality in the Morality of War', *Philosophy and Public Affairs*, 33 (1) (2005): 34–66, at 45; Jeff McMahan, *Killing in War*, Oxford: Oxford University Press, 2009: 197–8.

56. Michael N. Schmitt, '21st Century Conflict: Can the Law Survive?', *Melbourne Journal of International Law*, 8 (2007): 443–76, at 473.

57. See: James Turner Johnson, 'The Ethics of Insurgency', *Ethics & International Affairs*, 31 (3) (2017): 367–82, at 375; David Rodin and Henry Shue, 'Introduction', in *Just and Unjust Warriors: The Moral and Legal Status of Soldiers*, ed. David Rodin and Henry Shue, Oxford: Oxford University Press, 2008: 1–18, at 7.

58. Sune Engel Rasmussen, 'Suspected US drone strike targeting Isis killed civilians in Afghanistan, UN says', *The Guardian*, 29 September 2016, <https://www.theguardian.com/world/2016/sep/29/us-drone-strike-kills-civilians-isis-afghanistan>.

59. Reuters, 'US drone strike intended for Isis hideout kills 30 pine nut workers in Afghanistan', *The Guardian*, 19 September 2019, <https://www.theguardian.com/world/2019/sep/19/us-drone-strike-deaths-afghanistan-pine-nut-workers>.

60. Richard Luscombe, 'US drone strike mistakenly targeted Afghan aid worker, investigation finds', *The Guardian*, 11 September 2021, <https://www.theguardian.com/us-news/2021/sep/11/us-drone-strike-mistakenly-targeted-afghan-aid-worker-investigation-finds>.

61. In the 1977 First Additional Protocol to the Geneva Conventions, Article 51(2) provides: 'The civilian population as such, as well as individual civilians, shall not be the object of attack. Acts or threats of violence the primary purpose of which is to spread terror among the civilian population are prohibited. . . . Indiscriminate attacks are prohibited'. ICRC, 'Protocol Additional to the Geneva Conventions of 12 August 1949, and relating to the Protection of Victims of International Armed Conflicts (Protocol I)', Geneva, 8 June 1977. *International Committee of the Red Cross*, <https://ihl-databases.icrc.org/ihl/INTRO/470>.

62. Nils Melzer, *Interpretive Guidance on the Notion of Direct Participation in Hostilities under International Humanitarian Law*, Geneva: International Committee of the Red Cross, 2009.

63. In the 1977 Additional Protocol (I) to the 1949 Geneva Conventions, Article 51(5)(b) prohibits attacks 'which may be expected to cause incidental loss of civilian life, injury to civilians, damage to civilian objects, or a combination thereof, which would be excessive in relation to the concrete and direct military advantage anticipated'. ICRC, 'Protocol Additional to the Geneva Conventions of 12 August 1949, and relating to the Protection of Victims

of International Armed Conflicts (Protocol I)', Geneva, 8 June 1977. *International Committee of the Red Cross*, <https://ihl-databases.icrc.org/ihl/INTRO/470>.

64. Michael Walzer, *Just and Unjust Wars: A Moral Argument with Historical Illustrations*, 4th edn, New York: Basic Books 2006: 155.

65. In the 1977 Additional Protocol (I) to the 1949 Geneva Conventions, Article 57(2)(a)(ii) requires attackers to 'take all feasible precautions in the choice of means and methods of attack with a view to avoiding, and in any event to minimizing, incidental loss of civilian life, injury to civilians and damage to civilian objects'. ICRC, 'Protocol Additional to the Geneva Conventions of 12 August 1949, and relating to the Protection of Victims of International Armed Conflicts (Protocol I)', Geneva, 8 June 1977. *International Committee of the Red Cross*, <https://ihl-databases.icrc.org/ihl/INTRO/470>.

66. See: Jelena Pejic, 'Extraterritorial Targeting by Means of Armed Drones: Some Legal Implications', *International Review of the Red Cross*, 96 (893) (2014): 67–106, at 69.

67. Marcus Schulzke, 'The Morality of Remote Warfare: Against the Asymmetry Objection to Remote Weaponry', *Political Studies*, 64 (1) (2016): 90–105, at 93.

68. Michael W. Lewis, 'Drones: Actually the Most Humane Form of Warfare Ever', *The Atlantic*, 21 August 2013, <https://www.theatlantic.com/international/archive/2013/08/drones-actually-the-most-humane-form-of-warfare-ever/278746/>; Marcus Schulzke, *The Morality of Drone Warfare and the Politics of Regulation*. Cambridge: Polity Press, 2017: 117.

69. Daniel Byman, 'Why Drones Work: The Case for Washington's Weapon of Choice', *Foreign Affairs*, 92, (July/August 2013): 32–43, at 34.

70. Quoted in: Peter Lee, 'Rights, Wrongs and Drones: Remote Warfare, Ethics and the Challenge of Just War Reasoning', *Air Power Review*, 16 (3) (2013): 30–49, at 44.

71. Stuart Casey-Maslen, 'Pandora's Box? Drone Strikes under *Jus ad Bellum*, *Jus in Bello*, and International Human Rights Law', *International Review of the Red Cross*, 94 (886) (2012): 597–625, at 607.

72. Charles Blanchard, 'This is Not War by Machine', in *Drone Wars: Transforming Conflict, Law, and Policy*, ed. Peter L. Bergen and Daniel Rothenberg, New York: Cambridge University Press, 2015: 118–28, at 125.

73. Chris Church, 'Downrange operators keep drones flying over Iraq, Syria and Afghanistan', *Stars and Stripes*, 4 April 2017, <https://www.stripes.com/news/downrange-operators-keep-drones-flying-over-iraq-syria-and-afghanistan-1.461925>.

74. BBC, 'Syria war: MoD admits civilian died in RAF strike on Islamic State', *BBC News*, 2 May 2018, <https://www.bbc.co.uk/news/uk-43977394>.

75. Kevin Jon Heller, 'One Hell of a Killing Machine: Signature Strikes and International Law', *Journal of International Criminal Justice*, 11 (2013): 89–119, at 94.

76. Christof Heyns, Dapo Akande, Lawrence Hill-Cawthorne and Thompson Chengeta, 'The International Law Framework Regulating the Use of Armed Drones', *International and Comparative Law Quarterly*, 65 (2016): 791–827, at 813.

77. See: Michael B. Kelley, 'More evidence that drones are targeting civilian rescuers in Afghanistan', *Business Insider*, 25 September 2012, <https://www.businessinsider.com/drone-double-tap-first-responders-2012-9>; Conor Friedersdorf, 'Drone attacks at funerals of people killed in drone attacks', *The Atlantic*, 24 October 2013, <https://www.theatlantic.com/international/archive/2013/10/drone-attacks-at-funerals-of-people-killed-in-drone-strikes/280821/>; Samuel Alexander, 'Double-Tap Warfare: Should President Obama be Investigated for War Crimes?', *Florida Law Review*, 69 (1) (2017): 261–95; Dan Sabbagh, Jason Burke and Bethan McKernan, '"Libya is ground zero": drones on frontline in bloody civil war', *The Guardian*, 27 November 2019, <https://www.theguardian.com/news/2019/nov/27/libya-is-ground-zero-drones-on-frontline-in-bloody-civil-war>.

78. David Rodin, 'Terrorism without Intention', *Ethics*, 114 (July 2004): 752–71, at 768.

79. Mike Fowler, 'The Strategy of Drone Warfare', *Journal of Strategic Security*, 7 (4) (2014): 108–19, at 110.

80. See: Gordon Lubold and Warren P. Strobel, 'Secret U.S. missile aims to kill only terrorists, not nearby civilians', *Wall Street Journal*, 9 May 2019, <https://www.wsj.com/articles/secret-u-s-missile-aims-to-kill-only-terrorists-not-nearby-civilians-11557403411>; Eric Schmitt, 'U.S. Kills Qaeda leader with secretive missile', *New York Times*, 25 September 2020: A10; Peter Beaumont, 'US military increasingly using drone missile with flying blades in Syria', *The Guardian*, 25 September 2020, <https://www.theguardian.com/world/2020/sep/25/us-military-syria-non-explosive-drone-missile-blades>.

81. See: Arthur Holland Michel, 'Some cautionary notes on the new "Knife Missile"', *Defense One*, 10 May 2019, <https://www.defenseone.com/ideas/2019/05/some-cautionary-notes-new-knife-missile/156943/>.

82. Jean-Baptiste Jeangène Vilmer, 'France and the American Drone Precedent', in *The Ethics of War and Peace Revisited*, ed. Daniel R. Brunstetter and Jean-Vincent Holeindre, Washington, DC: Georgetown University Press, 2018: 97–116, at 104.

83. Bradley Jay Strawser, as quoted in: Scott Shane, 'The moral case for drones', *New York Times*, 15 July 2012: SR4.

84. Barack Obama, 'Remarks by the President in a Conversation on the Supreme Court Nomination', *The White House*, 8 April 2016, <https://obamawhitehouse.archives.gov/the-press-office/2016/04/08/remarks-president-conversation-supreme-court-nomination>.

85. Christof Heyns, Dapo Akande, Lawrence Hill-Cawthorne and Thompson Chengeta, 'The International Law Framework Regulating the Use of Armed Drones', *International and Comparative Law Quarterly*, 65 (2016): 791–827, at 813.

86. Bradley Jay Strawser, 'Moral Predators: The Duty to Employ Uninhabited Aerial Vehicles', *Journal of Military Ethics*, 9 (4) (2010): 342–68, at 353.

87. Marcus Schulzke, 'Rethinking Military Virtue Ethics in an Age of Unmanned Weapons, *Journal of Military Ethics*, 15 (3) (2016): 187–204, at 198.

88. Christof Heyns, 'Preface: Coming to Terms with Drones', in *Drones and the Future of Armed Conflict*, ed. David Cortright, Rachel Fairhurst and Kirsten Wall, Chicago and London: University of Chicago Press, 2015: vii–xi, at ix.

89. Janina Dill, 'The Informal Regulation of Drones and the Formal Legal Regulation of War', *Ethics and International Affairs*, 29 (1) (2015): 51–8, at 52.

90. Philip Alston, 'Report of the Special Rapporteur on extrajudicial, summary or arbitrary executions' (A/HRC/14/24/Add.6), Human Rights Council, United Nations General Assembly, 2010: para. 80.

91. All Party Parliamentary Group on Drones, *The UK's Use of Armed Drones: Working with Partners*, London: UK Parliament, July 2018: 5. See also: Dan Sabbagh, 'UK accused of "targeted killing" after drone strike on arms dealer to IS', *The Guardian*, 6 January 2022, <https://www.theguardian.com/world/2022/jan/06/uk-accused-of-targeted-killing-after-drone-strike-on-arms-dealer-to-is>.

92. Nils Melzer, *Interpretive Guidance on the Notion of Direct Participation in Hostilities under International Humanitarian Law*, Geneva: International Committee of the Red Cross, 2009: 34. See also: Philip Alston, 'Report of the Special Rapporteur on extrajudicial, summary or arbitrary executions' (A/HRC/14/24/Add.6), Human Rights Council, United Nations General Assembly, 2010: para. 60.

93. Stuart Casey-Maslen, 'Pandora's Box? Drone Strikes under *Jus ad Bellum*, *Jus in Bello*, and International Human Rights Law', *International Review of the Red Cross*, 94 (886) (2012): 597–625, at 612.

94. Rebecca J. Barber, 'The Proportionality Equation: Balancing Military Objectives with Civilian Lives in the Armed Conflict in Afghanistan', *Journal of Conflict and Security Law*, 15 (3) (2010): 467–500, at 481.

95. C. A. J. Coady, *Morality and Political Violence*, Cambridge: Cambridge University Press, 2008: 9.

96. See, for example: Eliav Lieblich, 'Beyond Life and Limb: Exploring Incidental Mental Harm under International Humanitarian Law', in *Applying International Law in Judicial and Quasi-Judicial Bodies*, ed. Derek Jinks, Jackson Nyamuya Maogoto and Solon Solomon, The Hague: Asser Press, 2014: 185–218; Sarah Holewinski, 'Just Trust Us: The Need to Know More about the Civilian Impact of US Drone Strikes', in *Drone Wars: Transforming Conflict, Law, and Policy*, ed. Peter L. Bergen and Daniel Rothenberg, New York: Cambridge University Press, 2015: 42–70, at 43; Steven P. Lee, 'The Ethics of Current Drone Policy', *International Journal of Applied Philosophy*, 30 (1) (2016): 115–32, at 122; Elke Schwarz, *Death Machines: The Ethics of Violent Technologies*, Manchester: Manchester University Press, 2018: 198; Alex Edney-Browne, 'The Psychosocial Effects of Drone Violence: Social Isolation, Self-Objectification, and Depoliticization', *Political Psychology*, 40 (6) (2019): 1341–56.

97. See: Alex Edney-Browne, 'What it's really like to live with drone warfare', *ABC Radio National*, 22 August 2017, <https://www.abc.net.au/news/2017-08-18/perspectives-from-the-front-line-of-the-drone-war/8793400>; Stefanie Glinski, 'Afghan families torn apart by drone strikes – picture essay', *The Guardian*, 6 December 2019, <https://www.theguardian.com/news/2019/dec/06/afghan-families-torn-apart-drone-strikes-picture-essay>.

98. See: Derek Gregory, 'Drone Geographies', *Radical Philosophy*, 183 (2014): 7–19, at 12.

99. Carl Schmitt, *The* Nomos *of the Earth: In the International Law of the* Jus Publicum Europaeum, trans. G. L. Ulmen, New York: Telos Press, 2003: 321.

100. Stephan Sonnenberg, 'Why Drones are Different', in *Preventive Force: Drones, Targeted Killing, and the Transformation of Contemporary Warfare*, ed. Kerstin Fisk and Jennifer M. Ramos, New York: New York University Press, 2016: 115–41, at 125.

101. See: Samuel Moyn, 'Drones and Imagination: A Response to Paul Kahn', *European Journal of International Law*, 24 (1) (2013): 227–33, at 229; Samuel Issacharoff and Richard Pildes, 'Drones and the Dilemma of Modern Warfare', in *Drone Wars: Transforming Conflict, Law, and Policy*, ed. Peter L. Bergen and Daniel Rothenberg, New York: Cambridge University Press, 2015: 388–420, at 391.

Chapter 3

VIOLENT LAW ENFORCEMENT

═══════════

Outside the paradigm of war, and beyond the reach of Just War morality, some instances of state violence can instead be conceptualised as
practices of law enforcement. Such practices, directed towards enforcing
a state's criminal law, range from the prevention of criminality through
to the punishment of criminals. Thus, 'law enforcement' in general can
be understood broadly to comprise the protecting of public safety, the
apprehending of suspects, the conducting of trials, the sentencing of con-
victs, and the carrying out of punishments. Violence, though, tends only
to be a potential feature of this process at its extreme ends. That is,
when a state agent is engaging in 'violent law enforcement', it usually
means that they are acting violently to prevent criminal wrongdoing (as
police do) or to punish it (as executioners do). In either case, however,
the conceptualising of violence as *law* enforcement does not necessarily
mean that that violence is itself *lawful* or morally permissible. Rather,
instances of police violence and punitive violence remain open to be
judged – as just or unjust – according to the moral expectations of violent state behaviour in peacetime.

In circumstances where combat is not going on, a morality featuring 'combatant' and 'non-combatant' categories can have no meaning in
guiding the conduct of state violence. When it comes to the morality of
violent law enforcement, then, there are only 'humans' to be considered,
and everyone involved is valued as a bearer of the human right to life. In
peacetime, the supreme moral importance of protecting life by restricting state-sanctioned killing is reflected in numerous international laws.
For present purposes, a good example is Article 2 of the 1950 European
Convention on Human Rights, which provides:

1. Everyone's right to life shall be protected by law. No one shall be
   deprived of his life intentionally save in the execution of a sentence
   of a court following his conviction of a crime for which this penalty is
   provided by law.

2. Deprivation of life shall not be regarded as inflicted in contravention of this Article when it results from the use of force which is no more than absolutely necessary:
   (a) in defence of any person from unlawful violence;
   (b) in order to effect a lawful arrest or to prevent the escape of a person lawfully detained;
   (c) in action lawfully taken for the purpose of quelling a riot or insur-rection.[1]

By comparison, killing people in war (intentionally or unintentionally) is a practice far less constrained by a moral concern for the right to life. And yet, for this very reason, there is a risk that some situations of violence will be wrongly classified as 'war' when a state would prefer to have more normative room to manoeuvre. In such cases, state violence that should be severely restricted according to rights-based law (if, for example, that violence serves a law enforcement purpose) can end up being subjected only to the more permissive rules of war. Consequently, based on a faulty conceptualisation of violence, there is potential for an excess of killing to occur because the wrong kind of morality has been brought into play. In this chapter, the problem of a mismatch between concept and morality is addressed by taking seriously the idea that some drone violence is, essentially, non-war violence. Specifically, it assesses the use of armed drones as a form of violent law enforcement by explor-ing two sub-paradigms of such violence: policing and punishment.

Regarding the latter, several authors have implicitly condemned some drone strikes in the course of distinguishing 'targeted killings' from warfare. For example, Christopher Fuller has described US intelligence agents who conduct strikes as performing the role of 'aerial execu-tioner'.[2] Michael Boyle has argued that drone-based 'targeted killings . . . operate on the logic of execution rather than combat'.[3] And Bernard Koch has observed that this type of killing is 'much closer to the execu-tion of capital punishment than to warfare and those who execute it [are] much closer to being hangmen than soldiers'.[4] However, it remains to consider why some drone violence is punitive in nature, why it might be morally wrong, and whether it could somehow be rendered morally acceptable as an exercise in violent law enforcement. Accordingly, the first section of the chapter assesses the long-range use of armed drones to conduct 'personality strikes' in remote parts of the world where the drone-using state is not party to an armed conflict. Focusing on past approaches taken by the US government, the discussion advances the idea that drone violence has sometimes amounted to a practice of bring-ing 'wild justice' to suspected terrorists abroad. Here, the main ethical concern is that, when lethal punishments are authorised by non-judicial agents of government and without the prior conduct of a fair trial, there is too much potential for unjust violation of a targeted person's right to life. In which case, the question arises: should punitive drone violence be judicially authorised, or should it instead be prohibited?[5]

In the future, armed drones might also be used to enforce criminal law in the domestic sphere, so the chapter's second section focuses on the sub-paradigm of police violence. As evidence of the rise of the 'public order drone',[6] governments worldwide are already making small drones available for a variety of policing purposes: border control, traffic management, search and rescue missions, criminal investigation, and the monitoring of public assemblies. Unarmed and controlled remotely (usually at short range), these camera-equipped aircraft have been shown to provide a powerful and mobile surveillance capacity that can be highly effective in detecting suspicious activity and guiding police operations. Beyond this, though, there is a possibility that some governments will become tempted to make greater use of drones in situations where criminal violence presents a danger to public safety. One option, then, might be to enable police to neutralise threats using drones equipped with weapons. In anticipation of that, it is important now to assess whether or how police should use armed drones. So, the present chapter does this by considering established principles governing police use of violence, and by exploring the hypothetical challenge of adhering to those principles as a 'tele-present' police officer.[7]

DRONE VIOLENCE FOR PUNISHING CRIME

On 12 October 2000, seventeen US Navy sailors were killed when the warship USS *Cole* was attacked in the Yemeni port of Aden by suicide bombers driving an explosive-laden boat. More than eighteen years later, in January 2019, the then-president of the United States confirmed that a man accused of organising this attack had recently been killed in a US drone strike in Yemen. Donald Trump tweeted: 'Our GREAT MILITARY has delivered justice for the heroes lost and wounded in the cowardly attack on the USS Cole. We have just killed the leader of that attack, Jamal al-Badawi. Our work against al Qaeda continues.'[8] Soon afterwards, US Central Command (which oversees military operations in the Middle East) confirmed that al-Badawi was killed in the strike while driving a vehicle alone in Yemen's Ma'rib region. A military spokesman later explained that in 2003 al-Badawi had been indicted by a federal grand jury, charged with fifty counts of various terrorism offenses, including the murder of US nationals. Moreover, before the 2019 strike, al-Badawi had been on a list of 'most wanted terrorists' maintained

by the Federal Bureau of Investigation, and the US State Department's
Rewards for Justice Program had offered up to five million dollars for
information leading to his arrest.[9]

At the time of writing, much remains to be discovered about the circumstances surrounding the killing of al-Badawi, but it is probable that
he was deliberately targeted in a so-called 'personality strike'. The purpose of this kind of drone strike is to eliminate named individuals, so
personality strikes are distinct from 'signature strikes' against unidenti-
fied individuals who are 'behaving in a manner considered . . . to resemble the actions of combatants'.[10] For the purposes of this chapter, four
features of al-Badawi's killing are worth highlighting: (1) Yemen was not
then a place where the United States was party to an armed conflict; (2)
it is at best unclear whether al-Badawi was regarded by the US government as a criminal or a combatant, or as both; (3) it is likewise unclear
whether the strike against al-Badawi was a preventive response to anticipated wrongdoing (terrorism) or a punitive response to past wrongdoing
(the attack on the *Cole*), or both; and (4) the killing of al-Badawi was
apparently done without judicial sanction from an American court or
any other. Together, these features suggest the possibility that the strike
against al-Badawi was essentially an act of punitive law enforcement.
And, if this is so, they further suggest that that act was performed in a
morally impermissible way.

The tasks of conceptualising and judging the personality strikes conducted under President Trump are made difficult by the fact that his
administration never publicly disclosed the 'parameters and principles'
of its drone policy.[11] By contrast, the preceding administration was more
transparent in this regard, and it eventually emerged that the US government under Barack Obama had conducted personality strikes as if these
were essentially practices of warfare (rather than law enforcement). In
early 2013, a Justice Department memo was leaked to NBC News that
had previously been sent to members of the US Senate's Intelligence Committee and Judiciary Committee. The document was relevant to the use
of armed drones, and it addressed 'the circumstances in which the U.S.
Government could use lethal force in a foreign country outside the area
of active hostilities against a US citizen who is . . . an al-Qaida leader
actively engaged in planning operations to kill Americans'. Among
the conditions under which, the memo argued, such a lethal operation
would be legal was: 'the operation would be conducted in a manner
consistent with *applicable* law of war principles'.[12] However, against this
assertion of the existence of a condition of war, several legal scholars
have suggested that the Obama administration mischaracterised some
of its drone strikes as 'warfare' to avoid the political inconvenience of

being subject to the strict morality and laws that govern state violence in peacetime.[13]

Within the sub-paradigm of punitive law enforcement, the most important rights-based restriction (based on the right to life) is the prohibition on killing arbitrarily. This is reflected, for example, in Article 6 of the 1966 International Covenant on Civil and Political Rights which provides that '. . . sentence of death . . . can only be carried out pursuant to a final judgement rendered by a competent court'.[14] And it exists in the domestic law of many states; for example, in the US Constitution's Fifth Amendment which provides that '[n]o person shall be . . . deprived of life . . . without due process of law'.[15] In practice, when the punitive law enforcement model applies to non-war violence, respect for the right to life and to due process involves the presumption of an accused person's innocence and the conduct of a fair trial.[16]

To follow legal processes carefully is to adhere to the principle of legalism which, in matters of criminal justice, helps to avoid arbitrariness in the killing of human beings who bear a presumptive right to life. The essential characteristic of legalism is orderliness. Through the conscientious and thorough application of a modern legal system's myriad rules and conventions, the practitioners and observers of criminal justice processes can potentially achieve a high level of certainty about the correctness of decision-making. By contrast, in the absence of a fair trial and conviction preceding an execution, it is more difficult to be confident that an executed individual really was criminally culpable and deserving of death. A common criticism of the US government's drone-based personality strikes outside war zones has been that they were done without recourse to legalism,[17] in which case they are difficult to justify as acts of punitive law enforcement. One way of thinking about this problem is to conclude immediately that the US government, outside the paradigm of war, wilfully perpetrated impermissible homicides (murders). However, a different approach is taken here: to consider first whether there is any scope to conceptualise and perhaps legitimise drone-based personality strikes within the law enforcement paradigm of state violence. On this basis, arguably, these strikes can begin to be understood as continuing an old American tradition of sometimes inflicting flawed methods of violent law enforcement ('wild justice') upon suspected criminals.

Wild justice and frontier violence

In their 2010 book *Revenge versus Legality*, Katherine Maynard and her colleagues explore the differences between wild justice and legalistic justice. On the one hand, they argue, there is 'extralegal, vigilante, or "wild" justice based upon revenge and driven by passion and grief' and, on the other hand, there is 'tamer, cooler, more rational and institutional legal justice'.[18] As a manifestation of violent law enforcement, wild justice is pursued self-righteously and vengefully. It tends to be untamed by adherence to formal legal constraints, and its wielders typically judge this wildness to be more effective in achieving just outcomes than is the practice of non-wild (legalistic) justice. Moreover, for these reasons, wild justice is historically more likely to occur in situations and territories where the rule of law is weak. In the United States, it is possible sometimes to discern an appetite for wild justice driven by a 'myth of redemptive violence' which runs deep in its popular and political culture.[19] This is revealed, as Maynard and her colleagues observe, by historical or fictional circumstances in which there are certain 'crimes or injuries that appear so mystifying or disturbing that ordinary, conventional legality – the usual, normative police procedures, judges' rulings, lawyers' motions, and jury verdicts – seems inadequate'.[20] Instead, therefore, 'a Dirty Harry is needed to solve or avenge such a crime; cruel or unusual procedures or punishments are called for; the law must be bent, broken or at least supplemented to achieve a just revenge'.[21]

To the extent that the idea of redemptive violence is an appealing one in the United States, its appeal can be traced to the country's early history. In the time of the American Old West (or Wild West), pioneering settlers were extending their nation's frontier westward. Across this vast and barely governed territory, law enforcement was generally a more violent and disorderly enterprise compared to that which obtained in the established urban settings of the east. Frontier justice was delivered by US government 'lawmen' like Wyatt Earp (1848–1929) who, in the Arizona Territory town of Tombstone, took part in the famous 'Gunfight at the O.K. Corral' during which lawmen shot and killed three outlaw cowboys.[22] Such real-life episodes from early American history have since been emulated abundantly in US popular culture. Between the 1930s and 1960s, in Hollywood, the filmscript writers for 'Westerns' frequently set narratives of violence in desert spaces 'where legality is so weak or non-existent that a good gunfight (or fistfight) is the only credible way to resolve differences or achieve justice'.[23]

Later, characters played by Clint Eastwood, Charles Bronson and Sylvester Stallone were variously depicted in popular US-made films as 'heroic avengers ridding the world of punks, thugs, rapists, homicidal maniacs, and other evildoers'.[24] These films contained the clear message that, in confronting evil-inspired dangers, the heroes' tactics sometimes needed to be ruthless. Moreover, a preference for lawless behaviour sometimes extended to a contempt for legalism as something that gets in the way of 'true' justice. For example, in the 1971 Eastwood film *Dirty Harry*, the eponymous hero is the 'off-the-leash cop' who will 'readily resort to violence in his work, [and is] not above a bit of crude torture to extract information from a perp with a bullet wound'.[25] He is depicted, moreover, as needing to contend with criminal *and* non-criminal antagonists. The latter include 'pusillanimous senior [police] officers and devious, vacillating, media-obsessed politicians',[26] as well as 'a variety of liberal twits and wusses who . . . castigate [Harry] for not following proper legal and police procedures'.[27]

The likely influence of popular culture that valorises wild justice should not, however, be overstated when it comes to US foreign policy. It is important to acknowledge that the US government has historically often acted as a champion of legalistic approaches to law enforcement, in contrast to other states (including enemies of the United States) that have sometimes preferred to reject legalism. When Hermann Göring was appointed (by Adolf Hitler) as Prussian Minister of the Interior in 1933, he boasted: 'my measures will not be crippled by any legalistic hesitation'.[28] And, in Nazi-ruled Germany more generally, due process and the rule of law were swiftly replaced by the straightforward *Führerprinzip*; the principle that a leader's commands equate to laws. After the end of the Second World War, when justice needed to be served in respect of alleged war crimes, the US government insisted upon legalism despite fierce urgings to the contrary by its allies. Joseph Stalin, for example, had wanted simply to kill up to 100,000 Nazi Germans in revenge for what they had done to the Soviet Union.[29] And the British foreign secretary, Anthony Eden, had favoured summary executions of top Nazi leaders, claiming: 'The guilt of such individuals is so black' that 'they fall outside and go beyond the scope of any judicial process'.[30] Under American leadership, though, the Nuremburg tribunals did eventually proceed to apply legalism and the judicial method of criminal justice to Nazi defendants.

A major disruption of the US government's attitude to legalism appeared to occur after 11 September 2001. America's people and politicians reacted to Al Qaeda's '9/11' terrorist attacks on US cities with shock and fear, and the political mood that descended upon the United States came to resonate with the cultural legacy of its frontier-pushing era. The popular myth of redemptive violence surged to the fore as the country set about confronting dreaded enemies inhabiting various disorderly settings of civil war, state failure and insurgency in North Africa, the Middle East and Central Asia.[31] One such 'terror frontier' was the Federally Administered Tribal Areas (FATA) of Pakistan, in the north-west of the country bordering Afghanistan, where the national government has relatively little control over the population or territory. Eventually, as will be discussed in Chapter 4, this area became the setting for extensive US use of drone strikes (including personality strikes) against suspected terrorists. For example, in August 2009 the Pakistani Taliban leader Baitullah Mehsud was killed (along with eleven other people) in a strike in the remote and mountainous region of South Waziristan. Mehsud had allegedly been guilty of organising, among other things, the 2007 assassination of Pakistan's former prime minister Benazir Bhutto.[32]

From the beginning of the US-led War on Terror, a prominent political attitude was that American counterterrorism would be more effective if it were conducted ruthlessly. In a television interview on 16 September 2001, US Vice President Dick Cheney explained:[33]

> I think the world increasingly will understand what we have here are a group of barbarians, that they threaten all of us . . . We also have to work, though, sort of the dark side, if you will. We've got to spend time in the shadows . . . That's the world these [terrorist] folks operate in, and so it's going to be vital for us to use any means at our disposal, basically, to achieve our objective.

The following day, President George W. Bush secretly authorised the CIA to hunt and kill Al Qaeda's leaders,[34] and he told journalists: 'I want justice, and there's an old poster out West, as I recall, saying "Wanted, Dead or Alive".'[35] In essence, arguably, this was an invocation of a national mythology of 'frontier justice'.[36] Soon afterwards, Bush promised the US Congress: 'whether we bring our enemies to justice, or bring justice to our enemies, justice will be done'.[37] Here, the bringing of enemies to justice implied the use of legal processes such as arrest and trial, but the alternative (bringing justice to enemies) seemed to threaten the use of non-legalistic (wild) and violent methods.

Bush subsequently made clear his conviction that the formal justice system lacked the capacity to adequately address the problem of terrorism. In his 2004 State of the Union speech, the president acknowledged: 'some people question if America is really in a war at all. They view terrorism more as a crime, a problem to be solved mainly with law enforcement and indictments'.[38] But he insisted: 'After the chaos and carnage of September 11th [2001], it is not enough to serve our enemies with legal papers.'[39] Legalism was then largely rejected in favour of wild justice, and so the Bush administration and its successors proceeded ruthlessly to achieve retribution for 9/11. In the zealous pursuit of Al Qaeda globally, over two decades, suspected terrorists were indefinitely detained (and sometimes tortured) by successive US administrations. And, after US special forces killed Al Qaeda leader Osama Bin Laden in Pakistan in May 2011, President Barack Obama boasted that 'justice has been done'.[40] However, armed drones soon became this president's preferred method of achieving retribution for known individuals' alleged crimes,[41] largely because of drones' capacity to strike a person – suddenly and with secrecy – in a remote location.

Personality strikes as administrative executions

In early 2011 the US Joint Special Operations Command authorised a squadron in control of drones flying over Yemen to kill Anwar al-Awlaki. At the time, 'Most Wanted' posters of this US citizen were displayed inside every ground control station at Cannon Air Force Base in New Mexico (home to the 3rd and 33rd Special Operations Squadron).[42] On 30 September 2011 the drones were flown from a base in Saudi Arabia into northern Yemen where they fired missiles at a car carrying al-Awlaki.[43] But not until May 2013 did the US Attorney General confirm publicly that this person was among four named US citizens who had been killed 'outside areas of active hostilities' in US drone strikes.[44] More than a year prior to this killing, CIA director Leon Panetta had used a television interview to identify al-Awlaki as a terrorist who posed a threat to the United States. In explaining the man's placement on a 'terrorist list', Panetta said: 'You can track Awlaki to the Detroit bomber. We can track him to other attacks in this country that have been urged by Awlaki.'[45] This highlighting of past wrongdoing suggests strongly that, when al-Awlaki was subsequently killed in a US drone strike, the killing was at least partly punitive in purpose. If so, this personality strike in a non-war setting was an example of drone violence manifesting as wild justice.

In 2012 President Obama's chief counterterrorism adviser, John Brennan, insisted that US use of lethal force was 'not about punishing terrorists for past crimes; we are not seeking vengeance'.[46] And yet, a few weeks earlier, in answer to the question 'How do we deliver justice to the enemy?', US State Department legal advisor Harold Koh had answered: 'I think there are different ways. It can be delivered through trials. Drones also deliver'.[47] In 2013 Obama himself explained that drone strikes are not undertaken 'to punish individuals – [rather] we act against terrorists who pose a continuing and imminent threat to the American people'.[48] However, the very phrase '*continuing* and imminent threat' implied that, when such an individual is targeted for a drone strike, their past actions are at issue. It is a phrase founded on the notion of 'elongated imminence', reportedly developed by Koh, which he compared to 'battered spouse syndrome'. In the same way that a spouse does not have to wait until a hand is being raised to strike before acting in self-defence if there is a pattern of past abuse, Koh argued, the US government does not have to wait to strike at terrorists.[49] If such was the thinking behind personality strikes conducted during the Obama administration, there is scope to regard these as instances of punitive drone violence within the law enforcement paradigm. Moreover, the method by which the US government reportedly made personality strike decisions at that time further suggests its application of a law enforcement mentality.

Wild justice involves a rejection of legalism, and sometimes this rejection manifests as a parodying or mimicking of legalistic approaches to criminal justice. Most obviously, there is the phenomenon of the show trial. In the Soviet Union, for example, the government would often stage public 'trials' in which defendants were coerced to make confessions, and guilty verdicts (to be used for propaganda purposes) were a foregone conclusion.[50] In the case of the Obama administration and its personality strikes, the mimicking of legalism instead involved unshown quasi-trials. The drone strikes resulting from these secret proceedings could thus be described as 'administrative executions'. Obama's government apparently regarded personality strikes as requiring less permissiveness than is allowed in the war paradigm, but not the high degree of restriction on state violence that accompanies full commitment to legalism within the law enforcement paradigm. The White House chief of staff, William Daley, explained in 2011: 'The president accepts as a fact that a certain amount of screw-ups are going to happen, and to him, that calls for a more judicious process.'[51] It did not, however, call for a *judicial* process, according to US Attorney General Eric Holder.[52] Rather, as Brennan suggested in 2012, it was enough that the right to life loomed large in Obama's thinking about personality strikes: 'the president, and I think all of us here, don't like the fact that people have to die. And so he wants to make sure that we go through a rigorous [pre-strike] checklist.'[53]

Accordingly, administrative decisions to authorise drone strikes against named individuals (suspected terrorists) located outside war zones were reportedly made only after lengthy deliberation and extensive consultation by officials across the US government. As such, these personality strikes could not be called 'summary' executions in the sense of being executions performed without delay and hesitation. Even so, they were undoubtedly extrajudicial decisions to kill, despite their bearing some resemblance to a proper criminal justice process: the involvement of lawyers, the weighing of 'evidence', the rendering of a 'verdict' and, if a person was 'convicted', the imposing of a punishment to fit the crime. In 2012 the *New York Times* first revealed what it called 'the strangest of bureaucratic rituals' in which more than 100 national security officials gathered via videoconference on a weekly basis 'to pore over terrorist suspects' biographies and recommend to the president who should be the next to die'.[54] In contrast to the predictability of a Soviet-style show trial, however, participants in these meetings reportedly did not hesitate to 'call out a challenge, pressing for the evidence behind accusations of ties to Al Qaeda'.[55] Prior to each meeting to consider lists of potential targets, the 'résumés' of individual terror suspects were put through a process of vetting, validation and evaluation. Then, at the White House, a committee chaired by the president would vote on who, where and when to strike.[56] In a 2014 article, Gregory McNeal described this administrative process as 'complex and time intensive, usually involving dozens of analysts from different agencies'.[57] And, to illustrate the high degree of care taken, he noted that 'target folders are continuously updated to reflect the most recent information regarding a target's status, [and] the compiled data is independently reviewed by personnel not responsible for its collection'.[58]

The occurrence of these practices was largely confirmed towards the end of Obama's presidency by the 2016 publication of the US government's drone 'playbook': 'Procedures for Approving Direct Action against Terrorist Targets Located outside the United States and Areas of Active Hostilities'.[59] As a basis for conducting personality strikes beyond the paradigm of war, these detailed procedures were probably intended to be followed also by Obama's successor, in the hope that they might continue his approach. And it could indeed be argued that 'playing' by the playbook prevented greater injustices that might otherwise have resulted from the US government's use of armed drones on its 'terror frontier'. Even so, a complex administrative approach to punishment can still only mimic a legalistic process of guilt-determination and sentencing. Thus, Obama's approach still morally impoverished drone violence as an exercise in punitive law enforcement. Critically, this was violence controlled entirely by the executive branch of government, allowing for none of the genuine impartiality that is expected of decision-making by an independent judiciary. Instead, the executive as a whole purported to play all the roles in what is ordinarily a highly distributed process of administering criminal justice: the 'prosecutor' who assembles a case, the 'jury' that makes a finding of fact, the 'judge' who imposes a sentence, and the 'executioner' who carries it out. This is fundamentally why US personality strikes outside war zones amounted to wild justice, and it raises the question of whether, in future, the 'wild' and drone-based punishment of capital crimes should be 'tamed' by involving a drone-using state's courts.

Taming punitive drone violence

After Donald Trump became president of the United States, he quickly sought to distance himself from his predecessor's approach to global counterterrorism. Whereas Obama had always insisted that his government's attacks against terrorists were not essentially punitive, in mid-2017 Trump appeared enthusiastically to favour the ruthless exercise of redemptive violence:[60]

> Terrorists . . . are nothing but thugs and criminals and predators, and that's right – losers. . . . These killers need to know they have nowhere to hide, that no place is beyond the reach of American might and American arms. Retribution will be fast and powerful as we lift restrictions and expand authorities.

The president's clear implication here was that legal or administrative restraints would only make US retribution for terrorist acts less effective. Accordingly, senior officials in the Trump administration reportedly pursued changes to the way drone strikes were conducted. In contrast to the Obama-era approach, Trump's reported preferences included: expanding the geographic scope for drone strikes to occur 'outside of areas of active hostilities', and lowering the evidential thresholds required to conduct strikes against terrorism suspects.[61] To the extent that these changes were enacted, the wild justice of US drone violence probably became even wilder under Trump than it had been under Obama. Moreover, Trump's conspicuous adoption of a vengeful rationale for drone use set an example to be potentially emulated by leaders of other drone-using states.[62] For example, before becoming the UK prime minister in 2019, Boris Johnson wrote in *The Spectator*: 'we legally justify these drone strike assassinations as preventative: to stop future acts of terror in Syria. But that scarcely masks the reality that killing them is also retributive – payback.'[63]

One suggested approach to taming such wildness is to accept that drone violence will sometimes be wielded for a punitive purpose and then allow states to restraint it themselves as a matter of law enforcement morality. That is, if the extrajudicial character of personality strikes is the problem, perhaps the solution is to arrange for judicial sanctioning of such killings in countries that already engage in capital punishment. In practice, this would mean that judges who are impartial (in the sense of being independent of the executive government) could conduct trials *in absentia* if an accused terrorist were unable to be extradited. The idea, then, is that these trials would aim fairly to establish whether the defendant (adequately represented in court) is guilty and, if so, a judge could subsequently sentence that individual to be targeted in a drone strike if no other method of execution was available. In this way, one could argue, genuine legalism would afford greater public confidence in the probity of drone-based, punitive law enforcement: that the verdict was correct, that the punishment was deserved, and that the risk of arbitrariness in the taking of human life was greatly reduced.

In a 2013 speech on counterterrorism, President Obama raised the idea of 'a special court to evaluate and authorize lethal action',[64] and the idea of running trials *in absentia* in a 'drone court' has attracted some scholarly support.[65] However, this idea has also been criticised for being impractical and/or unfair.[66] One feasibility-based objection is that courts are not institutionally equipped to be involved in time-critical decisions,[67] although this argument is strongest when contemplating drone violence in the war paradigm. If, instead, personality strikes against individuals located outside war zones were treated as a law enforcement matter, decisions on whether to authorise placing someone on a target list would not necessarily need to be made quickly. A court of criminal justice would be hard-pressed to decide exactly *when* an individual may be targeted in a drone strike, but it could still be feasible for a court to decide *whether* an individual should be strikable at some future time. Indeed, on this point it is worth noting that the executive branch of the US government did not decide to kill Anwar al-Awlaki at short notice or during a specific emergency. Rather, US officials had been discussing attacking him 'for well over a year', and this deliberation was so well known that al-Awlaki's father had time to seek (unsuccessfully) an injunction from a US judge.[68]

Beyond the issue of feasibility, a more serious concern is that any 'drone court' arrangements would not satisfy the moral requirement for a fair trial. Having the defendant physically present in court is an important fairness measure because there they can more readily receive legal advice and representation. Therefore, at the outset, it would be important for a prosecuting government to go to trial publicly so that an accused terrorist had an opportunity to surrender themselves and attend court. If they then chose to do so, and if they were subsequently convicted of a capital offence, that individual would also be available for execution by conventional means, and the very possibility of a judicially sanctioned drone strike would be avoided. Alternatively, that possibility could be avoided if the prosecuting government was able to capture an alleged terrorist, so a judge conducting a 'drone court' trial would arguably need to remain satisfied about the continued infeasibility (rather than the mere inconvenience) of effecting a capture.[69] If, though, an individual remained unavailable to be tried in person, fairness would then require that they be adequately represented. To this end, for example, a judge might also demand that a secure line of communication was in place between the absent accused and their in-court lawyer.

Satisfying such legalistic requirements – to maximise confidence in the fairness of a trial – could well prove highly onerous in practice. So, a government intent on using armed drones in this way to punish criminals abroad would likely be unable to conduct personality strikes as frequently as would be the case if these executions stemmed merely from executive decisions. Thus, from a human rights perspective, court-ordered drone strikes could seem to be a great improvement, compared to past US government practice, in reducing the overall risk of arbitrary killing. Nevertheless, even if a *sentence* of death could somehow be arrived at through a demonstrably fair process of decision-making, the *method* of execution could yet be what ultimately makes punitive drone violence morally impermissible. If it remained the case that large drones flying at long range were equipped only with explosive missiles, personality strikes directed accurately against convicted terrorists could still be condemned for posing too great a risk to the lives of innocent people nearby. The moral problem, then, would be one of disproportionate harm resulting from the conduct of violent law enforcement, and this alone could be reason enough to prohibit punitive drone strikes. On the other hand, if a differently armed drone were used closer to home for the primary purpose of protecting life (rather than killing), there might be more moral scope to permit drone violence within another sub-paradigm of law enforcement: policing.

ARMED DRONES AND DOMESTIC POLICING

A 'police drone' usually means a small, short-range, multirotor aircraft of the kind produced by civilian manufacturers and widely available commercially.[70] Already, their use has sometimes generated concerns about the intrusiveness of police surveillance and its impact on individual privacy and freedoms. For example, during the COVID-19 pandemic, police in several countries used drones equipped with cameras to monitor and enforce public compliance with social distancing rules.[71] Occasionally, this prompted accusations that aerial surveillance in locked-down societies was breaching people's privacy rights and exacerbating a 'police state' atmosphere.[72] The intrusiveness and privacy implications of drone use is an important and well-canvassed ethical issue on its own,[73] but the potential police use of drones equipped with weapons (as well as cameras) warrants special attention. Here, the concern for human rights extends to the right to life which underpins ethical principles for restraining police violence in a domestic context.

When US President Barack Obama insisted that none of his successors should 'deploy armed drones over U.S. soil',[74] he was probably envisaging large drones launching Hellfire missiles with deliberately deadly effect. This differs, though, from a scenario in which a police officer's intention is not (or not solely) to kill and where they are using a drone armed with a weapon not designed to be lethal. In such circumstances, how (if at all) might the use of an armed drone satisfy the ethical principles that guide police violence? And when (if ever) might it be morally permissible for police to use an armed drone against a criminal suspect or to protect public safety? At the time of writing, there have been no reports of armed drones being violently deployed by police anywhere in the world. Even so, the requisite technology already exists, and some corporations, legislators and non-government organisations have begun to anticipate the advent of police drone weaponisation. A potential moral advantage of this is that, if using drones reduces police exposure to danger, it could also reduce the risk of harm (caused by fearful officers) to criminal suspects and innocent bystanders. Weighing against this, however, is the possibility of an increased risk to others if distanced officers experience perception problems, and there might also be a danger of armed police drones provoking a violent escalation of public disorder.

Arming police drones

For policing purposes, the utility of a camera-equipped drone lies mainly in its mobility and capacity for dynamic observation. Although a small, battery-powered drone cannot remain airborne for a long time, it is quieter and often more practical than a piloted helicopter and much cheaper to acquire and maintain.[75] Such a drone can enter and remain in some spaces more easily than a police officer can and, in some circumstances, this capacity is preferable for a policing purpose. For example, a drone-based camera could be sent in place of an officer to observe a crime scene (looking for clues) in detail without as much risk of disturbing it.[76] Police drones have also been used extensively in some countries for a public safety purpose: surveilling crowds during outdoor events such as public demonstrations and sporting matches. Here, drones enable police on the ground to estimate the number of people attending, track group movements, anticipate overcrowding, and accordingly employ crowd-control techniques such as roadblocks.[77] In the United States, these small aircraft have sometimes been able to obtain evidence of criminality in real-time, such as when a Miami-Dade police drone flying at 3,100 feet (945 m) captured footage of a drug sale in Florida in late 2019.[78] The following year, in California, a drone despatched from the Chula Vista Police Department's Drone as First Responder programme filmed a suspect evading the police car pursuing him, throwing a gun away, and hiding a bag of what turned out to be heroin.[79] On another occasion, when a man was suspected of firing a gun at his family, a camera-equipped police drone was deployed to survey the situation and to keep officers 'out of harm's way'.[80]

In responding to threatened or actual violent crime, police officers sometimes do take physical risks in confronting suspects and might then carry some kind of weapon to protect themselves or others. The imagery obtained from an unarmed drone (of the position of an active shooter, for example) could vitally inform on-the-ground officers deciding when and how to take those risks for a threat-neutralisation purpose. However, the question that has arisen in some law enforcement circles is whether, if the drone itself were armed, a criminal threat could and should be neutralised in a way that exposes police to less danger.

As long ago as 2010, US border authorities were reportedly interested in equipping their drones with 'non-lethal weapons designed to immobilize' individuals identified as 'possibly involved in illegal activity'.[81] In 2014, in the United States, a company called Chaotic Moon publicly demonstrated the operation of a taser-armed drone, delivering a powerful electric shock to one of its interns (a volunteer), with a view to selling this technology to law enforcement personnel.[82] In the same year the South African company Desert Wolf launched sales of its Skunk Riot Control Copter, offering it to mining companies in the country as a means of responding to striking workers.[83] This small 'octocopter' drone is marketed as being 'designed to control unruly crowds without endangering the lives of the protestors or the security staff'.[84] It is equipped with four high-capacity paintball barrels that can rapidly fire a large quantity of solid plastic balls, dye marker projectiles, or pepper spray balls, and the drone also carries loudspeakers enabling the communication of warnings to a crowd below it.[85] In 2015, at the Milipol Paris homeland security exhibition, the French drone manufacturer Aero Surveillance unveiled its Multi-purpose Payload Launcher (MPL 30), which can reportedly carry up to eighteen tear gas grenades, for sale to law enforcement agencies.[86] And, earlier that year, police in the northern Indian city of Lucknow had reportedly purchased five of Desert Wolf's Skunk drones, which, according to police superintendent Yashasvi Yadav, 'can be used to shower pepper powder on an unruly mob in case of any trouble'.[87]

Meanwhile, North Dakota became the first US state to legislate in favour of police using drones armed with 'non-lethal' weapons,[88] whereas several other US states had by then expressly prohibited any kind of drone weaponisation.[89] Elsewhere, the issue of whether police may arm their drones remained largely unsettled, so in 2016 a team of researchers from Taser International (a company that supplies police with stun guns and body cameras) met with potential customers at the International Association of Chiefs of Police (IACP) conference in San Diego, California. Company spokesperson Steve Tuttle explained at the time:[90]

Following recent events, including the use of a robot to deploy lethal force in Dallas to eliminate a highly dangerous threat, we've received questions about whether it would be feasible to similarly deploy a TASER from an autonomous vehicle. One can certainly imagine high-risk scenarios such as terrorist barricades where such a capability could allow public safety officers to more rapidly incapacitate a threat and save many lives.

Tuttle was referring here to the Dallas Police Department's unprecedented use in July 2016 of a bomb-disposal robot (a land-based vehicle), armed with a bomb (C-4 explosive), to kill a gunman who had just targeted and killed five police officers.[91] The raising of this example, however, implied the possibility that a remotely controlled *aerial* vehicle too could be armed, and with the intention of causing death rather than temporary incapacitation.

The emergent temptation – operational and commercial – towards the use of armed drones for law enforcement purposes could be conceptualised as an example of what some authors call 'police militarization'.[92] According to Ian Shaw, for example, the drone has gradually evolved from being a surveillance platform to being an airstrike platform to being, most recently, 'a policing technology'.[93] Michael Salter has argued that 'drones represents a new stage in the militarisation of policing',[94] and for Oliver Davis the 'repatriation of the drone . . . follows a familiar pattern whereby coercive security technologies are tested abroad before finding their way 'home' to arm police forces that are becoming increasingly paramilitary in style and conduct'.[95]

From a technological perspective, such claims can be refuted by differentiating between the large drones used militarily in foreign territories and the small drones that some police departments have in fact been acquiring for domestic use. Part of the normal pattern of militarisation is that a state's police officers become armed with types of weapons that are also used (or have been used) by that state's military personnel. This process tends to be criticised where 'little thought [is] given to providing a weapon and ammunition specifically geared to the needs of civilian policing'.[96] An example is the 1033 Program in the United States (instituted by section 1033 of the National Defense Authorization Security Act of 1997) which facilitates transfers of surplus military equipment such as mine-resistant vehicles, amphibious tanks and grenade launchers to local police departments.[97] In the case of drones, by contrast, it has not been the case that US police have been receiving and repurposing ex-military drones and the associated heavy firepower (Hellfire missiles). Rather, police there and in some other countries have generally been purchasing smaller, commercially available drones of the kind used extensively by photographers and hobbyists.

Even so, a concern about militarisation remains valid in relation to another of its aspects: the potential for military ideas and attitudes to influence ideas and attitudes about policing. This influence is morally undesirable if, for example, police ethics begins to be replaced by military ethics (which affords a greater degree of permission for harming people) as a guide to police action. A concern that this might happen is reflected in the 'image problem' that drones in general continue to have. In the popular imagination, fed by media coverage of drone technology that focuses largely on air strikes in war zones, drones tend to be strongly associated with heavy-handed and military-style violence.[98] This perception, acknowledged by the IACP, informs the Association's current policy position that police drones 'shall not be equipped with weapons of any kind'.[99] The reasoning behind this position is couched in terms of likely public opposition to weaponisation: the 'public acceptance of airborne use of force is . . . doubtful', the IACP has explained, and this 'could result in unnecessary community resistance' to the use of *unarmed* police drones.[100] However, this assessment by the world's peak professional body for police leaders appears to be a pragmatic rather than principled argument against arming police drones; logically, the IACP's opposition seems liable to diminish in line with any shift in public opinion. A stronger foundation for a policy position on this issue would be one that is instead couched in terms of the established ethical principles for police violence (or 'use of force').

Ethics of police violence

Where there is public concern that police drones might be used violently in the same way as military drones, one source of reassurance is the long-standing expectation that police violence should be more restrained than military violence. The role of military personnel is (among other things) to be ready one day to fight or support fighters in war, but police use violence (on a more frequent basis) in the course of preventing crime and protecting public safety. This role difference is reflected in differing ethical standards for, on the one hand, police whose protective impulse is internally directed (to protect fellow citizens from each other) and, on the other hand, warriors whose defensive impulse is often externally directed (to protect citizens from foreign enemies). For example, while it is morally permissible in the context of armed conflict to attack and kill enemy soldiers without warning, no such moral permission is generally available against criminal suspects in the peacetime context of law enforcement. Also, whereas a police officer's use of force ought never to put the lives of innocent bystanders at risk, combatants guided by traditional military ethics may endanger civilians to a considerable extent on grounds of military necessity.[101] Moreover, there is an established expectation that police ethics and military ethics will remain distinct in their application, even in extreme cases of collective violence (such as riots) in a domestic setting where local authorities might feel tempted to respond aggressively.[102]

Other circumstances likely to warrant police possession and possible use of weapons include: shoot-outs between police and suspects during a bank robbery; the protection of government officials or foreign dignitaries; a police officer's chance encounter of a violent crime in progress; domestic violence involving emotionally disturbed individuals; sieges involving armed hostage-takers; and interceptions of suspected suicide bombers. Regardless of circumstances, however, the practice of policing is governed morally and fundamentally by respect for individual human rights, and especially for the right to life. Or, at least, this is how policing *ought* to be governed, according to a liberal notion of policing that assumes human rights are universal. It must be acknowledged that, in many illiberal societies throughout the world, policing is geared less towards serving and protecting the members of a policed community and more towards the (violent) domination of the local population.[103] In non-democracies, police are ethically disadvantaged by the fact that their position and role in society are not ultimately authorised by the people. This means that, instead of being democratically empowered to treat citizens with equal respect, those police find themselves bound instead to serve only a ruling elite which deploys them against domestic opposition groups. Police in this position are more liable to be regarded as 'enemies' rather than 'servants' of the people.[104] Here, the moral distinction between policing and warfare is most vulnerable to breaking down, making unethical police violence (drone-based or otherwise) more likely to occur.

Guidance for police action can be found in two influential 'soft law' documents drafted by law enforcement and human rights experts: the *Code of Conduct for Law Enforcement Officials*,[105] and the *Basic Principles on the Use of Force and Firearms by Law Enforcement Officials*.[106] The *Code of Conduct* includes a general 'serve and protect' principle to be observed at all times,[107] and a 'necessity' principle for when violence is a possibility.[108] The *Basic Principles* reinforce the latter principle, and they codify four other principles to guide police violence: legality, precaution, proportionality and accountability. Together, these interrelated principles establish a five-stage test applicable to any instance of police 'use of force': (1) whether force is being used in accordance with a domestic legal framework that satisfies the international human rights law prohibition of arbitrary killings (the legality principle); (2) whether, when planning and initially organising a police operation, the state seeks to minimise the possibility of recourse to lethal force as well as death and injury (the precaution principle); (3) whether it is absolutely necessary at the time for police to use a certain kind and degree of force to achieve a legitimate objective (the necessity principle); (4) whether the anticipated harm caused by police to the suspect and to bystanders is proportionate (not excessive) in comparison to the seriousness of the threat posed and the legitimate objective to be achieved (the proportionality principle); and (5) whether, if police caused serious injury or death, the state conducted an effective investigation of how this happened (the accountability principle).[109]

For present purposes, the principles of legality and accountability are not of central concern because these are essentially procedural. Although it is morally important to establish sets of legally binding rules for police use of force (legality) and for actual uses to be assessed accordingly (accountability), the content of those rules and assessments is critically informed by the three substantive principles: necessity, proportionality and precaution. The principle of necessity imposes a duty upon police to act non-violently wherever possible, to use force only for a legitimate purpose (for example, in self- or other-defence), and to use only as much force as is reasonable under the circumstances.[110] According to Christof Heyns, 'necessity' is a qualitative, quantitative and temporal concept.[111] A given use of force by police is qualitatively necessary if no other means (non-violent or less harmful) is available to achieve a legitimate objective. The amount of force is quantitatively necessary if it does not exceed the amount required to achieve that objective. And the use of force is temporally necessary if it must be used quickly (within 'seconds, not hours') against a person who presents an immediate threat.[112] When the instrument of force to be used is potentially lethal (a firearm, for example), the necessity threshold is very high: its use must be 'strictly unavoidable in order to protect life'.[113]

The latter requirement relates also to proportionality: the principle that the amount of force used, and its potential to cause harm, must be strictly proportionate to the seriousness of the crime and the legitimate objective to be achieved.[114] Accordingly, only the most serious of threats (potential loss of life) warrant the most serious (potentially lethal) uses of force by police. Preparing to use a certain type and degree of force 'proportionally' thus involves a balancing of the risks posed by a criminal suspect against the potential harm to that individual as well as to anyone else nearby. Force is or can become disproportionate where the harm caused outweighs the advantages of its use.[115] So, for example, shooting a firearm at a fleeing thief who poses no immediate danger to anyone is impermissible,[116] as is any police policy allowing lethal force to be used for a purpose other than to protect life.[117] Importantly, the proportionality principle is protective also of bystanders who might become unintended victims of police use of force. A bullet fired at a suspect on the street, for example, could pass through their body and go on to hit someone else. So, as a matter of proportionality, police are generally permitted to use low-velocity, expanding bullets which minimise the risk to bystanders from 'over-penetration'.[118]

When force is used, the principles of necessity and proportionality are more likely to be satisfied where policing operations have been carefully planned in a way that minimises the risk (to everyone involved) of death or injury.[119] Such planning is required by the principle of precaution which serves as a further safeguard of the human right to life. Taking reasonable precautions to respect life and prevent harm includes, for example: training police officers in the proper use of a variety of forceful techniques and instruments; requiring them (when appropriate) to issue a clear warning before using force; and ensuring that medical assistance is promptly available to potential victims.[120] Such precautious arrangements can be contrasted with operational plans that effectively lock police into taking forceful action, thereby potentially escalating criminal violence and risking a greater amount of injury and death.

The satisfaction of all three of the above principles is, in practice, supported by the 'differentiated' use of force. Ethical policing therefore critically involves the equipping of police with 'various types of weapons and ammunition,' including 'non-lethal incapacitating weapons for use in appropriate situations'.[121] So equipped, an officer is able to 'choose from a range of instruments and techniques to use force in order to opt for the least intrusive and most proportional one in the circumstances to achieve the legitimate policing objective'.[122] This means also that, where non-violent policing measures have been or are likely to be ineffective, the level of force used (ranging in effect from uncomfortable to injurious to deadly) can be 'escalated as gradually as possible'.[123] In the policing of a public assembly which has turned violent, for example, it might sometimes be ethically appropriate to apply 'less-lethal' force in the form of chemical irritants, electroshock weapons, rubber or plastic bullets, or water cannons.[124] Here, a key rationale for choosing these kinds of weapons is to reduce the risk of escalating the violence by avoiding the spectacle of fatalities. By contrast, when police encounter a suspected suicide bomber in a crowded place, a rapid resort to lethal weaponry might be justified if such force is the only way to prevent mass casualties from an exploding bomb.[125]

Tele-present police and permissible drone violence

When the platform for a weapon is a camera-equipped drone, the police user of force acts at a distance from a suspect. Yet the idea of distanced policing is already familiar in many parts of the world from the perspective of ordinary citizens. Technological changes have caused increasing police remoteness from the public as staffed desks and stations have given way to telephone and online services.[126] Now, drone technology too can enable police officers to spend less time interacting with citizens. This gives rise to broad concerns that such physical alienation might desensitise police to the concerns of the public,[127] and that police remoteness is inconsistent with a 'serve and protect' ethos.[128] If, in addition, an officer's 'tele-presence' was extended to the use of force,[129] satisfying ethical policing principles (necessity, proportionality and precaution) could be challenging. In considering that challenge, at least three factors are important: the reduction of risk to police; the quality of their drone-based perception of criminal threats; and the potential for weaponised drones to escalate public disorder.

Police risk and self-defence

The most obvious and immediate advantage of deploying a police drone, instead of a police officer, into a dangerous situation is that it spares that officer from exposure to physical risk. Risk avoidance is itself morally important because governments have a duty to protect the human rights of their police personnel. The provision of adequate training and equipment (including self-protective equipment), and the careful planning and command of police operations, helps to avoid the placing of officers in unnecessary danger.[130] It seems consistent with such efforts, then, to substitute a drone if its performance of a policing function is equivalent to (or better than) that of an on-scene officer. Less obvious, however, is whether reducing the risk to police in this way – removing them physically from the tense environment of an unfolding crime – is also essentially protective of suspects and bystanders. In this regard, when it comes to the police use of force, is deploying a tele-present officer better because they are less likely to act desperately, or is it worse because they are less likely to perceive enough of what is going on?

The *Basic Principles* provide that, for the purpose of 'restraining the application of means capable of causing death or injury to persons', police should 'be equipped with self-defence equipment such as shields, helmets, bullet-proof vests and bullet-proof means of transportation, *in order to* decrease the need to use weapons of any kind'.[131] Thus, as a matter of ethical policing, reducing risk to police is supposed to reduce the likelihood of their resorting to force, to the ultimate benefit of the public being policed. This ideal of mutual risk reduction has been demonstrated, for example, in Northern Ireland where 'a drastic reduction in the use of force' was achieved after police officers there were issued body-length shields and fireproof overalls.[132] Similarly, one could argue, protecting the bodies of armed police by sometimes replacing them with armed drones is essentially precautious and therefore ethically justified. A tele-present officer need not act in self-defence and, in remaining unexposed to danger, they cannot *fearfully* use a weapon. As Kyle Stelmack has argued, that officer would be spared 'direct contact with environmental factors that lead to the stress and anxiety that oftentimes results in the use of force, especially excessive force'.[133] From a safely remote position, and viewing imagery captured by their drone's camera, police would perhaps have more opportunity to refrain from using force unless or until it would clearly be necessary and proportionate. And, in the meantime, a drone equipped with loudspeakers could broadcast an officer's warning to a person acting dangerously to cease their actions, thus preserving the availability of a non-violent route to neutralising a public safety threat. The overall effect, then, of raising the practical threshold for permissible use of force would be a reduction in the likelihood of violence being used by police and of suspects or bystanders suffering harm.

Against this position, however, one could argue that drone based reduction of risk to police would be detrimental to the public *because* an officer is not physically present. With regard to the precaution principle and the importance of differentiated force, a tele-present officer (being at no risk) would probably feel less pressured to escalate quickly towards the use of a (lethal) weapon. Even so, the overall range of response options available to police would be reduced if an armed drone were deployed in place of an on-scene officer. The option of non-violently persuading a dangerous suspect to surrender to an immediate arrest is unavailable where police commanders have arranged for arrest-performing personnel to be kept at a distance. And a tele-present officer is also operationally locked out of using the various, less-lethal bodily techniques which are the most commonly used techniques in policing: for example, pushing with the palm of the hand or holding someone's arm behind their back. In addition, the use of an armed drone renders impossible the police use of instruments including batons, truncheons, shields (to push someone) and handcuffs.[134] Instead, the application of force with a drone could only *begin* with the use of ranged instruments (such as tasers, rubber bullets and sprayed chemicals) even though the circumstances of a police encounter might mean it is necessary and proportionate only to use milder techniques. Any temptation felt by police, then, to use force only as they can (rather than as they should) is one that would tend to make policing actions riskier (to suspects and bystanders alike) and therefore less justifiable.

Police perception of circumstances

In the application of bodily force, the on-scene officer can literally feel what they are doing to another person. And, prior to their use of any kind of violence, potentially all of that officer's other senses can be engaged in the perception of circumstances. The idea of deploying armed police drones has been criticised, in this regard, as an inferior form of violent policing because it only affords the drone's remote operator an attenuated sense of the harm they are causing. Arguably, 'being there' matters. The dangerousness of a situation might not be adequately assessable if, for example, a (potentially) violent suspect's demeanour cannot be observed up close.[135] And, to the extent that good perception relies upon police presence and proximity, a potential problem with the drone-based distancing of police officers is, as Jay Stanley has suggested, that 'their judgment about when to apply force is more likely to be flawed . . . and excessive amounts of force are more likely to be applied'.[136]

In the United States, some scholars have considered the potential police use of a drone-based weapon from the perspective of whether this would legally constitute a 'reasonable seizure'.[137] The US Constitution's Fourth Amendment provides that '[t]he right of the people to be secure in their persons . . . against unreasonable searches and seizures, shall not be violated'. Sometimes, when US police have been accused of using excessive force in attempting to apprehend a suspect, such force has been alleged to be an unreasonable seizure in violation of the Fourth Amendment. In the case of *Graham* v. *Connor*, the US Supreme Court established the constitutional standard that 'governs a free citizen's claim that law enforcement officials used excessive force in the course of making an arrest . . . or other 'seizure' of his person'.[138] This standard is that '[t]he 'reasonableness' of a particular use of force must be judged from the perspective of a reasonable officer *on the scene*'.[139] And, as the Court explained, 'reasonableness must embody allowance for the fact that police officers are often forced to make split-second judgments – in circumstances that are tense, uncertain, and rapidly evolving – about the amount of force that is necessary in a particular situation'.[140]

If an armed, camera-equipped drone were the only police asset 'on the scene', the legal question that would arise is whether the drone's controlling officer would be able to use force reasonably. According to a strict interpretation of the *Graham* standard, the defence of reasonableness is simply unavailable to any officer who uses force remotely rather than 'on the scene'.[141] From an ethical perspective, however, the broader issue is whether a tele-present officer would be sufficiently capable of judging whether a particular use of force would be necessary and proportionate under the circumstances. Could that officer, from a remote position, '*truly* assess the situation and administer the proper amount of force'?[142] In some cases, discerning the truth of what is going on might be made easier by absenting an at-risk officer from the scene and replacing them with a tele-present drone operator. For example, when it comes to police shooting mistakes, these have sometimes occurred when an observed suspect makes a sudden movement that is perceived as their reaching for a weapon. It later becomes known that the person was in fact reaching for a phone or other object, and a police officer's hasty resort to the use of a firearm is then explained by a concern for their own safety.[143] Such a concern cannot arise if an officer is merely tele-present, in which case that officer could instead afford to refrain from the use of force while taking time to confirm the true nature of a suspect's observed actions.

Even so, there could still be operational pressure to use drone violence quickly for the sake of *other*-defence, and here the tele-present officer would still face an ethical challenge: to obtain (via their drone's camera) an adequate understanding of the severity of a criminal threat to human life and to decide what forceful response (if any) would be necessary and proportionate. In circumstances where the threat appeared to be of moderate severity and there were many bystanders visible on the scene, the perception deficit from reliance upon drone vision alone might militate against the swift resort to violence. That is, a police decision-maker might decide it would be more precautious to await the acquisition (by additional means) of a stronger understanding of the unfolding situation. A more urgent decision to respond forcefully might yet be justified, though, if a drone on the scene was transmitting imagery of a severe and ongoing threat to life, and if there appeared to be no bystanders in the vicinity of a violent suspect.

If, for example, a lone sniper in a tall building were spotted firing on a crowd below, sending up an armed drone to neutralise that threat would likely be both necessary and proportionate. Or, in the presence of bystanders, the risk of bullet overpenetration (a proportionality problem) might be less if it is fired from a drone directly overhead (compared to an on-scene officer firing laterally), although this could still present a ricochet risk (another proportionality problem) if the suspect is standing on a hard surface. In more complicated circumstances, the necessity and proportionality principles might be even harder to satisfy when an armed drone alone is used. Where a targeted hostage-taker is surrounded by

hostages, using a drone-based weapon would present a greater proportionality challenge (the risk of police harm to innocents), just as would
the presence of a suspected suicide bomber in a crowd. And, in both
kinds of cases, the necessity of using force would arguably be more easily
judged by an armed officer who is physically on the scene. That officer
is in a better position to converse and negotiate with a hostage-taker
(perhaps obviating the need for any police violence) and is able immediately to accept a surrender. Or, in encountering a suspected bomber,
the on-scene officer is able to observe closely the suspect's demeanour
and actions, and to bring a firearm quickly to within point-blank range
(and less conspicuously than a drone can) if lethal force becomes necessary.[144] In such circumstances, for policing to be both effective and
ethical, officers need to be present (and thus at risk), because deploying
a tele-present officer's drone instead would be a less suitable and less
precautious approach.

Escalation risk

Precaution is just as important when police use of force is not intended
to be lethal, and a police drone could also be armed with less-lethal
weapons. As described earlier, the companies seeking to sell weaponised
drones to law enforcement authorities often emphasise the potential utility of this technology in the forceful policing of public assemblies. One
envisaged scenario is that police could use a drone's weapons to control
a large crowd's movement, 'employing pepper spray or rubber bullets to
prevent the crowd from moving past certain points'.[145] Deploying tele-
present officers to respond to a riot, for example, would obviate the need
to expose on-scene officers to the risk of harm, and the former would not
feel a need to act desperately in self-defence. Even so, an ethical problem
that might yet remain is that this policing tactic carries too great a risk of
escalating (worsening) the overall threat to public safety. Planning to use
police drones forcefully against assemblies of people would, then, not be
sufficiently precautious with regard to protecting everyone's right to life.

In 2016 the UN Human Rights Council published a report on the
proper management of assemblies, jointly authored by the Special Rapporteur on the rights to freedom of peaceful assembly and of association and the Special Rapporteur on extrajudicial, summary or arbitrary
executions. The report advised that, on the basis of a risk assessment,
'equipment for law- enforcement officials deployed during assemblies
should include . . . appropriate less-lethal weapons', and it recommended
police use of weapons and tactics which 'allow for a graduated response
and de-escalation of tensions'.[146] With regard to the availability of a

'growing range of weapons that are remote controlled', the report urged the exercise of '[g]reat caution' in the context of the policing of assemblies,[147] but it offered no detail on the meaning of this recommendation. Subsequently, guidance published by the UN Human Rights Commissioner recommended only that '[l]ess-lethal weapons and related equipment that deliver force by remote control . . . should be authorized only if, in the context of their intended or ordinary use, it can be ensured that such use would comply with international human rights law'.[148] The guidance did not, however, go on to explain how police drones armed with less-lethal weapons could be used in a necessary, proportionate and precautious way.

A good starting point for further considering this ethical challenge is the application of the precaution principle, which, in the planning of police operations, is important as an ethical precursor to satisfying the necessity and proportionality principles. For police commanders thinking of deploying drones during public assemblies, there would probably be at least two kinds of escalation risk worth anticipating in operational policies and plans. In considering drones armed with riot-control chemicals (tear gas), for example, commanders would need first to recall the potential for such weapons (delivered by any means) to cause a crowd to panic and perhaps stampede.[149] Second, they would need to consider any additional escalation risk associated specifically with police using *drones* as the means of weapon delivery. From the perspective of the policed public, in the context of an assembly, the necessity of police wielding even less-lethal weapons via drone might seem doubtful if no officers (requiring protection) are on the scene. And, because dispersed tear gas is inherently indiscriminate in generating debilitating effects, using drones for high-altitude dispersal might be (and appear) all the more excessive (disproportionate). It seems likely, moreover, that members of a crowd would react differently to drone use than they would to on-scene officers using force to control them. Perhaps, for example, a crowd's outrage and despair at being unable to 'fight back' could add to whatever sense of grievance has inspired the assembly, thus leading to a worse escalation of violent disorder.

CONCLUSION

When the use of armed drones cannot plausibly be conceptualised as warfare and Just War morality is thus unavailable, such violence is left open to be condemned as impermissible homicide unless a non-war basis for justification can be found. In some circumstances, a state's drone violence might instead be approached and justified as a practice of violent law

enforcement (punishment or policing), although here the moral requirements for restraint are stricter than they are during war. To the extent that
the US government's drone-based personality strikes have essentially been
a means of punishing crime, the main problem with these has been that
they are a morally flawed way of bringing criminals to justice. Without
recourse to genuine legalism, punitive drone strikes against unconvicted
terrorists will only ever amount to wild justice, and the associated moral
risk of arbitrary killing will remain high. It does not necessarily follow,
however, that involving a state's independent judges in strike decisions
would sufficiently tame drone violence of this kind. Pre-strike trials *in
absentia* of accused terrorists could, in practice, be extremely difficult to
conduct fairly. And, even if fair adjudication could somehow be achieved,
the long-range use of a missile-armed drone as the method of execution
would arguably carry too great a risk of harming any innocent people in
the vicinity of a punitive strike.

In the practice of domestic policing, 'violent law enforcement' functions primarily to protect rather than extinguish human life, and in this
regard any future arming of police drones could have moral advantages
and disadvantages. When criminal threats to public safety arise, reducing physical risk to police officers is important for its own sake. And,
to the extent that police who feel protected are less likely to use force
excessively, that risk-reduction can also benefit suspects and bystanders.
If, arguably, weapons controlled remotely by tele-present officers are less
likely to be used in haste or desperation, the arming of drones could be
justified as enabling greater adherence to the ethical principles of police
violence. On the other hand, there is a risk that the camera mounted on
a police drone might not provide a tele-present officer with a sufficiently
rich perception of events and circumstances. In which case, unnecessary
and/or disproportionate uses of force by police might become more likely
to occur because of misunderstandings and mistakes. Moreover, in the
policing of an unfolding crime, substituting a drone for an on-scene officer could sometimes generate a precaution problem because a drone is
less able to apply the full spectrum of violent and non-violent response
options. This could be especially problematic in public assembly contexts
(even if drones were armed only with less-lethal weapons) where it is
morally important for police to avoid aggravating crowds and thereby
inducing an escalation of violence.

NOTES

1. European Court of Human Rights, 'Convention for the Protection of
   Human Rights and Fundamental Freedoms', Rome, 4 November 1950,
   <https://www.echr.coe.int/Pages/home.aspx?p=basictexts&c>.

2. Christopher J. Fuller, *See It / Shoot It: The Secret History of the CIA's Lethal Drone Program*, Yale University Press, 2017: 15.

3. Michael J. Boyle, *The Drone Age: How Drone Technology Will Change War and Peace*, New York: Oxford University Press, 2020: 23.

4. Bernhard Koch, 'Moral Integrity and Remote-Controlled Killing: A Missing Perspective', in *Drones and Responsibility: Legal, Philosophical, and Sociotechnical Perspectives on Remotely Controlled Weapons*, ed. Ezio Di Nucci and Filippo Santoni de Sio, London: Routledge, 2016: 83–100, at 86.

5. The first section of this chapter develops ideas that originally featured in: Christian Enemark, 'Drone Violence as Wild Justice: Administrative Executions on the Terror Frontier', in *Ethics of Drone Strikes: Restraining Remote-Control Killing*, ed. Christian Enemark, Edinburgh: Edinburgh University Press, 2021: 74–92.

6. Kristin Bergtora Sandvik, 'The Public Order Drone: Promises, Proliferation and Disorder in Civil Airspace', in *The Good Drone*, ed. Kristin Bergtora Sandvik and Maria Gabrielsen Jumbert, London: Ashgate, 2016: 109–28.

7. The second section of this chapter develops ideas that originally featured in: Christian Enemark, 'Armed Drones and Ethical Policing: Risk, Perception, and the Tele-Present Officer', *Criminal Justice Ethics*, 40 (2) (2021): 124–44.

8. Ryan Browne and Barbara Starr, 'Trump: US military killed terrorist behind USS *Cole* bombing', *CNN*, 6 January 2019, <https://edition.cnn.com/2019/01/04/politics/uss-cole-al-badawi-killed/index.html>.

9. Ibid.

10. Bruce Cronin, *Bugsplat: The Politics of Collateral Damage in Western Armed Conflicts*, New York: Oxford University Press, 2018: 108–9.

11. Charlie Savage and Eric Schmitt, 'Biden quietly limits drone strikes away from war zones', *New York Times*, 4 March 2021: A12.

12. Quoted in: Jameel Jaffer, 'The Justice Department's white paper on targeted killing', *American Civil Liberties Union*, 4 February 2013, <https://www.aclu.org/blog/national-security/targeted-killing/justice-departments-white-paper-targeted-killing> (emphasis added).

13. See: Sebastian Wuschka, 'The Use of Combat Drones in Current Conflicts: A Legal Issue or a Political Problem?', *Goettingen Journal of International Law*, 3 (2011): 891–905, at 905; Chantal Meloni, 'State and Individual Responsibility for Targeted Killings by Drones', in *Drones and Responsibility: Legal, Philosophical, and Sociotechnical Perspectives on Remotely Controlled Weapons*, ed. Ezio Di Nucci and Filippo Santoni de Sio, London: Routledge, 2016: 47–64, at 47; Christian Schaller, 'Using Force against Terrorists "Outside Areas of Active Hostilities": The Obama Approach and the Bin Laden Raid Revisited', *Journal of Conflict & Security Law*, 20 (2) (2015): 195–227, at 195.

14. International Covenant on Civil and Political Rights. Adopted and opened for signature, ratification and accession by General Assembly resolution 2200A (XXI) of 16 December 1966, entry into force 23 March 1976, Office of the High Commissioner for Human Rights, United Nations, <https://www.ohchr.org/en/professionalinterest/pages/ccpr.aspx>.

15. Fifth Amendment – U.S. Constitution, *FindLaw*, <https://constitution.findlaw.com/amendment5.html>.

16. Michael Ramsden, 'Targeted Killings and International Human Rights Law: The Case of Anwar Al-Awlaki', *Journal of Conflict & Security Law*, 16 (2) (2011): 385–406, at 395.

17. See: Scott Shane, 'Judging a long, deadly reach', *New York Times*, 1 October 2011: A1; Steven P. Lee, 'Human Rights and Drone "Warfare"', *Peace Review* 27 (2015): 432–9, at 434.

18. Katherine Maynard, Jarod Kearney and James Guimond, *Revenge versus Legality: Wild Justice from Balzac to Clint Eastwood and Abu Ghraib*, Abingdon and New York: Birkbeck Law Press, 2010: 3.

19. Ibid. xii.

20. Ibid. 5.

21. Ibid. 5.

22. Paula Mitchell Marks. *And Die in the West: The Story of the O.K. Corral Gunfight*, New York: Morrow, 1989.

23. Katherine Maynard, Jarod Kearney and James Guimond, *Revenge versus Legality: Wild Justice from Balzac to Clint Eastwood and Abu Ghraib*, Abingdon and New York: Birkbeck Law Press, 2010: 167.

24. Ibid. 170.

25. Charles Bramesco, 'Dirty Harry at 50: Clint Eastwood's seminal, troubling 70s antihero', *The Guardian*, 23 December 2021, <https://www.theguardian.com/film/2021/dec/23/dirty-harry-clint-eastwood-70s-antihero>.

26. Maurice Punch, *Shoot to Kill: Police Accountability, Firearms and Fatal Force*, Bristol: Policy Press, 2011: 79.

27. Katherine Maynard, Jarod Kearney and James Guimond, *Revenge versus Legality: Wild Justice from Balzac to Clint Eastwood and Abu Ghraib*, Abingdon and New York: Birkbeck Law Press, 2010: 172–3.

28. Quoted in: Robert E. Conot, *Justice at Nuremburg*, New York: Carroll & Graf, 1993: 121.

29. Katherine Maynard, Jarod Kearney and James Guimond, *Revenge versus Legality: Wild Justice from Balzac to Clint Eastwood and Abu Ghraib*, Abingdon and New York: Birkbeck Law Press, 2010: 186.

30. Gary Jonathan Bass, *Stay the Hand of Vengeance: The Politics of War Crimes Tribunals*, Princeton, NJ: Princeton University Press, 2000: 185.

31. See: Jason Motlagh, 'U.S. takes terror fight to Africa's "Wild West"', *SFGate*, 27 December 2005, <https://www.sfgate.com/politics/article/U-S-takes-terror-fight-to-Africa-s-Wild-West-2555454.php>. Reuters, 'A wild frontier', *The Economist*, 18 September 2008, <https://www.economist.com/asia/2008/09/18/a-wild-frontier>.

32. Reuters, 'Obama: We took out Pakistani Taliban chief', *ABC News*, 22 August 2009, <https://www.abc.net.au/news/2009-08-21/obama-we-took-out-pakistani-taliban-chief/1399370>.

33. The White House, 'The Vice President appears on *Meet the Press* with Tim Russert', *The White House, President George W. Bush*, 16 September 2001, <https://georgewbush-whitehouse.archives.gov/vicepresident/news-speeches/speeches/vp20010916.html>.

34. See: Barton Gellman, 'CIA weighs "targeted killing" missions: administration believes restraints do not bar singling out individual terrorists', *Washington Post*, 28 October 2001: A01; Andrew Cockburn, *Kill Chain: Drones and the Rise of High-Tech Assassins*, London: Verso, 2016: 115.

35. Toby Harnden, 'Bin Laden is wanted: dead or alive, says Bush', *The Telegraph*, 18 September 2001, <https://www.telegraph.co.uk/news/worldnews/asia/afghanistan/1340895/Bin-Laden-is-wanted-dead-or-alive-says-Bush.html>.

36. Jeffrey S. Bachman and Jack Holland, 'Lethal Sterility: Innovative Dehumanisation in Legal Justifications of Obama's Drone Policy', *The International Journal of Human Rights*, 23 (6) (2019): 1028–47, at 1032.

37. Ian Christopher McCaleb, 'Bush vows justice will be done', *CNN*, 21 September 2001, <http://edition.cnn.com/2001/US/09/21/gen.president.speech/>.

38. George W. Bush, 'State of the Union Address', *The White House*, 20 January 2004, <https://georgewbush-whitehouse.archives.gov/news/releases/2004/01/20040120-7.html>.

39. Ibid.

40. Macon Phillips, 'Osama Bin Laden Dead', *The White House*, 2 May 2011, <https://obamawhitehouse.archives.gov/blog/2011/05/02/osama-bin-laden-dead>.

41. See: Peter L. Bergen and Jennifer Rowland, 'Decade of the Drone: Analyzing CIA Drone Attacks, Casualties, and Policy', in *Drone Wars: Transforming Conflict, Law, and Policy*, ed. Peter L. Bergen and Daniel Rothenberg, New York: Cambridge University Press, 2015: 12–41, at 33–8.

42. Chris Woods, *Sudden Justice: America's Secret Drone Wars*, London: Hurst & Co., 2015: 119.

43. Mark Mazzetti, Eric Schmitt and Robert F. Worth, 'C.I.A. strike kills U.S.-born militant in a car in Yemen', *New York Times*, 1 October 2011: A1.

44. Chris Woods, *Sudden Justice: America's Secret Drone Wars*, London: Hurst & Co., 2015: 137.

45. ABC News, '"This Week" Transcript: Panetta', *ABC News*, 27 June 2010, <https://abcnews.go.com/ThisWeek/week-transcript-panetta/story?id=11025299>. The 'Detroit bomber' is Umar Farouk Abdulmutallab, a Nigerian man convicted of attempting to detonate explosives hidden in his underwear while on board a flight from Amsterdam to Detroit, Michigan, in late 2009.

46. John O. Brennan, 'The Efficacy and Ethics of U.S. Counterterrorism Strategy', *Woodrow Wilson International Center for Scholars*, 30 April 2012, <https://www.wilsoncenter.org/event/the-efficacy-and-ethics-us-counterterrorism-strategy>.

47. Tara McKelvey, 'Interview with Harold Koh, Obama's defender of drone strikes', *Daily Beast*, 8 April 2012, <https://www.thedailybeast.com/interview-with-harold-koh-obamas-defender-of-drone-strikes>.

48. Barack Obama, 'Remarks by the President at the National Defense University', *The White House*, 23 May 2013, <https://obamawhitehouse.archives.gov/the-press-office/2013/05/23/remarks-president-national-defense-university>.

49. Daniel Klaidman, *Kill or Capture: The War on Terror and the Soul of the Obama Presidency*, Boston, MA: Houghton Mifflin Harcourt, 2012: 219–20.

50. Katherine Maynard, Jarod Kearney and James Guimond, *Revenge versus Legality: Wild Justice from Balzac to Clint Eastwood and Abu Ghraib*, Abingdon and New York: Birkbeck Law Press, 2010: 164.

51. Jo Becker and Scott Shane, 'Secret "kill list" proves a test of Obama's principles and will', *New York Times*, 29 May 2012: A1.

52. Charlie Savage, 'Relatives sue officials over U.S. citizens killed by drone strikes in Yemen', *New York Times*, 19 July 2012: A7.

53. Jo Becker and Scott Shane, 'secret "kill list" proves a test of Obama's principles and will', *New York Times*, 29 May 2012: A1.

54. Ibid. A1.

55. Ibid. A1.

56. Bruce Cronin, *Bugsplat: The Politics of Collateral Damage in Western Armed Conflicts*, New York; Oxford University Press, 2018: 116.

57. Gregory McNeal, 'Targeted Killing and Accountability', *Georgetown Law Journal*, 102 (2014): 681–794, at 708.

58. Ibid. 721.

59. Spencer Ackerman, '"Drones playbook" shows key role played by White House staff in deadly strikes', *The Guardian*, 6 August 2016, <https://www.theguardian.com/world/2016/aug/06/drones-playbook-white-house-nsc-obama-clinton-trump>; Cora Currier, 'White House finally releases its "playbook" for killing and capturing terror suspects', *The Intercept*, 6 August 2016, <https://theintercept.com/2016/08/06/white-house-finally-releases-its-playbook-for-killing-and-capturing-terror-suspects/>. The word 'playbook', used in the context of American football, refers to a book containing descriptions of the different offensive and defensive plays used by a football team.

60. Donald Trump, 'Remarks by President Trump on the Strategy in Afghanistan and South Asia', *The White House*, 21 August 2017, <https://www.whitehouse.gov/briefings-statements/remarks-president-trump-strategy-afghanistan-south-asia/>.

61. Rachel Stohl, *An Action Plan on U.S. Drone Policy. Recommendations for the Trump Administration*, Washington, DC: Stimson Center, 2018: 5.

62. See: Jennifer Gibson, 'We're quickly moving toward a world where drone executions are the norm', *Los Angeles Times*, 13 November 2019, <https://www.latimes.com/opinion/story/2019-11-13/drone-killings-war-syria-turkey>.

63. Boris Johnson, 'Why we should chuck Chequers', *The Spectator*, 28 July 2018, <https://www.spectator.co.uk/2018/07/boris-johnson-why-we-should-chuck-chequers/>.

64. Barack Obama, 'Remarks by the President at the National Defense University', *The White House*, 23 May 2013, <https://obamawhitehouse.archives.gov/the-press-office/2013/05/23/remarks-president-national-defense-university>.

65. See, for example: Amos Guoira and Jeffrey Brand, 'The Establishment of a Drone Court: A Necessary Restraint on Executive Power', in *Legitimacy and Drones: Investigating the Legality, Morality and Efficacy of UCAVs*, ed. Steven J. Barela, Farnham: Ashgate, 2015: 323–58; John Emery and Daniel R. Brunstetter, 'Restricting the Preventive Use of Force: Drones, the Struggle against Non-State Actors, and *Jus ad Vim*', in *Preventive Force: Drones, Targeted Killing, and the Transformation of Contemporary Warfare*, ed. Kerstin Fisk and Jennifer M. Ramos, New York: New York University Press, 2016: 257–82, at 259; Christian Nikolaus Braun, 'The Morality of Retributive Targeted Killing', *Journal of Military Ethics*, 18 (3) (2019): 170–88, at 179.

66. See, for example: Zeke Johnson, 'Why drone death courts are a terrible idea', *Amnesty International*, 25 February 2012, <http://blog.amnesty-usa.org/us/why-drone-death-courts-are-a-terrible-idea/>; Steve Vladeck, 'Drone courts: the wrong solution to the wrong problem', *Just Security*, 2 December 2014, <https://www.justsecurity.org/17914/drone-courts-wrong-solution-wrong-problem/>.

67. Neal K. Katyal, 'Who will mind the drones?', *New York Times*, 21 February 2013: A27; Garrett Epps, 'Why a secret court won't solve the drone-strike problem', *The Atlantic*, 16 February 2013, <https://www.theatlantic.com/politics/archive/2013/02/why-a-secret-court-wont-solve-the-drone-strike-problem/273246/>.

68. H. Jefferson Powell, *Targeting Americans: The Constitutionality of the U.S. Drone War*, New York: Oxford University Press, 2016: xvi.

69. Amos N. Guiora and Jeffrey S. Brand, 'Establishment of a Drone Court: A Necessary Restraint on Executive Power', in *Legitimacy and Drones: Investigating the Legality, Morality and Efficacy of UCAVs*, ed. Steven J. Barela, New York: Routledge, 2017: 323–57, at 349.

70. See: Faine Greenwood, 'Can a police drone recognize your face?', *Slate*, 8 July 2020, <https://slate.com/technology/2020/07/police-drone-facial-recognition.html>.

71. Kari Soo Lindberg and Colum Murphy, 'Drones take to China's skies to fight coronavirus outbreak', *Bloomberg*, 4 February 2020, <https://www.bloomberg.com/news/articles/2020-02-04/drones-take-to-china-s-skies-to-fight-coronavirus-outbreak>; Helena Smith, 'Greece to use drones to stop crowds gathering for Orthodox Easter', *The Guardian*, 17 April 2020, <https://www.theguardian.com/world/2020/apr/17/greece-to-use-drones-to-stop-crowds-gathering-for-orthodox-easter-covid-19>; Rebecca Ratcliffe, 'Police in Malaysia use drones to detect high temperatures amid Covid surge', *The Guardian*, 7 June 2021, <https://www.theguardian.com/world/2021/jun/07/police-in-malaysia-use-drones-to-detect-high-temperatures-amid-covid-surge>.

72. Thomas Gaulkin, 'Drone pandemic: will coronavirus invite the world to meet Big Brother?', *Bulletin of the Atomic Scientists*, 1 April 2020, <https://thebulletin.org/2020/04/drone-pandemic-will-coronavirus-invite-the-world-to-meet-big-brother>; Michael Richardson, '"Pandemic Drones": useful for enforcing social distancing, or for creating a police state?',

The Conversation, 31 March 2020, <https://theconversation.com/pandemic-drones-useful-for-enforcing-social-distancing-or-for-creating-a-police-state-134667>; Rick Noack, 'In victory for privacy activists, France is banned from using drones to enforce coronavirus rules', *Washington Post*, 14 January 2021, <https://www.washingtonpost.com/world/in-victory-for-privacy-activists-france-is-banned-from-using-drones-to-enforce-covid-rules/2021/01/14/b384eb40-5658-11eb-acc5-92d2819a1ccb_story.html>.

73. See: Andrew B. Talai, 'Drones and *Jones*: The Fourth Amendment and Police Discretion in the Digital Age', *California Law Review*, 102 (3) (2014): 729–80; Jonathan P. West and James S. Bowman, 'The Domestic Use of Drones: An Ethical Analysis of Surveillance Issues', *Public Administration Review*, 76 (4) (2016): 649–59; Rob Davies, 'Civil liberty fears as police consider using drones that film from 1,500ft', *The Guardian*, 29 October 2021, <https://www.theguardian.com/uk-news/2021/oct/29/police-england-wales-long-range-drone-footage-tender-filming>.

74. Barack Obama, 'Remarks by the President at the National Defense University', *The White House*, 23 May 2013, <https://obamawhitehouse.archives.gov/the-press-office/2013/05/23/remarks-president-national-defense-university>.

75. One type of drone used by British police is the DJI Mavic 2 Enterprise, which weighs less than one kilogram, has a battery life of twenty-nine minutes, operates at a range of five kilometres, and costs around £2,800: Eleanor Langford, 'Home Office plans to use military-grade drones to pursue suspects and monitor protests are raising privacy concerns', *PoliticsHome*, 17 September 2020, <https://www.politicshome.com/news/article/military-grade-drones-home-office>.

76. Bart Engberts and Edo Gillissen, 'Policing from Above: Drone Use by the Police', in *The Future of Drone Use: Opportunities and Threats from Ethical and Legal Perspectives*, ed. Bart Custers, The Hague: TMC Asser Press, 2016: 93–113, at 105.

77. Ibid. 101–2.

78. David Ovalle, 'From above, Miami-Dade police drone recorded crack cocaine sale live. It's a first, cops say', *Miami Herald*, 16 January 2020, <https://www.miamiherald.com/news/local/crime/article239246988.html>.

79. Cade Metz, 'Police drones are starting to think for themselves', *New York Times*, 7 December 2020: B1.

80. Judith Prieve, 'East Bay police department adds drones to crime-fighting arsenal', *The Mercury News*, 20 July 2019, <https://www.mercurynews.com/2019/07/20/east-bay-police-department-adds-drones-to-its-crime-fighting-arsenal/>.

81. Philip Bump, 'The border patrol wants to arm drones', *The Atlantic*, 2 July 2013, <https://www.theatlantic.com/national/archive/2013/07/border-patrol-arm-drones/313656/>.

82. Kyle Chayka, 'Watch this drone taser a guy until he collapses', *Time*, 11 March 2014, <https://time.com/19929/watch-this-drone-taser-a-guy-until-he-collapses/>.

83. Leo Kelion, 'African firm is selling pepper-spray bullet firing drones', *BBC News*, 18 June 2014, <https://www.bbc.co.uk/news/technology-27902634>; David Smith, 'Pepper-spray drone offered to South African mines for strike control', *The Guardian*, 20 June 2014, <https://www.theguardian.com/world/2014/jun/20/pepper-spray-drone-offered-south-african-mines-strike-control>.

84. Desert Wolf, 'Skunk Riot Control Copter', *Desert Wolf*, no date, <http://www.desert-wolf.com/dw/products/unmanned-aerial-systems/skunk-riot-control-copter.html> (accessed 5 January 2021).

85. Ibid.

86. Michael Crowley, *Tear Gassing by Remote Control: The Development and Promotion of Remotely Operated Means of Delivering or Dispersing Riot Control Agents*. London: Oxford Research Group, 2015: 28.

87. Luke Hurst, 'Indian police buy pepper spraying drones to control "unruly mobs"', *Newsweek*, 7 April 2015, <https://www.newsweek.com/pepper-spraying-drones-control-unruly-mobs-say-police-india-320189>.

88. Marco Della Cava, 'Police taser drones authorized in N.D.', *USA Today*, 28 August 2015, <https://eu.usatoday.com/story/tech/2015/08/28/police-taser-drones-authorized--north-dakota/71319668/>. The legality of using drone-based 'non-lethal' weapons in North Dakota is implied by the legislative provision that: '[a] law enforcement agency may not authorize the use of . . . an unmanned aerial vehicle armed with any *lethal* weapons'. H. 1328, 2015 Leg., 64th Sess. (N.D. 2015) (emphasis added).

89. See: Eric Brumfield, 'Armed Drones for Law Enforcement: Why It Might Be Time to Re-Examine the Current Use of Force Standard', *McGeorge Law Review*, 46 (3) (2014): 543–72, at 554.

90. Zusha Elinson, 'Taser explores concept of drone armed with stun gun for police Use', *Wall Street Journal*, 20 October 2016, <https://www.wsj.com/articles/taser-explores-concept-of-drone-armed-with-stun-gun-for-police-use-1476994514>.

91. Sam Thielman, 'Use of police robot to kill Dallas shooting suspect believed to be first in US history', *The Guardian*, 8 July 2016, <https://www.theguardian.com/technology/2016/jul/08/police-bomb-robot-explosive-killed-suspect-dallas>.

92. See, for example: Radley Balko. *Rise of the Warrior Cop: The Militarization of America's Police Forces*, New York: Public Affairs, 2013; Caroline Holmqvist, *Policing Wars: On Military Intervention in the Twenty-first Century*, Basingstoke: Palgrave Macmillan, 2014.

93. Ian G. R. Shaw, *Predator Empire: Drone Warfare and Full Spectrum Dominance*, Minneapolis: University of Minnesota Press, 2016: 22.

94. Michael Salter, 'Toys for the Boys? Drones, Pleasure and Popular Culture in the Militarisation of Policing', *Critical Criminology*, 22 (2) (2014): 163–77, at 164.

95. Oliver Davis, 'Theorizing the Advent of Weaponized Drones as Techniques of Domestic Paramilitary Policing', *Security Dialogue*, 50 (4) (2019): 344–60, at 344.

96. Maurice Punch, *Shoot to Kill: Police Accountability, Firearms and Fatal Force*, Bristol: Policy Press, 2011: 77.

97. See: Elizabeth E. Joh, 'Policing Police Robots', *UCLA Law Review*, 2 November 2016, <https://www.uclalawreview.org/policing-police-robots/>; Brian Barrett, 'The Pentagon's hand-me-downs helped militarize police. Here's how', *Wired*, 2 June 2020, <https://www.wired.com/story/pentagon-hand-me-downs-militarize-police-1033-program/>.

98. Maria Valdovinos, James Specht and Jennifer Zeunik, *Law Enforcement & Unmanned Aircraft Systems (UAS): Guidelines to Enhance Community Trust*. Washington, DC: Office of Community Oriented Policing Services, US Department of Justice, 2016: 1.

99. International Association of Chiefs of Police, 'Unmanned Aircraft', April 2019, <https://www.theiacp.org/resources/policy-center-resource/unmanned-aircraft>.

100. International Association of Chiefs of Police, 'Recommended Guidelines for the Use of Unmanned Aircraft', August 2012, <https://www.theiacp.org/sites/default/files/all/i-j/IACP_UAGuidelines.pdf>: 2.

101. Seumas Miller, *Shooting to Kill: The Ethics of Police and Military Use of Lethal Force*, New York: Oxford University Press, 2016: 11.

102. See: United Nations, 'Basic Principles on the Use of Force and Firearms by Law Enforcement Officials', Adopted by the Eighth United Nations Congress on the Prevention of Crime and the Treatment of Offenders, Havana, Cuba, 27 August to 7 September 1990. *Office of the High Commissioner for Human Rights*. <https://www.ohchr.org/en/professionalinterest/pages/useofforceandfirearms.aspx>. Principle 8 provides: 'Exceptional circumstances such as internal political instability or any other public emergency may not be invoked to justify any departure from these basic principles.'

103. See: Febriana Firdaus, 'Global protests throw spotlight on alleged police abuses in West Papua', *The Guardian*, 11 June 2020, <https://www.the-guardian.com/global-development/2020/jun/11/global-protests-throw-spotlight-on-alleged-police-abuses-in-west-papua>; BBC, 'End SARS protests: People "shot dead" in Lagos, Nigeria', *BBC News*, 21 October 2020, <https://www.bbc.co.uk/news/world-africa-54624611>; Tom Phillips, 'Heavily armed police launch bid to reclaim control of Rio de Janeiro favela', *The Guardian*, 20 January 2022, <https://www.theguardian.com/world/2022/jan/19/hundreds-of-armed-police-storm-rio-de-janeiro-favela>.

104. Tim Prenzler, *Ethics and Accountability in Criminal Justice: Towards a Universal Standard*, 1st edn, Brisbane: Australian Academic Press, 2009: 30.

105. United Nations, 'Code of Conduct for Law Enforcement Officials', adopted by General Assembly Resolution 34/169. 17 December 1979. *Office of the High Commissioner for Human Rights*. <https://www.ohchr.org/EN/ProfessionalInterest/Pages/LawEnforcementOfficials.aspx>.

106. United Nations, 'Basic Principles on the Use of Force and Firearms by Law Enforcement Officials', adopted by the Eighth United Nations Congress on the Prevention of Crime and the Treatment of Offenders, Havana,

Cuba, 27 August to 7 September 1990. *Office of the High Commissioner for Human Rights.* <https://www.ohchr.org/en/professionalinterest/pages/useofforceandfirearms.aspx>.

107. Article 1 of the Code provides: 'Law enforcement officials shall at all times fulfil the duty imposed upon them by law, by serving the community and by protecting all persons against illegal acts.'

108. Article 3 of the Code provides: 'Law enforcement officials may use force only when strictly necessary and to the extent required for the performance of their duty.'

109. Gloria Gaggioli, 'Lethal Force and Drones: The Human Rights Question', in *Legitimacy and Drones: Investigating the Legality, Morality and Efficacy of UCAVs*, ed. Steven J. Barel, New York: Routledge, 2017: 91–115, at 105.

110. See: United Nations, 'Basic Principles on the Use of Force and Firearms by Law Enforcement Officials', adopted by the Eighth United Nations Congress on the Prevention of Crime and the Treatment of Offenders, Havana, Cuba, 27 August to 7 September 1990. *Office of the High Commissioner for Human Rights.* <https://www.ohchr.org/en/professionalinterest/pages/useofforceandfirearms.aspx>: Principle 4.

111. Christof Heyns, 'Report of the Special Rapporteur on Extrajudicial, Summary or Arbitrary Executions' (A/HRC/26/36), 1 April 2014. New York: Human Rights Council, United Nations General Assembly, 2014: para. 60.

112. Ibid. para. 59.

113. United Nations, 'Basic Principles on the Use of Force and Firearms by Law Enforcement Officials', adopted by the Eighth United Nations Congress on the Prevention of Crime and the Treatment of Offenders, Havana, Cuba, 27 August to 7 September 1990. *Office of the High Commissioner for Human Rights.* <https://www.ohchr.org/en/professionalinterest/pages/useofforceandfirearms.aspx>: Principle 9.

114. Ibid. Principle 5.

115. See: United Nations, *Resource Book on the Use of Force and Firearms in Law Enforcement*, New York: United Nations Office on Drugs and Crime and Office of the United Nations High Commissioner for Human Rights, 2017: 18.

116. See: Christof Heyns, 'Report of the Special Rapporteur on Extrajudicial, Summary or Arbitrary Executions' (A/HRC/26/36), 1 April 2014. New York: Human Rights Council, United Nations General Assembly, 2014: para. 72.

117. United Nations, *Resource Book on the Use of Force and Firearms in Law Enforcement*, New York: United Nations Office on Drugs and Crime and Office of the United Nations High Commissioner for Human Rights, 2017: 22.

118. Ibid. 97.

119. See: United Nations, 'Basic Principles on the Use of Force and Firearms by Law Enforcement Officials', adopted by the Eighth United Nations Congress on the Prevention of Crime and the Treatment of Offenders, Havana, Cuba, 27 August to 7 September 1990. *Office of the High*

Commissioner for Human Rights. <https://www.ohchr.org/en/profes-sionalinterest/pages/useofforceandfirearms.aspx>: Principle 3.

120. See: Christof Heyns, 'Report of the Special Rapporteur on Extrajudicial, Summary or Arbitrary Executions' (A/HRC/26/36), 1 April 2014. New York: Human Rights Council, United Nations General Assembly, 2014: para. 51; United Nations, *Resource Book on the Use of Force and Firearms in Law Enforcement*, New York: United Nations Office on Drugs and Crime and Office of the United Nations High Commissioner for Human Rights, 2017: 20.

121. United Nations, 'Basic Principles on the Use of Force and Firearms by Law Enforcement Officials', adopted by the Eighth United Nations Congress on the Prevention of Crime and the Treatment of Offenders, Havana, Cuba, 27 August to 7 September 1990. *Office of the High Commissioner for Human Rights.* <https://www.ohchr.org/en/professionalinterest/pages/useofforceandfirearms.aspx>: Principle 2.

122. United Nations, *Resource Book on the Use of Force and Firearms in Law Enforcement*, New York: United Nations Office on Drugs and Crime and Office of the United Nations High Commissioner for Human Rights, 2017: 18.

123. Christof Heyns, 'Report of the Special Rapporteur on Extrajudicial, Summary or Arbitrary Executions' (A/HRC/26/36), 1 April 2014. New York: Human Rights Council, United Nations General Assembly, 2014: para. 61.

124. Although the *Basic Principles* refer to 'non-lethal incapacitating weapons,', the term 'less-lethal' is now widely preferred. The latter term acknowledges that these instruments can be lethal (to suspects and bystanders) in cases of misuse or malfunction, or where a victim's underlying health condition makes them more vulnerable to a weapon's effect. See: United Nations, *Resource Book on the Use of Force and Firearms in Law Enforcement*, New York: United Nations Office on Drugs and Crime and Office of the United Nations High Commissioner for Human Rights, 2017: 66 (note 145).

125. Seumas Miller, *Shooting to Kill: The Ethics of Police and Military Use of Lethal Force*, New York: Oxford University Press, 2016: 139.

126. See: M. R. McGuire, 'The Laughing Policebot: Automation and the End of Policing', *Policing & Society*, 31 (1) (2021): 20–36, at 27.

127. Maria Valdovinos, James Specht and Jennifer Zeunik, *Law Enforcement & Unmanned Aircraft Systems (UAS): Guidelines to Enhance Community Trust*, Washington, DC: Office of Community Oriented Policing Services, US Department of Justice, 2016: 2.

128. Gloria Gaggioli, 'Remoteness and Human Rights Law', in *Research Handbook on Remote Warfare*, ed. Jens David Ohlin, Cheltenham: Edward Elgar, 2017: 133–85, at 134.

129. See: Noel Sharkey, 'Are we prepared for more killer police robots?', *The Guardian*, 12 July 2016, <https://www.theguardian.com/commentisfree/2016/jul/12/killer-police-robots-legal-consequences-dallas>.

130. United Nations, *Resource Book on the Use of Force and Firearms in Law Enforcement*, New York: United Nations Office on Drugs and Crime and Office of the United Nations High Commissioner for Human Rights, 2017: 15.

131. United Nations, 'Basic Principles on the Use of Force and Firearms by Law Enforcement Officials', Adopted by the Eighth United Nations Congress on the Prevention of Crime and the Treatment of Offenders, Havana, Cuba, 27 August to 7 September 1990. *Office of the High Commissioner for Human Rights.* <https://www.ohchr.org/en/professionalinterest/pages/useofforceandfirearms.aspx>: Principle 2 (emphasis added).

132. Christof Heyns, 'Report of the Special Rapporteur on Extrajudicial, Summary or Arbitrary Executions' (A/HRC/17/28), 23 May 2011. New York: Human Rights Council, United Nations General Assembly, 2011: para. 104.

133. Kyle Stelmack, 'Weaponized Police Drones and Their Effect on Police Use of Force', *Pittsburg Journal of Technology Law & Policy*, 15 (2) (2015): 276–92, at 286.

134. See: United Nations, *Resource Book on the Use of Force and Firearms in Law Enforcement*, New York: United Nations Office on Drugs and Crime and Office of the United Nations High Commissioner for Human Rights, 2017: 65–66.

135. Kyle Stelmack, 'Weaponized Police Drones and Their Effect on Police Use of Force', *Pittsburg Journal of Technology Law & Policy*, 15 (2) (2015): 276–92, at 286.

136. Jay Stanley, 'Five reasons armed domestic drones are a terrible idea', *American Civil Liberties Union*, 27 August 2015, <https://www.aclu.org/blog/privacy-technology/surveillance-technologies/five-reasons-armed-domestic-drones-are-terrible>.

137. See: Eric Brumfield, 'Armed Drones for Law Enforcement: Why It Might Be Time to Re-Examine the Current Use of Force Standard', *McGeorge Law Review*, 46 (3) (2014): 543–72; Kyle Stelmack, 'Weaponized Police Drones and Their Effect on Police Use of Force', *Pittsburg Journal of Technology Law & Policy*, 15 (2) (2015): 276–92; Amanda A. Porter, 'Law Enforcement's Use of Weaponized Drones: Today and Tomorrow', *Saint Louis University Law Journal*, 61 (2) (2017): 351–70.

138. *Graham* v. *Connor* et al., 490 U.S. 386, 388 (1989).

139. Ibid. 388 (emphasis added).

140. Ibid. 388.

141. See: Eric Brumfield, 'Armed Drones for Law Enforcement: Why It Might Be Time to Re-Examine the Current Use of Force Standard', *McGeorge Law Review*, 46 (3) (2014): 543–72, at 565–6.

142. Amanda A. Porter, 'Law Enforcement's Use of Weaponized Drones: Today and Tomorrow', *Saint Louis University Law Journal*, 61 (2) (2017): 351–70, at 370 (emphasis added).

143. See: United Nations, *Resource Book on the Use of Force and Firearms in Law Enforcement*, New York: United Nations Office on Drugs and Crime

and Office of the United Nations High Commissioner for Human Rights, 2017: 70.

144. In a suicide bomber or 'active shooter' scenario, when an identified suspect poses an immediate threat to life and there are no other means available to neutralise the threat, a police officer may follow a 'shoot-to-kill' order: Stuart Casey-Maslen, 'Pandora's Box? Drone Strikes under *Jus ad Bellum, Jus in Bello*, and International Human Rights Law', *International Review of the Red Cross*, 94 (886) (2012): 597–625, at 618. In 2005 the former Commissioner of London's Metropolitan Police, John Stevens, told journalists the 'terrible truth' that the only way to stop a suicide bomber was to 'destroy his brain instantly, utterly': BBC, 'Debate rages over "shoot-to-kill"', *BBC News*, 24 July 2005, <http://news.bbc.co.uk/1/hi/uk/4711769.stm>.

145. Kyle Stelmack, 'Weaponized Police Drones and Their Effect on Police Use of Force', *Pittsburg Journal of Technology Law & Policy*, 15 (2) (2015): 276–92, at 280.

146. Maina Kiai and Christof Heyns, 'Joint Report of the Special Rapporteur on the Rights to Freedom of Peaceful Assembly and of Association and the Special Rapporteur on Extrajudicial, Summary or Arbitrary Executions on the Proper Management of Assemblies' (A/HRC/31/66), 4 February 2016. New York: Human Rights Council, United Nations General Assembly, 2016: para. 53.

147. Ibid. para. 56.

148. United Nations. *United Nations Human Rights Guidance on Less-Lethal Weapons in Law Enforcement*, New York and Geneva: Office of the High Commissioner for Human Rights, United Nations, 2020: 15.

149. See: United Nations, *Resource Book on the Use of Force and Firearms in Law Enforcement*, New York: United Nations Office on Drugs and Crime and Office of the United Nations High Commissioner for Human Rights, 2017: 88; United Nations. *United Nations Human Rights Guidance on Less-Lethal Weapons in Law Enforcement*, New York and Geneva: Office of the High Commissioner for Human Rights, United Nations, 2020: 24.

Chapter 4

THE PROBLEM OF 'GREY' DRONE VIOLENCE

In the discussion thus far, the use of armed drones has been assessed on the assumption that warfare and violent law enforcement are alternative concepts of state violence, and that these are the only such concepts capable of attracting moral justification. It might sometimes be the case, however, that drone violence is conceptualised as 'grey' violence. That is, a drone-using state might be tempted to blur or transcend existing paradigms of justifiable violence when it is not clearly 'at war' but wishes to avoid the strict morality of law enforcement. To explore such a scenario from an ethical perspective, this chapter focuses on circumstances in which a foreign government's armed drones are a constant presence overhead.[1]

On 20 January 2021, the day of Joe Biden's inauguration as president of the United States, the incoming national security adviser issued an order for tighter controls on counterterrorism operations outside war zones (away from where there are US troops present). Under the Trump administration, military commanders and the CIA had reportedly been allowed to decide for themselves when to conduct drone strikes against suspected terrorists. Henceforth, by contrast, permission for such attacks needed first to be obtained from the White House, pending an internal review of policy and procedures.[2] These largely secret 'rules' on US drones strikes, originally formulated during Barack Obama's presidency, formed part of an ongoing attempt by the US government to control and legitimise a largely unprecedented form of extraterritorial state violence.

In continuing the covert use of armed drones outside war zones, successive US administrations have apparently been unwilling or unable to assign this activity to either of the two existing paradigms for legitimately using force – war and law enforcement – wherein there is a ready supply of internationally agreed rules. Rather, the US government has seemed content to convey the idea that some of its drone violence is essentially neither warfare nor policing and thus beyond the ordinary sanction of humanitarian and human rights law. However, the vagueness of this conceptualisation – the contrived 'greyness' of such violence – has generated a concern about state impunity: that injustices caused by drone-based campaigns against suspected terrorists might escape notice and remedy. Amnesty International has argued, for example, that US policy and practice sets 'a dangerous precedent' for other drone-using states to 'avoid responsibility' for potentially unlawful killings.[3]

For drone strikes occurring outside areas of armed conflict to be properly judged and governed, an important first step is to arrive at a plausible conceptualisation of such violence. Accordingly, this chapter sets out to assess the nature and morality of US drone campaigns along America's 'terror frontier', which include the recent experience of CIA operations in the Federally Administered Tribal Areas (FATA) of north-western Pakistan. Here, for many years, drone violence was directed against a series of suspected terrorists identified according to behavioural signatures deemed to indicate threats to US security. Although CIA 'signature strikes' in FATA appeared to have ceased at the time of writing, this form of violence remains worthy of consideration because of its potential to recur, not least because the number of states using armed drones has lately been increasing.[4]

Several authors have already sought to engage with the moral problem of 'grey' drone violence by offering conceptualisations beyond 'war' or 'law enforcement'. One suggestion has been to conceptualise some drone strikes as a form of *vim* ('force short of war') and to govern such force according to a *jus ad vim* framework adapted from Just War theory.[5] Another approach has been to condemn US drone strikes outside war zones, in a way that combines conceptualisation with adverse judgement. According to some authors taking this approach, who emphasise the harmful effects of drone use upon innocents in the vicinity of strikes, this is essentially terroristic violence.[6] And other authors, focusing on US foreign policy and behaviour in the world, have argued that drone violence against suspected terrorists is imperialistic in nature.[7]

All three conceptualisations are assessed in later sections, but *vim*, terrorism and imperialism are ultimately rejected here as unhelpful or inaccurate. Instead, this chapter proposes a conceptual reorientation, introducing the idea that the US use of armed drones in non-war circumstances (for example, in FATA) is 'quasi-imperialistic' violence. In essence, drone violence of this kind is wielded in the pursuit only of thin domination, and without taking responsibility for the welfare of the dominated, and as such it functions merely as an instrument for policing emergent terrorist risks. Even so, and because of these features, quasi-imperialistic drone violence is open to condemnation as a violation of the human right to life.

THE 'GREYING' OF DRONE VIOLENCE

When the US government uses armed drones in places where there are conflicts going on (Afghanistan, Iraq, Libya and Syria), these aircraft are among numerous tools used together in a wider military effort. Drone-launched missile strikes are often used to provide close air support in defence of friendly troops who are in contact with or otherwise threatened by enemy troops. Here, the conceptualising of drone violence is generally not a problem. It is the violence of war, and war is generally understood to be one of two established paradigms for legitimate state violence. The other paradigm is law enforcement. Armed drones could one day be used for a domestic policing purpose (although no police department anywhere appears yet to have done so), or they could be used to punish criminal wrongdoing. For each of these paradigms, a set of principles and laws is available to be applied in determining whether an instance of state violence is just or unjust. There is human rights law which mainly applies in peacetime (for example, to criminal justice matters) and severely restricts killing, and there is humanitarian law which applies in wartime and is more permissive.

Sometimes, however, armed drones are used in non-war circumstances and without obviously serving a policing or punitive purpose. Here, on the one hand, a concern arises that drone violence appears to lack any potential for legitimacy and thus amounts to impermissible homicide in violation of the right to life. On the other hand, as the US government has claimed, it raises the possibility that such violence can be legitimate despite being neither war nor law enforcement. To assess these rival propositions, this chapter focuses on the maintaining of drone programmes that involve the conduct of signature strikes in a foreign territory. Also known as 'terrorist attack disruption strikes',[8] these are a 'grey' form of drone violence in the sense of being uncategorised or conceptually uncertain.

US signature strikes, unlike 'personality strikes' against named individuals (as discussed in Chapter 3), are conducted and justified based on pattern-of-life analysis of information about people and places collected from various sources. This analysis is undertaken to spot patterns that match one or more signature activities deemed to be indicative of a terrorist threat. Examples of suspicious activities, gleaned from public statements by US government officials, include 'planning attacks', 'transporting weapons', 'handling explosives', and 'consorting with known militants'.[9] The information used to identify these and other signatures reportedly includes metadata from computers and mobile phones, aerial surveillance footage, and voice patterns of callers which can be compared to thousands of other stored voice samples linked to suspected terrorists.[10] Under the Obama administration, as a guide for the conduct of signature strikes, the US government developed not a simple list of names but rather a 'disposition matrix'; a 'single, continually evolving database in which biographies, locations, known associates and affiliated organizations are all catalogued'.[11]

The US government has reportedly conducted signature strikes in at least three territories where it is neither party to an armed conflict nor enforcing the local criminal law: in Yemen, Somalia and, most of all, in Pakistan's north-western FATA region (which shares a highly porous border with Afghanistan). In these places, the sustaining of drone violence against a series of suspected terrorists has been intended to achieve a continuously disruptive effect. The apparent rationale is that, by forcing members of 'terrorist groups' inside targeted territories to spend time and resources on trying to avoid detection and stay alive, they have less of an opportunity to recruit, train, organise and execute attacks against US interests.[12]

Even if signature strikes are thus effective in suppressing perceived threats to the United States, part of the moral difficulty associated with drone violence of this kind is that innocents sometimes end up being harmed as well. In mid-2016 the Director of National Intelligence reported that, during the previous seven years, the US government had conducted 473 counterterrorism strikes outside areas of active hostilities. These had resulted in an estimated total of between 2372 and 2581 'combatant deaths' and between 64 and 116 'non-combatant deaths'.[13] There are uncertainties about the accuracy of these numbers and about who the US government counts as 'combatants' and 'non-combatants' in the first place. However, for present purposes the most interesting feature of this report (and related official pronouncements) is that these categories of victim are used at all. The idea of being either a 'combatant' or a 'non-combatant' arises only in war circumstances, but on its own account the US government has sometimes used armed drones 'outside areas of active hostilities'.[14]

Military ethics and humanitarian law traditionally permit the unintentional and proportional killing of non-combatants when enemy combatants are being targeted, so the US government is possibly making a claim on such permission when it employs *some* of the language of war in this way. The alternative to be avoided, presumably, is a default to the ethics applicable in the only other established paradigm of legitimate state violence – the peacetime business of law enforcement – where there are no 'combatants' (only people) and there is a stronger presumption against killing. Accordingly, because the US government is unable plausibly to claim it is at war but is unwilling to have its signature strikes judged according to the ethical expectations that obtain in peacetime, it has instead engaged in an expedient 'greying' of this form of drone violence. This has been done in a geographical sense and through legal innovation: by blurring the distinction between zones of war and zones of peace, and by asserting the existence of a category of legitimate state violence ('self-defence targeting') beyond the established categories of war and peacetime law enforcement.

The claimed legitimacy of wielding drone violence neither in war nor for a law enforcement purpose rests in part upon an argument that conditions in certain parts of the world are 'in between' the conditions of war and peace. In such territories, the argument goes, the law enforcement paradigm (and its associated framework of criminal justice ethics) does not apply *in principle* because law enforcement cannot *in practice* be conducted there. That is, some places where armed conflict is not occurring are nevertheless not to be regarded as zones of peace because, against the threat of terrorism, 'law enforcement mechanisms . . . are not a viable option'.[15] The perceived problem, in what Seumas Miller has labelled 'disorderly jurisdictions', is that 'there is no *effective* law enforcement in relation to terrorists conducting attacks on liberal democratic states'.[16] The discourse accompanying this argument is one of dangerous 'ungoverned spaces', from which terrorist threats to the United States emanate.[17] These places, as Majed Akhter has observed, are the 'global periphery' towards which armed drones proliferate 'despite the absence of a declared battlefield'.[18] Indeed, most CIA drone strikes have occurred in Pakistan's FATA, a frontier region historically scripted as 'ungoverned'.[19]

Another way in which the US government has sought to create normative space for its non-war drone violence has been to engage in legal innovation. In response to accusations that it was illegally using force in Pakistan, Somalia and Yemen, the Obama administration moved to reframe humanitarian and human rights law obligations to expand the legal scope for violent action.[20] Ordinarily, from a legal perspective, 'armed conflict' is limited to situations of intense and organised fighting, and only in such situations is humanitarian law (which is more permissive of killing than is human rights law) applicable. Where there is greater doubt about whether a specific operation counts as armed conflict, the more difficult it is to claim that killing individual terrorist suspects in this context is lawful.[21] So, to get around this difficulty while targeting suspected terrorists in signature strikes 'outside areas of active hostilities',[22] the US government has asserted that killings do not need to be justified under human rights law as long as they represent legitimate acts of national self-defence. On this basis, drone violence has been presented not as falling into a legal vacuum between the war and law enforcement paradigms (where no moral and legal basis for killing is available), but rather as an example of a third kind of legitimate state violence: 'self-defence targeting'.

In 2010 US State Department legal adviser Harold Koh argued publicly that '[n]ot every resort to force in self-defense by a state is necessarily undertaken through the conduct of armed conflict', and that 'a state that is engaged in an armed conflict *or* in legitimate self-defense is not required to provide targets with legal process before the state may use lethal force'.[23] This was an assertion that states can legitimately engage in extraterritorial violence and yet *not* be engaged in an armed conflict (at least in the legal sense of that term). Six years later, this legal innovation appeared also in an executive order issued by President Obama which stated: 'Civilian casualties are a tragic and at times unavoidable consequence of the use of force in situations of armed conflict *or* in the exercise of a state's inherent right of self-defense.'[24] Here, official US reasoning extended to implying that non-combatants ('civilians') can be considered to exist (as a category) even in non-war circumstances (where US troops are not involved in combat).

This attempt at legally inventing a 'grey' version of drone violence (between the black and white bodies of law on war and law enforcement) attracted widespread criticism for its potential to weaken humanitarian and rights-based protections for individuals in international law.[25] Two months after Koh's speech, Philip Alston (then the UN Special Rapporteur on Extrajudicial, Summary or Arbitrary Executions) warned, in reference to armed drones, of 'a highly problematic blurring and expansion of the boundaries of the applicable legal frameworks – human rights law, the laws of war, and the law applicable to the use of inter-state force'.[26] The principal concern here, which still endures, is that emphasising self-defence to justify violence at the interstate level might enable a bypassing of established legal standards governing violence against individual persons. If this were to happen, the issue of the permissibility of violating a targeted individual's right to life (as a matter of *conducting* violence) would collapse, leaving only the issue of whether *resorting* to force in world affairs is permissible.

While ever the US idea of 'self-defence targeting' is unaccepted as an additional category of legitimate state violence, the conduct of non-war drone strikes against suspected terrorists in 'ungoverned' territories is conceptually unsatisfactory. And the related problem of suspected injustice which remains is that unlawful killings might be occurring with impunity. In response to concerns that a drone-using state cannot be held accountable for the consequences of its 'grey' violence,[27] a promising approach is to give another name to drone violence outside war zones in order to gain some moral and governance traction upon it. Alternatives include conceptualising signature strikes as *vim* ('force short of war') or terroristic violence, or as imperialistic or quasi-imperialistic violence.

DRONE VIOLENCE AS *VIM*

In response to the US resorting to 'legal ambiguity' to justify some drone violence, one suggestion is to accommodate this by introducing a 'hybrid moral framework'.[28] This is needed, it is argued, to cover 'limited force that lies somewhere between law enforcement and just war, and combines elements of both'.[29] If counterterrorist drone strikes were conceptualised as a third category of legitimate state violence – as *vim* ('force short of war') – they could then be either defended as just *vim* or condemned as unjust *vim*. In other words, 'outside the "hot" battlefield',[30] drone violence could be judged according to a framework of *jus ad vim* (the justice of resorting to 'force short of war'). Advocates of such a framework are motivated by a concern to see that state violence, which putatively emerges in 'a gray area between law enforcement and war',[31] does not escape subjection to ethical judgement and principled regulation. Assuming that this greyness is real (rather than merely a government's self-interested assertion), the purported advantage of conceptualising 'grey' drone violence as *vim* is to gain more moral leverage and bring about greater restraint of it than has thus far been achieved.

For example, the labelling of some kinds of drone strikes as *vim* (non-war) rather than *bellum* (war) would bring into play a more restrictive ethics – *jus in vi* (the justice of conducting 'force short of war') – which is more protective of civilians than is *jus in bello* (incorporating the military ethics principles of necessity, discrimination and proportionality). Accordingly, even the unintended killing of civilians could be entirely proscribed by a *jus in vi* requirement of 'zero incidental civilian harm'.[32] Or, as Shannon Ford has suggested, 'foreseeable collateral [civilian] deaths' could be 'either not permissible or equivalent to what we would be willing to accept in a standard [domestic] policing operation'.[33] Nevertheless, according to its critics, the idea of a *jus ad vim* framework might yet be undesirable or unnecessary. One policy argument against introducing a third (hybrid) paradigm of legitimate state violence is that this would weaken the theoretical protections enjoyed by civilians and criminal suspects 'in areas that, under the current dichotomous framework [war or law enforcement], generally are characterised as non-conflict zones'.[34] Or, according to some moral theorists, *jus ad vim* might simply be redundant because Just War theory can already deal adequately with different magnitudes of force.[35] If so, it would make no analytical difference if a *jus ad vim* morality were introduced for evaluating drone violence.

In any event, the more important issue for present purposes is the strength of the *vim* concept itself as a basis for making moral judgements about political violence. The concept rests critically upon the notion that, when it comes to categorising force, size (and size alone) matters. *Vim* is force 'short of' war; it differs from war because it involves a lesser quantum of violence. Thus, the difference appears only to be one of degree rather than kind. Although *jus ad vim* advocates are admirably keen to plug what they see as a gap in the principled governance of violence in the world, they have arguably not completed the conceptual groundwork that is necessary to open up space for normative analysis. Despite their insistence that *vim* is not war (because a *jus ad vim* framework makes no sense otherwise), those advocates have not addressed adequately the challenge of determining whether a given instance of state violence counts as *vim* or war. As yet, there is no underlying 'falling short' (of war) theory addressing, for example, what the *essential* difference is between, on the one hand, war on a small scale or of short duration and, on the other hand, force 'short of' war. So, while ever the concept of *vim* remains vague in general, it is difficult to proceed confidently towards moral judgement on the basis that drone violence in particular is *vim*.

Promoters of a *jus ad vim* framework have had much to say about what *vim*'s characteristics are from time to time – how much violence is involved, where it occurs, who resorts to it, and why – but they have not offered a compelling definition of its *nature*. Rather, *vim* has tended only to be (under-)described in negative and relative terms. As non-war violence it tends, moreover, to be compared only to 'full-scale', 'widespread' and 'large-scale' war.[36] And so, when *vim* is discussed in this way, a distinction ends up being drawn not between 'war' and 'force short of war' but rather between 'large-scale war' and 'force short of large-scale war'. The trouble, then, with trying to equate the *amount* of violence with its *essence* is that *vim* becomes radically susceptible to conceptual contestation, and the original problem returns: determining which (if any) moral framework is applicable to 'grey' violence. For example, violence that seemed small-scale to the stronger side in a political confrontation (the self-styled deliverer of *vim*) could plausibly seem large scale to the weaker side (the self-styled recipient of *bellum*).

If the *vim* concept is thus too weak a foundation upon which to base moral judgements about drone strikes, only war and law enforcement remain as concepts of legitimate state violence. In which case, outside of war, any lethal violence not wielded for a law enforcement purpose could reasonably be presumed by default to be unjustly homicidal. After all, when thinking morally about violence, the human right to life is the starting point and it can sometimes be the endpoint too (in the sense that the permissibility or excusability of killing is never established). As Michael Walzer has put it, the problem in moral theory 'is not to describe how immunity is gained, but how it is lost. We are all immune to start with; our right not to be attacked is a feature of normal human relationships.'.[37] Accordingly, without a law enforcement or *vim* concept available to support it, non-war drone violence (signature strikes against suspected terrorists outside conflict zones) could be condemned for involving attacks against persons whose immunity to attack remains in place. One possible explanation that then arises is that drone violence of this kind is essentially terroristic.

DRONE STRIKES AS TERRORISTIC VIOLENCE

Most drone strikes conducted by the CIA, a civilian agency of the US government, have taken place in Pakistan's FATA region.[38] Here, according to numerous reports, the population at large was collectively terrified during periods (occurring between 2004 and 2017) when armed drones were a constant overhead presence.[39] The maintaining of the threat of aerial violence was intended to have a continuously suppressing effect on the activities of 'militants' in that part of the world, but this effect was inevitably also oppressive of everyone else who was made to experience mortal fear from one day to the next. Ordinary people were caused to think that they could suddenly become a victim – seemingly anywhere and at any time – and sometimes the fear of this eventuality was so great as to cause psychological harm.[40]

The fact of a widespread feeling of terror in FATA has occasioned several authors to conceptualise US drone use there as an example of terroristic violence. In contrast to war, law enforcement and *vim*, the 'terrorism' concept traditionally comes with its own built-in judgement framework. To describe violence in this way is also to condemn it as being necessarily unjust. So, when confronted with the moral problem of 'grey' drone violence apparently going on in the world unchecked, a frequent response among some scholars has been to frame this phenomenon as 'terrorism'. A 2018 issue of *Critical Studies on Terrorism* carried a collection of papers which all 'situate drone-inflicted violence within the wider context of state terrorism'.[41] According to Afxentis Afxentiou, 'drone warfare should be investigated as a form of terrorist violence',[42] and for Laurie Calhoun it is a 'fact' that 'drone campaigns terrorise entire communities of people, just as did the plane attacks of 11 September 2001'.[43] Along similar lines, arguments have been advanced that the use of armed drones follows a 'logic of terrorizing a population',[44] that drones 'may be considered a form of terrorism' to the extent that they 'produce terror in civilian populations',[45] that drones 'inflict mass terror upon entire populations',[46] and that the US drone programme is 'a contemporary manifestation' of 'imperial state terrorism'.[47]

Arguably, there is a problem with claims of this kind. Although drone violence can indeed have a generally terrifying effect where it occurs, it cannot properly be condemned as terroristic violence without evidence of deliberate targeting of civilians. In other words, for analytical purposes a distinction should be drawn: the fact of civilians *feeling* threatened by violence does not equate to the moral wrong of deliberately *threatening* with violence people who are understood to be civilians. As the latter is not the only possible cause of the former, the terrifying use of drones is potentially not an essentially terroristic act. Here it must be acknowledged that the meaning of 'terrorism' remains highly contested and, perhaps, has in some instances become 'too ideologically freighted to have any analytic value'.[48] Even so, in the careful assessment of a drone-using state's violence, it seems reasonable to proceed as non-ideologically as possible by using an object-focused definition of terrorism. Such a definition, unlike an agent-focused definition,[49] can encompass non-state *and* state agents of violence. And it has the advantage also of emphasising that feature which is morally most distinctive about terrorism: the employing of violence, for a political purpose, against civilian (or non-combatant) targets.[50]

In the case of US drone violence that has occurred extraterritorially, outside war zones, and without a law enforcement purpose, conceptualising and judging it as terroristic is made difficult by the sparseness of the empirical record. Little, if any, evidence of deliberate targeting of civilians has come to light, if indeed it has been going on at all. There have been some reports of so-called 'double-tap' (or 'second strike') drone attacks occurring, which appear to involve the killing of people who are seen coming to the rescue of victims of the first strike.[51] If true, this killing has probably been done on the assumption that the rescuers too are members of the same group being targeted by the US government. But it seems implausible to frame these secondary targets as dangerous (non-innocent) allies of the individuals who were struck first, especially in the moment when a drone's mounted camera shows them providing medical assistance rather than busily posing a threat to the United States. At least in theory, then, 'double-tap' drone strikes in non-war contexts are open to be condemned as instances of terroristic violence.

In the absence of a wrongful intention, violence might still be properly described as terroristic if innocents are harmed by a violent actor's recklessness. David Rodin has characterised the latter as 'the culpable bringing about of unintentional evil consequences (or the risk thereof) that are in fact unreasonable and unjustified in the circumstances'.[52] And, with regard to war contexts, he has argued that this issue arises particularly in the case of 'aerial bombardment against targets within or adjacent to civilian populations which is almost certain to generate noncombatant casualties'.[53] On one occasion, in early 2010, a US drone was reportedly used to kill an al-Qaeda commander in Miram Shah, a small town in FATA's North Waziristan district,[54] and this could reasonably be described as a 'recklessly terroristic' drone strike in the sense that it almost certainly endangered many other people in the town. However, as with allegedly intentional 'double-tap' drone strikes, there is a paucity of evidence that the US government has been *generally* reckless by routinely conducting drone strikes in heavily populated urban areas. In any event, the notion of 'reckless' terrorism is not as well established in moral theory as is the straightforwardly intentional kind. The latter, arguably, is of greater moral significance (and perhaps it is the *only* proper notion of terrorism) because it involves bringing a 'guilty mind' to bear upon one's violence.

On the whole, then, it is difficult to conceptualise and condemn the US government's wider counterterrorist drone programme as terroristic in nature. In contrast to the view of some early theorists of airpower who claimed that this *should* be directed against an enemy state's civilian population (to terrorise them into submission),[55] the US government's drone violence in FATA and elsewhere has proceeded according to a stated determination to *avoid* targeting innocents.[56] Although this alone does not prove the absence of any terroristic intent, it is nevertheless worth noting that scholarly denunciations of US drone violence as 'terrorism' have thus far not been founded on evidence of intentional targeting of civilians. Some scholars have instead argued that, because the effects (on civilians) of drone strikes *resemble* the effects of terroristic applications of airpower that undoubtedly occurred in the past, contemporary drone violence amounts to terrorism too. Yet, even if it is a historical 'fact' that 'organised terror has always been a component of regimes of aerial control',[57] it does not follow that terrorism must be the essence of any or all drone violence today. Unless or until evidence of intentional wrongdoing emerges, it is fairer to presume that the US government has not in fact wilfully engaged in a sustained enterprise – extending from one drone strike to the next – of wielding terroristic violence.

DRONE STRIKES AS IMPERIALISTIC VIOLENCE

If there are insufficient grounds to conceptualise drone violence outside war zones as terrorism, another concept worth considering as a basis for condemnation is imperialism. In much of the academic literature on armed drones, it has often been implied that contemporary US drone violence is wrong in the same way that 'air policing' in colonial history was wrong. Here, the 'newness' (and potential legitimacy) of drone violence tends to be disputed by claims about historical continuity and, for a number of authors, historicising such violence is a way of criticising it. This can be a quite persuasive approach given that so many violent acts from the past were either wrong at the time or would not be morally acceptable today. It is an approach mostly encountered in postcolonial and critical geography literature that situates the use of armed drones 'in a lineage of colonial technologies of pacification'.[58] And this situating usually involves the drawing of 'parallels' between the rationales and technologies underpinning drone strikes and those underpinning the use of airpower by European imperial powers in the early twentieth century.[59]

According to Priya Satia, the use of armed drones exhibits 'critical continuities with earlier [colonial] uses of air power',[60] and Campbell Munro has argued that drones 'undoubtedly mark a further evolution in imperial air policing' by functioning as 'a means to exercise asymmetric imperial violence'.[61] Similarly, others authors have claimed that the deployment of armed drones 'resembles' colonial war,[62] that the drone 'reactivates a colonial form of power',[63] and that the US drone programme for the targeted killing of terror suspects 'builds directly on the British experience of imperial policing through air power'.[64] Such arguments find circumstantial support in the fact that almost all drone violence to date has occurred in many of the same places which were previously the scene of imperial European air policing. Derek Gregory has noted, for example, 'numerous dispiriting parallels' between contemporary US drone campaigns and British aerial counterinsurgency efforts in the 1920s along the North-West Frontier (later part of Pakistan) and in Mesopotamia (later Iraq).[65] Other 'wild spaces of the imperial periphery' once subjected to 'imperial control from above',[66] where armed drones have also since appeared, include Afghanistan, Libya, Palestine (now part of Israel), Somaliland (now part of Somalia), Syria and Yemen.

After the end of the First World War, the victorious European powers found that their imperial governance responsibilities had increased, but the material means of sustaining all of them had declined. Pre-war imperial garrisons around the world needed to be maintained, but the 1919 Treaty of Versailles required Britain and France to govern also their post-Ottoman 'mandate' territories in the Middle East. It was Britain's Royal Air Force (RAF) which introduced to the world the practice of using airpower to maintain civil order. This was done mainly because it seemed to be a cheaper means of maintaining the 'imperial peace' than the older, army-based method of sending punitive expeditions to quell local unrest.[67]

It is less certain, however, that the US government too has lately been using airpower for an imperial purpose in the sense that this has been part of a 'process of establishing and maintaining an empire'.[68] There is perhaps a broader debate to be had about whether the United States is an empire,[69] but the narrower issue in this chapter is whether US drone violence outside war zones is imperialistic. Arguably, this kind of non-war violence, unlike colonial air policing of old, cannot be conceptualised (and thereby condemned) as imperialistic. Although the 'empire' concept, like 'terrorism', remains a subject of definitional debate,[70] one of the most frequently cited formulations is Michael Doyle's: that empire is 'a relationship . . . in which one state controls the effective political sovereignty of another political society'.[71] Historically, such control is what critically enables imperial acquisition (of territory or other resources) and it manifests in 'civilizatory' rule by the imperial power. For present purposes, then, a fair theoretical assumption is that imperialistic violence is essentially an instrument of exploitative acquisition and transformative administration.

In the 1920s, for example, British imperial control of Mesopotamia was both acquisitive and administrative in nature. The colonial administration, led by the RAF and reliant upon airpower, was geared towards the extraction of local oil wealth.[72] And, according to Peter Lieb, Britain's aerial operations there were influenced by a view of Arabs and Kurds as 'semi-civilized' peoples who had remained 'savages' while under Ottoman imperial, but who could yet be civilised by superior colonial rulers.[73] Satia has described aerial 'bombardment' in British-ruled Iraq as 'a permanent method of colonial administration'.[74] Thomas Hippler has observed that RAF airpower there had 'established a genuine government from the sky'.[75] And meanwhile, in British-ruled Sudan, Governor-General Sir John Maffey had reportedly described British airstrikes as a 'swift agent of government'.[76]

By contrast, US drone violence against suspected terrorists in Pakistan, Somalia and Yemen has been instrumental neither for resource acquisition nor local administration. The use of armed drones in these places has undoubtedly had a fearsome and coercive effect, but it has not risen to the level of 'control' (over 'another political society')[77] such as would warrant conceptualising such violence as imperialistic.[78] US drone violence evidences little by way of an imperial impulse to conquer, occupy, colonise and plunder these territories over which drones fly, and it does not support any broader US attempt at on-the-ground rule there.[79] On the contrary, armed drones seem perfectly suited to avoiding those things while the US government instead restricts itself to the mere management of terrorism risks emerging along its 'terror frontier'.

The taking of the latter approach also suggests strongly that the US government's drone violence is not instrumental in an imperial *mission civilisatrice*. Although the United States might well see itself as 'a premier guardian of civilisation', perceiving terrorists as 'threats to a civilized way of life',[80] US drones do not practically support any effort to 'civilise' the Pakistani, Somali or Yemeni 'wildernesses' from which those threats supposedly emanate. The drones are not, in other words, instruments to force 'progress' in those places towards a 'superior' condition of being. Rather, US drone violence does not aim for the eventual improvement of local life but only for the constant containment of individualised dangerousness and the suppression of security risks to a manageable level. Whereas once the American idea of a frontier imagined 'a spatially expansive progression of [European] civilization into the wilderness of the American continent',[81] the 'terror frontier' territories where US drones fly today do not seem destined to be brought into the fold of 'civilisation'. Instead, there appears to be an acceptance by the US government that these are places to be merely policed – remotely, violently and perhaps in perpetuity.

QUASI-IMPERIALISM AND US DRONE VIOLENCE

If drone violence of the kind described above is not genuinely imperialistic, it may yet be conceptualised and criticised for being almost (quasi) imperialistic. Some authors have hinted at this, offering suggestions (laced with paradox) that the constant overhead presence of armed drones amounts to 'aerial occupation',[82] or 'nonterritorial occupation',[83] or even a 'distinctly ambiguous' form of occupation.[84] A more straightforward approach, however, is to acknowledge that the exclusive use of armed drones by a foreign power really involves *non*-occupation. This reality can then be addressed as a defining characteristic of quasi-imperialistic violence as well as a source of its moral problems.

In the study of international relations, the term 'quasi-imperial' has previously been applied by Martin Shaw. Writing in 2002, he used it while trying to employ the 'empire' concept in an analytical (value-neutral) way and to encourage scholars to be 'sharper about what is really imperial and what is not'.[85] Shaw described some larger, non-Western states in the modern, postcolonial world as 'reconstitutions of historic pre-European or European empires'.[86] In places like China, India, Indonesia, Russia and Turkey, he observed national politics dominated by 'quasi-imperial relations of rule' involving 'internal colonialism' and the violent domination of one nation by another *within* state borders.[87] Pakistan too could thus be described as exercising quasi-imperial rule over its FATA region, where formerly the ruling was done imperially. As was the case during the time of British colonial rule, when the 1901 Frontier Crimes Regulation (FCR) was introduced, the FATA remains to this day an exceptional legal space where (as a legacy of the FCR) human rights are not nearly as protected as they are in the rest of Pakistan.[88] Inside what Madiha Tahir has called the FATA 'containment zone',[89] any violence enacted by the *Pakistani* military is, on Shaw's definition, quasi-imperialistic. However, US (drone) violence there is not, because the power dynamic this introduces is international rather than internal in character.

Or, *pace* Shaw, political violence could instead be conceptualised as quasi-imperialistic in an alternative sense: when it is wielded in furtherance of a 'temporary' episode of liberal imperialism. The latter is the kind of quasi-imperialism implied by Michael Ignatieff's idea of 'empire lite'. Here, US rule of foreign territories is understood to be less than genuinely imperial because it is not intended to be permanent. Rather, its purported aim is to foster democratic nation-building in other countries. In his 2003 book *Empire Lite*, Ignatieff observed of the 'Afghans', for example, that 'their best hope for freedom lies in a temporary experience of [US] imperial rule'.[90] Through US-sponsored nation-building, that is, his idea was that the state of Afghanistan would soon become 'strong enough to keep al-Qaeda from returning'.[91] At the time, the US government was heavily engaged in a ground-based counterinsurgency effort in Afghanistan, with some air support provided by armed drones. By contrast, in Pakistan, Somalia and Yemen, where drone violence (often used exclusively) has ostensibly served only a counterterrorism purpose, the US government has not pursued the 'empire lite' (nation-building) version of quasi-imperialism either.

For present purposes, then, the term 'quasi-imperialism' needs to be understood differently: as a transnational political exercise in thin domination motivated by an open-ended commitment to anti-responsibility. In comparison to the use of piloted aircraft making short sorties, the long-endurance capacity of armed drones is much more conducive to achieving a continuous disruption of emerging and perceived threats.

Drone violence that is quasi-imperialistic in this sense is the violence of risk-management rather than rule, and it essentially avoids the responsibility (for the welfare of the dominated) that is required (morally and legally) to be assumed by an occupying power.

In the broader context of counterterrorism, some authors have already identified a US preference for aiming only to managing risks rather than to solve problems.[92] And the armed drone in particular, as an instrument for killing suspected terrorists, has appeared to be well-suited to the inherently indefinite task of terrorism 'management'.[93] For other authors, drone violence of this kind is best captured by the notion of 'policing'. Here, though, that notion tends to be employed not in the narrow (liberal) sense of fighting crime but instead to describe a process of ordering.[94] On this understanding, the use of armed drones is certainly not policing as a community service, much less policing by popular consent. It is rather undertaken solely for the benefit of the drone-using state as it seeks to minimise risks to its national security. And meanwhile, from the perspective of local populations who are 'policed', the practice of such violence carries the potential for privation (not provision) of personal security.

Maintaining internal security, ensuring public safety and providing basic services are among the obligations the United States would assume if it acted imperially in Pakistan, Somalia and Yemen.[95] But by only employing armed drones in a quasi-imperialistic way, the US government has managed to avoid the responsibilities of occupation (as well as the associated financial costs and political risks). If, by contrast, it donned the mantle of the state and laid claim to the monopoly of legitimate force within the foreign territories where US drones fly, this would run the risk of triggering the law enforcement paradigm of state violence. And, in turn, the ethical expectations arising in that paradigm would require the wielding of (drone) violence to be much more restrained.

This is not to suggest, however, that quasi-imperialistic drone violence can truly escape any moral judgement at all. The fact of non-occupation does not affect the fundamental presumption that every person (qua potential victim) has a right to life, so such violence remains open to be judged according to rights-based principles which are applicable by default. Even if the US government's use of armed drones against suspected terrorists located outside war zones does not amount to violent law enforcement, the principles of necessity, proportionality and discrimination remain available for the purpose of moral assessment. Accordingly, as the next section shows, such drone use can be judged as morally unacceptable for three reasons that relate to the essential open-endedness of quasi-imperialistic violence: it is temporally unnecessary, excessively harmful over time, and eventually indiscriminate as between the 'dangerous' and the innocent.

THE INJUSTICE OF QUASI-IMPERIALISTIC DRONE VIOLENCE

The right to life includes the right not to be killed arbitrarily. When killing is done for a public purpose (on a state's behalf), it is not 'arbitrary', in the sense that it is not done as a matter of private (personal) whim. Beyond that, though, there needs to be a sound *reason* for taking a human life, and the most basic reason is that it is somehow 'necessary' to do so. In a war context, the relevant principle is military necessity, and this can generally be satisfied if violence is expected to achieve an advantage or reduce a risk. The use of an armed drone could be deemed militarily necessary because friendly ground troops are under fire and in need of air support. A necessity principle applies in law enforcement contexts too, although here it has a more restricted meaning: for example, a police officer may only use a lethal weapon against a criminal suspect if there is no other available way to save the life of a person who is in immediate danger. Outside of these two established paradigms of legitimate state violence, it is more difficult to establish the necessity of killing someone.

Indeed, in attempting to legitimise its quasi-imperialistic drone violence against suspected terrorists, the US government has been able to approach this task only by relying heavily on a critical but dubious claim about temporal necessity (the lack of any later opportunity to respond) and the 'imminence' of a threat. In 2011 White House advisor John Brennan argued that 'a more flexible understanding of "imminence" may be appropriate when dealing with terrorist groups'.[96] And the following year US Attorney General Eric Holder claimed that the imminence of a terrorist attack depends on 'considerations of the relevant window of opportunity to act, the possible harm that missing the window would cause to civilians, and the likelihood of heading off future disastrous attacks'.[97] This official effort to stretch the ordinary meaning of imminence was roundly criticised (sometimes to the point of ridicule) for being so obviously wrong from a conceptual standpoint.[98] Rosa Brooks observed, for example, that the Obama administration's definition of imminence 'does not require actual *imminence*', thus making the concept 'as loose, ill defined, and self-serving as might be imagined'.[99]

The moral problem with conducting a drone strike well before a terrorist attack is genuinely imminent (about to happen) is that it restricts the scope for non-violent response options to be brought to bear, and thus it makes the occurrence of state violence more likely and more frequent. Such violence, when conducted so far in advance of a threat materialising, can appear to be essentially preventive, or even 'merely "preferential"',[100] rather than necessary. And so there is room to conclude that the US government's quasi-imperialistic drone violence is arbitrarily abusive of the right to life in the sense that it occurs without a sufficiently good reason (from a temporal perspective) to kill a targeted individual *now*.

When the necessity of state violence is doubtful, it follows that the security benefit (threat reduction) to be derived from it might only be slight or negligible. It takes little foreseeable harm, then, to outweigh the moral value of that benefit and render the violence disproportionate (excessive). Empirically, the exact balance of benefits and harms derived from drone strikes outside war zones has been difficult to determine, especially over the long term.[101] Even so, several factors appear to reduce the security benefit to be gained by US signature strikes. First, most of those killed in such strikes are reportedly not the most influential terrorists (commanders) but rather are low-level ones.[102] Second, the use of 'signatures' (an assemblage of probable indices of dangerousness) still leaves plenty of room for mistakes and misunderstandings, such that too few strikes might be killing people who in fact pose a threat to the United States.[103] Third, the intelligence-led character of drone strikes against suspected terrorists creates perverse incentives for other actors in the foreign territories where targeting occurs. That is, local governments might secure forceful US assistance only by exaggerating the internal threat they face from insurgent ('terrorist') groups,[104] or individual CIA informants might fabricate allegations and thereby encourage US drone strikes against individuals in furtherance of personal feuds.[105] And fourth, even if a drone strike kills someone who really poses a threat, the very killing of that person precludes the gaining of a further benefit: actionable intelligence on terrorist operations they were planning with others who are still alive.[106]

If, in combination, these factors make quasi-imperialistic drone violence an enterprise that brings few or dubious benefits, they have the moral effect also of making it harder to excuse any harm which drones incidentally inflict upon innocents in the vicinity of targeted individuals. Moreover, the longer such violence persists, the more likely it is to become disproportionate (or more disproportionate). This is an especially serious moral risk given that the operational logic of quasi-imperialistic drone strikes against suspected terrorists located in remote areas is to *continuously* disrupt their plans. To be achieving this effect on an ongoing basis is also to be continually running the risk that the imperfect, signature-based strike process will cause the wrong people to die. Armed drones already have the powerful potential to be a persistent presence in places where airspace is uncontested, and technological developments might increase this potential in the future.[107] In addition, to the extent that US drone strikes *fuel* the anti-US terrorist threat, they have the capacity to generate ever more targets in 'a seemingly inescapable loop'.[108] Morally, because violence cannot *always* be a good thing, the harm that results from it can only begin to be legitimised by trading it off *temporarily* against an expected benefit. Thus, the indefinite exposing of people in a foreign territory to the risk of harm (intended or unintended) presents a problem of temporal disproportionality. In this way too, then, quasi-imperialistic drone violence can unjustly imperil the human right to life.

When a campaign of drone violence involves the indefinite endangerment of innocents, it becomes 'eventually' indiscriminate. This is so even if, from one strike to the next, there is an intention only to kill the non-innocent (suspected terrorists). The US government has repeatedly issued assurances that its drone strikes are conducted with great care to avoid 'civilian' casualties,[109] and in so doing it has highlighted the 'precision' capability of an armed drone.[110] It is undoubtedly the case that, unlike piloted aircraft, drones can loiter above a prospective target for hours 'waiting for the ideal moment to strike'.[111] However, innocents too are nevertheless sometimes killed unintentionally by exposure to the wider effects (blast waves and flying shrapnel) of 'pinpoint' missile strikes. Or, the death of an innocent who suddenly appears on the scene might result from the drone operator's inability to steer away a descending missile in time (because of the delay of several seconds as a signal bounces between a drone, a satellite and the control station).

In the context of US drone violence that aims to be continually disruptive (of emergent 'terrorist' threats), such deaths are not a moral problem because of any wrongful intention. Rather, they are a problem because the US government must know, after long experience, that innocents will almost certainly *keep* getting killed in its signature strikes. Strictly speaking, these killings are accidental in the sense of being unintended and undesired, and yet their occurrence is also the result of sustained and systematic endangerment. Eventually, and because quasi-imperialism essentially involves an open-ended commitment to violent risk management, a pattern sets in of 'routinely knowing' that drone strikes in aggregate *will* kill innocents.[112] And, once the morally undesirable outcome of a certain kind of violent action has become so highly predictable, it is arguably wrong to keep performing that action in the same way without trying hard to improve it.

The knowledge that innocents keep dying in signature strikes establishes a duty to take greater and greater precautions in the face of a highly foreseeable risk, but the US government has arguably neglected this duty by making too little effort to increase the *degree* to which its drone violence is discriminate in practice. When it comes to judging the permissibility of state violence, Rodin has advocated using the concept of negligence (rather than intention) in order to focus attention on 'what constitutes an appropriate standard of care' in the use of force.[113] And, in accordance with this alternative process of moral reasoning, Coady has suggested that 'a number of drone attacks deployed by the United States in the war on terror . . . have been insufficiently concerned with the non-combatant deaths they cause collaterally'.[114] Such concern could manifest in a serious effort to count and report the number of innocents killed and to be ever striving to improve targeting practices.

Against this, in 2019 the Trump administration stopped disclosing estimates of how many suspected terrorists and innocent bystanders are killed in US drone strikes outside war zones.[115] However, in the practice of quasi-imperialistic drone violence, the problem of insufficient care extends further than this. By using armed drones in remote areas, the US government *arranges* for itself to be largely incapable of morally improving this violence. Careful, on-the-ground evaluations of distant drone strikes are deemed infeasible, so there is limited scope to learn lessons (about the accuracy of targeting) which could immediately be applied (for the benefit of innocents) to the conduct of future strikes. It is arguably not enough, then, for a US president to set as 'the *highest* standard' a requirement of '*near*-certainty that no civilians will be killed or injured' before any drone strike is taken.[116] Rather, because a campaign of quasi-imperialistic violence is essentially an open-ended one, there needs also to be a sincere and unrelenting effort to get ever nearer to *actual* certainty. To carry on running the risk of making the same mistakes, without trying constantly to reduce the number of mistakes, is effectively to accept an unreduced risk to innocents. Such a negligent disposition, towards violence that must *eventually* be indiscriminate, is destined to involve violations of the human right to life.

CONCLUSION

In using armed drones against suspected terrorists located far away and outside war zones, the US government has struggled to claim successfully that drone strikes count as war, and it has been unwilling to accept the restrictions on violence that apply in the peacetime law enforcement paradigm. So, it has sought instead to claim that another ('grey') paradigm of legitimate state violence exists in between the established paradigms of war and law enforcement. Unless or until this notion is generally accepted, however, the greyness of some drone violence will keep generating concern that unjust killings are able to occur with impunity because there is no recourse to traditional principles of restraint. Gaining some governance purchase on violence of this kind is an increasingly urgent task as more states acquire armed drones and look to the example set by the US government on how to use them. To this end, it is important first to establish a plausible conceptualisation of non-war drone violence which can then serve as a basis for moral judgement.

To conceptualise such violence as *vim*, with a view to judging it according to a *jus ad vim* framework, is unhelpful because the *vim* concept remains under-described and radically vague. As such, its use might only compound the problem of categorical greyness. However, two better-understood concepts – terrorism and imperialism – cannot plausibly be applied to US drone violence outside war zones either. According to an object-focused definition of terrorism, a campaign of drone strikes is not essentially terroristic if it does not involve the deliberate targeting of innocents. And nor is drone violence imperialistic if it is not wielded by a foreign power that is imposing imperial rule, imperially acquiring resources and assuming imperial responsibilities.

In Pakistan, Somalia and Yemen, the US use of signature strikes against suspected terrorists is better conceptualised as quasi-imperialistic in nature. Foreign armed drones have only thinly dominated the populations of these parts of the world, and the drone-using state has not been acting there out of a sense of responsibility to those populations. Rather, the United States has been engaging in an ongoing exercise of merely and aerially policing terrorist risks to its national security. Conceptualised in this way, US drone use can nevertheless be assessed as a source of injustice, even if it has the immediate appearance of being less harmful than the heavy domination that characterises imperialistic violence. The essential open-endedness of quasi-imperialistic drone violence still carries the potential for abuse of the right to life when it is temporally unnecessary, excessively harmful over time, and eventually indiscriminate. While ever violence of this kind endures, it is morally unacceptable so it ought to be avoided.

NOTES

1. The content of this chapter was previously published as: Christian Enemark, 'The Enduring Problem of "Grey" Drone Violence', *European Journal of International Security* (2021): 1–18, DOI:10.1017/eis.2021.24) © Christian Enemark. It is reproduced here with kind permission from Cambridge University Press.
2. Charlie Savage and Eric Schmitt, 'Biden quietly limits drone strikes away from war zones', *New York Times*, 4 March 2021: A12.
3. Amnesty International, *'Will I Be Next?': US Drone Strikes in Pakistan*, London: Amnesty International Publications, 2013: 56.

4. Drone Wars, 'Who has armed drones?', *Drone Wars*, updated July 2021, <https://dronewars.net/who-has-armed-drones/> (accessed 25 April 2022).

5. See: John Emery and Daniel R. Brunstetter, 'Restricting the Preventive Use of Force: Drones, the Struggle against Non-State Actors, and *Jus ad Vim*', in *Preventive Force: Drones, Targeted Killing, and the Transformation of Contemporary Warfare*, ed. Kerstin Fisk and Jennifer M. Ramos, New York: New York University Press, 2016: 257–82.

6. See: Laurie Calhoun, 'Totalitarian Tendencies in Drone Strikes by States', *Critical Studies on Terrorism*, 11 (2) (2018): 357–75; Ian G. R. Shaw, *Predator Empire: Drone Warfare and Full Spectrum Dominance*, Minneapolis and London: University of Minnesota Press, 2016: 136.

7. See: Majed Akhter, 'The Proliferation of Peripheries: Militarized Drones and the Reconfiguration of Global Space', *Progress in Human Geography*, 43 (1) (2019): 64–80; Timothy Vasko, 'Solemn Geographies of Human Limits: Drones and the Neocolonial Administration of Life and Death', *Affinities: A Journal of Radical Theory, Culture, and Action*, 6 (1) (2013): 83–107.

8. Greg Miller, 'CIA didn't know strike would hit Al-Qaeda leader', *Washington Post*, 17 June 2015, <https://www.washingtonpost.com/world/national-security/al-qaedas-leader-in-yemen-killed-in-signature-strike-us-officials-say/2015/06/17/9fe6673c-151b-11e5-89f3-61410da94eb1_story.html>.

9. Kevin Jon Heller, 'One Hell of a Killing Machine: Signature Strikes and International Law', *Journal of International Criminal Justice*, 11 (1) (2013): 89–119, at 94–5 and 97.

10. Dan Gettinger, 'The Disposition Matrix', *Center for the Study of the Drone*, Bard College, 25 April 2015, <http://dronecenter.bard.edu/the-disposition-matrix/>.

11. Greg Miller, 'Plan for hunting terrorists signals U.S. intends to keep adding names to kill lists', *Washington Post*, 23 October 2012, <http://articles.washingtonpost.com/2012-10-23/world/35500278_1_drone-campaignobama-administration-matrix>.

12. Jacqueline L. Hazelton, 'Drone Strikes and Grand Strategy: Toward a Political Understanding of the Uses of Unmanned Aerial Vehicle Attacks in US Security Policy', *Journal of Strategic Studies*, 40 (1–2) (2017): 68–91, at 78–9.

13. Director of National Intelligence, 'Summary of Information Regarding U.S. Counterterrorism Strikes Outside Areas of Active Hostilities', *Office of the Director of National Intelligence*, US Government, 1 July 2016, <https://www.dni.gov/files/documents/Newsroom/Press%20Releases/DNI+Release+on+CT+Strikes+Outside+Areas+of+Active+Hostilities.PDF>.

14. Ibid.

15. Megan Braun and Daniel R. Brunstetter, 'Rethinking the Criterion for Assessing CIA-targeted Killings: Drones, Proportionality and *Jus ad Vim*', *Journal of Military Ethics*, 12 (4) (2013): 304–24, at 316.

16. Seumas Miller, *Shooting to Kill: The Ethics of Police and Military Use of Lethal Force*, New York: Oxford University Press, 2016: 265 (emphasis added).

17. Janosch Prinz and Conrad Schetter, 'Conditioned Sovereignty: The Creation and Legitimation of Spaces of Violence in Counterterrorism Operations of the "War on Terror"', *Alternatives: Global, Local, Political*, 41 (3) (2016): 119–36, at 119.

18. Majed Akhter, 'The Proliferation of Peripheries: Militarized Drones and the Reconfiguration of Global Space', *Progress in Human Geography*, 43 (1) (2019): 64–80, at 66.

19. Christine Agius, 'Ordering without Bordering: Drones, the Unbordering of Late Modern Warfare and Ontological Insecurity', *Postcolonial Studies*, 20 (3) (2017): 370–86, at 371.

20. Rebecca Sanders, 'Legal Frontiers: Targeted Killing at the Borders of War', *Journal of Human Rights*, 13 (4) (2014): 512–36, at 513.

21. Christian Schaller, 'Using Force against Terrorists "Outside Areas of Active Hostilities": The Obama Approach and the Bin Laden Raid Revisited', *Journal of Conflict & Security Law*, 20 (2) (2015): 195–227, at 197–8.

22. Director of National Intelligence, 'Summary of Information Regarding U.S. Counterterrorism Strikes Outside Areas of Active Hostilities', *Office of the Director of National Intelligence*, US Government, 1 July 2016, <https://www.dni.gov/files/documents/Newsroom/Press%20Releases/DNI+Release+on+CT+Strikes+Outside+Areas+of+Active+Hostilities.PDF>.

23. Harold Hongju Koh, 'The Obama Administration and International Law', *US Department of State*, 25 March 2010, <https://2009-2017.state.gov/s/l/releases/remarks/139119.htm> (emphasis added).

24. Government Publishing Office, '3 CFR 13732 – Executive Order 13732 of July 1, 2016. United States Policy on Pre- and Post-Strike Measures to Address Civilian Casualties in U.S. Operations Involving the Use of Force', *US Government Publishing Office*, <https://www.govinfo.gov/app/details/CFR-2017-title3-vol1/CFR-2017-title3-vol1-eo13732/summary> (emphasis added).

25. See: Laurie R. Blank, 'Targeted Strikes: The Consequences of Blurring the Armed Conflict and Self-Defense Justifications', *William Mitchell Law Review*, 38 (5) (2012): 1655–700; Max Brookman-Byrne, 'Drone Use "Outside Areas of Active Hostilities": An Examination of the Legal Paradigms Governing US Covert Remote Strikes', *Netherlands International Law Review*, 64 (1) (2017): 3–41.

26. Philip Alston, 'Report of the Special Rapporteur on Extrajudicial, Summary or Arbitrary Executions. Addendum: Study on Targeted Killings' (A/HRC/14/24/Add.6), Human Rights Council, United Nations General Assembly, 28 May 2010: para. 3. See also: Rosa Brooks, *How Everything Became War and the Military Became Everything: Tales from the Pentagon*, New York: Simon & Schuster, 2016.

27. Scott H. Englund, 'A Dangerous Middle-Ground: Terrorists, Counter-terrorists, and Gray-Zone Conflict', *Global Affairs*, 5 (4–5) (2019): 389–404, at 391.

28. John Emery and Daniel R. Brunstetter, 'Restricting the Preventive Use of Force: Drones, the Struggle against Non-State Actors, and *Jus ad Vim*', in *Preventive Force: Drones, Targeted Killing, and the Transformation of Contemporary Warfare*, ed. Kerstin Fisk and Jennifer M. Ramos, New York: New York University Press, 2016: 257–82, at 258; S. Brandt Ford, '*Jus ad Vim* and the Just Use of Lethal Force-Short-of-War', in *Routledge Handbook of Ethics and War: Just War Theory in the Twenty-First Century*, ed. Fritz Allhoff, Nicholas G. Evans and Adam Henschke, New York: Routledge, 2013: 63–75, at 68.

29. John Emery and Daniel R. Brunstetter, 'Restricting the Preventive Use of Force: Drones, the Struggle against Non-State Actors, and *Jus ad Vim*', in *Preventive Force: Drones, Targeted Killing, and the Transformation of Contemporary Warfare*, ed. Kerstin Fisk and Jennifer M. Ramos, New York: New York University Press, 2016: 257–82, at 258.

30. Daniel R. Brunstetter, 'Wading Knee-Deep into the Rubicon: Escalation and the Morality of Limited Strikes', *Ethics & International Affairs*, 34 (2) (2020): 161–73, at 162.

31. Daniel Brunstetter, '*Jus ad Vim*: A Rejoinder to Helen Frowe', *Ethics & International Affairs*, 30 (1) (2016): 131–6, at 132.

32. Ibid. 135.

33. S. Brandt Ford, '*Jus ad Vim* and the Just Use of Lethal Force-Short-of-War', in *Routledge Handbook of Ethics and War: Just War Theory in the Twenty-First Century*, ed. Fritz Allhoff, Nicholas G. Evans and Adam Henschke, New York: Routledge, 2013: 63–75, at 67.

34. Ben Jones and John M. Parrish, 'Drones and Dirty Hands', in *Preventive Force: Drones, Targeted Killing, and the Transformation of Contemporary Warfare*, ed. Kerstin Fisk and Jennifer M. Ramos, New York: New York University Press, 2016: 283–312, at 299.

35. C. A. J. Coady, *Morality and Political Violence*, Cambridge: Cambridge University Press, 2008: 7; Helen Frowe, 'On the Redundancy of *Jus ad Vim*: A Response to Daniel Brunstetter and Megan Braun', *Ethics & International Affairs*, 30 (1) (2016): 117–29, at 117.

36. See: Daniel Brunstetter and Megan Braun, 'From *Jus ad Bellum* to *Jus ad Vim*: Recalibrating Our Understanding of the Moral Use of Force', *Ethics & International Affairs*, 27 (1) (2013): 87–106.

37. Michael Walzer, *Just and Unjust Wars*, 4th edn, New York: Basic Books, 2006: 145. See also: Mary Ellen O'Connell, 'The Law on Lethal Force Begins with the Right to Life', *Journal on the Use of Force and International Law*, 3 (2) (2016): 205–9.

38. Bureau of Investigative Journalism, 'Drone Strikes in Pakistan', *Bureau of Investigative Journalism*, February 2020, <https://www.thebureauinvesti-gates.com/projects/drone-war/Pakistan>.

39. Jessica Purkiss and Jack Serle, 'US Drones Appear to Have Returned to Pakistan', *Bureau of Investigative Journalism*, 6 March 2017, <https://

www.thebureauinvestigates.com/stories/2017-03-06/us-drones-return-to-pakistan>. Reports include: Conor Friedersdorf, '"Every Person is Afraid of the Drones": The Strikes' Effect on Life in Pakistan', *The Atlantic*, 25 September 2012, <https://www.theatlantic.com/international/archive/2012/09/every-person-is-afraid-of-the-drones-the-strikes-effect-on-life-in-pakistan/262814/>; International Human Rights and Conflict Resolution Clinic at Stanford Law School and Global Justice Clinic at NYU School of Law, *Living Under Drones: Death, Injury, and Trauma to Civilians from US Drone Practices in Pakistan*, September 2012, <http://www.livingunderdrones.org/>; Human Rights Clinic at Columbia Law School and the Center for Civilians in Conflict, *The Civilian Impact of Drones: Unexamined Costs, Unanswered Questions*, 11 September 2012, <https://civiliansinconflict.org/publications/research/civilian-impact-drones-unexamined-costs-unanswered-questions/>.

40. Taylor Owen, 'Drones don't just kill. their psychological effects are creating enemies', *The Globe and Mail*, 13 March 2013, <https://www.theglobeandmail.com/opinion/drones-dont-just-kill-their-psychological-effects-are-creating-enemies/article9707992/>.

41. Marina Espinoza and Afxentis Afxentiou, 'Editors' Introduction: Drones and State Terrorism', *Critical Studies on Terrorism*, 11 (2) (2018): 295–300, at 295.

42. Afxentis Afxentiou, 'A History of Drones: Moral(e) Bombing and State Terrorism', *Critical Studies on Terrorism*, 11 (2) (2018): 301–20, at 305.

43. Laurie Calhoun, 'Totalitarian Tendencies in Drone Strikes by States', *Critical Studies on Terrorism*, 11 (2) (2018): 357–75, at 370.

44. Ian G. R. Shaw, *Predator Empire: Drone Warfare and Full Spectrum Dominance*, Minneapolis and London: University of Minnesota Press, 2016: 136.

45. Steven P. Lee, 'Human Rights and Drone "Warfare"', *Peace Review*, 27 (4) (2015): 432–9, at 436.

46. Grégoire Chamayou, *Drone Theory*, trans. Janet Lloyd, London: Penguin, 2015: 45.

47. Ruth Blakeley, 'Drones, State Terrorism and International Law', *Critical Studies on Terrorism*, 11 (2) (2018): 321–41, at 323.

48. Samuel Scheffler, 'Is Terrorism Morally Distinctive?' *The Journal of Political Philosophy*, 14 (1) (2006): 1–17, at 1.

49. See: Ruth Blakeley, 'State Terrorism in the Social Sciences: Theories, Methods and Concepts', in *Contemporary State Terrorism: Theory and Practice*, ed. Richard Jackson, Eamon Murphy and Scott Poynting, London: Routledge, 2010: 12–27.

50. Mitja Sardoč, 'Re-thinking Violence: An Interview with C. A. J. Coady', *Critical Studies on Terrorism*, 12 (4) (2019): 735–47, at 739.

51. Zulfiqar Ali, 'Two US drone strikes kill 6 militants in North Waziristan: officials', *The Express Tribune*, 19 August 2012, <https://tribune.com.pk/story/424117/us-drone-strike-kills-four-militants-in-pakistan-officials>; Glenn Greenwald, 'US drone strikes target rescuers in Pakistan – and the West

stays silent', *The Guardian*, 20 August 2012, <https://www.theguardian.
com/commentisfree/2012/aug/20/us-drones-strikes-target-rescuers-
pakistan>; Amnesty International, *'Will I Be Next?': US Drone Strikes in
Pakistan*, London: Amnesty International Publications, 2013: 20.

52. David Rodin, 'Terrorism without Intention', *Ethics*, 114 (4) (2004): 752–71,
    at 764.
53. Ibid. 762.
54. Joby Warrick and Peter Finn, 'CIA Director says secret attacks in Pakistan
    have hobbled al-Qaeda', *Washington Post*, 18 March 2010: A01.
55. See: Afxentis Afxentiou, 'A History of Drones: Moral(e) Bombing and State
    Terrorism', *Critical Studies on Terrorism*, 11 (2) (2018): 301–20, at 311.
56. See: John Brennan, 'The Ethics and Efficacy of the President's Counterter-
    rorism Strategy', *Wilson Center*, 30 April 2012, <https://www.wilsoncenter.
    org/event/the-efficacy-and-ethics-us-counterterrorism-strategy>.
57. Marina Espinoza and Afxentis Afxentiou, 'Editors' Introduction: Drones
    and State Terrorism', *Critical Studies on Terrorism*, 11 (2) (2018): 295–300,
    at 297.
58. Majed Akhter, 'The Proliferation of Peripheries: Militarized Drones and
    the Reconfiguration of Global Space', *Progress in Human Geography*, 43
    (1) (2019): 64–80, at 64.
59. Oliver Kearns, 'Secrecy and Absence in the Residue of Covert Drone
    Strikes', *Political Geography* 57 (1) (2017): 13–23, at 18.
60. Priya Satia, 'Drones: A History from the British Middle East', *Humanity*, 5
    (1) (2014): 1–31, at 1.
61. Campbell Munro, 'The Entangled Sovereignties of Air Police: Mapping
    the Boundary of the International and the Imperial', *Global Jurist*, 15 (2)
    (2015): 117–38, at 127 (emphasis removed).
62. Samuel Moyn, 'Drones and Imagination: A Response to Paul Kahn', *Euro-
    pean Journal of International Law*, 24 (1) (2013): 227–33, at 227.
63. Derek Gregory, 'Dirty Dancing: Drones and Death in the Borderlands',
    in *Life in the Age of Drone Warfare*, ed. Lisa Parks and Caren Kaplan,
    Durham, CT, and London: Duke University Press, 2017: 25–58, at 45.
64. Ruth Blakeley, 'Drones, State Terrorism and International Law', *Critical
    Studies on Terrorism*, 11 (2) (2018): 321–41, at 327.
65. Derek Gregory, 'From a View to a Kill: Drones and Late Modern War',
    Theory, Culture & Society, 28 (7–8) (2011): 188–215, at 189.
66. Campbell Munro, 'The Entangled Sovereignties of Air Police: Mapping
    the Boundary of the International and the Imperial', *Global Jurist*, 15 (2)
    (2015): 117–38, at 125.
67. See: Michael Paris, 'Air Power and Imperial Defence 1880-1919', *Jour-
    nal of Contemporary History*, 24 (2) (1989): 209–25; David E. Omissi,
    Air Power and Colonial Control: The Royal Air Force, 1919–1939,
    Manchester: Manchester University Press, 1990.
68. Michael W. Doyle, *Empires*, Ithaca, NY: Cornell University Press, 1986: 19.
69. See: Desmond King, 'When an Empire is Not an Empire: The US Case',
    Government and Opposition, 41 (2) (2006): 163–96; Alfred W. McCoy,

Policing America's Empire: The United States, the Philippines, and the Rise of the Surveillance State, Madison, WI: University of Wisconsin Press, 2009; David Harvey, *The New Imperialism*, Oxford: Oxford University Press, 2003.

70. Dominic Alessio and Wesley Renfro, 'Empire?', *European Journal of American Studies*, 15 (2) (2020): 1–22, at 13.

71. Michael W. Doyle, *Empires*, Ithaca, NY: Cornell University Press, 1986: 45.

72. Oliver Davis, 'Theorizing the Advent of Weaponized Drones as Techniques of Domestic Paramilitary Policing', *Security Dialogue*, 50 (4) (2019): 344–60, at 348.

73. Peter Lieb, 'Suppressing Insurgencies in Comparison: The Germans in the Ukraine, 1918, and the British in Mesopotamia, 1920', *Small Wars & Insurgencies*, 23 (4) (2012): 627–47, at 634–5.

74. Priya Satia, *Spies in Arabia: The Great War and the Cultural Foundation of Britain's Covert Empire in the Middle East*, Oxford: Oxford University Press, 2008: 240.

75. Thomas Hippler, *Governing from the Skies: A Global History of Aerial Bombing*, trans. David Fernbach, London: Verso, 2017: 68–9.

76. David Killingray, '"A Swift Agent of Government": Air Power in British Colonial Africa, 1916–1939, *Journal of African History*, 25 (4) (1984): 429–44, at 431.

77. Michael W. Doyle, *Empires*, Ithaca, NY: Cornell University Press, 1986: 45.

78. Article 42 of the 1907 Hague Regulations states that a territory is considered 'occupied' when 'it is actually placed under the authority of the hostile army' and the 'occupation extends only to the territory where such authority has been established and can be exercised'. Here, the exercise of 'effective control' of territory is understood to be essential because this substantiates the notion of 'authority'. See: Tristan Ferraro, 'Determining the Beginning and End of an Occupation under International Humanitarian Law', *International Review of the Red Cross*, 94 (885) (2012): 133–63, at 134 and 140.

79. According to Derek Gregory, US drone violence is thus distinguishable from the use of armed drones in the occupied Palestinian territories where the state of Israel exercises effective control: Derek Gregory, 'Dirty Dancing: Drones and Death in the Borderlands', in *Life in the Age of Drone Warfare*, ed. Lisa Parks and Caren Kaplan, Durham, CT, and London: Duke University Press, 2017: 25–58, at 41.

80. Ian G. R. Shaw, *Predator Empire: Drone Warfare and Full Spectrum Dominance*, Minneapolis and London: University of Minnesota Press, 2016: 126.

81. Sonja Schillings, *Enemies of All Humankind: Fictions of Legitimate Violence*, Hanover, NH: Dartmouth College Press, 2017: 127.

82. John Emery and Daniel R. Brunstetter, 'Drones as Aerial Occupation', *Peace Review*, 27 (4) (2015): 424–31, at 424; Campbell A. O. Munro, 'Mapping the Vertical Battlespace: Towards a Legal Cartography of Aerial Sovereignty', *London Review of International Law*, 2 (2) (2014): 233–61, at 238.

83. Ian G. R. Shaw, *Predator Empire: Drone Warfare and Full Spectrum Dominance*, Minneapolis and London: University of Minnesota Press, 2016: 256.

84. Derek Gregory, 'Dirty Dancing: Drones and Death in the Borderlands', in *Life in the Age of Drone Warfare*, ed. Lisa Parks and Caren Kaplan, Durham, CT, and London: Duke University Press, 2017: 25–58, at 30.

85. Martin Shaw, 'Post-Imperial and Quasi-Imperial: State and Empire in the Global Era', *Millennium: Journal of International Studies*, 31 (2) (2002): 327–36, at 329.

86. Ibid. 333.

87. Ibid. 334.

88. Ian Shaw and Majed Akhter, 'The Unbearable Humanness of Drone Warfare in FATA, Pakistan', *Antipode*, 44 (4) (2012): 1490–509, at 1498.

89. Madiha Tahir, 'The Containment Zone', in *Life in the Age of Drone Warfare*, ed. Lisa Parks and Caren Kaplan, Durham, CT, and London: Duke University Press, 2017: 220–40.

90. Michael Ignatieff, *Empire Lite*, London: Vintage, 2003: 107.

91. Ibid. 79.

92. See: Yee-Kuang Heng, 'The "Transformation of War" Debate: Through the Looking Glass of Ulrich Beck's *World Risk Society*', *International Relations*, 20 (1) (2006): 69–91, at 70; Elke Schwarz, *Death Machines: The Ethics of Violent Technologies*, Manchester: Manchester University Press, 2018: 4.

93. Christine Agius, 'Ordering without Bordering: Drones, the Unbordering of Late Modern Warfare and Ontological Insecurity', *Postcolonial Studies*, 20 (3) (2017): 370–86, at 370–71; Alex Danchev, 'Bug Splat: The Art of the Drone', *International Affairs*, 92 (3) (2016): 703–13, at 706.

94. Mark Neocleous, 'Air Power as Police Power', *Environment and Planning D: Society and Space*, 31 (4) (2013): 578–93; Campbell Munro, 'The Entangled Sovereignties of Air Police: Mapping the Boundary of the International and the Imperial', *Global Jurist*, 15 (2) (2015): 117–38.

95. The fulfilment of these occupier obligations does not render imperialism per se morally acceptable. See: Rahul Rao, 'The Empire Writes Back (to Michael Ignatieff)', *Millennium: Journal of International Studies*, 33 (1) (2004): 145–66, at 161.

96. John O. Brennan, 'Strengthening our security by adhering to our values and laws', *The White House*, 16 September 2011, <https://obamawhitehouse. archives.gov/the-press-office/2011/09/16/remarks-john-o-brennan-strengthening-our-security-adhering-our-values-an>.

97. Eric Holder, 'Attorney General Eric Holder speaks at Northwestern University School of Law', *US Department of Justice*, 5 March 2012, <https://www.justice.gov/opa/speech/attorney-general-eric-holder-speaks-northwestern-university-school-law>.

98. See: Dennis R. Schmidt and Luca Trenta, 'Changes in the Law of Self-Defence? Drones, Imminence, and International Norm Dynamics', *Journal on the Use of Force and International Law*, 5 (2) (2018): 201–45, at 202; Aiden Warren and Ingvild Bode, 'Altering the Playing Field: The U.S. Redefinition of the Use-of-Force', *Contemporary Security Policy*, 36 (2) (2015): 174–99, at 186.

99. Rosa Brooks, 'Drones and Cognitive Dissonance', in *Drone Wars: Transforming Conflict, Law, and Policy*, ed. Peter L. Bergen and Daniel Rothenberg, New York: Cambridge University Press, 2015: 230–52, at 244 (original emphasis).

100. Neil C. Renic, 'A Gardener's Vision: UAVs and the Dehumanisation of Violence', *Survival*, 60 (6) (2018): 57–72, at 64.

101. Jacqueline L. Hazelton, 'Drone Strikes and Grand Strategy: Toward a Political Understanding of the Uses of Unmanned Aerial Vehicle Attacks in US Security Policy', *Journal of Strategic Studies*, 40 (1–2) (2017): 68–91, at 71–72; Patrick B. Johnston and Anoop K. Sarbahi, 'The Impact of US Drone Strikes on Terrorism in Pakistan', *International Studies Quarterly*, 60 (2) (2016): 203–19, at 203.

102. In a media report on signature strikes in Yemen, an anonymous US official reasoned: 'they might not be big names now . . . but these were the guys that would have been future leaders': Eric Schmitt, 'Embassies open, but Yemen stays on terror watch', *New York Times*, 12 August 2013: A1.

103. Grégoire Chamayou, *Drone Theory*, trans. Janet Lloyd, London: Penguin, 2015: 49; Neil C. Renic, 'A Gardener's Vision: UAVs and the Dehumanisation of Violence', *Survival*, 60 (6) (2018): 57–72, at 67.

104. James Igoe Walsh, *The Effectiveness of Drone Strikes in Counterinsurgency and Counterterrorism Campaigns*, Carlisle, PA: Strategic Studies Institute, 2013: 4–5.

105. Hillel Ofek, 'The Tortured Logic of Obama's Drone War', *The New Atlantis*, Spring (2010): 35–44, at 37; Azhar Masood, 'Pakistani tribesmen settle scores through US drones', *Arab News*, 23 May 2011, <www.arabnews.com/node/378426>.

106. Audrey Kurth Cronin, 'The Strategic Implications of Targeted Drone Strikes for US Global Counterterrorism', in *Drones and the Future of Armed Conflict*, ed. David Cortright, Rachel Fairhurst and Kirsten Wall, Chicago and London: University of Chicago Press, 2015: 99–120, at 119.

107. Clive Blount, 'Useful for the Next Hundred Years? Maintaining the Future Utility of Airpower', *The RUSI Journal*, 163 (3) (2018): 44–51, at 46.

108. Jameel Jaffer, *The Drone Memos: Targeted Killing, Secrecy and the Law*, New York: The New Press, 2016: 20.

109. In 2014 President Obama stated his administration's commitment to carry out counterterrorist drone strikes 'only where . . . there is near certainty of no civilian casualties': Barack Obama, 'Remarks by the President at the United States Military Academy Commencement Ceremony', *The White House*, 28 May 2014, <https://obamawhitehouse.archives.gov/the-press-office/2014/05/28/remarks-president-united-states-military-academy-commencement-ceremony>.

110. In 2012 John Brennan claimed that the 'surgical precision' of drone strikes gave the US government the ability to kill 'an al-Qaida terrorist' with 'laser-like focus': John Brennan, 'The Ethics and Efficacy of the President's Counterterrorism Strategy', *Wilson Center*, 30 April 2012, <https://www.wilsoncenter.org/event/the-efficacy-and-ethics-us-counterterrorism-strategy>.

111. Daniel Byman, 'Why Drones Work: The Case for Washington's Weapon of Choice', *Foreign Affairs*, July/August (2013): 32–43, at 34.

112. James DeShaw Rae, 'Drones and a Culture of Death', *Peace Review*, 27 (4) (2015): 477–83, at 478.

113. David Rodin, 'Terrorism without Intention', *Ethics*, 114 (4) (2004): 752–71, at 765.

114. Mitja Sardoč, 'Re-thinking Violence: An Interview with C. A. J. Coady', *Critical Studies on Terrorism*, 12 (4) (2019): 735–47, at 741.

115. Charlie Savage and Eric Schmitt, 'Biden quietly limits drone strikes away from war zones', *New York Times*, 4 March 2021: A12.

116. Barack Obama, 'Remarks by the President at the National Defense University', *The White House*, 23 May 2013, <https://obamawhitehouse.archives.gov/the-press-office/2013/05/23/remarks-president-national-defense-university> (emphasis added).

Chapter 5

TELE-INTIMATE VIOLENCE

═══════════

A practical problem associated with the perceived 'greyness' of some drone violence is that the individuals assigned to wield it on a state's behalf might struggle to find a source of justification. In his 2021 book *On Killing Remotely*, retired US Marine Corps officer Wayne Phelps recorded what appears to be an instance of this struggle, which arose from uncertainty about whether war or law enforcement was the proper conceptual basis for determining the permissibility of state violence. Before 30 September 2011, when the US Government used an armed drone flying in Yemen to kill US citizen and suspected terrorist Anwar al-Awlaki, members of a US military drone unit had refused to perform this task. Their commander in chief, President Barack Obama, had decided that this man should be killed, but the assigned killers reportedly 'thought it was illegal' to kill an American without trial.[1] In their view, it seemed, this was a matter of criminal justice, not warfare. The unit commander was consequently dismissed, the job was instead 'given to the CIA . . . [which] had different rules to fight under',[2] and, in Phelps's assessment, this case of principled disobedience was '[o]ne of those legendary moments' of 'moral courage' within the military profession.[3] As a matter of individual judgement, refusing to kill had been the right thing to do, even though refraining from such action carried a personal cost. And yet, arguably, those drone operators might thus have avoided a more serious cost: the moral self-harm potentially incurred by acting in a way that they personally judged to be wrong.

In much of the discussion of drone violence thus far, attention has focused on state agency in the use of armed drones and on the victimhood of targeted individuals (and others in the vicinity of a strike). This chapter shifts the focus towards the individual agency of drone operators and to the potential for these perpetrators of state-sanctioned violence to be included among its victims. When approached from this direction, the conceptualisation of drone violence becomes less a matter of its political nature (as

123

war or violent law enforcement) and more a matter of the human experience of being violent. In this regard, the critically important feature of an armed drone is that it enables a person not only to be killed from afar but also to be closely observed. This remotely controlled and camera-equipped weapon system has an unprecedented capacity to reveal the humanity of a distant human target, and such revelation is morally significant in two potentially dissonant ways. It can facilitate a drone operator's efforts to adhere to ethical principles for restraining violence, but it can also undermine that operator's moral willingness to kill another person.

To explore this tension, the chapter proceeds upon a concept of drone violence as 'tele-intimate' violence. As 'tele' (distanced) violence, it presents no physical risk to the individual user of force, but as 'intimate' violence it carries a moral risk. It is well established that humans, on a personal level, generally think it is wrong to kill each other, although a reluctance to do so can be overcome through a process of justification. To kill in a way that adheres to principles of military ethics or police ethics, for example, is often adequate to this end. However, such adherence is sometimes not enough on its own to make a killer *feel* justified in their actions, in which case they might then judge themselves as having betrayed their own sense of what it means to be a good person. To suffer badly from adverse self-judgement is to incur 'moral injury', and this is the kind of injustice with which this chapter is primarily concerned.

Only recently has it begun to be recognised that drone violence is potentially injurious to the moral well-being of drone operators. Part of the reason for this delay is that, during the last two decades of drone use, advocates and critics alike have tended instead to focus their arguments on the geographical aspect of distanced killing and on the removal of state personnel from the *physical* risk of proximity to other violent actors. Daniel Byman, for example, has observed that 'drones have done their job remarkably well' and 'at no risk to U.S. forces'.[4] Dennis Blair has described drone strikes as 'politically advantageous' because they involve 'no U.S. casualties'.[5] And Michael Walzer has envisaged future wars fought with drones 'in which there won't be any casualties (on our side), no veterans who spend years in VA [Veterans Affairs] hospitals'.[6] Added to this, some scholars have insisted that, if there is an individual-level problem with drone operators, it is rather that they are not capable of being *morally* harmed by their own drone strikes either. One such argument is that, by situating the killer 'at maximum range' from the victim, 'killing is made extremely easy' (and thus *too* easy) from an emotional standpoint.[7] Or, as another argument goes, the operation of armed drones introduces new humanitarian risks because operators watching their on-screen kills are as morally disengaged from reality (and thus as immune to moral harm) as the players of violent computer games.[8]

Gradually, though, such assertions have become discredited as more empirical evidence to the contrary has emerged. To an increasing extent, and despite the access difficulties faced by non-military researchers, individuals' accounts of their experience of operating armed drones have come to light.[9] These accounts have tended to show that drone operators are morally engaged, and often deeply so. Numerous operators have reported experiencing a sense of intimacy towards the real people who are prospective targets, and sometimes those operators appear to find it personally difficult to justify the killing they do.[10] This occasional difficulty suggests a plausible connection between wielding drone violence and incurring moral injury, and it establishes the possibility of drone operator 'victimhood' as a valid subject of normative inquiry.[11]

Even so, before embarking on that inquiry, it is worth anticipating the concern that doing so might afford undue prominence to the drone operator in relation to other kinds of victim. A scholarly focus on the perpetrators of drone violence, and on whether they 'lose sleep at night',[12] could be rightly criticised if it were intended to draw attention away from the 'real' (physically affected) victims at the receiving-end of a missile strike.[13] However, this is not the intention here. The purpose of this chapter is not to restrict the scope of moral concern but rather to cast the net wider in the search for potential *loci* of injustice that might otherwise remain obscure and unexplored. Inquiring into the experiences and judgements of drone operators is necessary if the morality of drone violence, in all its aspects, is to be comprehensively assessed and debated. To consider that a drone operator might be the victim of one kind of injustice (moral injury) does not necessarily demote or displace the consideration of other kinds. On the contrary, as later sections of the chapter will show, a regard for the humanity of people who are (or might be) physically harmed in drone strikes is at the heart of *why* a drone operator is at risk of moral injury and should therefore exercise restraint.

The discussion begins with an account of the 'tele-intimate violence' concept, and attention then turns to the issues of individual moral agency and moral injury as they relate to the perpetration of violence on behalf of the state. The core issue to be addressed in the chapter is why one person might be morally injured by wielding drone violence against another person, especially after closely observing them. Following on from this, a question of prospective moral responsibility arises: what should a drone-using state do, as an employer of drone operators, to address this potential form of injustice? In response, the chapter concludes with a suggestion that that state should safeguard killer-employees' moral well-being in the workplace by empowering them to exercise discretion and by valorising moral courage. However, a crucial condition for any efforts to prevent moral victimhood in this way is that they should tend also to reduce the risk of injustices occurring among the physical victims of drone violence. Short of avoiding the perpetration of such violence altogether, it is argu-ably important not to eliminate the risk of moral injury, because these other victims benefit from this risk as a source of extra-legal restraint upon the individual agency of a conscientious drone operator.

CONCEPTUALISING DRONE VIOLENCE AS TELE-INTIMATE VIOLENCE

One perspective on the advent of armed drones, and on their use for war or counterterrorism purposes, is that this is merely another step in a historical process of removing a violent actor further away from their opponent and thus making that actor safer.[14] According to this view, drone violence is neither new nor especially interesting because its evident effects (damage, injuries and deaths) are readily comparable to those generated by other weapons, and the moral imperative to pro-tect victims from any *unjust* effects is the same. A humanitarian lawyer would probably claim, moreover, that the remoteness that character-ises drone violence is unremarkable too. A missile fired from a drone is no different, they might argue, from any other weapon in common use; all that matters, legally, is whether specific uses comply with the rules of international humanitarian law (assuming a drone strike occurs where a war is going on).[15] What such a perspective lacks, however, is an account of a camera-equipped drone's capacity to bring its operator *closer* – visually – to a prospective human target, notwithstanding the fact of geographical separation. Even if drone violence technology is not revolutionary, it is undoubtedly revelatory, and moral reasoning needs to engage with this characteristic.

In the contemplation of armed drones, there is an understandable temptation to obsess over physical distancing, because the control of these aircraft from potentially thousands of miles away seems to achieve remoteness to the maximum possible extent. And yet, when it comes to considering the experience of those individuals who directly engage in remote-control violence, a quite different conceptual emphasis is more relevant. Geography is effectively transcended by the rapid transmission of data between drones and controllers via satellite. Physical distance then becomes less important, conceptually speaking. Rather, as a mat-ter of 'hands-on' practice, what matters most is that drones are 'deadly *surveillance* platforms'.[16] The operator of an armed drone can, in real-time, watch and respond to the imagery captured by a faraway drone-mounted camera. A lot of the time, that means watching video footage of the actions of people in foreign territories. The humanity of those people is thereby revealed repeatedly to a drone operator, sometimes to the point of establishing a one-sided familiarity with their habits and relationships. Thus, when a remotely located but closely observed person is subsequently targeted in a drone strike, it arguably makes sense to conceptualise what the drone operator *experiences* as 'tele-intimate' violence.

Based on reports of how the US and UK governments conduct drone strikes, the term 'drone operator' refers here to either of two people who work closely together in a ground station filled with data screens and control instruments. One person is the sensor operator, who controls the drone's cameras and related technologies, and the other person is the drone's pilot (seated immediately adjacent) who controls its flight. In the moment of executing a strike, the pilot acts to trigger the release of a missile from the drone, and the sensor operator then maintains aim with a targeting laser as the missile descends.[17] Before and after this, though, the greater part of each drone operator's work consists of watching other people. In media interviews with ex-operators,[18] and in a variety of academic analyses of drone violence, a prominent idea is that a drone operator can come to experience feelings of intimacy with those watched and targeted individuals. Nicholas Brown has observed, for example, that a 'deep level of intimacy' arises when a drone operator conducts 'panopticon-like surveillance' and so becomes 'privy to the most quotidian and personal details of the everyday lives' of prospective targets.[19] Bianca Baggiarini has argued that drone-based killing involves 'a battle space . . . where the enemy is intimately known'.[20] And Dave Blair and Karen House have described a drone operator's 'relational attachment to a human target' as 'Cognitive Combat Intimacy'.[21]

Importantly, the achievable degree of intimacy is not uniform across all types of missions. When a drone strike occurs while providing air support to friendly troops who are under attack (or at risk of attack), the pre-strike observation of enemies to be targeted might only be fleeting or of short duration. By contrast, in the long-planned 'targeted killing' of a suspected terrorist, that individual will often have been watched for a prolonged period until the emergence of a favourable opportunity to attack (when it would not also harm too many innocents). In which case, the drone operators assigned to do this will have perceived (over consecutive days, weeks or months) an abundance of the prosaic and familiar features of the targeted individual's life. When or if the time comes for drone operators to kill a person whose humanity has thus been so constantly and richly revealed to them, the drone violence to be wielded then is of a highly tele-intimate nature. But, regardless of how long a target was watched previously, after any strike the drone operators also observe what the extinguishing of humanity means in grisly detail. Unlike others who kill from a distance, they are prevented from conceiving their causation of death in abstract terms only. Rather, the human consequences of drone operators' lethal actions are immediately and clearly displayed to them on a video screen. Whereas, historically, artillery soldiers and high-altitude bombardiers, for example, have merely supposed that they killed 'some people', today's drone operators *know* it. And, sometimes, in the routine post-strike surveillance of severed body parts and the evident anguish of a victim's nearby family members, they know also that they have killed someone they came to 'know' in their own tele-intimate way.

STATE VIOLENCE, INDIVIDUAL AGENCY AND THE PROBLEM OF MORAL INJURY

Intimacy is a useful concept, not only in accounting for drone operators' novel and peculiar experience of killing, but also in the way it partially draws attention away from 'the state' as an abstract agent of violence. Strictly speaking, states don't kill; people do. So, to build a more complete picture of the true meaning of political violence, it is important to understand the agency of individuals who act violently on the state's behalf. And, for the purpose of ethical assessment, their *moral* agency is of particular interest. According to Seumas Miller, it is possible to distinguish institutional and noninstitutional cases of the use of lethal force. The first kind involves killing by 'institutional actors in their capacity as institutional actors', and the second kind of killing is done by 'ordinary human beings in their noninstitutional, *natural* capacities'.[22] Miller points to 'police officers and military combatants' as paradigmatic cases of institutional actors who deploy lethal force.[23] However, it is arguably the case that people who come to wield violence from within state institutions do not entirely cease to be the natural (noninstitutional) actors that they were before. A member of the military or law enforcement profession may be licensed to kill, under certain circumstances, by a public authority. Even so, their individual agency might not be entirely subsumed by performing an institutional role. If, instead, a person's pre-institutional sense of self endures, they cannot be regarded as being *only* an instrument of the state when it comes to the use of force.

Competent performance of an institutional role involves dutiful adherence to the institution's rules, and this effort will often be in harmony with a person's original sense of what it means to do the right thing. For many institutional killers, who *would* feel averse to killing in the course of their private lives, the knowledge that they are acting violently as an agent of the state might be a great and sufficient source of moral comfort. Some other killers, though, struggle morally with what they do, even if it is done in strict accordance with externally imposed rules. Killings that are permitted or excused by others remain open to be condemned by the killers themselves, because a person's sense of 'being ethical' does not necessarily equate to the fact of rule-following. That is, acts or omissions which are legally right (or not unlawful) can sometimes be (or seem to be) morally wrong. Some killers (or would-be killers) in a state's employ thus seek to ascribe moral meaning to lethal action on a personal (non-institutional) level, even though state institutions are sometimes not well prepared for facilitating this. For example, according to one former commander of a British nuclear missile submarine, his 'sailors . . . would want to discuss and understand *personally* the ethical ramifications of our mission', which was 'not something covered in official publications'.[24]

On the other hand, within Western militaries more generally, there is a strong tradition of applying Aristotelian virtue ethics to decisions about violence.[25] Here, the emphasis is on individual moral agency and the cultivation of a good (virtuous) character, and the expectation is that a person will increasing know (through education and practice) what virtue to exhibit when confronting morally challenging situations.[26] Martial virtues are commonly understood to include courage, loyalty and self-sacrifice,[27] and a warrior who exhibits these is seen (and can often see themselves) as a 'good warrior'. Moreover, ethics training provided by military institutions often emphasises virtues (as distinct from written rules) as a useful basis for making important decisions quickly.[28] In war, this cultivated habit of being virtuous can nevertheless reinforce decision-making by reference to international laws of warfare and national rules of engagement. For example, whereas the deliberate killing of civilians in war is to be avoided because it is illegal, it is morally undesirable *also* because it is vicious (anti-virtuous): a cruel and cowardly act.[29] At other times, however, virtue ethics and individual moral agency might lead a decision-maker away from rule-following. 'Being ethical', then, involves decisions to act beyond or against rules; doing less or more than is permitted or required. Such a situation can arise where the rule to be followed is itself unjust, or where it would obviously be immoral under the circumstances to follow a general rule (such as 'obey orders').[30] Alternatively, an individual's sense of virtue might sometimes occasion them to refrain from doing what a rule permits (for example, killing an enemy soldier) because that individual alone judges this to be what a virtuous (merciful) person would do.[31]

Perpetration and moral injury

To act against one's own sense of right is, in severe cases, to run the risk of 'moral injury'. This term derives from the narrower idea of 'moral distress' which Andrew Jameton first used in 1984 to describe what some nurses feel when institutional regulations prevent them from acting in what they believe to be an ethically appropriate manner.[32] A decade later, Jonathan Shay's book *Achilles in Vietnam* introduced the idea of moral injury to the study of military working environments,[33] and this expanded analytical attention towards the distress a person might experience as a result of their own (not others') wrongdoing. The term has since been used by other psychologists seeking to describe emotional problems that are not captured by 'trauma' or other diagnostic terms,[34] yet moral injury is also widely understood *not* to be a clinical diagnosis. Rather, it has remained an essentially *ethical* concept which informs analyses of individual experience from within and beyond the field of psychology.[35] Moral injury as an injustice has been assessed when it arises out of a sense of betrayal by others.[36] However, when assessing the experience of people who are employed to kill, a more suitable focus is the potential for lethal action to generate profound and debilitating feelings of self-betrayal. Such feelings include guilt (if a person perceives that their actions were vicious) and/or shame (if they believe that this is what other people perceive).

In a widely cited article from 2009, Brett Litz and his colleagues defined moral injury as involving 'an act of transgression that creates dissonance and conflict because it violates assumptions and beliefs about right and wrong and personal goodness'.[37] Since then, other studies have sustained a particular interest in the causal relationship between perpetrating transgressive acts and suffering moral injury. For example, William Nash and others have referred to the perpetrating of acts that 'transgress deeply held, communally shared moral beliefs'.[38] Kent Drescher and his colleagues have argued that moral injury is brought about by 'perpetration of immoral acts, in particular actions that are inhumane, cruel, depraved, or violent, bringing about pain, suffering, or death of others'.[39] And Shay, for whom the moral injury of a person begins with the 'betrayal of what's right', has maintained that such injury is 'the soul wound inflicted by doing something that violates one's own ethics, ideals, or attachments'.[40]

Previously, the idea that a perpetrator of wrongdoing could also become a victim had been explored by Rachel MacNair in her 2002 study of 'perpetration-induced traumatic stress'.[41] Although this was done in the narrower context of post-traumatic stress disorder (PTSD), MacNair made clear that PTSD symptoms can emerge in the absence of guilty feelings, and vice versa.[42] Consistent with that finding, a recurrent theme in the literature on moral injury is that it is not the same as PTSD (a diagnosis related to a person's loss of safety).[43] So, any conflation of the two when considering the experience of killers would tend to obscure rather than illuminate the potential moral self-harm produced by the physical harming of other people.

Moral disengagement and the 'problem' of humanisation

The prohibition on people killing each other is deeply entrenched in the ordinary moral thinking of social human beings. It can often be a profound challenge, then, for individual agents of state violence to somehow overcome a personal sense of its wrongness. In the military profession, for example, Karl Marlantes has observed that 'warriors of good conscience' have struggled for centuries to reconcile 'the moral conduct we are taught as children with the brutal actions of war'.[44] This struggle has also been acknowledged by the military historian Samuel Marshall, who argued in his 1961 book *Men against Fire*:[45]

> [The American soldier] is what his home, his religion, his schooling, and the moral code and ideals of his society have made him. The Army cannot unmake him. It must reckon with the fact that he comes from a civilization in which aggression, connected with the taking of life, is prohibited and unacceptable. The teaching and ideals of that civilization are against killing, against taking advantage. The fear of aggression has been expressed to him so strongly and absorbed by him so deeply and pervadingly – practically with his mother's milk – that it is part of a normal man's emotional makeup.

For the person raised and socialised to cherish life, both dying *and* killing are potentially fearsome prospects. Physically, we fear dying, but we morally fear killing. If the latter fear cannot somehow be overcome by a would-be killer, to go on and kill anyway is to run the risk of moral injury. Often, in human experience, such harm does not occur, because sufficient 'moral disengagement' is achieved as to avoid subsequent distress and guilt. Sometimes, though, this approach fails, and the killer remains vulnerable to the injurious effect of adverse self-judgement. For present purposes, moral disengagement and the object of it (killing) need not be regarded as inherently bad things. Rather, this concept is merely used analytically here to help identify circumstantial factors that are relevant to the risk of falling victim to moral injury.

From within a social cognitive theory of morality, Albert Bandura has identified eight mechanisms of moral disengagement which, individually or in various combinations, enable people to 'do harm and live with themselves'.[46] Beyond the restraining effect on transgressive conduct generated by social sanctions (fear of external punishment), each of these mechanisms can be conceived as a way of loosening the purchase of personal sanctions (self-condemnation of bad behaviour). One mechanism is *moral justification*, whereby an ordinarily bad act is made personally acceptable by situating it in the service of a morally worthy purpose. *Euphemistic labelling*, in the form of sanitised or complicated language, can be a mechanism for downplaying the malign character of activities or making them sound benign. *Advantageous comparison* of one's harmful conduct with something 'much worse' can be used in attempting to excuse that conduct. Through *displacement of responsibility*, one is spared from self-censure by viewing another agent (such as a public authority) as fully responsible for an action. Or, though *diffusion of responsibility*, one's involvement in an act is diluted and rendered morally acceptable by highlighting how other people were involved in it too. *Disregarding or distorting consequences* is a mechanism for avoiding personal responsibility by ignoring, misrepresenting or denying the harmful effects of one's actions. *Attribution of blame* involves self-exculpation by claiming that one's victims somehow deserved to be harmed. And self-censure can be blunted also by *dehumanisation* which, by divesting victims of their human qualities, makes them seem easier (morally) to harm.[47]

Regarding the specific harm of killing, it is unlikely that all these mechanisms of moral disengagement are always invoked by all killers. And, when it comes to individuals who kill on behalf of the state, some mechanisms might be more applicable than others. Moreover, the relevant state institution might try to facilitate moral disengagement for the sake of achieving a public and greater good. Even so, the state-sanctioned killing that is done for a war or law enforcement purpose could still entail a residual risk of moral injury to warriors and law enforcers respectively, especially when circumstances make it difficult to dehumanise victims.

Executioners

Capital punishment is widely regarded as wrong in principle, and more than half the world's countries have abolished it.[48] Where this practice persists, though, state authorities require executioners who are willing to enforce the law by lethally punishing criminal wrongdoing. For example, when Sri Lankan prison authorities sought to fill two hangman positions in 2019, the advertisement in the state-run *Daily News* stated that applicants should have 'an excellent moral character' and should pass a test of their 'mental strength'.[49] In the past, an executioner's moral confidence in performing their lethal role in society was sometimes and partly derived from a personal commitment to ensuring the victim's physical comfort. When James Berry worked as an executioner in England in the late nineteenth century, he developed the 'long drop' technique of hanging ('by varying the length of [the rope] in accordance with the physical characteristics of the criminal') while striving for 'dislocation without mutilation'.[50] And the English executioner Albert Pierrepoint is remembered for refining a technique of hanging that 'snapped the spinal cord at exactly the correct place to bring about a death that was instant and painless'.[51] However, even without making such a commitment (to achieve 'a good kill'), an executioner might be able to take some moral comfort from the fact that their killing of a criminal was preceded and justified by a process of adjudication and sentencing.[52] Provided that the victim's trial was fair, and any appeals against the death sentence were fairly rejected, the executioner could then feel somewhat reassured that the victim truly deserved to be killed.

Sometimes, when there is concern that such reassurance is not enough, additional measures are needed to safeguard the moral well-being of a state executioner and thus smooth the way towards punitive killing. In particular, the state might seek to facilitate moral disengagement by arranging for the killing to be done under conditions conducive to diffusing responsibility. As was noted in a 2015 UN report, the tendency among wealthier states that retain the death penalty is to carry it out 'in an increasingly organized, technical, and bureaucratic manner, favouring teamwork and a piecemeal approach, without thorough reflection, emotion or individual responsibility'.[53] Within the United States, this has been described as an effort by governments to ensure that, in the design of execution practices, 'nobody is responsible for everything'.[54] In the case of execution by firing squad, for example, moral disengagement by diffusing responsibility can involve the use of a dummy round inserted randomly into one of the rifles used by a squad of volunteer marksmen. Each squad member is thus enabled potentially to derive some moral comfort from not knowing for sure whether the shot *they* fired was a deadly one.[55]

Even when moral disengagement is pursued in this way, an executioner might nevertheless remain morally burdened by feeling *mainly* responsible for causing another person's death. In the context of a complex criminal justice process, a sentenced victim is not killed *because* of the executioner, but he or she is undoubtedly 'killed *by* the executioner'.[56] This truth might be bearable if, previously, an executioner becomes convinced that the victim has 'a bestial [inhuman] aspect to their nature'.[57] But, alternatively, if a victim's perceived humanity remains intact and is confirmed by personal interaction, their life might be much harder for an executioner to extinguish without afterwards experiencing moral anguish. In one execution in Oregon in the 1990s, for example, Semon Frank Thompson struggled with giving up some of his virtue ('empathy') in the process.[58] Part of the 'problem' was the exquisite humanity he encountered in one of his victims who, immediately prior to receiving a lethal injection, asked for the straps binding him to the gurney to be loosened because they were hurting him. After the straps were adjusted, 'he looked [Thompson] in the eye' and touchingly said: "Thanks, boss".'[59] At Jerry Givens's first execution (involving an electric chair) in Virginia in 1982, he could 'smell the burning flesh', and he later recalled how difficult it was 'to transform myself into someone who could go and take the life of another person'.[60] And, for Allen Ault, a psychologist who supervised executions for the US State of Georgia, close involvement in such killing became a source of unrelenting regret. He later insisted: 'No-one has the right to ask a public servant to take on a life-long sentence of nagging doubt, shame and guilt.'[61]

Killer-warriors

Other servants of the state who run the risk of moral injury are its warriors. In war circumstances, too, the perceiving of victims' humanity can sometimes thwart attempts at moral disengagement. But, even when a warrior's act of killing is not as intimate an experience as an executioner's, some killer-warriors still struggle morally with what they must do or have done. As a matter of intention, state authorities do not send their warriors to *die* in war, though there is often an acknowledged risk of this. Dying is not the essential purpose of warriors. Rather, they are sent to war to *kill* people (and break things) for a political reason (good or bad), and this task can be morally significant on an individual level too. As Nancy Sherman has observed, 'having to kill others' is seen by some soldiers as 'the greatest threat of war', because '[b]ecoming a killer is what's evil, even if sanctioned by wearing a uniform'.[62] Some forms of killing in war, such as the intentional slaughter of civilians, might be especially degrading,[63] so the humanitarian laws that prohibit this can be regarded as protective of both victims and perpetrators. From a protection perspective, however, a more challenging prospect is that a risk of moral injury might also accompany lethal acts that are within the established rules of warfare.

For many warriors, the moral question about killing ('Is it right?') is perfectly answered by recourse to the Just War morality that underpins humanitarian law; lawful action *is* right action. However, for some others who seek to make moral sense of killing, it is not enough to receive assurances that they acted in accordance with prescribed standards of warfighting. Rather, these external sources of justification (related to the *jus in bello* principles of discrimination and proportionality) fail to dispel these warriors' sense of guilt and self-betrayal about taking a human life. For them, killing 'justly' still *feels* wrong. Thus, for example, causing the death of an innocent person might be morally injurious, even though a limited amount of 'collateral damage' is generally regarded as permissible in war.[64] That is, after unintentionally killing a civilian, a self-judging warrior might not feel morally exculpated by a reminder that only an *intentional* killing of this kind is a *jus in bello* violation. Moreover, as Timothy Kudo has suggested, such a reminder could make matters worse: 'You can't [just] *tell* someone who has killed an innocent person that he did the right thing even if he followed all the proper procedures before shooting.'[65]

A risk of moral injury might also arise if a warrior intentionally kills a non-civilian, especially if that victim's humanity had previously become conspicuous. In military training and subsequent warfighting, dehumanisation is a critical and often successful mechanism for overcoming warriors' reluctance to kill.[66] The euphemistic labelling of enemies (for example, as 'targets', 'bastards', 'bad guys' or 'madmen') can facilitate this, because it effectively deprives them of individuality and humanity.[67] Then, when the killing occurs, many warriors are thereby enabled to remain morally untroubled by the experience. Occasionally, however, dehumanisation fails, the reluctance to kill resurges, and a warrior risks morally harming themselves if they proceed to kill someone anyway. According to Sherman, killing is hardest at moments when an enemy individual 'seems most clearly to suggest the shared role of fellow human'.[68] Katherine Baggaley and her colleagues have observed that military personnel tend to refrain from killing 'when their antagonists evince a human side'.[69] And, in exploring the phenomenon of the 'naked soldier', Walzer has argued that an empathetic sniper might become morally inclined to spare an enemy from death after watching them behave in unthreatening and familiar ways. In witnessing an enemy's 'prosaic acts', the would-be killer's sense of 'common humanity' is restored, and so killing becomes more difficult to justify (as a matter of individual agency).[70] This element of pre-kill witnessing is present also in the case of violence emanating from a camera-equipped drone. And, as discussed in the next section, it likely forms part of the reason why some drone operators are at risk of incurring moral injury.

WIELDING DRONE VIOLENCE AND RISKING MORAL INJURY

Even before the morality of killing is considered, the practical experience of operating a drone for prolonged periods can itself be highly stressful. In the United States, where this problem is well documented, drone operators routinely risk boredom, fatigue and other mentally unhealthy outcomes by working long sequences of long shifts.[71] This high-tempo work practice has resulted from the US government's constant and heavy demand for drone deployments in operations worldwide, and from the chronic difficulty of recruiting and retaining enough personnel to service that demand.[72] Sometimes, the US government has described work-related stress among drone operators as merely a 'burnout' problem,[73] perhaps to avoid turning it into a medical matter that might endanger a much-needed operator's position and career.[74] However, there have also been clinical diagnoses of PTSD recorded among US drone operators, albeit not at a high rate relative to the US military as a whole.[75]

In 2020 an Independent Medical Expert Group, which the UK Ministry of Defence had tasked to investigate the impact of drone use on operators, reported that 'moral injury' was another possible risk.[76] In so doing, it noted that drone operators are 'required to kill . . . without risk to themselves' and face the risk of 'direct visual exposure to atrocities', and it recommended further study in this context of 'the impact on mental health of killing humans'.[77] Previously, a variety of authors had suggested that moral injury was a worthwhile area of inquiry. From within the US military, USAF officer Joseph Chapa has acknowledged that moral injury among drone operators is something 'one can easily see' as a possibility.[78] And Douglas Pryer has predicted that 'cases of moral injury will only increase as sensors become more advanced and killing becomes more intimate for drone operators'.[79] Other authors have argued that moral injury is 'a harm that drone combat is especially prone to cause',[80] that the circumstances of drone-based killing are 'corroding the souls' of operators,[81] and that 'the concept of moral injury has provided the ideational means' for drone operators 'to express the harm they feel'.[82]

It is difficult to substantiate such claims empirically by, for example, counting the number of operators who judge themselves harshly and incur moral injury when they kill. This is partly because that community of individuals – heavily shrouded in official secrecy – is notoriously difficult for non-military researchers to access.[83] Also, the few ex-operators who speak publicly (and mostly negatively) about their experience of killing might not provide a representative picture of what drone violence feels like for most of those who wield it. Even so, for present purposes, it is worthwhile to consider a few reasons why drone-based killing could (in theory) be morally injurious to the killer.

It must first be acknowledged, though, that an individual drone operator might in fact manage to avoid moral injury entirely. Some operators have sometimes publicly expressed pride in the moral importance of their work.[84] For others, being confident in their adherence to *jus in bello* principles might be enough to overcome any feelings of guilt or shame. And moral disengagement, too, could be a factor in reducing a drone operator's reluctance to kill. Diffusion of responsibility, for example, might be achieved by emphasising the involvement of many other people in the whole process of executing a drone strike.[85] Although, as Chapa has pointed out, the numerous intelligence analysts involved in that process do not share with a drone pilot the specific experience of pulling a trigger to release a weapon that causes death.[86] The dehumanisation of human targets could be facilitated by institutional language which instead refers simply to 'targets'.[87] Or, as in the case of US targeting parlance, potential victims' humanity could be obscured by using standard acronyms like 'MAM (military-age male)',[88] and by referring to a drone strike's destructive effect as its 'bugsplat'.[89] In addition, there is evidence that drone operators sometimes invent their own dehumanising language. According to former USAF airman Michael Haas, for example, young children appearing in video footage captured by drones have sometimes been labelled 'TITS' (terrorists in training) because, as he has explained, the drone operators watching these children have felt compelled 'to remove their humanity'.[90]

If such efforts to morally disengage fail, there are arguably at least three factors which could underpin drone operators' reluctance to kill and the risk of moral injury if they do kill. First, there is the potential for a drone's powerful video-camera to restore a targeted individual's humanity and thus increase the moral weight of taking a human life. The second factor is the requirement for drone operators to maintain violent (military) and peaceful (civilian) identities, and the difficulty of constantly transitioning between these identities. The third factor is the traditional notion that warriors' assumption of physical risk is what affords them some moral permission to harm others physically.

Humanity revealed and knowingly destroyed

When drone violence is conceptualised as war and Just War morality is accordingly applied, the power of a drone's camera can readily be regarded as an asset. For the purpose of adhering to *jus in bello* principles, there is arguably a moral advantage in an armed drone's ability to hover over an area for lengthy periods while relaying imagery via satellite to its ground control station. In the context of deciding when or whether to release a missile, drone operators are able to obtain and maintain a vivid picture of what is happening in that area. So, if the observed situation suddenly altered (for example, a small child wandered into view), a planned strike against an enemy could be quickly aborted and an unintended harm avoided. An armed *and* camera-equipped drone thus appears to provide a strong basis for applying force in a discriminate manner. However, when drone violence is conceptualised differently – as tele-intimate violence – a powerful capacity for observation can be understood to impose a great moral weight upon the conscience of the individual who is positioned to kill. Even if a drone operator tries to dehumanise a targeted person, this effort is liable to be thwarted by the camera's revelation of that person's humanity.[91] Revealed humanity, being hard to deny, might then be hard to extinguish. Compared to other forms of distanced killing, drone violence perpetrated against a physically remote victim does not have the same capacity to reduce a person's ordinary resistance to killing. Thus, a tele-intimate killing with an armed drone is arguably more likely to feel wrong on an individual level and to cause moral injury to the killer.

In his book *On Killing*, Dave Grossman referred to a spectrum of 'distance and ease of aggression' to illustrate the 'direct relationship between the empathic and physical proximity of the victim, and the resultant difficulty and trauma of the kill'.[92] At one extreme, Grossman argued, is the cold-blooded, close-range, execution-style killing of someone who represents no significant or immediate threat to the killer. This, the worst kind of killing, is intensely traumatic for the killer, who 'has limited internal motivation to kill the victim', and the 'close range of the kill severely hampers the killer in his attempts to deny the humanity of the victim and . . . [his] personal responsibility for the kill'.[93] At the other extreme on Grossman's spectrum is the situation of bomber aircraft crews who, during the Second World War, were able to bring themselves to kill civilians (by droppings bombs from high altitude) 'primarily through application of the mental leverage provided to them by the [vertical] distance factor'.[94] Although the crews understood at an intellectual level the horror of what they were doing, the distance factor 'permitted them to deny it' emotionally.[95] In other words, those high-flying bombardiers killed easily with only abstract knowledge, because they never *observed* the physical characteristics and emotional behaviours of particular people before killing them.

According to Grossman's scheme, physical remoteness can facilitate killing that would otherwise feel morally difficult to do, but this holds true only if increased remoteness reduces killers' sensory perception of victims. This is not the case when a camera guides and illuminates the application of drone violence. Rather, the camera puts the drone operator on notice that real humans are at stake in moral decision-making; not just the abstract concepts of 'legitimate targets' and 'collateral damage'. Prior to engaging in tele-intimate violence, a drone operator can 'experience the 'human face' of their target',[96] acquiring intimate knowledge of what it means for a watched individual to live a life. And, by witnessing the many and repeated prosaic acts that confirm a prospective victim's humanity, the human object of an operator's violence is concretised and contextualised. For example, in published comments from US drone operators, a common theme is their witnessing of a prospective target's ordinary, familiar and peaceful acts: drinking tea and shopping for cigarettes,[97] attending evening prayers,[98] doing laundry and having sex.[99] According to USAF officer Hernando Ortega, witnessing these 'regular old life things' can be distressing for drone operators because 'some of the stuff [you watch] might remind you of stuff you did yourself', and he has suggested that gaining that familiarity 'makes it a little difficult to pull the trigger'.[100]

A feeling of wrongness about a killing might also arise from an appreciation of the kind of human relationships that the killer and the would-be victim have in common. For example, in his First World War memoir, *Storm of Steel*, Ernst Jünger recounted the moment when he was about to kill a panicking French soldier. At the last moment, the soldier held up a photograph of himself surrounded by family, and Jünger (who then refrained from killing) described this revelation as 'a plea from another world';[101] a peaceful 'world' of home life from which both men had come and to which both presumably hoped to return. In the case of today's drone violence, when an individual selected for killing continues to live among the local population, they often remain enmeshed within a family and neighbourhood. This means that, prior to attacking, a drone operator's perception of that individual's humanity includes the ordinary elements of familial and neighbourly connections. The operator witnessing these might thus be reminded of their own parents, children and friends, and of why those relationships are morally valuable. Consequently, it might become morally more difficult to kill a *father*, for example, than it is to kill a mere 'target'.[102] And, in proceeding with a missile strike anyway, the potential to incur moral injury could then be all the greater, especially if the drone operator later observes family members' anguish at the swift transformation of a living person into a ruined corpse.[103]

Alternation of violent and peaceful selves

A second factor relevant to the risk of moral injury among drone opera-tors is the peculiar circumstance of repeatedly transitioning, from one day to the next, between two radically different 'worlds': the violent world of professional life and the peaceful world of private life. An operator working at the USAF's Creech Base, for example, can travel daily from and to a family home in the northern suburbs of Las Vegas. One part of their day then involves wielding and witnessing violence in a foreign territory, and another part involves the peaceful activities of ordinary civilian life in the United States. As between each situation, the moral expectations regarding the permissibility of killing are poles apart. And, arguably, if these expectations are constantly being thrown into contrast, it could become gradually more difficult for a drone operator to reconcile them within a single sense of moral selfhood.

For soldiers who have experienced combat in the army, transitioning out of military life can sometimes produce the distressing experience of identity 'fragmentation'. This involves the splitting of a soldier's self by their inability to regard a military identity and violent actions as mor-ally reconcilable with a civilian identity and the attendant social norm of non-violence. As Paul Berghaus and Nathan Cartagena have observed, a combat veteran returning from deployment in a war zone can later find it 'extremely difficult to integrate their professional and personal moral selves',[104] especially if they killed someone while deployed. That killer's moral self might then remain fragmented if, while continuing to identify as 'a good soldier', they cannot also identify as 'a good person'. Such is the challenge, as Sherman has described it, of acquiring 'a moral self capacious enough for both civilian and warrior sensibilities';[105] somehow, that is, one must 'overcome one's aversion to killing while in uniform but then regain it in the return to civilian life'.[106]

It seems likely that fragmentation could also become a problem for the operator of an armed drone who remains 'at home' when they go 'to war'.[107] When that operator kills, they do something that is unacceptable in the peaceful life of a civilian. And yet, in contrast to the experience of a deployed soldier, the moral expectations that go along with civilian life are being constantly reinforced by the drone operator's daily return to it. Thus, it could become harder, at the level of individual moral agency, to justify killing another person when one is being frequently reminded that this is ordinarily forbidden. A soldier who deploys abroad for long peri-ods can have a settled sensation of living (and killing) in 'a world apart'. However, the drone operator who stays behind must instead endure what Shane Riza has called the 'two-lives paradigm' and the 'two-worlds phenomenon',[108] involving 'the constant yo-yo of emotion between gearing up for the business of death and winding down so as not to bring it home'.[109] Other authors have described this as an experience of '"whiplash" between war fighter and civilian roles',[110] of struggling to adapt to 'highly antithetical environments',[111] or of being 'caught up in two very different moral worlds' that pull the lives of drone operators in different directions.[112]

Although deployed soldiers who survive combat do eventually return home, they do not return *regularly* to a civilian milieu steeped in peacetime morality. Only drone operators do that, and only they must be always readjusting to the exquisite tranquillity of 'normality'. Their situation involves being called upon to do something (killing) that is both acceptable and encouraged in a world of violence, but they must then eschew and condemn that same thing immediately because it is impermissible in their between-shifts world of peace. Moreover, for the drone operator who moves quickly out of and back into a civilian-like existence, there might not be as much time available as there is for a soldier deployed abroad to reflect (with colleagues) on whether it felt right to kill another person. In which case, drone-based killing can end up being done, but never deeply discussed, amid 'a daily routine that involves the sights and sounds of a normal . . . life'.[113] This routine has the capacity to serve as a constant reminder that killing is normally wrong, which could then make it increasingly harder for some drone operators to judge their violence and themselves favourably. And if, instead, adverse self-judgement is the result of wielding drone violence, it carries a risk of moral injury.

Physical risk and moral permission

The third factor worth considering as a basis for moral injury is physical risk, to which many drone operators are notoriously not exposed. Despite the normal prohibition on killing *within* the peaceful context of civilian society, killing *on behalf* of that society is often encouraged, and citizens who volunteer to wage war are often admired by their fellows. This admiration stems partly from an attitude that the killing of dangerous enemies is a valuable service to society. But it is also based on ascribing moral value to the way warriors sometimes put their bodies and lives at risk in the process. In turn, by exposing themselves to some degree of physical risk, they are arguably better able to justify endangering other people. In this way, traditionally, risk-taking and endangerment are morally packaged together, and the practice of war emerges as an exceptional moral circumstance that affords each at-risk warrior a special permission to kill. As Martin Cook has observed, volunteer military personnel enter into a morally unique 'contract' with the state.[114] One part of this contract is an acceptance of 'the obligation to put their lives and bodies at grave risk', and another part 'requires them to kill other human beings'.[115] Critically, according to this view, an attribute that warriors on either side of a conflict have in common is potential victimhood, in the sense that they all have a bodily stake in the same violent contest. That *mutual* physical risk is what effectively 'buys' permission for lethal violence; a preparedness to die is given in exchange for a licence to kill.

Where a killer-warrior is instead highly unlikely to become a victim of some physical harm, they are arguably more likely to feel personally that the traditional justification for killing in war is unavailable to them. Absent mutual victimhood, that is, their lethal violence could seem to lose its moral value if it more closely resembled mere slaughter. An aversion to such killing was apparent, for example, among some US military pilots during the Gulf War. In February 1991 a road between Kuwait and Iraq became known as the Highway of Death after repeated air strikes against Iraqi soldiers who were using the road to retreat. One US pilot reportedly compared flying missions against these fleeing people to 'shooting fish in a barrel',[116] and other pilots expressed misgivings about 'shooting up Iraqi troops who were powerless to defend themselves'.[117] Nevertheless, in this instance of extremely asymmetric violence, where there was little immediate risk of retaliation, the killers still had to endure a degree of danger. Even without suffering an enemy's anti-aircraft fire, it is inherently hazardous for a person to be airborne. For example, a pilot sitting in a cockpit is at risk from mechanical failure that forces a descent by parachute into hostile territory, or they might crash due to loss of consciousness at high altitude.

By contrast, none of these things endangers the ground-based and often remotely located operators of armed drones, so it is hard to secure for themselves the additional moral cover that physical risk-taking traditionally bestows upon killers in war. Even if individual instances of killing were deemed by others to have adhered to *jus in bello* principles, for example, the one-sidedness of physical risk (experienced only by the targeted person) could remain a 'burden' to the drone operator,[118] leading to adverse self-judgement and possibly to moral injury. However, it would be wrong to presume that the weight of this burden must be equal in all circumstances and that the risk of becoming morally injured will always be high. Although a drone operator does not directly experience danger, it might be somewhat easier (morally speaking) for them to kill if this were protective of *someone else* who is immediately at risk of attack. That is, urgent other-defence could feel more justifiable (and could thus be less likely to be morally injurious) than drone violence which does not seem to be essentially defensive.

A drone strike can be conducted in an established conflict zone to protect at-risk civilians or to support friendly (or allied) troops. Or, it can be directed against someone who is far away from an ongoing conflict and therefore not immediately threatening to anyone. To the extent that drone operators tend to prefer the former, this might indicate that urgent other-defence feels to them like a firmer moral basis for killing. Some UK drone operators have 'prioritized the protecting of allied troops on the ground above the killing of the enemy',[119] by individually and collectively adopting a 'guardian' identity.[120] And other operators, in the United States, reportedly 'love' the feeling that they are 'protecting our people'.[121] There, according to USAF officer Lewis Pine, 'success' for a drone operator means being able to say: 'Hey, I just saved guys on the ground today because I was able to put one of my missiles into a group of bad guys that were shooting at them.'[122] In this way, it seems, the faraway drone operator can come to invest self-justification with the deployed soldier's immediate experience of physical risk. Accordingly, for them, the moral value in killing *now* is that others may *now* be spared death. Moreover, there is relatively little opportunity in a swift tactical encounter with an enemy for their humanity to be revealed via video camera. So, the 'protective' drone operator's feeling of moral rectitude is less likely to be undermined by a humane reluctance to take a targeted person's life, thus also possibly lowering further the risk that killing them will cause moral injury.

That risk is probably greater, though, when drone operators kill people who are located away from a conflict zone. When an armed drone is flying over a scene in which friendly and enemy troops are exchanging fire, the tactical and moral imperative to protect others is clear. So too is the dangerousness of prospective victims and the legitimacy of killing them in other-defence. By contrast, in circumstances where targeted humans are 'outside of active firefights' and 'not behaving like combatants',[123] it is arguably harder for an operator to characterise and justify their lethal violence as essentially defensive, because it has no immediate life-saving value. And, if a long-planned killing (of a suspected terrorist, for example) was preceded by prolonged observation, the drone operator might have added to their own moral burden by becoming highly cognisant of the targeted victim's humanity.

A STATE EMPLOYER'S RESPONSIBILITY TO THE MORALLY AT-RISK DRONE OPERATOR

Once it is established that the wielding of drone violence in different ways can carry a greater or lesser risk of moral injury, one challenge this generates is to address that type of injustice in the context of drone operators' work practices. The idea that drone violence victims can include its perpetrators might seem at first to be politically unpalatable for drone-using states, as this idea goes to the heart of why governments send armed drones into dangerous places: to spare their personnel from exposure to risk. From an ethical perspective, however, the idea of drone operator victimhood cannot easily be dismissed by a government that aims to be a caring and responsible employer. If trying to avoid physical injury among individuals who act violently for the state is important, it is arguably important also to protect them against any moral injury possibly arising from that violence. Accordingly, when tele-intimate killing with an armed drone is acknowledged as being morally hard labour, a question of policy worth exploring is: how should a state employer protect drone operators' moral well-being?

Although military and law enforcement personnel are servants of the state, as human beings they have inherent as well as instrumental value. State authorities have a prospective moral responsibility towards those they place at risk in pursuit of the state's objectives. This is why it is reasonable for police officers to expect not to be placed in unnecessary danger by authorities, and for soldiers to expect that their lives will not be squandered by commanders and political leaders. In wartime, the moral concern to spare civilians from harm is well known, but it is worth recalling that the global humanitarian movement to protect war's victims originated in response to the battlefield sufferings of wounded combatants.[124] Today, the notion of regarding military personnel as mere 'cannon fodder' is widely regarded as a vile anachronism, and in many parts of the world this attitude has been replaced with a concern to protect the rights of individuals who violently serve the state. This concern derives partly from an understanding that the state owes a reciprocal responsibility of care to 'the people who voluntarily put themselves in harm's way for the protection and defense of their compatriots'.[125] In addition, in some Western countries, such service to the state has increasingly come to be treated more as a technical occupation rather than as a heroic vocation,[126] with recruitment efforts often focused upon economic incentives and career advantages.[127] And, in this sociological turn towards state violence as 'work', the state has increasingly acquired a responsibility for safeguarding the 'occupational' well-being of its killer-employees.[128]

Since the advent of armed drones, some states have elected to care for their military pilots' bodies and lives by no longer requiring them to climb into a cockpit and fly. Moreover, from the perspective of occupational well-being, it could be argued that the state (as a responsible employer) *should* sometimes use armed drones. Indeed, this might be regarded as the 'healthier' choice if the only other way of achieving a necessary objective involves using a riskier, functionally equivalent, non-drone method of violence. In advocating this choice, Bradley Strawser has referred to a 'principle of unnecessary risk (PUR)'.[129] His argument is that, if a state can arrange for its military to use armed drones to carry out missions instead of 'inhabited' weapons systems, with no loss of capability (including the capacity to act justly), then 'via PUR . . . the state has a clear ethical obligation to do so'.[130] Here, though, it would need to be the case that a state was determined to use some kind of violence anyway, to the exclusion of non-violent methods of problem-solving. Otherwise, the choice to use armed drones would be harder to justify as an exercise in caring for state personnel, because *not* resorting to force at all would be another available way to reduce the risk of physical harm.

Once a government has committed itself to drone violence, its responsibility to care for the violent agents it employs is arguably not fully discharged by locating them in ground control stations far away from where a drone strike occurs. Rather, a state employer that reduces employee risk *by* using drones has a responsibility also to reduce the risk *of* using drones. Specifically, a concern to reduce the physical risk of dying should be accompanied by attention to the non-physical risks of killing. In countries where the risk to drone operators' occupational well-being of perpetrating violence is a concern at all, it has mainly been approached as a psychology and mental health challenge. In the United States the Air Force recruits operators by reference to suitable 'psychological attributes',[131] incorporating stringent 'behavioural requirements' into the selection process.[132] Then it continues to investigate drone operators' 'psychophysical performances' for the purpose of optimising the military effectiveness of drone technologies.[133] Such investigation is also undertaken in the United Kingdom to anticipate and remedy psychological problems. For example, in 2019 when the UK Ministry of Defence asked medical experts to investigate the impact of drone use on British operators, it was motivated by a concern that financial claims for 'mental health disorders' under the UK's Armed Forces Compensation Scheme were continuing to increase.[134] Some academic researchers, too, have highlighted the risk of mental illness, by referring to the 'psychological needs . . . specific to drone operators',[135] and to the 'special therapeutic needs' that arise from 'killing and witness the impact of their confirmed killing on screen'.[136]

Consistent with such framing of occupational well-being as a mental health matter, at Creech Air Force Base in the United States there is reportedly a policy requiring drone operators to contact a psychologist every time they deploy a weapon.[137] That psychologist is part of a Human Performance Team on the base, and all team members possess security clearances that allow them to confer freely with drone operators working there.[138] It is reasonable, then, to conclude that any emergent mental illness among the operators of US armed drones has the potential to be spotted early and that swift treatment of symptoms would be available. However, as the root cause of mental illness, or in the absence of it, a drone operator who has killed might yet experience a *moral* difficulty, and psychological methods alone cannot resolve that. If so, where a state employer is focused only on the *psychological* risk that attends the perpetration of drone violence, there is a danger that a killer-employee's moral injury will remain unaddressed or be mischaracterised as sickness. In this scenario, an individual drone operator's guilt could end up being unduly pathologised,[139] and their expressions of ethical concern about why and how a drone strike occurred could more easily be dismissed by institutional superiors as the worthless outpourings of a diseased mind.[140] Indeed, a government might be keen to suppress in this way the 'subversive' notion of individualised *moral* costs being incurred 'on the home front', especially if it is struggling to maintain popular confidence that its outward engagement in drone violence is justified.[141]

For the sake of drone operators themselves, it is arguably better to approach moral well-being as something that is inherently worthy of protection, regardless of whether it is connected to mental health. This would be consistent with the 'shield approach' to military ethics whereby, through the personal exercise of restraint, a wartime killer's humanity is protected as against the killing they do (so they can 'live with themselves afterwards').[142] Already, in the United States and the United Kingdom there has been some movement beyond the mental health paradigm of caring for state-employed drone operators. Specifically, an American or British operator's moral concern about killing can also be explored as a spiritual matter with the help of military chaplains embedded within drone units.[143] In increasingly secular societies, however, the availability of religious guidance will probably have a declining capacity to address the risk of moral injury. A more durable alternative might be to approach the avoidance of moral injury among drone operators as a matter of professional empowerment. A state employer's responsibility, then, would be to enable moral self-care by allowing greater individual autonomy in the hands-on practice of drone violence.

Within military units, obedience is ordinarily very important. Through combat training individuals are conditioned to act reflexively in response to commands, and this disciplined capacity for swift action can often be critically protective of fellow combatants when exchanging fire with an enemy. By contrast, in the wielding of drone violence, it is sometimes not as urgent for commanders to be able to bypass an individual's moral autonomy in this way. If, for example, an armed drone is flying where there are no friendly personnel in immediate need of protection, it is harder to claim that a drone operator *must* (obediently) kill a targeted person *now*. Rather, in this circumstance, there may be a temporal opportunity and therefore a moral requirement for the would-be killer to reflect upon whether a planned drone strike is justified.

Reportedly, members of UK Reaper crews have been allowed to refuse (and have sometimes actually refused) to release a missile when civilian deaths could result.[144] And, in the provision of close air support by US drones, a USAF Reaper pilot must 'consent to release' a weapon upon receiving clearance from a ground commander for a drone strike.[145] Given the deep secrecy that typically surrounds these states' military and counterterrorist operations, it is difficult to know whether the exercise of such discretion by drone operators is generally permitted or only occasionally tolerated. But, in any event, drone operators who receive mere authorisation (rather than an order) to kill might still find themselves under heavy pressure to 'obey'. For example, if a government's political urge to kill a 'high value target' were strong, this might occasion senior commanders to take a close interest in a planned drone strike. This institutional pressure could limit a drone operator's ability to account for any individual experience of tele-intimacy towards a prospective victim, and they might then find it harder to avoid killing *reluctantly* and incurring moral injury.

A suggested alternative is that the state employer of drone operators could instead arrange to empower them, institutionally, by formally encouraging the discussion of moral doubts.[146] And, arising from this, as Janina Dill has proposed, any refusals to kill could be respected and protected by instituting 'a rule of conscientious objection on a strike-by-strike basis'.[147] Such an arrangement would provide more scope for a drone operator to act according to their own judgement of what is right, and it could make feelings of self-betrayal less likely to emerge. Even so, in conscientiously refusing to wield drone violence, there might yet be a professional risk associated with thereby angering fellow personnel. In which case, a state employer's responsibility would need to extend also to the valorising of moral courage as a key virtue for the operator of an armed drone.[148] Here, though, the emphasis would not be upon *killing* (perhaps tele-intimately) as a courageous thing to do,[149] because that would tend to encourage increased exposure to the risk of moral injury. Rather, as a matter of workplace culture, the morally courageous drone operator would be the one who can *refrain* from killing when it feels wrong, even if everyone else watching disagrees.

CONCLUSION

Among the many kinds of injustice that might result from the use of armed drones, the victimhood of drone operators themselves deserves some consideration, even though theirs is clearly less severe than what is experienced by victims at the receiving-end of a missile strike. By conceptualising drone violence as tele-intimate violence, the potential injustice of perpetration-induced moral injury is brought to the fore, and this can then be added to the other reasons why restraint of such violence is required. As a matter of military ethics, if being 'a good warrior' is approached only in terms of rules and rule-following, there is a risk of failing to capture all the morally significant aspects of an individual's experience of killing another person. In the case of drone operators, the making of moral judgements needs to account for the distinctive capacity of a camera-equipped weapon platform to reveal the humanity of a distant target in real time. To the extent that such revelation can undermine an operator's willingness to kill, the state that employs them has a responsibility to minimise the risk of moral injury. And, as dehumanisation is unlikely to be an effective risk-reduction measure in these circumstances, a better approach is needed if a government is unwilling to abandon drone violence altogether.

In future, the provision of psychological and spiritual support might not be enough to protect drone operators while they undertake the morally hard labour of tele-intimate killing. In which case, one approach to addressing the risk to these employees' well-being in the workplace could be to enable greater self-protection through the exercise of discretion. This would involve the fostering of a professional culture of encouraging moral courage and the allowing of courageous refusals to kill. Thus, an individual charged with wielding drone violence would be empowered with more control over their exposure to the risk of moral injury, but a degree of moral vulnerability would nevertheless be preserved as a source of restraint for the benefit of others. In an alternative future scenario, however, protecting drone operators' well-being might be approached by instead *reducing* their involvement in the operation of armed drones. That is, if some functions within drone-based weapon systems were able to be performed by artificial intelligence (AI) technologies instead of humans, this too could be a way for the latter to avoid the most disturbing aspects of the experience of killing. And yet, as the next chapter will show, the notion of 'devolving' drone violence from humans to AI is one that raises an additonal set of moral concerns.

NOTES

1. From an interview with '[a]n RPA [remotely piloted aircraft] pilot within a special operations squadron', quoted in: Wayne Phelps, *On Killing Remotely: The Psychology of Killing with Drones*, New York: Little, Brown and Company, 2021: 238. See also: Lauren Walker, 'Death from above: confessions of a killer drone operator', *Newsweek*, 19 November 2015, <http://europe.newsweek.com/confessions-lethal-drone-operator-396541>.

2. Wayne Phelps, *On Killing Remotely: The Psychology of Killing with Drones*, New York: Little, Brown and Company, 2021: 238.

3. Ibid. 237.

4. Daniel Byman, 'Why Drones Work: The Case for Washington's Weapon of Choice', *Foreign Affairs* (July/August 2013): 32–43, at 32.

5. Jo Becker and Scott Shane, 'Secret 'Kill List' Proves a Test of Obama's Principles and Will', *New York Times*, 29 May 2012: A1.

6. Michael Walzer, 'Just and Unjust Targeted Killing and Drone Warfare', *Daedalus*, 145 (4) (2016): 12–24, at 15.

7. Jai C. Galliott, *Military Robots: Mapping the Moral Landscape*, Farnham: Ashgate, 2015: 140.

8. See: Philip Alston, 'Report of the Special Rapporteur on Extrajudicial, Summary or Arbitrary Executions. Addendum: Study on targeted killings' (A/HRC/14/24/Add.6), Human Rights Council, United Nations General Assembly, 28 May 2010: para. 84; Lambèr Royakkers and Rinie van Est, 'The Cubicle Warrior: The Marionette of Digitalized Warfare', *Ethics and Information Technology* 12 (2010): 289–96; Chris Cole, Mary Dobbing and Amy Hailwood, *Convenient Killing: Armed Drones and the 'Playstation' Mentality*, Oxford: Fellowship of Reconciliation, 2010; Laurie Calhoun, *We Kill Because We Can: From Soldiering to Assassination in the Drone Age*, London: Zed Books, 2015: 189.

9. Examples include: Matthew Power, 'Confessions of a Drone Warrior', *GQ*, 23 October 2013, <http://www.gq.com/story/drone-uav-pilot-assassination>; Heather Linebaugh, 'I worked on the US drone program. The public should know what really goes on', *The Guardian*, 29 December 2013: <http://www.theguardian.com/commentisfree/2013/dec/29/drones-us-military>; Drone Pilot (US) interviewed by Daniel Rothenberg, 'It Is War at a Very Intimate Level', in *Drone Wars: Transforming Conflict, Law, and Policy*, ed. Peter L. Bergen and Daniel Rothenberg, New York: Cambridge University Press, 2015: 113–28.

10. Two books that include multiple drone operators' accounts of this kind are: Peter Lee, *Reaper Force: The Inside Story of Britain's Drone Wars*. London: John Blake, 2019; Wayne Phelps, *On Killing Remotely: The Psychology of Killing with Drones*, New York: Little, Brown and Company, 2021.

11. See: Jacob Holz, 'Victimhood and Trauma within Drone Warfare', *Critical Military Studies* (2021): 1–16, <DOI: 10.1080/23337486.2021.1953738>.

12. Christopher Coker, 'Ethics, Drones, and Killer Robots', in *The Oxford Handbook of International Political Theory*, ed. Chris Brown and Robyn Eckersley. Oxford: Oxford University Press, 2018: 247–58, at 255.

13. See: Alex Edney-Browne, 'Embodiment and Affect in a Digital Age: Understanding Mental Illness among Military Drone Personnel', *Krisis: Journal for Contemporary Philosophy*, Issue 1 (2017): 18–32, at 20; Christine Agius, 'Ordering without Bordering: Drones, the Unbordering of Late Modern Warfare and Ontological Insecurity', *Postcolonial Studies*, 20 (3) (2017): 370–86, at 379.

14. Bradley Jay Strawser, 'Moral Predators: The Duty to Employ Uninhabited Aerial Vehicles', *Journal of Military Ethics*, 9 (4), 2010: 342–68, at 343; Lambèr Royakkers and Rinie van Est, 'The Cubicle Warrior: The Marionette of Digitalized Warfare', *Ethics and Information Technology*, 12 (2010): 289–96, at 291.

15. See, for example: Philip Alston, 'Report of the Special Rapporteur on Extrajudicial, Summary or Arbitrary Executions. Addendum: Study on targeted killings' (A/HRC/14/24/Add.6), Human Rights Council, United Nations General Assembly, 28 May 2010: para. 79; Ryan R. Vogel, 'Drone Warfare and the Law of Armed Conflict', *Denver Journal of International Law and Policy*, 39 (1) (2010): 101–38, at 133.

16. Harry van der Linden, 'Drone Warfare and Just War Theory', in *Drones and Targeted Killing: Legal, Moral, and Geopolitical Issues*, 2nd edn, ed. Marjorie Cohn, Northampton MA, Olive Branch Press, 2018: 179–204, at 200 (original emphasis).

17. Marc Pitzke, 'How drone pilots wage war', *Spiegel International*, 12 March 2010, <https://www.spiegel.de/international/world/remote-warriors-how-drone-pilots-wage-war-a-682420.html>; Peter Lee, 'The Distance Paradox: Reaper, the Human Dimension of Remote Warfare, and Future Challenges for the RAF', *Air Power Review*, 21 (3) (2018): 106–30.

18. See, for example: Richard Engel, 'Former drone operator says he's haunted by his part in more than 1,600 deaths', *NBC News*, 6 June 2013, <http://investigations.nbcnews.com/_news/2013/06/06/18787450-former-drone-operator-says-hes-haunted-by-his-part-in-more-than-1600-deaths>; Sophie Shevardnadze and Bruce Black, 'Former drone pilot, Lieutenant-Colonel: Obama personally orders drone killings', *RT*, 29 November 2013, <https://www.rt.com/shows/sophieco/weapon-drones-industry-demand-465/>.

19. Nicholas R. Brown, 'Unmanned? The Bodily Harms and Moral Valor of Drone Warfare', in *The Future of Drone Use: Opportunities and Threats from Ethical and Legal Perspectives*, ed. Bart Custers, The Hague: TMC Asser Press, 2016: 189–207, at 202.

20. Bianca Baggiarini, 'Drone Warfare and the Limits of Sacrifice', *Journal of International Political Theory*, 11 (1) (2015): 128–44, at 129.

21. Dave Blair and Karen House, 'Avengers in Wrath: Moral Agency and Trauma Prevention for Remote Warriors', *Lawfare*, 12 November 2017, <https://www.lawfareblog.com/avengers-wrath-moral-agency-and-trauma-prevention-remote-warriors>. For other discussions of 'intimacy',

see: Derek Gregory, 'From a View to a Kill: Drones and Late Modern War', *Theory, Culture & Society*, 28 (7–8) (2011): 188–215; John Williams, 'Distant Intimacy: Space, Drones, and Just War', *Ethics and International Affairs*, 29 (1) (2015): 93–110.

22. Seumas Miller, *Shooting to Kill: The Ethics of Police and Military Use of Lethal Force*, New York: Oxford University Press, 2016: 3 (original emphasis).

23. Ibid. 3.

24. Andrew Corbett, 'Military Virtues', *Journal of Military Ethics*, 18 (3) (2019): 263–65, at 263 (emphasis added).

25. See: Peter Olsthoorn, *Military Ethics and Virtues: an Interdisciplinary Approach for the 21st Century*, London: Routledge, 2010; Peer de Vries, 'Virtue Ethics in the Military: An Attempt at Completeness', *Journal of Military Ethics*, 19 (3) (2020): 170–85.

26. Aristotle called this acquired knowledge *phronesis* (practical wisdom): Aristotle, *The Ethics of Aristotle: The Nicomachean Ethics*, trans. J. A. K. Thomson, London: Penguin, 1953: 209.

27. See: H. R. McMaster, 'Remaining True to Our Values – Reflections on Military Ethics in Trying Times', *Journal of Military Ethics*, 9 (3) (2010): 183–94, at 193.

28. See: Paul Robin, Nigel De Lee and Don Carrick, *Ethics Education in the Military*, Aldershot: Ashgate, 2008.

29. Christopher Coker, *Humane Warfare*, London: Routledge, 2001: 37.

30. See: Jean-François Caron, 'Exploring the Extent of Ethical Disobedience through the Lens of the Srebrenica and Rwanda Genocides: Can Soldiers Disobey Lawful Orders?', *Critical Military Studies*, 5 (1) (2019): 1–20, at 1.

31. See: Neil C. Renic, 'Battlefield Mercy: Unpacking the Nature and Significance of Supererogation in War', *Ethics and International Affairs*, 33 (3) (2019): 343–62, at 353.

32. Andrew Jameton, *Nursing Practice: The Ethical Issues*, Englewood Cliffs, NJ: Prentice Hall, 1984. See also: Elizabeth Gingell Epstein and Ann Baile Hamric, 'Moral Distress, Moral Residue, and the Crescendo Effect', *Journal of Clinical Ethics*, 20 (4) (2009): 330–42; Edgar Jones, 'Moral Injury in Time of War', *The Lancet*, 391 (2018): 1766–7, at 1767; Mariam Alexander, 'NHS staff are suffering from "moral injury", a distress usually associated with war zones', *The Guardian*, 12 April 2021, <https://www.theguardian.com/commentisfree/2021/apr/12/nhs-staff-moral-injury-distress-associated-with-war-zones-pandemic>.

33. Jonathan Shay, *Achilles in Vietnam: Combat Trauma and the Undoing of Character*, New York: Atheneum, 1994.

34. Jeremy Jinkerson, 'Moral Injury as a New Normal in the Modern Wars', *The Military Psychologist*, October 2014, <http://www.apadivisions.org/division-19/publications/newsletters/military/2014/10/moral-injury.aspx>.

35. Warren Kinghorn, 'Combat Trauma and Moral Fragmentation: A Theological Account of Moral Injury', *Journal of the Society of Christian Ethics*, 32 (2) (2012): 57–74; Joseph M. Currier, Jason M. Holland and Jesse

Malott, 'Moral Injury, Meaning Making, and Mental Health in Returning Veterans', *Journal of Clinical Psychology*, 71 (3) (2015): 229–40; Chris J. Antal and Kathy Winings, 'Moral Injury, Soul Repair, and Creating a Place for Grace', *Religious Education*, 110 (4) (2015): 382–94; Sheila Frankfurt and Patricia Frazier, 'A Review of Research on Moral Injury in Combat Veterans', *Military Psychology*, 28 (5) (2016): 318–30.

36. See, for example: Jessica Wolfendale, 'Military sexual assault is a moral injury', *War on the Rocks*, 21 May 2021, <https://warontherocks.com/2021/05/the-military-justice-improvement-act-and-the-moral-duty-owed-to-sexual-assault-victims/>.

37. Brett T. Litz, Nathan Stein, Eileen Delaney, Leslie Lebowitz, William P. Nash, Caroline Silva and Shira Maguen, 'Moral Injury and Moral Repair in War Veterans: A Preliminary Model and Intervention Strategy', *Clinical Psychology Review*, 29 (8) (2009): 695–706, at 698.

38. William P. Nash, Jennifer Vasterling, Linda Ewing-Cobbs, Sarah Horn, Thomas Gaskin, John Golden and Patricia Lester, 'Consensus Recommendations for Common Data Elements for Operational Stress Research and Surveillance: Report of a Federal Interagency Working Group', *Archive of Physical Medicine and Rehabilitation*, 91 (11) (2010): 1673–83, at 1676.

39. Kent D. Drescher, David W. Foy, Caroline Kelly, Anna Leshner, Kerrie Schutz and Brett Litz, 'An Exploration of the Viability and Usefulness of the Construct of Moral Injury in War Veterans', *Traumatology*, 17 (1) (2011): 8–13, at 9.

40. Jonathan Shay, 'Moral Injury', *Intertexts*, 16 (1) (2012): 57–66, at 58.

41. Rachel M. MacNair, *Perpetration-Induced Traumatic Stress: The Psychological Consequences of Killing*, Westport CT: Praeger, 2002: 7.

42. Ibid. 8.

43. Brett T. Litz, Nathan Stein, Eileen Delaney, Leslie Lebowitz, William P. Nash, Caroline Silva and Shira Maguen, 'Moral Injury and Moral Repair in War Veterans: A Preliminary Model and Intervention Strategy', *Clinical Psychology Review* 29 (8) (2009): 695–706, at 699; Rita Nakashima Brock, 'Moral Injury: The Crucial Missing Piece in Understanding Soldier Suicides', *Huffpost*, 22 September 2012, <https://www.huffpost.com/entry/moral-injury-the-crucial-missing-piece-in-understanding-soldier-suicides_b_1686674>; Maggie Puniewska, 'Healing a Wounded Sense of Morality', *The Atlantic*, 3 July 2015, <http://www.theatlantic.com/health/archive/2015/07/healing-a-wounded-sense-of-morality/396770/>.

44. Karl Marlantes, *What It Is Like to Go to War*, New York: Grove Press, 2011: 51.

45. S. L. A. Marshall, *Men against Fire: The Problem of Battle Command in Future War*, New York: William Morrow, 1961: 78.

46. Albert Bandura, *Moral Disengagement: How People Do Harm and Live with Themselves*, New York: Macmillan, 2016.

47. See: Albert Bandura, 'Moral Disengagement in the Perpetration of Inhumanities', *Personality and Social Psychology Review*, 3 (3) (1999): 193–209.

48. Amnesty International, 'Death sentences and executions 2020', *Amnesty International*, 21 April 2021, <https://www.amnesty.org/en/documents/act50/3760/2021/en/>.

49. Associated Press, 'Sri Lanka advertises for two hangmen as country resumes capital punishment', *The Guardian*, 14 February 2019, <https://www.theguardian.com/world/2019/feb/14/sri-lanka-advertises-for-two-hangmen-as-country-resumes-capital-punishment>.

50. Gerald D. Robin, 'The Executioner: His Place in English Society', *The British Journal of Sociology*, 15 (3) (1964): 234–53, at 243.

51. Jeffrie G. Murphy, 'People We Hire as Executioners: Who Are They? Who Are We?, *Criminal Justice Ethics*, 35 (2) (2016): 87–99, at 92.

52. See: Gerald D. Robin, 'The Executioner: His Place in English Society', *The British Journal of Sociology*, 15 (3) (1964): 234–53, at 245; Rachel M. MacNair, *Perpetration-Induced Traumatic Stress: The Psychological Consequences of Killing*, Westport, CT: Praeger, 2002: 9.

53. United Nations, *Moving Away from the Death Penalty: Arguments, Trends and Perspectives*, 2nd edn, New York: United Nations, Office of the High Commissioner for Human Rights, 2015: 18.

54. Mike Pearl, 'What it's like to be a death row executioner in America', *Vice*, 27 May 2015, <https://www.vice.com/en/article/bnpxp5/how-do-you-get-a-job-as-an-executioner-in-america-526>.

55. See: Kathryn Westcott, 'How and why Gardner was shot', *BBC News*, 18 June 2010, <http://www.bbc.co.uk/news/10254279>.

56. Gerald D. Robin, 'The Executioner: His Place in English Society', *The British Journal of Sociology*, 15 (3) (1964): 234–53, at 245–46 (emphasis added).

57. Michael J. Osofsky, Albert Bandura and Philip G. Zimbardot, 'The Role of Moral Disengagement in the Execution Process', *Law and Human Behavior* 29 (4) (2005): 371–93, at 386–7.

58. Semon Frank Thompson, 'What I learned from executing two men', *New York Times*, 18 September 2016: SR3.

59. Ibid. SR3.

60. Sarah Macdonald, 'An interview with an executioner', *Daily Life*, 27 March 2012, <http://www.dailylife.com.au/news-and-views/news-features/an-interview-with-an-executioner-20120326-1vu0a.html>.

61. Stephen Sackur, 'Electric chair haunts US former executions chief', *BBC News*, 23 February 2014, <https://www.bbc.co.uk/news/magazine-26273051>.

62. Nancy Sherman, *Stoic Warriors: The Ancient Philosophy behind the Military Mind*, Oxford: Oxford University Press, 2007: 118–19.

63. Shannon E. French, *The Code of the Warrior*, Lanham, MD: Rowman & Littlefield, 2003: 121–22.

64. Nancy Sherman, *The Untold War: Inside the Hearts, Minds, and Souls of Our Soldiers*, New York: Norton, 2010: 107.

65. Timothy Kudo, 'How we learned to kill', *New York Times*, 1 March 2015: SR1 (emphasis added).

66. See: Morten Braender, 'Deployment and Dehumanization: A Multi-Method Study of Combat Soldiers' Loss of Empathy', *Res Militaris*, 5 (2) (2015): 1–18.

67. Katherine Baggaley, Olga Marques and Phillip C. Shon, 'An Exploratory Study of the Decision to Refrain from Killing in the Accounts of Military and Police Personnel', *Journal of Military Ethics*, 18 (1) (2019): 20–34, at 30.

68. Nancy Sherman, *Stoic Warriors: The Ancient Philosophy behind the Military Mind*, Oxford: Oxford University Press, 2007: 121.

69. Katherine Baggaley, Olga Marques and Phillip C. Shon, 'An Exploratory Study of the Decision to Refrain from Killing in the Accounts of Military and Police Personnel', *Journal of Military Ethics*, 18 (1) (2019): 20–34, at 21.

70. Michael Walzer, *Just and Unjust Wars: A Moral Argument with Historical Illustrations*, 4th edn, New York: Basic Books, 2006: 142.

71. Elisabeth Bumiller, 'A day job waiting for a kill shot a world away', *New York Times*, 30 July 2012: A1; Dave Majumdar, 'U.S. drone fleet at "breaking point," Air Force says', *The Daily Beast*, 5 January 2015, <http://www.thedailybeast.com/articles/2015/01/04/exclusive-u-s-drone-fleet-at-breaking-point-air-force-says.html>; Cherie Armour and Jana Ross, 'The Health and Well-Being of Military Drone Operators and Intelligence Analysts: A Systematic Review', *Military Psychology*, 29 (2) (2017): 83–98; Alaa Hijazi, Christopher J. Ferguson, F. Richard Ferraro, Harold Hall, Mark Hovee and Sherrie Wilcox, 'Psychological Dimensions of Drone Warfare', *Current Psychology*, 38 (2019): 1285–96.

72. GAO, *Actions Needed to Strengthen Management of Unmanned Aerial System Pilots* (GAO-14-316), Washington DC: United States Government Accountability Office, 2014: 35; Jeff Schogol, 'Air Force losing more drone pilots than it trains', *Military Times*, 9 January 2015, <http://www.militarytimes.com/story/military/careers/2015/01/09/air-force-losing-drone-pilots/21503301/>; Chaitra M. Hardison, Eyal Aharoni, Christopher Larson, Steven Trochlil and Alexander C. Hou, *Stress and Dissatisfaction in the Air Force's Remotely Piloted Aircraft Community: Focus Group Findings*, Santa Monica, CA: RAND, 2017: xi.

73. Aaron Retica, 'Drone-pilot burnout', *New York Times*, 14 December 2008: MM55.

74. Peter M. Asaro, 'The Labor of Surveillance and Bureaucratized Killing: New Subjectivities of Military Drone Operators', *Social Semiotics*, 23 (2) (2013): 196–224, at 214; Cherie Armour and Jana Ross, 'The Health and Well-Being of Military Drone Operators and Intelligence Analysts: A Systematic Review', *Military Psychology*, 29 (2) (2017): 83–98, at 94.

75. See: Jean L. Otto and Bryant J. Webber, 'Mental Health Diagnoses and Counselling among Pilots of Remotely Piloted Aircraft in the United States Air Force', *Medical Surveillance Monthly Reports* (US Armed Forces Health Surveillance Branch), 20 (3) (2013): 3–8; Wayne L. Chappelle, Tanya Goodman, Laura Reardon and William Thompson, 'An Analysis of

Post-Traumatic Stress Symptoms in United States Air Force Drone Operators', *Journal of Anxiety Disorders*, 28 (2014): 480–7.

76. IMEG, 'The Independent Medical Expert Group (IMEG) 5th Report: Report and recommendations on medical and scientific aspects of the Armed Forces Compensation Scheme', *UK Government*, February 2020, <https://assets.publishing.service.gov.uk/government/uploads/system/uploads/attachment_data/file/865824/20200213_IMEG_FIFTH_REPORT___FINAL_VERSION.pdf>: 2.

77. Ibid. 2.

78. Joseph O. Chapa, 'Remotely Piloted Aircraft, Risk, and Killing as Sacrifice: The Cost of Remote Warfare', *Journal of Military Ethics*, 16 (3–4) (2017): 256–71, at 262.

79. Douglas A. Pryer, 'Moral Injury: What Leaders Don't Mention When They Talk of War', *Army*, 14 August 2014, <http://www.armymagazine.org/2014/08/14/moral-injury-what-leaders-dont-mention-when-they-talk-of-war/>.

80. Nicholas R. Brown, 'Unmanned? The Bodily Harms and Moral Valor of Drone Warfare', in *The Future of Drone Use: Opportunities and Threats from Ethical and Legal Perspectives*, ed. Bart Custers, The Hague: TMC Asser Press, 2016: 189–207, at 203.

81. Laurie Calhoun, *We Kill Because We Can: From Soldiering to Assassination in the Drone Age*, London: Zed Books, 2015: 312.

82. Michelle Bentley, 'Fetishised Data: Counterterrorism, Drone Warfare and Pilot Testimony', *Critical Studies on Terrorism*, 11 (1) (2018): 88–110, at 97.

83. Alison J. Williams, 'Enabling Persistent Presence? Performing the Embodied Geopolitics of the Unmanned Aerial Vehicle Assemblage', *Political Geography*, 30 (2011): 381–90, at 382; Cherie Armour and Jana Ross, 'The Health and Well-Being of Military Drone Operators and Intelligence Analysts: A Systematic Review', *Military Psychology*, 29 (2) (2017): 83–98, at 93.

84. See, for example: Brian Everstine, 'Inside the Air Force's drone operations', *Air Force Times*, 22 June 2015, <https://www.airforcetimes.com/news/your-air-force/2015/06/22/inside-the-air-force-s-drone-operations/>; T. Mark McCurley, 'I was a drone warrior for 11 years. I regret nothing', *Politico Magazine*, 18 October 2015, <https://www.politico.com/magazine/story/2015/10/drone-pilot-book-213263/>.

85. Albert Bandura, 'Disengaging Morality from Robotic War', *The Psychologist* (February 2017): 38–43, at 41–42.

86. Joseph O. Chapa, 'Remotely Piloted Aircraft, Risk, and Killing as Sacrifice: The Cost of Remote Warfare', *Journal of Military Ethics*, 16 (3–4) (2017): 256–71, at 267.

87. Jeffrey S. Bachman and Jack Holland, 'Lethal Sterility: Innovative Dehumanisation in Legal Justifications of Obama's Drone Policy', *The International Journal of Human Rights*, 23 (6) (2019): 1028–47, at 1035–6.

88. Andrew Cockburn, *Kill Chain: Drones and the Rise of High-Tech Assassins*, London: Verso, 2016: 16.

89. Walter Pincus, 'Are drones a technological tipping point in warfare?', *Washington Post*, 24 April 2011, <http://www.washingtonpost.com/world/are-predator-drones-a-technological-tipping-point-in-warfare/2011/04/19/AFmC6PdE_story.html>; Jennifer Robinson, '"Bugsplat": The ugly US drone war in Pakistan', *Al Jazeera*, 29 November 2011, <https://www.aljazeera.com/opinions/2011/11/29/bugsplat-the-ugly-us-drone-war-in-pakistan/>.

90. Lauren Walker, 'Death from above: confessions of a killer drone operator', *Newsweek*, 19 November 2015, <http://europe.newsweek.com/confessions-lethal-drone-operator-396541>.

91. See: Mark Coeckelbergh, 'Drones, Information Technology, and Distance: Mapping the Moral Epistemology of Remote Fighting', *Ethics and Information Technology*, 15 (2013): 87–98, at 97; Alex Edney-Browne, 'Embodiment and Affect in a Digital Age: Understanding Mental Illness among Military Drone Personnel', *Krisis: Journal for Contemporary Philosophy*, Issue 1 (2017): 18–32, at 20; Peter Lee, 'The Distance Paradox: Reaper, the Human Dimension of Remote Warfare, and Future Challenges for the RAF', *Air Power Review*, 21 (3) (2018): 106–30, at 115.

92. Dave Grossman, *On Killing: The Psychological Cost of Learning to Kill in War and Society*, rev. edn, Boston, MA: Back Bay Books, 2009: 97.

93. Ibid. 203.

94. Ibid. 101–2.

95. Ibid. 102.

96. Jesse Kirkpatrick, 'Drones and the Martial Virtue Courage', *Journal of Military Ethics*, 14 (3–4) (2015): 202–19, at 212.

97. Patrick Tucker, 'America's drone pilot shrink says they need a vacation from war', *Defense One*, 18 June 2015, <http://www.defenseone.com/management/2015/06/americas-drone-pilot-shrink-says-they-need-vacation-war/115498/>.

98. Greg Jaffe, 'The watchers: airmen who surveil the Islamic State never get to look away', *Washington Post*, 6 July 2017, <https://www.washingtonpost.com/world/national-security/the-watchers-airmen-who-surveil-the-islamic-state-never-get-to-look-away/2017/07/06/d80c37de-585f-11e7-ba90-f5875b7d1876_story.html>.

99. Nicola Abé, 'Dreams in infrared: the woes of an American drone operator', *Der Spiegel*, 14 December 2012, <http://www.spiegel.de/international/world/pain-continues-after-war-for-american-drone-pilot-a-872726.html>.

100. Elisabeth Bumiller, 'A day job waiting for a kill short a world away', *New York Times*, 30 July 2012: A1.

101. Ernst Jünger, *Storm of Steel*, trans. Michael Hoffman, New York: Penguin, 2004: 234.

102. See: Mark Hookham, '"Killing jihadist fathers is hard": RAF drone pilots reveal stress of taking out targets', *The Sunday Times*, 18 June 2017, <https://www.thetimes.co.uk/article/killing-jihadist-fathers-is-hard-

british-drone-operators-reveal-stress-they-face-in-taking-out-targets-s7pnvfbt2>.

103. See: Drone Pilot (US) interviewed by Daniel Rothenberg, 'It is War at a Very Intimate Level', in *Drone Wars: Transforming Conflict, Law, and Policy*, ed. Peter L. Bergen and Daniel Rothenberg, New York: Cambridge University Press, 2015: 113–28, at 115; Peter Lee, *Reaper Force: The Inside Story of Britain's Drone Wars*, London: John Blake, 2019: 179.

104. Paul T. Berghaus and Nathan L. Cartagena, 'Developing Good Soldiers: The Problem of Fragmentation within the Army', *Journal of Military Ethics*, 12 (4) (2013): 287–303, at 290.

105. Nancy Sherman, *The Untold War: Inside the Hearts, Minds, and Souls of Our Soldiers*, New York: Norton, 2011: 4.

106. Nancy Sherman, *Stoic Warriors: The Ancient Philosophy behind the Military Mind*, Oxford: Oxford University Press, 2007: 121.

107. See: Will Pavia, 'Diary of a drone pilot', *The Times*, 23 April 2016, <https://www.thetimes.co.uk/article/diary-of-a-drone-pilot-wfg50mkb7>; Vin Ray, 'The US Air Force's commuter drone warriors', *BBC News*, 8 January 2017, <https://www.bbc.co.uk/news/magazine-38506932>.

108. M. Shane Riza, 'Two-Dimensional Warfare: Combatants, Warriors, and Our Post-Predator Collective Experience', *Journal of Military Ethics*, 13 (3) (2014): 257–73, at 262 and 264.

109. M. Shane Riza, *Killing without Heart: Limits on Robotic Warfare in an Age of Persistent Conflict*, Washington, DC: Potomac Books, 2013: 96.

110. Alaa Hijazi, Christopher J. Ferguson, F. Richard Ferraro, Harold Hall, Mark Hovee and Sherrie Wilcox, 'Psychological Dimensions of Drone Warfare', *Current Psychology*, 38 (2019): 1285–96, at 1288.

111. Robert Jay Lifton, 'The Dimensions of Contemporary War and Violence: How to Reclaim Humanity from a Continuing Revolution in the Technology of Killing', *Bulletin of the Atomic Scientists*, 69 (4) (2013): 9–17, at 15.

112. Grégoire Chamayou, *Drone Theory*, trans. Janet Lloyd, London: Penguin, 2015: 121.

113. Thomas Gibbons-Neff, 'Killing and the drone warrior', *War on the Rocks*, 6 November 2013, <http://warontherocks.com/2013/11/killing-and-the-drone-warrior/>.

114. Martin L. Cook, *The Moral Warrior: Ethics and Service in the U.S. Military*, Albany, NY: State University of New York Press, 2004: 123.

115. Ibid. 123–4.

116. D. Keith Shurtleff, 'The Effects of Technology on Our Humanity', *Parameters* (Summer 2002): 100–12, at 107.

117. Christopher Coker, *Waging War without Warriors? The Changing Culture of Military Conflict*, Boulder, CO: Lynne Rienner, 2002: 68.

118. Scott Beauchamp, 'Can drone pilots be heroes?', *The Atlantic*, 23 January 2016, <https://www.theatlantic.com/politics/archive/2016/01/can-drone-pilots-be-heroes/424830/>.

119. Peter Lee, 'Remoteness, Risk and Aircrew Ethos', *Air Power Review*, 15 (1) (2015): 1–19, at 16.

120. Peter Lee, 'The Distance Paradox: Reaper, the Human Dimension of Remote Warfare, and Future Challenges for the RAF', *Air Power Review*, 21 (3) (2018): 106–30, at 118.

121. Elisabeth Bumiller, 'Air Force drone operators report high levels of stress', *New York Times*, 19 December 2011: A8.

122. Paul D. Shinkman, 'Military stalls on efforts to repair drone troubles depicted in "good kill"', *U.S. News and World Report*, 13 May 2015, <http://www.usnews.com/news/articles/2015/05/13/military-stalls-on-efforts-to-repair-drone-pilots-troubles>.

123. Joseph O. Chapa, 'Remotely Piloted Aircraft, Risk, and Killing as Sacrifice: The Cost of Remote Warfare', *Journal of Military Ethics*, 16 (3–4) (2017): 256–71, at 267 and 263.

124. See: Caroline Moorhead, *Dunant's Dream: War, Switzerland and the History of the Red Cross*, London: Harper Collins, 1998.

125. Jesse Kirkpatrick, 'State Responsibility and Drone Operators', in *Drones and Responsibility: Legal, Philosophical, and Sociotechnical Perspectives on Remotely Controlled Weapons*, ed. Ezio Di Nucci and Filippo Santoni de Sio, London and New York: Routledge, 2016: 101–16, at 102.

126. See: Charles C. Moskos and Frank R. Wood (ed.), *The Military: More Than Just a Job?* Oxford: Pergamon-Brassey's, 1988.

127. Ned Dobos, 'War as a Workplace: Ethical Implications of the Occupational Shift', *Journal of Military Ethics*, 18 (3) (2019): 248–60, at 250.

128. See: Malcolm Braithwaite, Graeme Nicholson, Rob Thornton, David Jones, Robin Simpson, David McLoughin and David Jenkins, 'Armed Forces Occupational Health – A Review', *Occupational Medicine*, 59 (8) (2009): 528–38; Martin Bricknell and Paul Cain, 'Understanding the Whole of Military Health Systems: The Defence Healthcare Cycle', *RUSI Journal*, 165 (3) (2020): 40–9, at 45.

129. Bradley J. Strawser, 'Moral Predators: The Duty to Employ Uninhabited Aerial Vehicles', *Journal of Military Ethics*, 9 (4) (2010): 342–68, at 344.

130. Ibid. 348.

131. Wayne Chappelle, Kent McDonald and Katharine McMillan, *Important and Critical Psychological Attributes of USAF MQ-1 Predator and MQ-9 Reaper Pilots According to Subject Matter Experts* (AFRL-SA-WP-TR-2011-0002), Air Force Research Laboratory, May 2011: 1.

132. Cherie Armour and Jana Ross, 'The Health and Well-Being of Military Drone Operators and Intelligence Analysts: A Systematic Review', *Military Psychology*, 29 (2) (2017): 83–98, at 94.

133. Peter M. Asaro, 'The Labor of Surveillance and Bureaucratized Killing: New Subjectivities of Military Drone Operators', *Social Semiotics*, 23 (2) (2013): 196–224, at 197.

134. IMEG, 'The Independent Medical Expert Group (IMEG) 5th Report: Report and recommendations on medical and scientific aspects of the Armed Forces Compensation Scheme', *UK Government*, February 2020, <https://assets.publishing.service.gov.uk/government/uploads/system/

uploads/attachment_data/file/865824/20200213_IMEG_FIFTH_
REPORT__FINAL_VERSION.pdf>: 1.

135. Jesse Kirkpatrick, 'State Responsibility and Drone Operators', in *Drones and Responsibility: Legal, Philosophical, and Sociotechnical Perspectives on Remotely Controlled Weapons*, ed. Ezio Di Nucci and Filippo Santoni de Sio, London and New York: Routledge, 2016: 101–16, at 109.

136. Alaa Hijazi, Christopher J. Ferguson, F. Richard Ferraro, Harold Hall, Mark Hovee and Sherrie Wilcox, 'Psychological Dimensions of Drone Warfare', *Current Psychology*, 38 (2019): 1285–96, at 1286 and 1287.

137. Sara Reardon, 'I spy, with my faraway eye', *New Scientist*, (26 January 2013): 46–9, at 48.

138. Brian Everstine, 'Inside the Air Force's drone operations', *Air Force Times*, 22 June 2015, <https://www.airforcetimes.com/news/your-air-force/2015/06/22/inside-the-air-force-s-drone-operations/>.

139. See: Tine Molendijk, Eric-Hans Kramer and Désirée Verweij, 'Moral Aspects of "Moral Injury": Analyzing Conceptualizations on the Role of Morality in Military Trauma', *Journal of Military Ethics*, 17 (1) (2018): 36–53, at 38.

140. See: Robert Jay Lifton, *Home from the War: Learning from Vietnam Veterans*, New York: Other Press, 2005: 166; Laurie Calhoun, 'The Silencing of Soldiers', *The Independent Review*, 16 (2) (2011): 247–70, at 264.

141. See: Eyal Press, 'The Wounds of the Drone Warrior', *New York Times*, 13 June 2018, <https://www.nytimes.com/2018/06/13/magazine/veterans-ptsd-drone-warrior-wounds.html>.

142. Stephen Coleman, *Military Ethics: An Introduction with Case Studies*, New York: Oxford University Press, 2013: 272. See also: Christopher Toner, 'Military Service as a Practice: Integrating the Sword and Shield Approaches to Military Ethics', *Journal of Military Ethics*, 5 (3) (2006): 183–200.

143. Eyal Press, 'The wounds of the drone warrior', *New York Times*, 13 June 2018, <https://www.nytimes.com/2018/06/13/magazine/veterans-ptsd-drone-warrior-wounds.html>; Lucy Fisher, 'Soldiers get lessons in morality of drone killings', *The Times*, 25 September 2018, <https://www.thetimes.co.uk/article/soldiers-get-lessons-in-morality-of-drone-killings-52zqt2ckc>.

144. Chris Cole, '"It was incessant." Former RAF Reaper pilot speaks to *Drone Wars*', *Drone Wars*, 30 May 2017, <https://dronewars.net/2017/05/30/justin-thompson-interview/>; Peter Lee, 'Drone crews and moral engagement', *The Psychologist*, June 2017, <https://thepsychologist.bps.org.uk/volume-30/june-2017/drone-crews-and-moral-engagement>.

145. Joe Chapa, 'Inside Britain's Reaper force: human stories and ethical dilemmas', *War on the Rocks*, 18 October 2018, <https://warontherocks.com/2018/10/inside-britains-reaper-force-human-stories-and-ethical-dilemmas/>.

146. Shannon E. French, Victoria Sisk and Caroline Bass, 'Drones, Honor, and Fragmented Sovereignty', in *The Ethics of War and Peace Revisited*, ed. Daniel R. Brunstetter and Jean-Vincent Holeindre, Washington, DC: Georgetown University Press, 2018: 201–19, at 216.

147. Janina Dill, 'The Informal Regulation of Drones and the Formal Legal Regulation of War', *Ethics and International Affairs* 29 (1) (2015): 51–8, at 53.
148. See: Peter Olsthoorn, 'Ethics for Drone Operators: Rules versus Virtues', in *Ethics of Drone Strikes: Restraining Remote-Control Killing*, ed. Christian Enemark, Edinburgh: Edinburgh University Press, 2021: 115–29, at 120.
149. See: Peter Lee, 'Remoteness, Risk and Aircrew Ethos', *Air Power Review*, 15 (1) (2012): 1–19, at 17; Grégoire Chamayou, *Drone Theory*, trans. Janet Lloyd, London: Penguin, 2015: 102; Jesse Kirkpatrick, 'Drones and the Martial Virtue Courage', *Journal of Military Ethics*, 14 (3–4) (2015): 202–19, at 211.

Chapter 6

DEVOLVED VIOLENCE

In 2014 a USAF officer named Michael Byrnes, who then had over 2,000 hours of experience operating MQ-1 (Predator) and MQ-9 (Reaper) drones, published his ideas about a hypothetical aircraft (FQ-X) which could bring 'unmatched lethality to air-to-air combat'.[1] Freed from the remote-control of human pilots in ground stations, the purpose of this 'machine-piloted aircraft' would be 'to find and destroy enemy aircraft'.[2] Incorporating 'computer vision software' to 'positively identify the target', the FQ-X itself would execute 'the underlying mathematical truths of what human combat pilots do in the cockpit, doing so more quickly and with more precision'.[3]

Byrnes' vision at the time was of a future in which control of drone violence had passed from humans to artificial intelligence (AI), and the technology that might enable such a change has since been advancing. In late 2018 increasing capacities to apply AI for violent purposes prompted European Commission vice-president Federica Mogherini to observe that '[w]e are entering a world where drones could independently search for a target and kill without human intervention'.[4] Then, less than two years later, a technological breakthrough was achieved: an AI fighter pilot virtually 'killed' a human fighter pilot. In August 2020 the US Defense Advanced Research Projects Agency had organised the AlphaDogfight contest to demonstrate the potential for AI to perform critical military tasks that are ordinarily performed by humans. In one demonstration, an algorithm controlling an F-16 fighter aircraft in virtual reality (VR) competed with a real F-16 pilot using a VR headset and a simulated set of F-16 controls. The notional aircraft under AI control was repeatedly able to outmanoeuvre and 'destroy' the human's aircraft with a well-timed and long-distance shot, showing clearly (in theory) that an AI system is capable of prevailing in a 'dogfight' even against highly trained humans.[5]

It is currently far from clear, however, whether such a capability would be ethically acceptable if it were ever to become a reality in world affairs. The violent use of aircraft without a human controller on board is a practice that already generates serious ethical challenges associated with physical human–machine distancing. Beyond that, if humans were to become further 'distanced' from drone violence by a technology-driven reduction in their control over it, this development too could arguably become a source of injustice. Accordingly, in this chapter attention turns to the morality of drone violence conceptualised as violence devolved from humans to AI.

For present purposes, the key characteristic of an armed drone is that it is a multifunction system. Within this system, certain 'critical' functions (for example target identification and fire control) relate to violence and thus are especially significant from an ethical perspective. Other, less significant functions (for example take-off, landing and aerial manoeuvring) are already able to be performed by AI in some experimental drone systems. For example, the X-47B (made by Northrup Grumman) has been able to perform tasks by itself that are difficult for human pilots (aerial refuelling and landing on an aircraft carrier),[6] and the MQ-20 Avenger (made by General Atomics) has performed 'basic aviation behaviors . . . while reacting to geo-fences' under the control of the USAF's AI-based Skyborg system.[7] In addition, there is now a reasonable prospect of AI also controlling or dominating the function of deciding whether or how to apply violence. And, as some governments have continued to pursue plans to incorporate more and better AI technology into various weapon systems, this has fuelled an ethical debate among scholars and policymakers about how to respond.

The chapter begins with an explanation of what 'devolving' drone violence from humans to AI means, and then situates this potential development within the ongoing ethical debate about 'lethal autonomous weapon systems'. A critical issue in that debate is whether any system can or should incorporate ethical decision-making by AI (functioning as an artificial moral agent), but progress has arguably been inhibited by confusion over the meaning of 'autonomous'. In response, the chapter outlines an alternative, differentiated approach to the ethical assessment of armed drones incorporating AI, based upon the emergent principle of 'meaningful human control'. It is an approach that focuses on the performance (by humans or AI) of functions within weapon systems, and it involves assessing AI function-performance as an enabler of drone violence against human and non-human targets, for different purposes, in armed conflict or law enforcement circumstances.

DEVOLVING DRONE VIOLENCE TO ARTIFICIAL INTELLIGENCE

In contrast to dystopic fantasies about machines seizing power from humans (for example the *Terminator* scenario),[8] a common idea in recent literature addressing AI and violence is that humans *choose* to empower AI. Some authors have called this a process of 'delegating' to AI some of the powers and functions ordinarily controlled by humans,[9] but the notion of devolving control is arguably more useful because it better describes something that can occur in degrees. That is, as in matters of government, the devolution of functions within a multifunction system can be either partially or completely achieved. If every governmental function were devolved to a substate territorial authority within a larger state's territory, that would amount to complete devolution (the granting of independence). A more familiar arrangement, however, is the devolving of some functions and the reserving of others. The idea of devolution is usually understood in the context of the governance of a sovereign territory comprising multiple region-based identities. Under the United Kingdom's current devolution settlement, for example, some governmental functions (including health, policing and education) are devolved from the UK government to the Northern Irish, Scottish and Welsh governments, while other functions (including defence and foreign policy) are reserved. Moreover, such partial devolution is open to be understood either as an endpoint or as a pathway towards the eventual granting of full governmental control.

Similarly, in a technological system (such as a weapon system) comprising multiple functions which might each be (or become) performable either by a human or AI, devolution can involve the performance by AI of one, some or all functions previously performed by humans. Incorporating AI *into* a system does not necessarily render the *whole* of that system AI-controlled, and what it usually achieves is the establishment of a new distribution of function-performance roles among the AI and human elements of the system. This is to assume, though, a 'narrow' (functional) notion of AI. Consistent with the current reality that most AI research aims to 'provide useful tools',[10] AI is understood here as a technology for substituting human control of a specific function with control by a narrowly intelligent machine (qua information-processor). The broader notion of a single AGI (artificial general intelligence) entity, exhibiting 'human-level' intelligence and independently controlling a complex combination of functions, is highly speculative and thus is less relevant to the present discussion.[11]

Among the many types of weapon systems in the world that might incorporate AI technology to some degree, armed drones deserve special attention. For at least two reasons, they are likely to be prioritised for AI incorporation, especially when it comes to the use of violence on an air-to-air basis. First, from an operational perspective, securing dominance of the air domain is always a priority, and incorporating one or more AI elements within a drone-based weapon system might afford a critical advantage to that end. Assuming that some governments will continue sometimes to prefer using armed drones over placing on-board human pilots at risk, AI incorporation seems likely to be seen as a way of increasing the resilience and effectiveness of an armed drone (for example by making it faster and more manoeuvrable) in a contested aerial environment. This is fundamentally important because, once air control has been fought for and secured, any surface-based weapon systems (on land or at sea) are spared the risk of enemy attack from above, and it also enables other air power roles (strike, transportation and surveillance) to be performed without aerial interference.

The second reason for prioritising drones for AI incorporation is tied more closely to ethical concerns, and it relates to the relatively 'uncluttered' nature of the air domain. To the extent that incorporating AI into a weapon system brings or increases the risk of causing unintended harm, the open sky is a relatively low-risk and ethically less complicated environment in the sense that it typically contains very few humans. Something could go wrong when deploying an experimental AI technology intended to enhance, for example, a drone's ability to evade or strike airborne enemy assets (personnel or materiel). However, any damage caused during such deployment would probably be less than if a new AI technology were incorporated into a ground-based weapon system designed to operate in the land domain where potential human victims are generally more plentiful.

Unless or until AGI technology emerges, incorporating AI into a drone-based weapon system will continue to involve assembling different types of narrow AI technology that are tailored to particular functions within the system. Those functions fall into five categories of capability for an armed drone. In the category of *mobility* (the ability to govern and direct a system's motion within its environment), AI might perform a take-off, navigation or collision-avoidance function. *Health management* (the ability to manage system functioning and survival) might include AI performance of a fault detection or self-repair function. *Interoperability* (the ability for the system to collaborate with other machines or humans) might involve AI performance of a mass coordination (drone swarming) function. In the category of *intelligence* (ability to collect and process relevant data), AI might perform data collection or data analysis. And *use of force* (the ability to search for, identify, track, select or attack targets) might involve the devolution, from a human to AI, of control over a target-detection, target-selection or fire-control function for a particular on-board weapon.[12]

For present purposes, the capability categories of intelligence and use of force are of greatest relevance because the various functions therein relate most directly to the potential devolution of drone *violence*. Moreover, when considering the possibility of AI incorporation, it is important to acknowledge that such violence is not a single act but rather a multifunction process. This is reflected, for example, in the USAF concept of a 'kill chain', known also as 'F2T2EA' ('find, fix, track, target, engage, and assess').[13] The chain describes a sequence of steps that is followed before and after striking targets, and it provides a structure for thinking about the placement of human or AI function-performers at each step of the process. To 'find' is to find a target within surveillance or reconnaissance data, or using other intelligence means. To 'fix' is to obtain specific coordinates for the target either from existing data or by collecting additional data. To 'track' is to keep track of the target until either a decision is made not to 'engage' the target, or the target is in fact engaged. To 'target' is to select an appropriate weapon to use on the target to create a desired effect, and then to assess the value of the target and the availability of appropriate weapons. To 'engage' is to use the weapon against the target. And to 'assess' is to evaluate, using intelligence means, the effects of the engagement.[14]

From an operational perspective, a desire to devolve some pre-violence and violence-enabling functions from humans to AI is understandable in the light of at least four factors: personnel, speed, communication and data. Although an armed drone flies without a pilot on board, a large number of people on the ground can be involved in sustaining its operation,[15] and for the USAF especially this has persistently presented a serious staffing challenge. Despite heavy demand from US ground commanders for drone overflights in support of deployed soldiers, recruiting and retaining drone operators has sometimes been difficult.[16] Thus, the prospect of being able to achieve the same military benefits with fewer personnel – because more functions within a drone system would be performed by AI instead – is one that understandably appeals to some commanders.

Even so, human contributors to a weapon system can be perceived as a problem not only because they are scarce but also because they are *human*. Here, one concern is that the cognitive limits of the human brain (as a processor of information) might in future 'delay' the operation of a system when there is an operational imperative to keep outpacing an enemy. AI could seem like an attractive substitute, then, if it afforded a capacity for performing a certain function at superhuman speed.[17] For example, a drone with an AI-controlled manoeuvre function might be valued for its ability to execute an evasive response to an incoming missile more quickly than could an on-board pilot or a ground-based controller.

Moreover, from this perspective, the ability to achieve further increases in operational speed (by devolving more functions to AI) would become increasingly significant if an enemy too were using a weapon system that similarly incorporated AI.[18]

A third operational factor driving support for devolution to AI is the current challenge of maintaining communication (via satellite) between armed drones and their distanced operators. One downside of removing a pilot from an aircraft is that *remote* control is more vulnerable to being lost or compromised, potentially leading to crashes and mission failures. However, that vulnerability could in theory be overcome if enough functions were devolved to on-board AI technologies so that, in the event of a communication breakdown, an armed drone could carry on flying a mission. Or, if a commander simply wished to avoid *trying* to maintain communication in an environment that made this difficult, they might be attracted to the idea of having AI obviate any need for the 'tethering' (by data links) of drones to human operators.[19]

Lastly, there is the matter of the data itself which, if collected in vast quantities by drone-mounted cameras (and other sensors), must be transmitted, analysed and exploited. Here, devolution could seem like an attractive remedy to a self-inflicted and risk-laden problem of information overload.[20] In devolving intelligence-related functions from humans to AI, a drone-user might hope to make data analysis timelier and exploitation of analyses more effective. For example, one idea is that AI could somehow be rapidly applied to cross-checking imagery of a person's face (captured by a drone's camera) against a database of 'suspected terrorist' face images.[21] Indeed, former US Deputy Defense Secretary Bob Work appears to have had such capabilities in mind when, in 2017, he established Project Maven and directed it to 'rapidly develop and field technology to automate the processing, exploitation, and dissemination . . . of data from tactical-scale drones and full motion video from Predator and Reaper systems in support of US military operations'.[22] The following year, however, Project Maven lost a major corporate partner (Google) when its employees (including many AI engineers) publicly objected, on moral grounds, to helping the US military conduct drone strikes.[23] On this occasion, a concern for the operational utility of AI had collided with a concern for its ethical application.

ETHICAL DEBATE OVER 'LETHAL AUTONOMOUS WEAPON SYSTEMS'

For the purpose of morally assessing the devolution of drone violence functions from humans to AI, a useful starting point is the broader and ongoing controversy over so-called 'lethal autonomous weapon systems' (LAWS). The debate about whether or how AI should be combined with violence (drone-based or otherwise) has, in recent years, been pursued most prominently in formal diplomatic meetings. These have been convened in Geneva, Switzerland, under the auspices of the 1980 Convention on Prohibitions or Restrictions on the Use of Certain Conventional Weapons Which May be Deemed to be Excessively Injurious or to Have Indiscriminate Effects (the Convention on Certain Convention Weapons, or 'CCW'). In December 2016, at the Fifth CCW Review Conference, representatives of member states decided to establish 'an open-ended Group of Governmental Experts (GGE) related to emerging technologies in the area of lethal autonomous weapons systems (LAWS) in the context of the objectives and purposes of the Convention'.[24] Since then, at meetings held from late 2017 onwards, discussions at GGE meetings have traversed a range of issues that had earlier been brought to public attention by human rights lawyers and arms control activists calling for the legal regulation or prohibition of LAWS.[25] Before that, however, an ethical debate among academics had begun in which proponents of machine 'autonomy' in weapon systems have generally claimed that this will produce ethically better outcomes than those expected when humans retain control over violence. Opponents have usually insisted that weapons can only be sufficiently restrained by the exercise of human moral agency.[26]

The debate is driven by different and possibly irreconcilable understandings of what it means to be ethical and to achieve moral progress, and it has often focused on the performance of the most morally significant function when it comes to state violence: decision-making. Contributors who are agency-focused tend to argue that only *humans* are capable of making moral decisions, and contributors who are outcome-focused tend to be open to the idea that AI involvement might result in *better* moral decisions overall. Vincent Boulanin and his colleagues have highlighted this divide in the context of international humanitarian law (IHL) rules (derived from military ethics principles), observing that there are diverging deontological and consequentialist perspectives on what the fundamental purpose of IHL is. The first perspective emphasises the importance of 'ensuring the non-delegable role of humans in . . . deliberative processes' because they are essential to IHL rule-adherence.[27] And the second perspective deemphasises rule-adherence by agents (human or AI) in favour of maximising 'the avoidance of unlawful effects'.[28] Accordingly, the 'regime' of IHL is either to be approached as one that '*mandates* evaluations and judgements by human beings in the conduct of military operations' or as 'solely an effects-based regime, *permitting* militaries to use any combination of humans and machines to undertake military action as long as the anticipated or actual effects are not unlawful'.[29]

The consequentialist case for using LAWS (in which AI performs the decision-making function) is simple and intuitively appealing: it could reduce the risk of injustices resulting from state violence. Given humans' historically poor record of adhering to relevant ethical principles, it seems plausible not only that AI could somehow be made to do a better job of this but also that states have a duty to allow and pursue such moral improvement for the benefit of potential victims in the future. Whereas the committing of atrocities is often driven by humans' physical and emotional responses to violence, so the argument goes, AI would be incapable of feeling these responses (such as fear and anger) and so would be less likely overall than humans are to generate unjust effects. Keith Abney, for example, has highlighted 'bloodlust' and desires for 'revenge' as being among 'human characteristics that lead to war crimes'.[30] Ron Arkin has argued, therefore, that 'lethal autonomous unmanned systems . . . will potentially be capable of performing more ethically on the battlefield than are human soldiers'.[31] And, with regard to the problem of 'excessive use of force' in law enforcement, Michael McGuire has suggested that automated 'policebots' could bypass the 'emotion, bias . . . and other human frailties' which 'distort [police] performance – often with tragic results'.[32]

In approaching an unpredictable future, these and all other consequentialist claims remain open to contestation. For example, one outcome-focused counterargument is that, even if the introduction of AI-controlled violence demonstrably caused a reduction of unjust harms on an incident-by-incident basis, this benefit might yet be outweighed by the harm of an AI-driven increase in the overall risk of violence occurring in the world. Such an objection to LAWS reflects a fear that, if AI were to increase the tempo of attack and defence dynamics beyond humans' capacity to comprehend, violent conflicts would be more likely to escalate quickly, to the overall detriment of stability and peace worldwide.[33] On consequentialist grounds, one could also criticise the 'superior performance' justification for replacing humans with AI as one that carries the potential for *lowering* the standard of acceptable ethical conduct in the exercise of state violence. LAWS proponents tend to use as their moral benchmark the record of human frailty rather than the potential for human improvement. So, if the ethical standard of violent human behaviour were to decline in the future (hastened perhaps by an AI-induced moral deskilling effect), there would be room (according to proponents' logic) to tolerate a deterioration in the relative 'performance' of LAWS too.

In any ethical debate, countervailing consequentialist claims are by nature difficult to substantiate and reconcile. Even if introducing AI into weapon systems can reasonably be anticipated to usher in some moral improvement, this is clearly not the only pathway for reducing human-authored injustices in the world,[34] and it might not turn out to be the best way. Setting anticipated outcomes aside, however, opponents of LAWS have also deployed deontological arguments, and here again the focus has been on AI performance of a weapon system's decision-making function. Such performance, it is argued, would in principle (and thus in all circumstances) be morally unacceptable for one or more of three reasons: to be killed by AI would offend human dignity; AI is incapable of moral agency; and AI cannot bear moral responsibility for wrongdoing.

The making of dignity-based argument against LAWS sometimes begins with the intuition that there is something 'morally repugnant' about the idea of affording machines a discretion to kill humans.[35] This potential and purported substitution of agency is regarded as a problem by those who suggest, for example, that the very minimum of respect a prospective human victim deserves is to have 'another human' decide to harm them.[36] Were this not to occur, because AI had instead performed that function, killing would have become no more respectful than 'setting a mousetrap'[37] and treating human beings 'like vermin'.[38] Robert Sparrow has gone so far as to argue that '[k]illing people with robots would be disrespectful in (roughly) *the same way* that – but to a much *higher degree* than – spitting or urinating on people would be or . . . mutilating their corpses would be'.[39] However, the drawing of such comparisons raises the questions of whether or why the involvement of AI in lethal decision-making is *more* offensive to human dignity than any other mode of killing. Other authors have suggested that it is not,[40] in which case dignity-based arguments do not weigh more heavily against LAWS in particular. So, it might rather be more accurate to claim that violence per se is degrading and that violence in any form, when applied contrary to a person's desire to remain unharmed, is what essentially violates human dignity to some or other degree.

Other objections to LAWS focus instead on the inherent capacities of AI and humans to exercise moral agency. Capacity-based objections tend to be based on the claim that any promise of AI performing 'ethically' is a non-starter because only *humans* can ever exercise moral judgement, choose whether to act in accordance with ethical requirements, and then be meaningful recipients of praise or blame. To the contrary, some authors have considered the general possibility of artificial moral agents,[41] and this has sometimes extended to suggestions that it might become more appropriate to conceptualise LAWS as warriors rather than as weapons. Such agents have accordingly been foreshadowed, for example, as an emergent 'class of combatants'[42] and as 'warfighters who are no longer merely human'.[43] However, the notion of AI being a *moral agent* (be it involved in violence or not) can be challenged on metaethical grounds. Such a notion necessarily relies on the assertion that moral properties are reducible to physical properties. And, relatedly, it purports to reduce 'ethics' itself to a radically thin concept.

As a matter of metaethics, an ethical 'naturalist' is open to reducing a moral property to a physical property. For example, a hedonist reduces 'goodness' to pleasure, such that their *feeling* of pleasure is at once a physical and morally desirable condition. But a 'non-naturalist' insists, by contrast, that moral properties exist independently of the natural world and are not reducible to anything that can be physically sensed.[44] This distinction is relevant to the LAWS debate because proponents of AI incorporation sometimes put great store in processes of sensing, measuring and calculating, when they are offering a justification.

In some predictions of how AI will 'behave ethically' in wartime, the achieving of *in bello* discrimination (between legitimate and illegitimate targets) is discussed in terms of the sensing (using cameras, laser scanners and/or other tools) of entities and phenomena in an environment of potential violence. One idea is that armed drones could incorporate 'machine vision' AI technology which is programmed, trained or enabled to learn not to target protected symbols (like the red cross) or small-statured people (like children).[45] Or AI could be tasked to distinguish, in video footage, an unarmed civilian from a motorcyclist carrying a machine gun.[46] Or AI could target 'enemy' weapons of a recognised type (like AK-47 rifles) which are presumed to be in the hands of hostile (targetable) individuals. In each such instance, however, AI would not be discriminating *morally* because it would not also be making contextual judgements, as a human agent would.[47] Merely sensing a thing which has the size and shape of a rifle, for example, does not involve judging who (what kind of person) is carrying that rifle and why (for what kind of purpose). Such judgement is an inherently imprecise rather than physically determinate thing, and it is also essentially reflective in the sense that it brings to bear both learned ideas and lived experiences.[48] The morality of a situation-in-context is thus only partially captured when dealing only with physical properties that stand as nonmoral proxies for moral requirements. Genuinely *moral* discrimination by AI alone is impossible, then, because the critical element of judgement is missing, and this irreducibility of moral properties to physical properties is arguably what makes AI-driven 'discrimination' impermissible.

When it comes to the principle of *in bello* proportionality, the purported exercise of moral agency by AI relies on an assumption that ethics is computable. One idea is that AI could be tasked with 'properly computing the minimal force necessary for military success',[49] which fits with a broader notion that increasing decision speed in the military requires the components of a decision to be 'computationally tractable'.[50] This would involve reducing 'to numbers' the alternative decisions available, the relevant possible results of decisions, the likelihood of each result, and the relative value of each result.[51] The proportionality principle would thus be approached as a kind of 'moral arithmetic',[52] with correct ethical conduct arrived at through 'algorithmic reasoning'.[53] From a scientific perspective, however, 'mathematical simplification' for the sake of computational tractability runs the risk, when tasking AI to find solutions to problems, of constructing 'an unrealistic . . . search space'.[54] An enduring reality which is bypassed in any strictly numerical approach to a proportionality challenge is the incommensurability of qualitatively different values (for example human lives and military objectives) to be counted and compared by a decision-maker. On this argument, judgement (about the instrumental and inherent worth of competing values) is, again, held to be an essential element of moral agency. And, as this element cannot be captured by AI (which is capable only of computation), it follows that 'doing' proportionality requires a human, and that non-human (AI) adherence to this principle is impossible to achieve.

Further to the issue of AI capacity for moral agency, another reason offered for rejecting the idea of an artificial moral agent is that this idea would impoverish the meaning of morality itself. That is, if the element of judgement were removed from our understanding of what it means to behave 'ethically' (such that the exercising of moral agency was reduced to abstraction and calculation), this would unhelpfully deny the essential contestability of ethics.[55] A thin concept of ethics could well appeal to an engineer or user of AI because it would seem to make the challenge of being 'ethical' more tractable.[56] However, it might not take long, then, for attempts by AI to 'do the right thing' (while denying the contestability of ethics) to run into trouble. Suppose, for example, that the rightness or wrongness of an AI decision were considered only to be a matter of following or violating rules, respectively. Even if such 'rules' as discrimination and proportionality were able to be encoded within a machine's operating system, a particular situation might yet prove that achieving good behaviour does not equate to rule-following.

In some situations where competing values are at stake, it will appear to be the case that both following *and* violating a rule will lead to a bad outcome. This problem of 'moral dilemmas' can often arise in war, for example, due to the irreconcilable tensions that exist between deontological and consequentialist modes of moral reasoning within military ethics.[57] Alternatively, good behaviour might be difficult to equate to

rule-following because a particular rule is itself unethical, either in principle or under certain circumstances. Here, the breaking of a rule can be
considered a good action because it is the *virtuous* thing to do. Throughout military history rule-breaking has occasionally taken the form of
disobeying orders or even betraying a leader for the sake of a greater
good, and it has taken moral courage for a person to do this.[58] Also,
people have sometimes refrained from doing what a rule permits them
to do (for example killing an enemy soldier) and have instead exhibited
the virtues of compassion and mercy towards a fellow human being.
Such transcendence of a rules-based concept of ethics can sometimes
be morally admirable in practice. And yet, as some opponents of LAWS
have argued, it is a form of goodness that is beyond the capacity of AI
to achieve.[59] For all that greater AI incorporation might seem to promise
a moral gain (increased civilian protection), there could also be a loss of
moral opportunity (to be virtuous) when humans are doing less.

Lastly, in the ethical debate over LAWS, there is the issue of AI capacity to bear moral responsibility. Some scholars have warned that the
reduction or removal of human involvement in decisions about violence
would render impossible the apportioning of blame and the administering of punishment for any wrongdoing.[60] That is, if AI cannot ever plausibly be held responsible, and if sometimes there is also no human who
can fairly be blamed, the danger then is that a responsibility gap emerges
whereby injustices caused by LAWS are able to occur and recur with
impunity. In the absence of any real moral agency being brought to bear
upon a situation, no wrong (or right) *acts* would be *done*; rather, '[t]
hings' would 'just happen'.[61] If a deployed AI technology was designed
to adapt its operation to a changing environment, that very unreliability
could render it impossible and unfair to ascribe blame for any wrongdoing to the humans who originally designed that technology.[62] Or, if an
AI technology being used by a military commander could not be shown
to be under their effective control when an injustice occurred, assigning
blame to that commander would likewise be a problem.[63]

Alex Leveringhaus has even suggested that incorporating AI into
armed drones could 'essentially take us back to a pre-Nuremberg
world'.[64] The now-defunct legal defence that 'I am not to blame for
wrongdoing because I only followed orders' would be replaced, he has
argued, by 'a similar defence: "I am not to blame because the drone did
it"'.[65] Alternatively, a human who is not genuinely responsible for the AI
performance of a function (because they cannot cognitively comprehend
such performance) could nevertheless be designated as a scapegoat for
any injustice caused, though here again the problem of a responsibility
gap would endure. Moreover, even if the blameworthiness of AI could

somehow be made plausible in theory,[66] the consequent requirement of punishment could never be fulfilled in practice. After all, *taking* moral responsibility means receiving praise and reward for good conduct or receiving criticism and punishment for wrongdoing. However, unless a 'culpable' AI technology were to become treated as a moral patient (by virtue of being sentient and able to suffer),[67] punishment of an unembodied entity would seem to be unavailable as a way for the victims of unjust harm to achieve 'meaningful retributive justice'.[68]

In the face of these various ethical objections to the idea of AI agency in state practices of violence, no government participating in the diplomatic debate over LAWS has unambiguously advocated the full devolution (from humans to AI) of weapon system functions. Some official pronouncements appear to leave room for a policy shift in that direction. For example, the US Defense Department stated in a 2018 report that it 'does not *currently* have an autonomous weapon system that can search for, identify, track, select, and engage targets independent of a human operator's input'.[69] However, even if such a high degree of devolution to AI never occurs, the use of a weapon system (such as an armed drone) that incorporates AI might still be morally unacceptable. When human moral agency is at stake, it is not straightforwardly the case that non-'autonomous' weapon systems may be used and 'autonomous' ones may not. Rather, much depends on the way in which a weapon system's multiple functions are distributed among AI or human elements of the system, and on the conditions under which each function is then performed. When approached in this way, moral permissibility becomes a matter of whether a weapon system is subject to 'meaningful human control'.

THE PRINCIPLE OF MEANINGFUL HUMAN CONTROL

At CCW meetings in Geneva about LAWS, progress in international negotiations has often been frustrated by problems of terminology. Specifically, some states have insisted upon adopting either narrower or broader definitions of 'autonomy' when considering what kinds of weapon systems would be covered by any future regime of international governance. For example, since 2012 the US government has defined an 'autonomous' weapon system narrowly as one that is able, after activation, to 'select and engage targets without further intervention by a human operator',[70] and the International Committee of the Red Cross adopted a similar definition in 2021.[71] The UK government, by contrast, has used a broader definition: an 'autonomous system is capable of understanding higher-level intent and direction ... [and] of deciding a course of action ... without depending on human oversight and control'.[72] According to the narrower definition, more systems (including some systems that already exist) would be covered, whereas the broader definition would seem to cover only systems that are under the overall control of some highly sophisticated AI that might emerge in the future.

Unfortunately, then, the question of *why* a particular type of weapon system ought to be permitted or prohibited (because of the *way* it incorporates AI) often gets overtaken by disagreement about what 'autonomy' in general ought to mean. This problem is only compounded when terms such as 'semi-autonomous' or 'partially autonomous' are used to describe a weapon system,[73] as they beg the question: which half or which parts of the system are autonomous? Moreover, these terms do not illuminate the important issue of whether the functions to be performed by AI (rather than humans) fall within the most morally significant 'half' or 'part' of the system. Sometimes, too, the use of a weapon system is held to be justified because it is not '*fully* autonomous' (in the manner of a 'killer robot'),[74] yet this term misses the point that even an increase in the number of weapon system functions performed by AI (falling short of all of them) might still reduce human control of that system to a morally unacceptable level.

The idea of ethically requiring a 'meaningful' level of human control was introduced into the LAWS debate discourse in 2014 by the UK-based organisation Article 36,[75] and it has since become a more tractable alternative to the tricky concept of 'autonomy' as a focus for discussions. The concept of meaningful human control (MHC) prompts consideration of whether, in the context of a given weapon system's operation, human control over violence is genuine or illusory, and it rejects the proposition that *any* form or degree of human involvement is necessarily a sufficient safeguard against injustice. In considering whether human control of a system is 'meaningful', the central issue is not whether humans or AI should exercise moral agency, but rather: how should AI technology be used in a way that assists (or avoids disrupting) the proper exercise of human moral agency? As a guiding principle for thus limiting the devolution of violence from humans to AI, the content of MHC has yet to be precisely defined and agreed upon internationally. However, there are arguably at least six indicators of meaningfulness. Human control of a weapon system is 'meaningful' if it: (1) involves control of the system's 'critical' functions; (2) is exercisable in a timely fashion; (3) does not involve excessive trust in AI; (4) avoids the anthropomorphism of AI; (5) is able fairly to attract the attribution of blame for any wrongdoing; and (6) is a feature of the system's design.

Regarding the control of a weapon system's 'critical' functions, in discussions of LAWS these are generally understood to include (but are not necessarily limited to) selecting targets and engaging (firing at) targets,[76] as these are the functions that most directly enable violence to occur. In the operation of an armed drone, for example, some other functions (take-off and landing, navigation, and in-flight manoeuvring) might be devolved to AI without raising any serious ethical concerns, but the drone's violence could still be regarded as remaining under meaningful human control if its critical functions were performed by humans. It is less certain, though, whether the non-violent functions of collecting and analysing intelligence are always 'critical' for MHC purposes. On one view, AI performance of these functions could be regarded as consistent with MHC because it merely provides a foundation for well-informed decisions by humans. Or, as some authors have argued, intelligence functions can be regarded as critical (and thus non-delegable) because they are morally significant as precursors to violence.[77] If so, it would not be permissible, as a matter of MHC, for an armed drone system to incorporate an on-board AI 'analyst' that identified targets based on data collected from the drone's sensors.[78]

The meaningfulness of human control can also be understood in a temporal sense. Here, adherence to the MHC principle requires that human function-performers within a system can understand and interact with its AI function-performers in a timely way. Human control of AI-assisted violence is temporally meaningful only if the opportunity exists to override AI and thus prevent or mitigate injustices resulting from malfunctions or mistakes.[79] This might involve, for example, having time for a human to check whether the AI performer of an intelligence function has correctly tagged a target as 'legitimate'. Or it might involve the preservation of an opportunity for careful checking of an AI-generated estimate of the damage likely to be caused if the weapon system were used under certain circumstances. Already, some weapon systems incorporating AI operate so quickly that their human 'controllers' feel outpaced and overwhelmed,[80] so the use of such systems could sometimes be hard to reconcile with the MHC principle. And this might especially be the case in complex situations where an accommodation of the 'slowness' of human deliberation is rather required for control over violence to be meaningful.

Another indicator of MHC is non-excessive trust in the AI components of a weapon system. From an operational efficiency perspective, it is well understood that human function-performers within that system need somehow to *establish* a sense of trust. However, an ethical concern can arise thereafter from the potential for humans to *over*trust AI. This is a problem if it precludes genuine moral agency in the exercise of violence, to the point perhaps of reducing the 'value add' from human involvement in a weapon system's operation to merely 'rubber stamp[ing] the decisions made by computers'.[81] Sometimes, excessive trust in AI might relate to undesirable behaviour (human complacency and overconfidence), and at other times this might be largely attributable to unfavourable circumstances (information overload). If human operators of weapon systems experience 'automation bias',[82] this can lead to an overestimation of the accuracy and reliability of information provided by AI. This form of overtrusting was probably the cause, for example, of some past incidents of friendly fire involving the Patriot air defence system, where human operators failed to override the false identification of an enemy target.[83] Alternatively, if humans become confused by situations that are fast-paced and complicated, they might feel that they have no choice but to trust in an AI-generated output that is possibly not trust*worthy*.[84] Here, too, the meaningfulness of human control and the purchase of moral agency are undermined, because the bestowing of 'trust' in AI (to enable good outcomes) is forced and therefore false.

The problem of overtrusting might be compounded if humans were somehow to infer humanity in an AI function-performer, so the avoidance of anthropomorphism is itself worth counting as an indicator of MHC. Historically, humans have a strong appetite for projecting human characteristics onto non-human creatures or objects. In the field of AI research, public demonstrations of technology have sometimes fed this tendency by featuring 'natural-sounding voices, facial expressions, and simulated displays of human emotions'.[85] Some AI-enabled communication technologies, for example, include a female-sounding voice as a way of encouraging and facilitating their use.[86] However, the risk in such 'fanciful anthropomorphisms of machines',[87] especially when applied to processes of direct human–AI interaction, is that humans will deceive themselves into thinking that something human-like should be treated 'just like a human'.[88] In practice, such treatment could involve affording to AI as much trust, protection and respect as a human deserves. And, in the operation of a weapon system, a possibility then is that automation bias could be reinforced by anthropomorphic bias. An anthropomorphised AI, as a function-performer within the system, would thus become positioned not only to be trusted excessively but also to be designated (erroneously or mendaciously) as a proper recipient of praise or blame. At that stage, though, a commitment to the importance of *meaningful* human control would be harder to sustain while also *pretending* that AI too can exercise moral agency and bear moral responsibility.

A capacity for moral responsibility, including the ability to be held accountable for wrongdoing, is yet another part of what it means to be genuinely in control.[89] As an indicator of MHC, a commitment to human accountability for the operation of a weapon system serves as a check against the purported blaming and punishing of an AI technology that is inherently unblameable and unpunishable. Beyond this, however, there needs to be more than a commitment only to make *any* human accountable. For human control to be *meaningfully* connected to moral responsibility, the holding of someone to account must still be fair. It would not satisfy the MHC principle if, for example, an instance of wrongdoing was *strictly* blamed upon one person who was clearly incapable of understanding and intervening in the performance of a certain function by AI. That predesignated scapegoat would not be genuinely responsible for the wrongdoing, and its true source (whatever it was) would remain unremedied. The violent effects of a weapon system operated in this way could not, then, be reasonably described as 'under control', because the *other* humans involved could not feel restrained in their conduct by the possibility of punishment.

The strength of a commitment to meaningful human control is indicated, lastly, by the way in which a weapon system is designed. Here, part of the challenge is to avoid excluding human operators from necessarily performing the system's critical functions. This could require designing the interfaces between human and non-human elements of the system to make the latter more understandable.[90] And achieving MHC *by design* could also involve 'built-in limitations' on AI behaviour,[91] including deliberately limiting the speed of AI information-processing so that human function-performers are less likely to be cognitively overwhelmed. In addition, an important consideration is whether a particular function within a system is set up (from a technical perspective) to be performed *only* by a human. Where this is not the case, because that function is performable by a human *or* AI, adherence to the MHC principle is merely a matter of choosing how to *use* a weapon system. But choices are more easily changed than are the engineered features of a system. So, if control over a critical function were instantly transferrable to an AI function-performer (perhaps by a human finger flicking a switch), that design feature would be one that enabled the rapid fulfilment of any temptation to release a weapon system from human restraint. The human control over such a system would thus be less meaningful because it could so easily be given away.

A weapon system incorporating AI can have built-in restraints and still *not* be under meaningful human control, and this problem is well illustrated by one type of 'loitering munition' (used by the Israeli Defence Force): the Harpy. Although it is sometimes referred to as a 'suicide' or 'kamikaze' drone, the non-reusable Harpy might more accurately be described as a flying mine. It is designed, once activated, to aerially survey a large area of land until it detects an enemy's radar signal, whereupon it responds by crashing itself into the source of the signal and explodes. Thus, the devolved performance of the Harpy's critical functions (target selection and engagement) does not require the maintenance of a communication link to a remote operator. Lacking such a continuous opportunity for human intervention, this loitering munition is still temporally and spatially restrained by design. That is, its operation cannot exceed a set time limit and it cannot fly outside set geographical boundaries. From the perspective of MHC, however, the risk is that this weapon system will be insufficiently sensitive to morally significant changes in its operating environment that might arise even within a short timeframe. Although, by design, a Harpy's only potential targets are non-human ones (radar installations), it is also not designed to deactivate itself (or to be always able to be deactivated remotely) if humans unexpectedly come close to its materiel target.[92] Here, the moral problem with a lack of meaningful human control would essentially be one of non-discrimination: the inability of the weapon system's targeting function (as devolved to AI) to spare *any* nearby human from harm, let alone a *civilian* human.

DRONE VIOLENCE AND HUMAN–MACHINE INTERACTION: A DIFFERENTIATED APPROACH TO ETHICAL ASSESSMENT

If it is accepted as a matter of principle that all weapon systems should operate under meaningful human control, it does not follow that achieving such control in practice always requires the same (one-size-fits-all) approach. Rather, because context is morally relevant,[93] there is potential for different systems operating in different situations to satisfy the MHC principle in different ways. Moving beyond discussions of whether the 'autonomy' of *whole* weapon systems is permissible, a differentiated approach to ethical assessment instead involves consideration of who (or what) performs certain functions *within* a system. In the remainder of this chapter, such an approach is demonstrated by focusing on the meaningful human control of one kind of weapon system – the armed drone – and by addressing the questions: which functions may (or may not) be devolved to AI, subject to what control arrangements, in what kind of circumstances, and why? A useful term for this purpose is 'human–machine interaction' (HMI), which usually refers more generally to the interaction between humans and computers.[94] Here, it is well suited to thinking about the distribution of functions to be performed, and it has the immediate linguistic advantage of locking in a minimal presumption against artificial moral agency: that AI is always in some way interacting with a human (and thus never acting on its own) when a weapon system is operating.

To satisfy the MHC principle in some contexts of drone violence, it will be morally more important to have HMI arrangements in place that are highly restrictive of AI function-performers within the drone system. And in other contexts, as Daniele Amoroso and Guglielmo Tamburrini have argued, 'milder forms of human control will suffice'.[95] Either way, though, attention needs to focus on the devolution of two functions that relate most directly to the justness or otherwise of drone violence: identifying and selecting targets, and violently engaging those targets. Sometimes, circumstances might require HMI in an armed drone system to be arranged on what could be called a 'green-light' basis. This would involve a built-in presumption against engaging a target selected or recommended by AI, whereby the engagement function could be performed only if or when a human operator decided to go ahead. In different circumstances, only a 'red-light' HMI arrangement would be morally required for MHC purposes. There would then be a built-in presumption in favour of proceeding towards engaging a selected target within a set timeframe, but this process could be overridden by a human operator deciding to stop it. Green-light HMI might be suitable where, for example, there is a higher moral risk associated with excessive human trust in AI, and red-light HMI might be suitable where a lengthy opportunity for human intervention is morally less important. In other kinds of situations, it might be the case that neither mode of HMI will suffice because it is too risky to devolve to AI the performance of any of an armed drone's critical functions.

Different targets, purposes and environments

When it comes to determining which (if any) mode of HMI is morally acceptable in the exercise of AI-assisted drone violence, it is worth considering a combination of contextual factors including the type of target, the purpose of the violence, and the prevailing environmental conditions. More specifically, the meaningfulness or otherwise of an arrangement for human control can be judged, firstly, according to whether an armed drone incorporating AI is to be used against materiel targets (for example, incoming missiles) or against human ones. Secondly, it is important to consider whether this is for an offensive purpose, for the purpose of defending the drone itself, or for the purpose of defending a human who is under attack or at immediate risk of attack. And thirdly, the permissibility of a mode of HMI can depend upon whether drone violence is to occur in an environment of armed conflict that is 'cluttered' (with civilians and/or friendly forces) or 'low-clutter', or whether it is instead to occur in a law enforcement environment in which stricter (peacetime) ethical standards apply to a state's violence.

Anti-materiel or anti-human targeting

Morally, it is a less serious matter to target inanimate objects than it is to target living human beings. So, to the extent that the MHC principle serves a humanitarian end, it is reasonable to distinguish anti-materiel targeting from anti-human targeting when determining what kind of HMI arrangement is permissible. Directing drone violence against materiel can, of course, carry a risk of harm to untargeted humans nearby. For example, a drone releasing on-board munitions to destroy an incoming missile might result in those munitions striking a civilian aircraft farther away. What matters more here, though, is that anti-materiel targeting by a specially designed weapon system is 'non-lethal' in the sense that it is not intended (by the designer) to kill anyone. Thus, it is unfortunate, for ethical assessment purposes, that this important distinction between non-lethal and deadly violence has sometimes been overlooked in the broader debate about LAWS, largely due to the efforts of some non-government organisations to raise awareness of the perceived need to prohibit 'killer robots'.[96]

A better, more expansive approach to addressing concerns about violence and AI is to ask: against what type of target is a weapon system to be used, and under what kind of arrangement for human control may AI perform the functions of selecting and engaging targets? Accordingly, it could be easier to justify a mode of HMI whereby human operators within a drone system exercise only low-level (supervisory) control over AI as it fires anti-missile missiles (or some other defensive anti-materiel countermeasure). This is because meeting the technical challenge of correct target-identification is relatively straightforward when dealing with missiles moving on a trajectory that can be tracked. By contrast, it is technically much more difficult, and perhaps impossible, for AI alone to correctly target humans whose relevant intentions and behaviours are more amenable to being accurately recognised by fellow humans.[97] In which case, assigning AI to perform an anti-human targeting function while under only low-level human control would be harder to justify by reference to the MHC principle.

Offensive, drone-defensive or human-defensive purposes

Beyond the issue of target type, it is useful also to draw distinctions regarding the purpose of a potential instance of AI-assisted drone violence. This, too, affects the permissibility of relying upon a particular mode of HMI. An armed drone could be used for an offensive purpose such as attacking another drone, a piloted aircraft or a human on the ground. Alternatively, drone violence could be applied for a drone-defensive purpose (to protect the drone itself) or a human-defensive purpose (to defend humans who are under attack or immediately threatened). The latter could include, for example, using an air-to-ground weapon in defence of friendly troops or using an air-to-air weapon to defend the pilots of friendly aircraft nearby.

From an ethical perspective, violence for offensive purposes tends to be harder to justify, especially if it is essentially aggressive. This is because the urgency of self-preservation (while under attack) does not arise at the moment of *offensive* violence occurring, and it is not available as an excuse for not taking more care (when acting violently) to avoid generating unjust effects. It follows, then, that adhering to the MHC principle in the offensive use of AI-assisted drone violence would tend to require a higher rather than lower level of human control. Similarly, violence with a drone-defensive purpose could be more difficult to justify where the HMI arrangement involves low-level human control. However, here the critical issue is a drone's lack of a morally valuable 'self' to defend. The benefit gained from such defence would carry little weight, potentially, against the risk of thereby causing unjust harm (to nearby civilians, for example).[98] By contrast, the successful defence of humans under attack is a benefit that carries more moral weight. And, for this reason, there could be a stronger moral case in some circumstances for permitting a mode of HMI in which there is a higher degree of devolution of an armed drone's critical functions.

Low-clutter, cluttered or law enforcement environments

The third factor to be considered when determining the permissibility of different HMI arrangements is the kind of environment in which AI-assisted drone violence is to occur. In the context of warfare, some operating environments can be described as 'low-clutter' in the sense that there are few or no civilians or friendly personnel present who would be endangered by a drone-based weapon system. Most aerial and maritime environments fit this description, although many land environments (such as cities) do not. Other environments are instead 'cluttered' with potential victims, so using an armed drone there against enemy targets (materiel or human) carries a greater risk of breaking the wrong things or killing the wrong people. Outside of warfare, such a risk is of even greater concern, so it is useful also to consider a third type of operating 'environment' in which state violence is only narrowly permissible: law enforcement.

Fewer ethical challenges would be likely to arise where an armed drone incorporating AI was used in a low-clutter environment, because here legitimate targets are more easily recognisable by analysing data derived from the drone's on-board sensors.[99] It could be morally more acceptable, then, to run the risk of having in place a mode of HMI in which less human control is exercisable over the drone system's critical functions. Even so, it would be important to ensure that that armed drone *stayed* in such an environment. Other AI-assisted weapon systems are designed to operate, under minimal human supervision, in low-clutter (aerial) environments against materiel targets (incoming air-to-surface missiles) – for example Israel's ground-based Iron Dome and the US Navy's ship-based Phalanx system – but these usually occupy a fixed position.[100] By contrast, an airborne drone is highly mobile, so it could more easily be moved into a cluttered environment where low-level human control of drone violence is riskier and harder to justify. Amid the 'clutter' of civilians and friendly forces who need to be spared from harm, target recognition (by AI or humans) is a more difficult function to perform. For this reason, HMI within a drone-based weapon system would arguably need to feature a greater degree of human control, and especially in instances of anti-human targeting.

Whatever 'meaningful' human control means in a war setting, it has a stricter meaning when the state uses a weapon system to violently enforce its domestic criminal law. Where an armed drone is to be used for this purpose, the moral expectation for taking care with human lives is greater, and the scope for permitting AI-assisted drone violence is likely to be much narrower (if there is any at all). This is partly because the political stakes when police encounter criminal suspects are generally far lower than they are when a military contest is ongoing, and also because a law enforcement environment is deeply and structurally 'cluttered' by the strong, rights-based moral presumption against killing in peacetime.[101] The essential objective of policing is neither to neutralise nor defeat enemies but rather to protect the lives of all citizens. Accordingly, as was discussed in Chapter 3, police violence is subject to ethical principles (of necessity, proportionality and precaution) that are less tolerant of human harm than are military ethics principles. When it comes to drone violence, adhering to the MHC principle should thus involve taking a stricter view of what system functions should count as 'critical' and of when (if ever) AI may perform such functions, even with humans being closely involved.[102] A mode of HMI that is permissible in war might, then, be harder to justify within a drone system that is to be used for violent law enforcement.

Permissible HMI in different circumstances

When the various combinations of contextual factors are accounted for, it remains to consider what (if any) mode of HMI is morally suitable under different circumstances of AI-assisted drone violence. Assuming that anti-materiel targeting does not apply to law enforcement environments, there are fifteen possible contexts (see Table 6.1). Arguably, in six of these contexts only a stricter arrangement for human control (green-light HMI) is justified. There are six other contexts in which a milder arrangement for human control (red-light HMI) is permissible as satisfying the MHC principle. And in three contexts, AI-assisted drone violence would not be permissible on any HMI basis.

Table 6.1 Different HMI requirements for human control of AI-assisted drone violence

Targeting:	Environment:	**Purpose of AI-assisted drone violence:**		
		Human-defensive ↓	Drone-defensive ↓	Offensive ↓
Anti-materiel	Low clutter →	RED-light HMI	RED-light HMI	RED-light HMI
Anti-materiel	Cluttered →	RED-light HMI	RED-light HMI	GREEN-light HMI
Anti-human	Low clutter →	RED-light HMI	GREEN-light HMI	GREEN-light HMI
Anti-human	Cluttered →	GREEN-light HMI	GREEN-light HMI	Not permitted
Anti-human	Law enforcement →	GREEN-light HMI (without devolution of target selection)	Not permitted	Not applicable

Anti-human, offensive drone violence (AI-assisted or otherwise) in a law enforcement environment is impermissible because the notion of attack (offense) is foreign to the protective essence and ethos of policing. 'Offensive' law enforcement is, if anything, more akin to extrajudicial execution. Also, it would be impermissible in a law enforcement context for drone violence to be wielded in defence of the drone itself. This is because the associated risk of harming any nearby humans would far outweigh the benefit of 'saving' a non-living thing. Similarly, in a cluttered wartime environment, AI performance of an armed drone's critical functions (even on a green-light HMI basis) would likely involve too great a risk of unjust harm when it is done for an offensive purpose (in the absence of an immediate threat). As aggressive violence is already more difficult generally to justify than is defensive violence, this factor would not weigh favourably against the MHC risks (such as overtrusting AI) that attend any HMI arrangement within a weapon system. Where a system incorporating AI was to be used very near to an enemy target (on a ground-based platform, for example), there might be more moral scope to permit offensive violence in a cluttered environment, because opportunities for timely human intervention in AI function-performance could be greater. However, in the case of drones strikes conducted over vast distances, the remoteness of a human controller from a prospective victim can weaken the temporal element of MHC. That is, when imagery data can take several seconds to transmit between a drone's camera and a human observer via satellite, some time to intervene (to prevent an injustice) is lost. In which case, even a stricter HMI arrangement would arguably not suffice to make AI-assisted drone violence permissible when that violence was merely offensive rather than essentially defensive in its purpose.

Red-light HMI permissions

In other circumstances, when contextual factors combine differently, the balance of ethical risks and benefits will differ too. While it will then, as always, be necessary to adhere to the MHC principle, it might sometimes be the case that such adherence is achievable by distributing a drone system's critical functions among humans and AI on a red-light HMI basis. In other words, some situations might justify deploying a system in which selecting and engaging targets are jointly controlled functions: able to be initiated by AI and halted by a human. Here, though, the human element of control would critically depend upon the maintenance of a reliable communication link. So, an important safeguard in any red-light HMI arrangement would be to ensure (by design) that drone violence could not continue if that link were ever broken or compromised.

In a low-clutter environment of warfare, anti-materiel drone violence based on red-light HMI would probably be permissible for any purpose (offensive, drone-defensive or human-defensive). Even if a human function-performer were prone to overtrust the drone system's AI, or if they had limited time in which to intervene, this arrangement could still constitute a morally acceptable degree of human control. This is because, under such circumstances, the likelihood of any human being harmed is extremely low. Humans would not be the target of drone violence, and few if any civilians and/or friendly personnel would be present and potentially endangered by AI-assisted drone violence operating on a red-light HMI basis. By contrast, in a cluttered environment, the risk of unjust harms occurring is greater, so there is less moral scope for permitting red-light HMI. Such an arrangement for human control is less open, in this situation, to be justified as sufficiently 'meaningful' if the purpose of AI-assisted drone violence is merely offensive. It would be easier, though, to justify heavier reliance upon rapid AI function-performance if anti-materiel targeting in a cluttered environment were done for a purpose with greater moral weight: the direct defence of humans who are under attack or immediately at risk.

Red-light HMI might also be permissible for a drone-defensive purpose, although here the building-in of a lengthier opportunity for human intervention in the weapon system's relevant functions would arguably be required. After all, quickly 'saving' a non-living drone is a morally less urgent objective than is taking more time (when responding violently to materiel threats) to avoid causing harm to humans. Similarly, a strengthening of the temporal element of MHC is also morally worthwhile when it comes to anti-human targeting in a low-clutter environment for a human-defensive purpose. Here, the risk of unintentional harms arising from AI-assisted drone violence is less than in a cluttered environment, and this affords more justification to allow speedy AI performance of targeting and engagement functions on a red-light HMI basis. Such a capability would be militarily valuable if, for example, the armed drone was flying in formation with a friendly inhabited aircraft under attack by a nearby enemy pilot.[103] However, when another human's life (rather than an inanimate object) is at stake, this arguably warrants allowing at least a little more time for that drone's human controller to override its AI if the wrong person would otherwise be killed.

Green-light HMI permissions

In other contexts, a temporally enhanced mode of red-light HMI would not suffice for human control of AI-assisted drone violence to count as meaningful, and only a stricter arrangement for distributing a drone system's critical functions would be permissible. Then, as Byrnes has explained, an armed drone system (with many functions performed by AI) would need to be designed to 'reach back to its human operator at key junctures' when circumstances created a 'moral need to limit the diffusion of responsibility to nonhuman actors'.[104] To this end, green-light HMI does not involve joint AI–human control over the selecting and engagement of targets. Instead, AI function-performance under this arrangement is more subordinate to human control because violence cannot proceed without a human function-performer deciding and acting to make this happen. Consequently, more time for human consideration of morally relevant circumstances can be taken beforehand, and the risk associated with excessive human trust in AI is potentially reduced. This is because, within a drone system designed for green-light HMI, a human function-performer can decide whether or when to *initiate* violence rather than possibly deciding in a rush to *stop* (with a 'red light' intervention) AI-initiated violence that is already under way. Moreover, when seeking to ensure MHC (and avoid overtrusting AI) in this stricter way, a drone's AI is better regarded as not 'deciding' but merely 'recommending' the selection of a target.[105]

In a low-clutter environment, anti-human targeting requires this extra care to be taken when its purpose is not as important as human-defence. At this point, because violence for a lesser (offensive or drone-defensive) purpose is harder to justify, it becomes morally necessary for a drone system incorporating AI to operate instead on a green-light HMI basis. In the absence of an immediate threat, from an operational perspective, the performance of a drone system's critical functions does not need to be especially speedy. Indeed, some USAF drone operators have reportedly appreciated how, currently, they are sometimes able to wield violence in a more deliberative manner and without the 'urgency of time'.[106] In any event, ethically speaking, the *introduction* of another physical risk (through offensive violence) to innocent or friendly humans is too serious a matter, even in a low-clutter environment, to be conducted according to a milder (red-light HMI) standard of MHC. And, in a cluttered environment, even if the targets of offensive violence are only materiel ones, the higher risk of unintended harms occurring there is a good reason for preferring green-light HMI in those circumstances too.

Where anti-human targeting is to serve a drone-defensive purpose, a key challenge while operating on a green-light HMI basis would be to avoid assigning too much value to drones in relation to human beings, especially within a cluttered environment. Here, a commitment to anti-anthropomorphism could rise in importance as one of the indicators of MHC. Although a drone is generally less likely to be anthropomorphised (and thus overvalued) than a humanoid weapon system, descriptions of some prototype drones as being 'loyal wingmen' to airborne human pilots reflect a slight tendency in this direction.[107] And, if the use of such language also increases the risk of excessive human trust in AI, this would add to the case for preferring the stricter (green-light) mode of HMI when drones alone are to be defended from human aerial attackers. If action is to be initiated to harm an enemy human pilot in order to protect a drone in a warfare context, it should at least be done (or not done) as matter of human (not AI) judgement.

The defence of one or more humans is, by contrast, a morally more important purpose for anti-human targeting in a cluttered environment. However, in such circumstances a green-light mode of HMI is arguably still required. As much as the urgency of fulfilling a human-defensive purpose might seem to warrant a milder approach to MHC, the lives of the many potential innocent victims of AI-assisted drone violence remain of sufficient moral worth as to demand a higher standard of care and control. If, instead, a drone system operated according to red-light HMI, there would be a high humanitarian risk associated with human controllers failing to stop AI-initiated violence when necessary to avoid unjust harms. Thus, it would be harder for such human control to be plausibly described as meaningful, so green-light HMI would be better.

When state violence is wielded, moral expectations for preserving human life are higher within a law enforcement environment where police are charged with confronting dangerous criminals and protecting public safety. Outside warfare, everyone is a 'civilian' and there is a strong presumption against killing people, so the scope to permit AI-assisted drone violence here is narrow: anti-human targeting, for a human-defensive purpose only, and always on a green-light HMI basis. For the reasons discussed in Chapter 3, there would likely be few circumstances in which police violence would be morally improved by using an armed drone. And there would perhaps be fewer still in which a police drone system would be morally improved by devolving the performance of a critical function to AI. For the most part, this is because an aerial platform is usually not well suited to police officers' professional need to make careful observation of human behaviour and then exercise their judgement. It is important to do this, for example, in determining whether a criminal suspect really poses a serious threat to the lives of others. And yet, observing and judging people is more easily done on the ground and up-close to where that suspect is, rather than remotely and from the air.

If circumstances clearly justify the use of violence in response to a suspect's ongoing threat to life, it might sometimes be the case that devolving *only* the function of target engagement to AI is permissible. For example, after a human involved in controlling a drone system has decided that only a lethal response can neutralise a particular hostage-taker or suicide bomber, having AI control over the precise timing of the 'kill shot' might be safer to bystanders than having human control.[108] However, beyond such rare and obvious instances of threat, it is doubtful whether any moral advantage could be derived from devolving a critical function to AI technology. Within a drone system operating in a law enforcement environment, the function of recommending a target is certainly critical, because there is less tolerance here than there is during a war of running the moral risk of harming the wrong person. The difficulty with devolving that function to AI, though, is that suspicious human behaviour is not apt to be recognised as such by a non-human function-performer.

AI image-processing technologies exist which purport to identify similarities between faces (facial recognition) and the emotional cause of facial expressions (affect recognition), and they have been widely criticised for being inaccurate and discriminatory.[109] But even if these forms of AI were to improve, they would arguably still fail to replicate the greater part of what it means for a police officer to exercise judgement about another person's likely intentions (criminally harmful or otherwise). Such judgement must be brought to bear also upon infinite varieties of bodily movement, spoken language and verbal intonation, and these can be especially challenging to 'decode' when police encounter vulnerable people (for example the mentally ill, intoxicated or disabled).[110] Moreover, that judgement critically draws upon an officer's lived experience and capacity for empathy, whereas AI is non-living and feels nothing. To devolve the function of recommending human targets to AI would, therefore, probably increase the risk of police violence being unjust. So, as a matter of system design, the HMI arrangement would need to be most restrictive of AI where an armed drone was operating in a law enforcement environment.

CONCLUSION

As armed drones continue to proliferate, and as they are increasingly deployed to seize or exploit the control of airspace, drone-using states are likely to remain interested in improving the capabilities of these aircraft. From an operational perspective, there appear to be clear advantages in devolving the performance of drone system functions from remote humans to on-board AI technologies. For example, devolution could be a way of easing the pressure to have sufficient personnel available for every drone mission. It could enable some functions (such as aerial manoeuvre or data analysis) to be performed at superhuman speed. And it could reduce the importance of maintaining strong and secure communication links between faraway drones and their on-the-ground controllers. For these and other reasons, it seems likely that the future operation of armed drones will feature the incorporation of AI to some degree. From an ethical perspective, though, what matters most in the pursuit of such 'improvement' is whether or how humans or AI should perform the critical function of making decisions about drone violence.

The consequentialist argument in favour of artificial moral agency is attractive, and one can readily imagine and desire a future in which humans suffer fewer unjust harms because armed drones (and other weapon systems) are controlled entirely by AI. Weighing against this merely *possible* humanitarian gain, however, it is certain that much would be lost from the meaning of 'being ethical' if humans became less involved in decision-making when other humans' lives are immediately at stake. Even if future AI technologies turned out to be better overall at following rules for restraining violence, it would remain the case that only humans possess the valuable capacities to make judgements based on lived experience, to disobey rules when this is morally required, and to bear moral responsibility for wrongdoing. Thus, to preserve the beneficial effect of these capacities, the better approach to incorporating AI into weapon systems is to ensure that it leaves room for violence to remain under meaningful human control.

In shifting attention away from the vexed issue of what weapon systems count as 'autonomous', the MHC concept is useful because it allows distinctions to be drawn between the technical characteristics and ethical acceptability of different kinds of systems operating under various conditions. Although, as discussed in this chapter, there are certain minimal indicators of whether human control is 'meaningful', it is also the case that context matters when making moral judgements about *how* AI should assist state violence. Standards of meaningfulness can and should differ, then, according to the type of target to be struck, the purpose that this would serve, and the kind of environment into which a weapon system is deployed. Accordingly, when it comes to any future incorporation of AI into armed drone systems, it can be anticipated that some higher-risk circumstances would require a stricter (green-light) mode of HMI when selecting and engaging targets. In other circumstances, when a lengthy opportunity for human intervention is morally less important, a milder (red-light) mode would suffice in the performance of these critical functions. And, sometimes, when the risk of unjust harm is especially high, AI assistance in the wielding of drone violence would never be morally permissible.

NOTES

1. Michael W. Byrnes, 'Nightfall: Machine Autonomy in Air-to-Air Combat', *Air & Space Power Journal* (May–June 2014): 48–75, at 48–9.
2. Ibid. 48 and 50.
3. Ibid. 56.
4. Federica Mogherini, 'Speech by High Representative/Vice-President Federica Mogherini at the Annual Conference of the European Defence Agency', *European Union External Action Service*, 29 November 2018, <https://eeas.europa.eu/headquarters/headquarters-homepage/54646/speech-high-representativevice-president-federica-mogherini-annual-conference-european-defence_en>.
5. Will Knight, 'A dogfight renews concerns about AI's lethal potential', *Wired*, 25 August 2020, <https://www.wired.com/story/dogfight-renews-concerns-ai-lethal-potential/>. See also: DARPA, 'AlphaDogfight trials foreshadow future of human–machine symbiosis', *Defense Advanced Research Projects Agency*, 26 August 2020, <https://www.darpa.mil/news-events/2020-08-26>.
6. Arash Heydarian Pashakhanlou, 'AI, Autonomy, and Airpower: The End of Pilots?', *Defence Studies*, 19 (4) (2019): 337–52, at 341 and 342.
7. Theresa Hitchens, 'Skyborg AI flies second drone; demos "Portability"', *Breaking Defense*, 30 June 2021, <https://breakingdefense.com/2021/06/skyborg-ai-flies-second-drone-demos-portability/>.
8. See: Hilary Swift, '"Terminator Conundrum": robots that could kill on their own', *New York Times*, 25 October 2016, <https://www.nytimes.com/2016/10/26/us/pentagon-artificial-intelligence-terminator.html>; Allegra Harpootlian and Emily Manna, 'The new face of American war is a robot', *The Nation*, 29 April 2019, <https://www.thenation.com/article/archive/tom-dispatch-american-warfare-drones-military-tech-robot/>.
9. See: Ian G. R. Shaw, *Predator Empire: Drone Warfare and Full Spectrum Dominance*, Minneapolis and London: University of Minnesota Press, 2016: 158; Alan Schuller, 'Autonomous Weapon Systems and the Decision to Kill', *Just Security*, 21 September 2017, <https://www.justsecurity.org/45164/autonomous-weapon-systems-decision-kill/>; Gjert Lage Dyndal, Tor Arne Berntsen and Sigrid Redse-Johansen, 'Autonomous military drones: no longer science fiction', *NATO Review*, 28 July 2017, <https://www.nato.int/docu/review/articles/2017/07/28/autonomous-military-drones-no-longer-science-fiction/index.html>.
10. Margaret A. Boden, *Artificial Intelligence: A Very Short Introduction*, Oxford: Oxford University Press, 2018: 107.
11. See: Alan Bundy, 'Preparing for the Future of Artificial Intelligence', *AI & Society*, 32 (2017): 285–7; Tannya D. Jajal, 'Distinguishing between Narrow AI, General AI and Super AI', *Medium*, 21 May 2018, <https://medium.com/mapping-out-2050/distinguishing-between-narrow-ai-general-ai-and-super-ai-a4bc44172e22>.
12. See: Vincent Boulanin, *Mapping the Development of Autonomy in Weapon Systems: A Primer on Autonomy*. Stockholm: Stockholm International Peace Research Institute, 2016: 7.

13. USAF, 'Annex 3-60 – targeting', *U.S. Airforce Doctrine*, updated 12 November 2021, <https://www.doctrine.af.mil/Portals/61/documents/AFDP_3-60/3-60-AFDP-TARGETING.pdf>: 27.

14. Ibid. 28–30.

15. Micah Zenko, 'The coming future of autonomous drones', *Council on Foreign Relations*, 4 September 2012, <https://www.cfr.org/blog/coming-future-autonomous-drones>.

16. Pratap Chatterjee, 'A chilling new post-traumatic stress disorder: why drone pilots are quitting in record numbers', *Salon*, 6 March 2015, <http://www.salon.com/2015/03/06/a_chilling_new_post_traumatic_stress_disorder_why_drone_pilots_are_quitting_in_record_numbers_partner/>. See also: Lucy Fisher, 'Stress of killing from afar creates shortage of MoD drone operators', *The Times*, 13 January 2020, <https://www.thetimes.co.uk/article/stress-of-killing-from-afar-creates-shortage-of-mod-drone-operators-0fnm36r6t>.

17. See: US Department of Defense, *Unmanned Systems Integrated Roadmap 2017–2042* (issued 28 August 2018): 20. Available at: US Naval Institute, 'Pentagon Unmanned Systems Integrated Roadmap 2017–2042', *USNI News*, 30 August 2018, <https://news.usni.org/2018/08/30/pentagon-unmanned-systems-integrated-roadmap-2017-2042>; Zach Hughes, 'Fog, friction, and thinking machines', *War on the Rocks*, 11 March 2020, <https://warontherocks.com/2020/03/fog-friction-and-thinking-machines/>.

18. See: Elsa B. Kania, 'Chinese Military Innovation in the AI Revolution', *RUSI Journal*, 164 (5–6) (2019): 26–34, at 30.

19. James J. Wirtz, 'The "Terminator Conundrum" and the Future of Drone Warfare', *Intelligence and National Security*, 32 (4) (2017): 433–5, at 434.

20. See: Thom Shanker and Matt Richtel, 'In new military, data overload can be deadly', *New York Times*, 17 January 2011: A1.

21. Henry McDonald, 'AI expert calls for end to UK use of "racially biased" algorithms', *The Guardian*, 12 December 2019, <https://www.theguardian.com/technology/2019/dec/12/ai-end-uk-use-racially-biased-algorithms-noel-sharkey>.

22. Robert O. Work, 'Establishment of an Algorithmic Warfare Cross-Functional Team (Project Maven)'. Memorandum from the Deputy Secretary of Defense. *US Department of Defense*, 26 April 2017, <https://www.govexec.com/media/gbc/docs/pdfs_edit/establishment_of_the_awcft_project_maven.pdf>.

23. Michael J. Boyle, *The Drone Age: How Drone Technology Will Change War and Peace*, New York: Oxford University Press, 2020: 117.

24. Fifth Review Conference of the High Contracting Parties to the Convention on Prohibitions or Restrictions on the Use of Certain Conventional Weapons Which May Be Deemed to Be Excessively Injurious or to Have Indiscriminate Effects, *Final Document of the Fifth Review Conference* (CCW/CONF.V/10), Geneva, 23 December 2016: 9.

25. See: Christof Heyns, 'Report of the Special Rapporteur on extrajudicial, summary or arbitrary executions' (A/HRC/23/47), New York: Human

Rights Council, United Nations General Assembly, 9 April 2013; Human Rights Watch, 'The Need for New Law to Ban Fully Autonomous Weapons: Memorandum to Convention on Conventional Weapons Delegates', *Human Rights Watch*, 13 November 2013, <https://www.hrw.org/news/2013/11/13/need-new-law-ban-fully-autonomous-weapons>; Samuel Gibbs, 'Musk, Wozniak and Hawking urge ban on warfare AI and autonomous weapons', *The Guardian*, 27 July 2015, <https://www.theguardian.com/technology/2015/jul/27/musk-wozniak-hawking-ban-ai-autonomous-weapons>.

26. Early contributions to this debate include: Robert Sparrow, 'Killer Robots, *Journal of Applied Philosophy*, 24 (1) (2007): 62–77; Ronald C. Arkin, 'Ethical Robots in Warfare', *IEEE Technology and Society* (Spring 2009): 30–3.

27. Vincent Boulanin, Laura Bruun and Netta Goussac, *Autonomous Weapon Systems and International Humanitarian Law: Identifying Limits and the Required Type and Degree of Human–Machine Interaction*, Stockholm: Stockholm International Peace Research Institute, June 2021: 15.

28. Ibid. 15.

29. Ibid. i (emphasis added).

30. Keith Abney, 'Autonomous Robots and the Future of Just War Theory', in *Routledge Handbook of Ethics and War: Just War Theory in the Twenty-First Century*, ed. Fritz Allhoff, Nicholas G. Evans and Adam Henschke, New York: Routledge, 2013: 338–51, at 342.

31. Ronald C. Arkin, 'The Case for Ethical Autonomy in Unmanned Systems', *Journal of Military Ethics*, 9 (4) (2010): 332–41, at 332. See also: Jeremy Rabkin and John Yoo, '"Killer robots" can make war less awful', *Wall Street Journal*, 1 September 2017, <https://www.wsj.com/articles/killer-robots-can-make-war-less-awful-1504284282>.

32. M. R. McGuire, 'The Laughing Policebot: Automation and the End of Policing', *Policing and Society*, 31 (1) (2021): 20–36, at 31.

33. Thomas K. Adams, 'Future Warfare and the Decline of Human Decision-making', *Parameters* (Winter 2001–02): 57–71, at 66; Jürgen Altmann and Frank Sauer, 'Autonomous Weapon Systems and Strategic Stability', *Survival*, 59 (5) (2017): 117–42, at 118.

34. See: Ryan Tonkens, 'The Case against Robotic Warfare: A Response to Arkin', *Journal of Military Ethics*, 11 (2) (2012): 149–68, at 150 and 160.

35. Adam Satariano, 'Will there be a ban on killer robots?', *New York Times*, 19 October 2018: F8.

36. Christof Heyns, 'Human Rights and the Use of Autonomous Weapons Systems (AWS) During Domestic Law Enforcement', *Human Rights Quarterly*, 38 (2016): 350–78, at 367. See also: Peter Asaro, 'On Banning Autonomous Weapon Systems: Human Rights, Automation, and the Dehumanization of Lethal Decisionmaking', *International Review of the Red Cross*, 94 (886) (2012): 687–709; Robert Hart, 'The Case for Banning Autonomous Weapons Rests on Morality, Not Practicality', *Bulletin*

of the Atomic Scientists, 24 April 2017, <http://thebulletin.org/case-banning-autonomous-weaponsrests-morality-not-practicality10707>.

37. Aaron Johnson, 'The Morality of Autonomous Robots', *Journal of Military Ethics*, 12 (2) (2013): 129–41, at 134.

38. Robert Sparrow, 'Robotic Weapons and the Future of War', in *New Wars and New Soldiers: Military Ethics in the Contemporary World*, ed. Jessica Wolfendale and Paolo Tripodi, Farnham: Ashgate, 2011: 117–36, at 125.

39. Robert Sparrow, 'Robots as "Evil Means"? A Rejoinder to Jenkins and Purves', *Ethics and International Affairs*, 30 (3) (2016): 401–3, at 402 (emphasis added).

40. Gloria Gaggioli, 'Remoteness and Human Rights Law', in *Research Handbook on Remote Warfare*, ed. Jens David Ohlin, Cheltenham: Edward Elgar, 2017: 133–85, at 170; Amanda Sharkey, 'Autonomous Weapons Systems, Killer Robots and Human Dignity', *Ethics and Information Technology*, 21 (2019): 75–87, at 75 and 85.

41. See: John P. Sullins, 'When Is a Robot a Moral Agent?', *International Review of Information Ethics*, 6 (2006): 23–30; Wendell Wallach and Colin Allen, *Moral Machines: Teaching Robots Right from Wrong*, New York: Oxford University Press, 2009.

42. Heather M. Roff, 'Killing in War: Responsibility, Liability, and Lethal Autonomous Robots', in *Routledge Handbook of Ethics and War: Just War Theory in the Twenty-First Century*, ed. Fritz Allhoff, Nicholas G. Evans and Adam Henschke, New York: Routledge, 2013: 352–64, at 352.

43. Keith Abney, 'Autonomous Robots and the Future of Just War Theory', in *Routledge Handbook of Ethics and War: Just War Theory in the Twenty-First Century*, ed. Fritz Allhoff, Nicholas G. Evans and Adam Henschke, New York: Routledge, 2013: 338–51, at 345.

44. See: Ralph Wedgwood, 'The Price of Non-reductive Moral Realism', *Ethical Theory and Moral Practice*, 2 (3) (1999): 199–215; Michael Ridge, 'Moral Non-Naturalism', *Stanford Encyclopedia of Philosophy*, ed. Edward N. Zalta (Fall 2019 Edition), <https://plato.stanford.edu/archives/fall2019/entries/moral-non-naturalism/>.

45. See: Jake Evans, 'Australian Defence Force invests $5 million in 'killer robots' research', *ABC News*, 28 February 2019, <https://www.abc.net.au/news/2019-03-01/defence-force-invests-in-killer-artificial-intelligence/10859398>.

46. Michael Auslin, 'Can the Pentagon win the AI arms race?', *Foreign Affairs*, 19 October 2018, <https://www.foreignaffairs.com/articles/united-states/2018-10-19/can-pentagon-win-ai-arms-race>.

47. See: Duncan Purves, Ryan Jenkins and Bradley J. Strawser, 'Autonomous Machines, Moral Judgment, and Acting for the Right Reasons', *Ethical Theory and Moral Practice*, 18 (2015): 851–72, at 851–2.

48. See: Michael Skerker, Duncan Purves and Ryan Jenkins, 'Autonomous Weapons Systems and the Moral Equality of Combatants', *Ethics and Information Technology*, 22 (2020): 197–209, at 198.

49. Keith Abney, 'Autonomous Robots and the Future of Just War Theory', in *Routledge Handbook of Ethics and War: Just War Theory in the Twenty-First Century*, ed. Fritz Allhoff, Nicholas G. Evans and Adam Henschke, New York: Routledge, 2013: 338–51, at 342.

50. Brad DeWees, Chris Umphres and Maddy Tung, 'Machine learning and life-and-death decisions on the battlefield', *War on the Rocks*, 11 January 2021, <https://warontherocks.com/2021/01/machine-learning-and-life-and-death-decisions-on-the-battlefield/>.

51. Ibid.

52. Susan Anderson, 'Philosophical Concerns with Machine Ethics', in *Machine Ethics*, ed. Michael Anderson and Susan Anderson, Cambridge: Cambridge University Press, 2011: 162–7, at 162.

53. Elke Schwarz, *Death Machines: The Ethics of Violent Technologies*, Manchester: Manchester University Press, 2018: 16.

54. Margaret A. Boden, *Artificial Intelligence A Very Short Introduction*, Oxford: Oxford University Press, 2018: 24.

55. Elke Schwarz, *Death Machines: The Ethics of Violent Technologies*, Manchester: Manchester University Press, 2018: 20.

56. See: Margaret A. Boden, *Artificial Intelligence: A Very Short Introduction*, Oxford: Oxford University Press, 2018: 19; John Kaag and Whitley Kaufman, 'Military Frameworks: Technological Know-How and the Legitimization of Warfare', *Cambridge Review of International Affairs*, 22 (4) (2009): 585–606, at 600.

57. Kareem Ayoub and Kenneth Payne, 'Strategy in the Age of Artificial Intelligence', *Journal of Strategic Studies*, 39 (5–6) (2016): 793–819, at 811.

58. See: Nigel Jones, *Countdown to Valkyrie: The July Plot to Assassinate Hitler*, Barnsley: Frontline Books, 2009.

59. Heather M. Roff, 'Killing in War: Responsibility, Liability, and Lethal Autonomous Robots', in *Routledge Handbook of Ethics and War: Just War Theory in the Twenty-First Century*, ed. Fritz Allhoff, Nicholas G. Evans and Adam Henschke, New York: Routledge, 2013: 352–64, at 360 (note 13); Christof Heyns, 'Human Rights and the Use of Autonomous Weapons Systems (AWS) During Domestic Law Enforcement', *Human Rights Quarterly*, 38 (2016): 350–78, at 370; Christopher Coker, 'Ethics, Drones, and Killer Robots', in *The Oxford Handbook of International Political Theory*, ed. Chris Brown and Robyn Eckersley, Oxford: Oxford University Press, 2018: 247–58, at 252; Human Rights Watch and Harvard Law School International Human Rights Clinic, *Losing Humanity: the Case against Killer Robots*, Human Rights Watch, 2012, <https://www.hrw.org/report/2012/11/19/losing-humanity/case-against-killer-robots>: 38; Peter Burt, *Off the Leash: The Development of Autonomous Military Drones in the UK*, Oxford: Drone Wars UK, November 2018: 14.

60. Robert Sparrow, 'Killer Robots', *Journal of Applied Philosophy*, 24 (1) (2007): 62–77, at 67; George R. Lucas Jr., 'Industrial Challenges of Military Robotics', *Journal of Military Ethics*, 10 (4) (2011): 274–95.

61. Nikil Mukerji, 'Autonomous Killer Drones', in *Drones and Responsibility: Legal, Philosophical, and Sociotechnical Perspectives on Remotely Controlled Weapons*, ed. Ezio Di Nucci and Filippo Santoni de Sio, London: Routledge, 2016: 197–214, at 208.

62. Dante Marino and Guglielmo Tamburrini, 'Learning Robots and Human Responsibility', *International Review of Information Ethics*, 6 (2006): 46–51, at 49.

63. See: Frank Sauer and Niklas Schörnig, 'Killer Drones: "The Silver Bullet" of Democratic Warfare?', *Security Dialogue*, 43 (4) (2012): 363–80, at 375.

64. Alex Leveringhaus, 'Drones, Automated Targeting, and Moral Responsibility', in *Drones and Responsibility: Legal, Philosophical, and Sociotechnical Perspectives on Remotely Controlled Weapons*, ed. Ezio Di Nucci and Filippo Santoni de Sio, London: Routledge, 2016: 169–81, at 172.

65. Ibid. 172.

66. See: Sean Coughlan, 'A-levels and GCSEs: Boris Johnson blames "mutant algorithm" for exam fiasco', *BBC News*, 26 August 2020, <https://www.bbc.co.uk/news/education-53923279>.

67. Robert Sparrow, 'Killer Robots', *Journal of Applied Philosophy*, 24 (1) (2007): 62–77, at 73.

68. Human Rights Watch and Harvard Law School International Human Rights Clinic, *Losing Humanity: the Case against Killer Robots*, Human Rights Watch, 2012, <https://www.hrw.org/report/2012/11/19/losing-humanity/case-against-killer-robots>: 4.

69. US Department of Defense, *Unmanned Systems Integrated Roadmap 2017-2042* (issued 28 August 2018): 22 (emphasis added). Available at: US Naval Institute, 'Pentagon Unmanned Systems Integrated Roadmap 2017-2042', *USNI News*, 30 August 2018, <https://news.usni.org/2018/08/30/pentagon-unmanned-systems-integrated-roadmap-2017-2042>.

70. US Department of Defense, 'Autonomy in Weapon Systems', Directive no. 3000.09 (21 November 2012), *Washington Headquarters Services*, <http://www.esd.whs.mil/Portals/54/Documents/DD/issuances/dodd/300009p.pdf>: 13.

71. ICRC, 'ICRC position on autonomous weapon systems', *International Committee of the Red Cross*, 12 May 2021, <https://www.icrc.org/en/document/icrc-position-autonomous-weapon-systems>.

72. Ministry of Defence, *Unmanned Aircraft Systems* (Joint Doctrine Publication 030.2), 12 September 2017, <https://www.gov.uk/government/uploads/system/uploads/attachment_data/file/673940/doctrine_uk_uas_jdp_0_30_2.pdf>: 13–15.

73. See: Defence Ethics Committee, 'Opinion on the Integration of Autonomy into Lethal Weapon Systems', *French Government*, 29 April 2021, <https://www.defense.gouv.fr/salle-de-presse/communiques/communique_le-comite-d-ethique-de-la-defense-publie-son-rapport-sur-l-integration-de-l-autonomie-des-systemes-d-armes-letaux>.

74. See: Jean-Baptiste Jeangène Vilmer, 'A French opinion on the ethics of autonomous weapons', *War on the Rocks*, 2 June 2021, <https://warontherocks.com/2021/06/the-french-defense-ethics-committees-opinion-on-autonomous-weapons/>.

75. Thompson Chengeta, 'Defining the Emerging Notion of "Meaningful Human Control" in Weapon Systems', *International Law and Politics*, 49 (2017): 833–90, at 854.

76. See, for example: European Parliament, Resolution of 12 September 2018 on autonomous weapon systems (2018/2752(RSP)), para. F.

77. Alex Leveringhaus, 'Drones, Automated Targeting, and Moral Responsibility', in *Drones and Responsibility: Legal, Philosophical, and Sociotechnical Perspectives on Remotely Controlled Weapons*, ed. Ezio Di Nucci and Filippo Santoni de Sio, London: Routledge, 2016: 169–81, at 174; Arthur Holland Michel, 'The killer algorithms nobody's talking about', *Foreign Policy*, 20 January 2020, <https://foreignpolicy.com/2020/01/20/ai-autonomous-weapons-artificial-intelligence-the-killer-algorithms-nobodys-talking-about/>; Tony Gillespie, 'Good Practice for the Development of Autonomous Weapons', *The RUSI Journal*, 165 (5–6) (2020): 58–67, at 60.

78. See: Greg Waldron, 'GA-ASI to conduct AI, machine learning work with MQ-9', *Flight Global*, 18 September 2019, <https://www.flightglobal.com/military-uavs/ga-asi-to-conduct-ai-machine-learning-work-with-mq-9/134362.article>; Peter Burt, 'US Reaper drones test Agile Condor: another step closer to "killer robots"', *Drone Wars*, 27 September 2019, <https://dronewars.net/2019/09/27/us-reaper-drones-test-agile-condor-another-step-closer-to-killer-robots/>.

79. Richard Moyes, 'Key Elements of Meaningful Human Control', *Article 36*, April 2016, <http://www.article36.org/wp-content/uploads/2016/04/MHC-2016-FINAL.pdf>: 2; Tony Gillespie, 'Good Practice for the Development of Autonomous Weapons', *The RUSI Journal*, 165 (5–6) (2020): 58–67, at 61; Daniele Amoroso and Guglielmo Tamburrini, 'Autonomous Weapons Systems and Meaningful Human Control: Ethical and Legal Issues', *Current Robotics Reports*, 1 (2020): 187–94, at 189.

80. Ingvild Bode and Tom Watts, 'Worried about the autonomous weapons of the future? Look at what's already gone wrong', *Bulletin of the Atomic Scientists*, 21 April 2021, <https://thebulletin.org/2021/04/worried-about-the-autonomous-weapons-of-the-future-look-at-whats-already-gone-wrong/>.

81. Christopher Coker, *Waging War without Warriors? The Changing Culture of Military Conflict*, Boulder, CO: Lynne Rienner, 2002: 174.

82. See: Raja Parasuraman and Victor Riley, 'Humans and Automation: Use, Misuse, Disuse, Abuse', *Human Factors*, 39 (2) (1997): 230–53.

83. Elsa B. Kania, 'The critical human element in the machine age of warfare', *Bulletin of the Atomic Scientists*, 15 November 2017, <https://thebulletin.org/2017/11/the-critical-human-element-in-the-machine-age-of-warfare/>; Peter Burt, *Off the Leash: The Development of Autonomous Military Drones in the UK*, Oxford: Drone Wars UK, 2018: 50.

84. Arthur Holland Michel, 'The killer algorithms nobody's talking about', *Foreign Policy*, 20 January 2020, <https://foreignpolicy.com/2020/01/20/ai-autonomous-weapons-artificial-intelligence-the-killer-algorithms-nobodys-talking-about/>; Ingvild Bode and Tom Watts, 'Worried about the autonomous weapons of the future? Look at what's already gone wrong', *Bulletin of the Atomic Scientists*, 21 April 2021, <https://thebulletin.org/2021/04/worried-about-the-autonomous-weapons-of-the-future-look-at-whats-already-gone-wrong/>.

85. Jerry Kaplan, 'Artificial Intelligence: Think Again', *Communications of the ACM*, 60 (1) (2017): 36–8, at 36.

86. See: Shira Levine, 'Why navigation apps have a gender issue', *BBC*, 3 March 2016, <http://www.bbc.com/autos/story/20160303-are-you-gps-gender-biased>; Emma Brockes, 'Help – I think I'm in an abusive relationship with Alexa', *The Guardian*, 20 September 2018, <https://www.theguardian.com/commentisfree/2018/sep/20/alexa-devices-amazon-echo>.

87. Seumas Miller, *Shooting to Kill: The Ethics of Police and Military Use of Lethal Force*, New York: Oxford University Press, 2016: 271.

88. Elke Schwarz, *Death Machines: The Ethics of Violent Technologies*, Manchester: Manchester University Press, 2018: 166. In 2021 the European Parliament called for prohibition of 'the anthropomorphisation of LAWS' in order to 'rule out any possibility of confusing humans with robots': European Parliament, Resolution of 20 January 2021 on artificial intelligence: questions of interpretation and application of international law in so far as the EU is affected in the areas of civil and military uses and of state authority outside the scope of criminal justice (2020/2013(INI)): para. 40.

89. Daniele Amoroso and Guglielmo Tamburrini, 'Autonomous Weapons Systems and Meaningful Human Control: Ethical and Legal Issues', *Current Robotics Reports*, 1 (2020): 187–94, at 189; European Parliament, Resolution of 20 January 2021 on artificial intelligence: questions of interpretation and application of international law in so far as the EU is affected in the areas of civil and military uses and of state authority outside the scope of criminal justice (2020/2013(INI)): para. 26.

90. Daniele Amoroso and Guglielmo Tamburrini, 'In Search of the "Human Element": International Debates on Regulating Autonomous Weapons Systems', *The International Spectator*, 56 (1) (2021): 20–38, at 27.

91. Tony Gillespie, 'Good Practice for the Development of Autonomous Weapons', *The RUSI Journal*, 165 (5–6) (2020): 58–67, at 62.

92. See: Daniele Amoroso and Guglielmo Tamburrini, 'Autonomous Weapons Systems and Meaningful Human Control: Ethical and Legal Issues', *Current Robotics Reports*, 1 (2020): 187–94, at 190.

93. Alex Leveringhaus, 'Drones, Automated Targeting, and Moral Responsibility', in *Drones and Responsibility: Legal, Philosophical, and Sociotechnical Perspectives on Remotely Controlled Weapons*, ed. Ezio Di Nucci and Filippo Santoni de Sio, London: Routledge, 2016: 169–81, at 177.

94. A similar term is 'human-machine teaming'. See: Ministry of Defence, 'Joint Concept Note 1/18: Human–Machine Teaming', *UK Government*, 21 May 2018, <https://www.gov.uk/government/publications/human-machine-teaming-jcn-118>.

95. Daniele Amoroso and Guglielmo Tamburrini, 'Autonomous Weapons Systems and Meaningful Human Control: Ethical and Legal Issues', *Current Robotics Reports*, 1 (2020): 187–94, at 192.

96. See: *Campaign to Stop Killer Robots*, <https://www.stopkillerrobots.org>; Human Rights Watch, 'Losing humanity: the case against killer robots', *Human Rights Watch*, 19 November 2012, <https://www.hrw.org/report/2012/11/19/losing-humanity/case-against-killer-robots>.

97. Erico Guizzo and Evan Ackerman, 'Do we want robot warriors to decide who lives or dies?', *IEEE Spectrum*, 31 May 2016, <https://spectrum.ieee.org/robotics/military-robots/do-we-want-robot-warriors-to-decide-who-lives-or-dies>.

98. See: Marcus Schulzke, 'Rethinking Military Virtue Ethics in an Age of Unmanned Weapons, *Journal of Military Ethics*, 15 (3) (2016): 187–204, at 199.

99. See: Peter Burt, *Off the Leash: The Development of Autonomous Military Drones in the UK*, Oxford: Drone Wars UK, 2018: 21.

100. BBC, 'How Israel's Iron Dome missile shield works', *BBC News*, 17 May 2021, <https://www.bbc.co.uk/news/world-middle-east-20385306>; Zachary Fryer-Biggs, 'Coming soon to a battlefield: robots that can kill', *The Atlantic*, 3 September 2019, <https://www.theatlantic.com/technology/archive/2019/09/killer-robots-and-new-era-machine-driven-warfare/597130/>.

101. See: Christof Heyns, 'Human Rights and the Use of Autonomous Weapons Systems (AWS) During Domestic Law Enforcement', *Human Rights Quarterly*, 38 (2016): 350–78.

102. See: Peter Asaro, '"Hands up, don't shoot!" HRI and the Automation of Police Use of Force', *Journal of Human-Robot Interaction*, 5 (3) (2016): 55–69, at 68.

103. See: Valerie Insinna, 'Under Skyborg program, F-35 and F-15EX jets could control drone sidekicks', *Defense News*, 22 May 2019, <https://www.defensenews.com/air/2019/05/22/under-skyborg-program-f-35-and-f-15ex-jets-could-control-drone-sidekicks/>.

104. Michael W. Byrnes, 'Nightfall: Machine Autonomy in Air-to-Air Combat', *Air & Space Power Journal* (May–June 2014): 48–75, at 63.

105. See: Daniele Amoroso and Guglielmo Tamburrini, 'Autonomous Weapons Systems and Meaningful Human Control: Ethical and Legal Issues', *Current Robotics Reports*, 1 (2020): 187–94, at 191; Alan Backstrom and Ian Henderson, 'New Capabilities in Warfare: An Overview of Contemporary Technological Developments and the Associated Legal and Engineering Issues in Article 36 Weapons Reviews', *International Review of the Red Cross*, 94 (2012): 483–514, at 497.

106. Michael J. Boyle, *The Drone Age: How Drone Technology Will Change War and Peace*, New York: Oxford University Press, 2020: 124.

107. See: Beth Stevenson, '"Loyal Wingman" part of the future of air combat', *AIN online*, 13 June 2019, <https://www.ainonline.com/aviation-news/defense/2019-06-13/loyal-wingman-part-future-air-combat>; Ewan Levick, 'Boeing's autonomous fighter jet will fly over the Australian Outback', *IEEE Spectrum*, 2 January 2020, <https://spectrum.ieee.org/aerospace/military/boeings-autonomous-fighter-jet-will-fly-over-the-australian-outback>.

108. See: Christof Heyns, 'Human Rights and the Use of Autonomous Weapons Systems (AWS) During Domestic Law Enforcement', *Human Rights Quarterly*, 38 (2016): 350–78, at 358.

109. United Nations High Commissioner for Human Rights, 'Impact of new technologies on the promotion and protection of human rights in the context of assemblies, including peaceful protests' (A/HRC/44/24), New York, Human Rights Council, United Nations General Assembly, 24 June 2020: paras 31–2; Jane Wakefield, 'AI emotion-detection software tested on Uyghurs', *BBC News*, 26 May 2021, <https://www.bbc.co.uk/news/technology-57101248>; Drew Harwell, 'Amazon extends ban on police use of its facial recognition technology indefinitely', *Washington Post*, 18 May 2021, <https://www.washingtonpost.com/technology/2021/05/18/amazon-facial-recognition-ban/>; Douglas Heaven, 'Expression of Doubt', *Nature* 578 (27 February 2020): 502–4, at 503.

110. See: Peter Asaro, '"Hands up, don't shoot!" HRI and the Automation of Police Use of Force', *Journal of Human-Robot Interaction*, 5 (3) (2016): 55–69, at 62.

Chapter 7

CONCLUSION: DRONE VIOLENCE AND THE SCOPE FOR FUTURE RESTRAINT

As more governments acquire armed drones, and as new opportunities to use them emerge, there will be a continuing need for ethical thinking about why and how drone violence occurs. In conceptualising such violence in a variety of ways, a range of approaches to moral judgement is made available, and this affords a broad basis for understanding and debating what it means to use armed drones justly or unjustly. Today, many instances of drone violence can be judged as acts of warfare against combatant enemies, but other instances might soon need to be judged as police efforts to neutralise criminal threats to public safety. In some circumstances, a drone strike against an individual might amount to punishment for a crime or the mere management of a security risk, and it might also feel (to the drone operator) like the murder of a fellow human being. Or, in future, there might be no human controller available to feel anything at all if a drone's critical functions are performed by AI.

When drone violence is warfare, the moral risks from a *jus ad bellum* perspective relate mainly to the notion that warfare of this kind might be or become too easy to wage. This is a potential concern, especially, if a state does not place some of its own personnel at physical risk while using drones violently in a conflict. From a *jus in bello* perspective, however, there is perhaps some moral progress to be achieved in the sense that drone warfare could be conducted according to higher standards of discrimination and proportionality. Armed drones equipped with video cameras bring a powerful and sometimes prolonged capacity for pre-strike observation of prospective victims. For this reason, their use could render more feasible the adoption of a normative basis for warfare that further reduces the risk of unjust victimhood: a narrowed concept of who really constitutes a military threat, and a broadened concept of civilian harm.

Violent law enforcement is an alternative concept of a state's drone violence, and here a risk of injustice accompanies drone-based practices of punishment or policing. To the extent that some strikes conducted by the US government have been essentially punitive, the moral problem with these is that they amounted only to wild justice. Notwithstanding the careful rendering of administrative determinations about certain individuals' liability to be targeted, the risk of arbitrary execution remained unacceptably high because independent judges were not involved. And yet, even if the drone-based punishment of a crime could somehow be fairly and judicially authorised, a prohibitive problem of proportionality would remain if a missile strike posed too great a risk of hitting the wrong person or harming innocent people. Likewise, in the practice of policing, one moral concern with any future arming of police drones is that this might sometimes be too dangerous to bystanders and thus inconsistent with protecting public safety. In the policing of an unfolding crime, substituting a drone for an on-the-scene officer could generate a precaution problem because a drone cannot bring to bear the full spectrum of violent and non-violent response options. Moreover, if the camera mounted on a police drone failed to provide its remote controller with adequate perception of relevant circumstances, unjust police violence might become more likely to occur because of mistakes and misunderstandings. On the other hand, the arming of police drones might also be beneficial to suspects and bystanders if police officers were thereby made to feel better protected (by remoteness), and if this then made them less likely to use weapons excessively.

Warfare and violent law enforcement are the only paradigms of state violence to which a ready supply of moral expectations and principle-based laws can be applied. However, a lesson from past US experience is that a state's possession of armed drones might feed a temptation to act violently in a 'grey' manner that is not obviously captured by the morality of either paradigm. Such action is morally problematic if it causes state violence to be judged according to the wrong standards of behaviour, and part of the required response to this is to define some drone violence in more concrete terms. For several years, the US government used long-range drones to manage national security risks emerging in remote parts of the world, by enabling violent effects to be constantly generated, for a seemingly indefinite period, and in relative secrecy. In doing this, the US government purported to draw upon the morality of war to excuse occasional harm to innocent people within targeted territories, but the conditions that obtained there were not those of warfare. Rather, the essential open-endedness of drone violence in this instance made it quasi-imperialistic in nature. And, as the moral importance of the human right to life was thus never diminished by the emergence of a genuine war condition, so the US government's quasi-imperialistic drone violence remained open to condemnation according to the stricter morality of peacetime.

Beyond the issue of a drone-using state's political purpose, drone violence can and should be considered from an individual operator's perspective too, as tele-intimate violence. On this basis, the potential for victimhood and injustice is open to be understood not only in terms of what physical harms are inflicted upon other people but also in terms of how killing might harm the killer's moral well-being. When killing is a highly visual experience – as it is when a camera-equipped drone is the instrument of death – the moral disengagement that traditionally enables killing can be substantially more difficult to achieve. Consequently, whether drone violence is wielded in the waging of war or in the enforcing of law, a drone operator runs the risk of incurring moral injury, especially when a targeted person's humanity has previously been revealed over time. If the injustice of moral injury were then to be addressed as a matter of occupational well-being, this would seem to require the provision of something more than medical care and spiritual support. In addition, perhaps, a drone-using state could act to morally empower its operators by valorising moral courage and formally affording them operational discretion over whether or when to use a drone-based weapon.

Even if a drone-using state were to champion individual agency in this way, future technological advancements might yet enable an alternative approach: the devolution of control over drone violence from humans to AI technologies. Here, though, any associated reduction in the risk of moral injury would be a relatively minor advantage. The greater moral concern would be to ensure that an armed drone's AI-assisted violence remained under meaningful human control. Failing that, the potential for highly devolved drone violence to harm humans unjustly would lie in the inherent inability of AI to make moral decisions and take moral responsibility for wrongdoing. Thus, if or when AI technology comes to be incorporated into drone-based weapon systems, adherence to the MHC principle would require engineered arrangements that guarantee a satisfactory degree of human–machine interaction in the performance of critical system functions. Such arrangements would need to account for the moral differences between different operational conditions. However, if this could be achieved, it would do much to preserve the restraining influence of human moral agency for the benefit of possible victims.

Into the future, as armed drones proliferate and related technologies advance, the potential for unjust victimhood seems likely to increase unless there is a countervailing effort to restrain drone-using states and the individual operators they employ. It will arguably remain important, then, to maximise the preventing of injustice by first thinking broadly about how and why it can be right or wrong to use these aircraft in different kinds of circumstances. To that end, the concepts of violence discussed here – warfare, violent law enforcement, tele-intimate violence and devolved violence – could usefully underpin a more comprehensive approach to rendering moral judgements and requiring adherence to diverse principles of restraint.

BIBLIOGRAPHY

ABC. '"This Week" Transcript: Panetta', *ABC News*, 27 June 2010, <https://abcnews.go.com/ThisWeek/week-transcript-panetta/story?id=11025299>.

Abé, Nicola. 'Dreams in Infrared: The Woes of an American Drone Operator', *Der Spiegel*, 14 December 2012, <http://www.spiegel.de/international/world/pain-continues-after-war-for-american-drone-pilot-a-872726.html>.

Abney, Keith. 'Autonomous Robots and the Future of Just War Theory', in *Routledge Handbook of Ethics and War: Just War Theory in the Twenty-First Century*, ed. Fritz Allhoff, Nicholas G. Evans and Adam Henschke. New York: Routledge, 2013: 338–51.

Ackerman, Spencer. '"Drones playbook" shows key role played by White House staff in deadly strikes', *The Guardian*, 6 August 2016, <https://www.theguardian.com/world/2016/aug/06/drones-playbook-white-house-nsc-obama-clinton-trump>.

Adams, Thomas K. 'Future Warfare and the Decline of Human Decisionmaking', *Parameters* (Winter 2001–02): 57–71.

AFP. 'French army carries out first-ever drone strike during Mali op', *France 24*, 23 December 2019, <https://www.france24.com/en/20191223-french-army-carries-out-first-ever-drone-strike-during-mali-op>.

AFP. 'Turning to Israel, Germany to get weaponized drones for the first time', *Times of Israel*, 6 April 2022, <https://www.timesofisrael.com/turning-to-israel-germany-to-get-weaponized-drones-for-the-first-time>.

Afxentiou, Afxentis. 'A History of Drones: Moral(e) Bombing and State Terrorism', *Critical Studies on Terrorism*, 11 (2) (2018): 301–20.

Agius, Christine. 'Ordering without Bordering: Drones, the Unbordering of Late Modern Warfare and Ontological Insecurity', *Postcolonial Studies*, 20 (3) (2017): 370–86.

Akhter, Majed. 'The Proliferation of Peripheries: Militarized Drones and the Reconfiguration of Global Space', *Progress in Human Geography*, 43 (1) (2019): 64–80.

Alessio, Dominic, and Wesley Renfro. 'Empire?', *European Journal of American Studies*, 15 (2) (2020): 1–22.

Alexander, Mariam. 'NHS staff are suffering from "moral injury", a distress usually associated with war zones', *The Guardian*, 12 April 2021, <https://www.theguardian.com/commentisfree/2021/apr/12/nhs-staff-moral-injury-distress-associated-with-war-zones-pandemic>.

Alexander, Samuel. 'Double-Tap Warfare: Should President Obama be Investigated for War Crimes?', *Florida Law Review*, 69 (1) (2017): 261–95.

Ali, Zulfiqar. 'Two US drone strikes kill 6 militants in North Waziristan: officials', *The Express Tribune*, 19 August 2012, <https://tribune.com.pk/story/424117/us-drone-strike-kills-four-militants-in-pakistan-officials>.

All Party Parliamentary Group on Drones. *The UK's Use of Armed Drones: Working with Partners*, London: UK Parliament, July 2018.

Alston, Philip. 'Report of the Special Rapporteur on Extrajudicial, Summary or Arbitrary Executions. Addendum: Study on Targeted Killings' (A/HRC/14/24/Add.6), Human Rights Council, United Nations General Assembly, 28 May 2010.

Altmann, Jürgen, and Frank Sauer. 'Autonomous Weapon Systems and Strategic Stability', *Survival*, 59 (5) (2017): 117–42.

Amnesty International. *'Will I Be Next?': US Drone Strikes in Pakistan*. London: Amnesty International Publications, 2013.

Amnesty International. 'Death Sentences and Executions 2020', *Amnesty International*, 21 April 2021, <https://www.amnesty.org/en/documents/act50/3760/2021/en/>.

Amoroso, Daniele, and Guglielmo Tamburrini. 'Autonomous Weapons Systems and Meaningful Human Control: Ethical and Legal Issues', *Current Robotics Reports*, 1 (2020): 187–94.

Amoroso, Daniele, and Guglielmo Tamburrini. 'In Search of the "Human Element": International Debates on Regulating Autonomous Weapons Systems', *The International Spectator*, 56 (1) (2021): 20–38.

Anderson, Susan. 'Philosophical Concerns with Machine Ethics', in *Machine Ethics*, ed. Michael Anderson and Susan Anderson. Cambridge: Cambridge University Press, 2011: 162–7.

Anonymous. 'USAF's Skyborg ACS flies onboard MQ-20 Avenger tactical UAV', *Air Force Technology*, 30 June 2021, <https://www.airforce-technology.com/news/usafs-skyborg-acs-flies-onboard-mq-20-avenger-tactical-uav/>.

Antal, Chris J., and Kathy Winings. 'Moral Injury, Soul Repair, and Creating a Place for Grace', *Religious Education*, 110 (4) (2015): 382–94.

Aristotle. *The Ethics of Aristotle: The Nicomachean Ethics*, trans. J. A. K. Thomson. London: Penguin, 1953.

Arkin, Ronald C. 'Ethical Robots in Warfare', *IEEE Technology and Society* (Spring 2009): 30–3.

Arkin, Ronald C. 'The Case for Ethical Autonomy in Unmanned Systems', *Journal of Military Ethics* 9 (4) (2010): 332–41.

Armour, Cherie, and Jana Ross. 'The Health and Well-Being of Military Drone Operators and Intelligence Analysts: A Systematic Review', *Military Psychology*, 29 (2) (2017): 83–98.

Asaro, Peter. 'On Banning Autonomous Weapon Systems: Human Rights, Automation, and the Dehumanization of Lethal Decisionmaking', *International Review of the Red Cross*, 94 (886) (2012): 687–709.

Asaro, Peter M. 'The Labor of Surveillance and Bureaucratized Killing: New Subjectivities of Military Drone Operators', *Social Semiotics*, 23 (2) (2013): 196–224.

Asaro, Peter M.. '"Hands up, don't shoot!": HRI and the Automation of Police Use of Force', *Journal of Human-Robot Interaction*, 5 (3) (2016): 55–69.

Associated Press. 'Sri Lanka advertises for two hangmen as country resumes capital punishment', *The Guardian*, 14 February 2019, <https://www.theguardian.com/world/2019/feb/14/sri-lanka-advertises-for-two-hangmen-as-country-resumes-capital-punishment>.

Atherton, Kelsey D. 'Grenade launching drone will be part of Army exercise in 2020', *C4ISRNET*, 19 November 2019, <https://www.c4isrnet.com/unmanned/2019/11/19/grenade-launcher-drone-is-backpackable-air-support/>.

Atherton, Kelsey D. 'One drone down and the new nuance of escalation', *Defense News*, 20 June 2019, <https://www.defensenews.com/unmanned/2019/06/20/one-drone-down-and-the-new-nuance-of-escalation/>.

Auslin, Michael. 'Can the Pentagon win the AI arms race?', *Foreign Affairs*, 19 October 2018, <https://www.foreignaffairs.com/articles/united-states/2018-10-19/can-pentagon-win-ai-arms-race>.

Ayoub, Kareem, and Kenneth Payne. 'Strategy in the Age of Artificial Intelligence', *Journal of Strategic Studies*, 39 (5–6) (2016): 793–819.

Bachman, Jeffrey S., and Jack Holland. 'Lethal Sterility: Innovative Dehumanisation in Legal Justifications of Obama's Drone Policy', *The International Journal of Human Rights*, 23 (6) (2019): 1028–47.

Backstrom, Alan, and Ian Henderson. 'New Capabilities in Warfare: An Overview of Contemporary Technological Developments and the Associated Legal and Engineering Issues in Article 36 Weapons Reviews', *International Review of the Red Cross*, 94 (2012): 483–514.

BAE. 'Taranis', *BAE Systems*, no date, <https://www.baesystems.com/en-uk/product/taranis1> (accessed 7 February 2022).

Baggaley, Katherine, Olga Marques and Phillip C. Shon. 'An Exploratory Study of the Decision to Refrain from Killing in the Accounts of Military and Police Personnel', *Journal of Military Ethics*, 18 (1) (2019): 20–34.

Baggiarini, Bianca. 'Drone Warfare and the Limits of Sacrifice', *Journal of International Political Theory*, 11 (1) (2015): 128–44.

Balko, Radley. *Rise of the Warrior Cop: The Militarization of America's Police Forces*. New York: Public Affairs, 2013.

Bandura, Albert. 'Moral Disengagement in the Perpetration of Inhumanities', *Personality and Social Psychology Review*, 3 (3) (1999): 193–209.

Bandura, Albert. *Moral Disengagement: How People Do Harm and Live with Themselves*. New York: Macmillan, 2016.

Bandura, Albert. 'Disengaging Morality from Robotic War', *The Psychologist* (February 2017): 38–43.

Barber, Rebecca J. 'The Proportionality Equation: Balancing Military Objectives with Civilian Lives in the Armed Conflict in Afghanistan', *Journal of Conflict and Security Law*, 15 (3) (2010): 467–500.

Barrett, Brian. 'The Pentagon's hand-me-downs helped militarize police. Here's how', *Wired*, 2 June 2020, <https://www.wired.com/story/pentagon-hand-me-downs-militarize-police-1033-program/>.

Bass, Gary Jonathan. *Stay the Hand of Vengeance: The Politics of War Crimes Tribunals*. Princeton: Princeton University Press, 2000.

Baudrillard, Jean. *The Gulf War Did Not Take Place*. Indianapolis: Indiana University Press, 1995.

BBC. 'Debate rages over "shoot-to-kill"', *BBC News*, 24 July 2005, <http://news.bbc.co.uk/1/hi/uk/4711769.stm>.

BBC. 'US drone strike in Pakistan "killed key al-Qaeda man",' *BBC News*, 18 March 2010, <http://news.bbc.co.uk/2/hi/americas/8573652.stm>.

BBC. 'UK drone carries out first strike in Iraq', *BBC News*, 10 November 2014, <https://www.bbc.co.uk/news/world-middle-east-29992686>.

BBC. 'Syrian pro-government drone shot down by US military', *BBC News*, 8 June 2017, <https://www.bbc.co.uk/news/world-middle-east-40206957>.

BBC. 'Syria war: MoD admits civilian died in RAF strike on Islamic State', *BBC News*, 2 May 2018, <https://www.bbc.co.uk/news/uk-43977394>.

BBC. 'Qasem Soleimani: US kills top Iranian general in Baghdad air strike', *BBC News*, 3 January 2020, <https://www.bbc.co.uk/news/world-middle-east-50979463>.

BBC. 'Syria war: Turkish drone strikes "kill 19 Syrian soldiers"', *BBC News*, 2 March 2020, <https://www.bbc.co.uk/news/world-middle-east-51701069>.

BBC. 'End Sars protests: People "shot dead" in Lagos, Nigeria', *BBC News*, 21 October 2020, <https://www.bbc.co.uk/news/world-africa-54624611>.

BBC. 'How Israel's Iron Dome missile shield works', *BBC News*, 17 May 2021, <https://www.bbc.co.uk/news/world-middle-east-20385306>.

BBC. 'Drone helps save cardiac arrest patient in Sweden', *BBC News*, 6 January 2022, <https://www.bbc.co.uk/news/technology-59885656>.

Beauchamp, Scott. 'Can drone pilots be heroes?', *The Atlantic*, 23 January 2016, <https://www.theatlantic.com/politics/archive/2016/01/can-drone-pilots-be-heroes/424830/>.

Beauchamp, Zack, and Julian Savulescu. 'Robot Guardians: Teleoperated Combat Vehicles in Humanitarian Military Intervention', in *Killing by Remote*

Control: The Ethics of an Unmanned Military, ed. Bradley Jay Strawser. New York: Oxford University Press, 2013: 106–25.

Beaumont, Peter. 'Making of a martyr: how Qassem Suleimani was hunted down', *The Guardian*, 5 January 2020, <https://www.theguardian.com/world/2020/jan/05/making-of-a-martyr-how-qassem-suleimani-was-hunted-down>.

Beaumont, Peter. 'US military increasingly using drone missile with flying blades in Syria', *The Guardian*, 25 September 2020, <https://www.theguardian.com/world/2020/sep/25/us-military-syria-non-explosive-drone-missile-blades>.

Becker, Jo, and Scott Shane. 'Secret "kill list" proves a test of Obama's principles and will', *New York Times*, 29 May 2012: A1.

Bentley, Michelle. 'Fetishised Data: Counterterrorism, Drone Warfare and Pilot Testimony', *Critical Studies on Terrorism*, 11 (1) (2018): 88–110.

Bergen, Peter L., and Jennifer Rowland. 'Decade of the Drone: Analyzing CIA Drone Attacks, Casualties, and Policy', in *Drone Wars: Transforming Conflict, Law, and Policy*, ed. Peter L. Bergen and Daniel Rothenberg. New York: Cambridge University Press, 2015: 12–41.

Berghaus, Paul T., and Nathan L. Cartagena. 'Developing Good Soldiers: The Problem of Fragmentation within the Army', *Journal of Military Ethics*, 12 (4) (2013): 287–303.

Blair, Dave. 'A Categorical Error: Rethinking "Drones" as an Analytical Category for Security Policy', *Lawfare*, 24 April 2016, <https://www.lawfareblog.com/categorical-error-rethinking-drones-analytical-category-security-policy>.

Blair, Dave, and Karen House. 'Avengers in Wrath: Moral Agency and Trauma Prevention for Remote Warriors', *Lawfare*, 12 November 2017, <https://www.lawfareblog.com/avengers-wrath-moral-agency-and-trauma-prevention-remote-warriors>.

Blakeley, Ruth. 'State Terrorism in the Social Sciences: Theories, Methods and Concepts', in *Contemporary State Terrorism: Theory and Practice*, ed. Richard Jackson, Eamon Murphy and Scott Poynting. London: Routledge, 2010: 12–27.

Blakeley, Ruth. 'Drones, State Terrorism and International Law', *Critical Studies on Terrorism*, 11 (2) (2018): 321–41.

Blanchard, Charles. 'This is Not War by Machine', in *Drone Wars: Transforming Conflict, Law, and Policy*, ed. Peter L. Bergen and Daniel Rothenberg. New York: Cambridge University Press, 2015: 118–28.

Blank, Laurie R. 'Targeted Strikes: The Consequences of Blurring the Armed Conflict and Self-Defense Justifications', *William Mitchell Law Review*, 38 (5) (2012): 1655–700.

Blount, Clive. 'Useful for the Next Hundred Years? Maintaining the Future Utility of Airpower', *The RUSI Journal*, 163 (3) (2018): 44–51.

Blum, Gabriella. 'The Individualization of War: From War to Policing in the Regulation of Armed Conflicts', in *Law and War*, ed. Austin Sarat, Lawrence

Douglas and Martha Merrill Umphrey. Stanford, CA: Stanford University Press, 2013: 48–82.

Bode, Ingvild, and Tom Watts, 'Worried about the autonomous weapons of the future? Look at what's already gone wrong', *Bulletin of the Atomic Scientists*, 21 April 2021, <https://thebulletin.org/2021/04/worried-about-the-autonomous-weapons-of-the-future-look-at-whats-already-gone-wrong/>.

Boden, Margaret A. *Artificial Intelligence: A Very Short Introduction*. Oxford: Oxford University Press, 2018.

Borg, Stefan. 'Assembling Israeli Drone Warfare: Loitering Surveillance and Operational Sustainability', *Security Dialogue*, 52 (5) (2021): 401–17.

Borger, Julian. 'The drone operators who halted Russian convoy headed for Kyiv', *The Guardian*, 28 March 2022, <https://www.theguardian.com/world/2022/mar/28/the-drone-operators-who-halted-the-russian-armoured-vehicles-heading-for-kyiv>.

Boulanin, Vincent. *Mapping the Development of Autonomy in Weapon Systems: A Primer on Autonomy*. Stockholm: Stockholm International Peace Research Institute, 2016.

Boulanin, Vincent, Laura Bruun and Netta Goussac. *Autonomous Weapon Systems and International Humanitarian Law: Identifying Limits and the Required Type and Degree of Human–Machine Interaction*. Stockholm: Stockholm International Peace Research Institute, June 2021.

Boyle, Michael J. 'The Legal and Ethical Implications of Drone Warfare', *The International Journal of Human Rights*, 19 (2) (2015): 105–26.

Boyle, Michael J. *The Drone Age: How Drone Technology Will Change War and Peace*. New York: Oxford University Press, 2020.

Braender, Morten. 'Deployment and Dehumanization: A Multi-Method Study of Combat Soldiers' Loss of Empathy', *Res Militaris*, 5 (2) (2015): 1–18.

Braithwaite, Malcolm, Graeme Nicholson, Rob Thornton, David Jones, Robin Simpson, David McLoughin and David Jenkins, 'Armed Forces Occupational Health – A Review', *Occupational Medicine*, 59 (8) (2009): 528–38.

Bramesco, Charles. 'Dirty Harry at 50: Clint Eastwood's seminal, troubling 70s antihero', *The Guardian*, 23 December 2021, <https://www.theguardian.com/film/2021/dec/23/dirty-harry-clint-eastwood-70s-antihero>.

Braun, Christian Nikolaus. 'The Morality of Retributive Targeted Killing', *Journal of Military Ethics*, 18 (3) (2019): 170–88.

Braun, Christian Nikolaus. '*Jus ad Vim* and Drone Warfare: A Classical Just War Perspective', in *Ethics of Drone Strikes: Restraining Remote-Control Killing*, ed. Christian Enemark. Edinburgh: Edinburgh University Press, 2021: 31–49.

Braun, Megan, and Daniel R. Brunstetter. 'Rethinking the Criterion for Assessing CIA-targeted Killings: Drones, Proportionality and *Jus ad Vim*', *Journal of Military Ethics*, 12 (4) (2013): 304–24.

Brennan, John O. 'Strengthening our security by adhering to our values and laws', *The White House*, 16 September 2011, <https://obamawhitehouse.archives. gov/the-press-office/2011/09/16/remarks-john-o-brennan-strengthening-our-security-adhering-our-values-an>.

Brennan, John O. 'The Efficacy and Ethics of U.S. Counterterrorism Strategy', *Woodrow Wilson International Center for Scholars*, 30 April 2012, <https:// www.wilsoncenter.org/event/the-efficacy-and-ethics-us-counterterrorism-strategy>.

Bricknell, Martin, and Paul Cain, 'Understanding the Whole of Military Health Systems: The Defence Healthcare Cycle', *RUSI Journal*, 165 (3) (2020): 40–49.

Brock, Rita Nakashima. 'Moral injury: the crucial missing piece in understanding soldier suicides', *Huffpost*, 22 September 2012, <https://www.huffpost. com/entry/moral-injury-the-crucial-missing-piece-in-understanding-soldier-suicides_b_1686674>.

Brockes, Emma. 'Help – I think I'm in an abusive relationship with Alexa', *The Guardian*, 20 September 2018, <https://www.theguardian.com/commentis-free/2018/sep/20/alexa-devices-amazon-echo>.

Brookman-Byrne, Max. 'Drone Use "Outside Areas of Active Hostilities": An Examination of the Legal Paradigms Governing US Covert Remote Strikes', *Netherlands International Law Review*, 64 (2017): 3–41.

Brooks, Rosa. 'Drones and Cognitive Dissonance', in *Drone Wars: Transforming Conflict, Law, and Policy*, ed. Peter L. Bergen and Daniel Rothenberg. New York: Cambridge University Press, 2015: 230–52.

Brooks, Rosa. *How Everything Became War and the Military Became Everything: Tales from the Pentagon*. New York: Simon & Schuster, 2016.

Brown, Nicholas R. 'Unmanned? The Bodily Harms and Moral Valor of Drone Warfare', in *The Future of Drone Use: Opportunities and Threats from Ethical and Legal Perspectives*, ed. Bart Custers. The Hague: TMC Asser Press, 2016: 189–207.

Browne, Ryan, and Barbara Starr. 'Trump: US military killed terrorist behind USS Cole bombing', *CNN*, 6 January 2019, <https://edition.cnn.com/2019/01/04/ politics/uss-cole-al-badawi-killed/index.html>.

Brumfiel, Geoff. 'In Yemen conflict, some see a new age of drone warfare', *NPR*, 29 May 2019, <https://text.npr.org/726760128>.

Brumfield, Eric. 'Armed Drones for Law Enforcement: Why It Might Be Time to Re-Examine the Current Use of Force Standard', *McGeorge Law Review*, 46 (3) (2014): 543–72.

Brunstetter, Daniel, and Megan Braun. 'From *Jus ad Bellum* to *Jus ad Vim*: Recalibrating Our Understanding of the Moral Use of Force', *Ethics & International Affairs* 27 (1) (2013): 87–106.

Brunstetter, Daniel. '*Jus ad Vim*: A Rejoinder to Helen Frowe', *Ethics & International Affairs*, 30 (1) (2016): 131–6.

Brunstetter, Daniel R. 'Wading Knee-Deep into the Rubicon: Escalation and the Morality of Limited Strikes', *Ethics & International Affairs*, 34 (2) (2020): 161–73.

Bulos, Nabih. 'Carnage escalates, options for U.S. diminish in new round of Yemeni civil war attacks', *Los Angeles Times*, 21 January 2022, <https://www.latimes.com/world-nation/story/2022-01-21/houthis-yemen>.

Bumiller, Elisabeth. 'Air Force drone operators report high levels of stress', *New York Times*, 19 December 2011: A8.

Bumiller, Elisabeth. 'A day job waiting for a kill shot a world away', *New York Times*, 30 July 2012: A1.

Bump, Philip. 'The border patrol wants to arm drones', *The Atlantic*, 2 July 2013, <https://www.theatlantic.com/national/archive/2013/07/border-patrol-arm-drones/313656/>.

Bundy, Alan. 'Preparing for the Future of Artificial Intelligence', *AI & Society* 32 (2017): 285–87.

Bureau of Investigative Journalism. 'Drone strikes in Pakistan', *Bureau of Investigative Journalism*, February 2020, <https://www.thebureauinvestigates.com/projects/drone-war/Pakistan>.

Burt, Peter. *Off the Leash: The Development of Autonomous Military Drones in the UK*. Oxford: Drone Wars UK, November 2018.

Burt, Peter. 'US Reaper drones test Agile Condor: another step closer to "Killer Robots"', *Drone Wars*, 27 September 2019, <https://dronewars.net/2019/09/27/us-reaper-drones-test-agile-condor-another-step-closer-to-killer-robots/>.

Bush, George W. 'State of the Union Address', *The White House*, 20 January 2004, <https://georgewbush-whitehouse.archives.gov/news/releases/2004/01/20040120-7.html>.

Byman, Daniel. 'Why Drones Work: The Case for Washington's Weapon of Choice', *Foreign Affairs*, 92 (July/August 2013): 32–43.

Byrnes, Michael W. 'Nightfall: Machine Autonomy in Air-to-Air Combat', *Air & Space Power Journal* (May–June 2014): 48–75.

Calhoun, Laurie. 'The Silencing of Soldiers', *The Independent Review*, 16 (2) (2011): 247–70.

Calhoun, Laurie. *We Kill Because We Can: From Soldiering to Assassination in the Drone Age*. London: Zed Books, 2015.

Calhoun, Laurie. 'Totalitarian Tendencies in Drone Strikes by States', *Critical Studies on Terrorism*, 11 (2) (2018): 357–75.

Callamard, Agnès. *Use of Armed Drones for Targeted Killings*. Report of the Special Rapporteur on extrajudicial, summary or arbitrary executions (A/HRC/44/38), Human Rights Council, United Nations General Assembly, 15 August 2020.

Caron, Jean-François. 'Exploring the Extent of Ethical Disobedience through the Lens of the Srebrenica and Rwanda Genocides: Can Soldiers Disobey Lawful Orders?', *Critical Military Studies*, 5 (1) (2019): 1–20.

Casey-Maslen, Stuart. 'Pandora's Box? Drone Strikes under *Jus ad Bellum*, *Jus in Bello*, and International Human Rights Law', *International Review of the Red Cross*, 94 (886) (2012): 597–625.

Chamayou, Grégoire. *Drone Theory*, trans. Janet Lloyd. London: Penguin, 2015.

Chandler, Katherine. *Unmanning: How Humans, Machines and Media Perform Drone Warfare*. New Brunswick: Rutgers University Press, 2020.

Chapa, Joseph O. 'Remotely Piloted Aircraft, Risk, and Killing as Sacrifice: The Cost of Remote Warfare', *Journal of Military Ethics*, 16 (3–4) (2017): 256–71.

Chapa, Joe. 'Inside Britain's Reaper force: human stories and ethical dilemmas', *War on the Rocks*, 18 October 2018, <https://warontherocks.com/2018/10/inside-britains-reaper-force-human-stories-and-ethical-dilemmas/>.

Chappelle, Wayne, Kent McDonald and Katharine McMillan. *Important and Critical Psychological Attributes of USAF MQ-1 Predator and MQ-9 Reaper Pilots According to Subject Matter Experts* (AFRL-SA-WP-TR-2011-0002), Air Force Research Laboratory, May 2011.

Chappelle, Wayne L., Tanya Goodman, Laura Reardon and William Thompson. 'An Analysis of Post-Traumatic Stress Symptoms in United States Air Force Drone Operators', *Journal of Anxiety Disorders*, 28 (2014): 480–7.

Chatterjee, Pratap. 'A chilling new post-traumatic stress disorder: why drone pilots are quitting in record numbers', *Salon*, 6 March 2015, <http://www.salon.com/2015/03/06/a_chilling_new_post_traumatic_stress_disorder_why_drone_pilots_are_quitting_in_record_numbers_partner/>.

Chayka, Kyle. 'Watch this drone taser a guy until he collapses', *Time*, 11 March 2014, <https://time.com/19929/watch-this-drone-taser-a-guy-until-he-collapses/>.

Chengeta, Thompson. 'Defining the Emerging Notion of "Meaningful Human Control" in Weapon Systems', *International Law and Politics*, 49 (2017): 833–90.

Church, Chris. 'Downrange operators keep drones flying over Iraq, Syria and Afghanistan', *Stars and Stripes*, 4 April 2017, <https://www.stripes.com/news/downrange-operators-keep-drones-flying-over-iraq-syria-and-afghanistan-1.461925>.

Clark, Ian. *Waging War: A New Philosophical Introduction*, 2nd edn. Oxford: Oxford University Press, 2015.

Clark, Lindsay C. *Gender and Drone Warfare: A Hauntological Perspective*. Abingdon: Routledge, 2019.

Clausen, Christian. 'Air Force to retire MQ-1 Predator drone, transition to MQ-9 Reaper', *US Defense Department*, 27 February 2017, <https://www.defense.gov/News/News-Stories/Article/Article/1095612/air-force-to-retire-mq-1-predator-drone-transition-to-mq-9-reaper/>.

Clausewitz, Carl von. *On War*. London: Penguin, 1982 [1832].

Coady, C. A. J. 'The Morality of Terrorism', *Philosophy*, 60 (231) (1985): 47–69.

Coady, C. A. J. *Morality and Political Violence*. New York: Cambridge University Press, 2008.

Cockburn, Andrew. *Kill Chain: Drones and the Rise of High-Tech Assassins*. London: Verso, 2016.

Coeckelbergh, Mark. 'Drones, Information Technology, and Distance: Mapping the Moral Epistemology of Remote Fighting', *Ethics and Information Technology*, 15 (2013): 87–98.

Cohen, Rachel S. 'MQ-9 Air-to-Air Missiles Postponed for Higher Priorities', *Air Force Magazine*, 21 June 2019, <https://www.airforcemag.com/MQ-9-Air-to-Air-Missiles-Postponed-for-Higher-Priorities/>.

Coker, Christopher. *Humane Warfare*. London: Routledge, 2001.

Coker, Christopher. *Waging War without Warriors? The Changing Culture of Military Conflict*. Boulder, CO: Lynne Rienner, 2002.

Coker, Christopher. 'Ethics, Drones, and Killer Robots', in *The Oxford Handbook of International Political Theory*, ed. Chris Brown and Robyn Eckersley. Oxford: Oxford University Press, 2018: 247–58.

Cole, Chris. 'Finally revealed: UK drone strikes in Afghanistan by province', *Drone Wars*, 2 April 2015, <https://dronewars.net/2015/04/02/finally-revealed-uk-drone-strikes-in-afghanistan-by-province/>.

Cole, Chris. '"It was incessant." Former RAF Reaper pilot speaks to *Drone Wars*', *Drone Wars*, 30 May 2017, <https://dronewars.net/2017/05/30/justin-thompson-interview/>.

Cole, Chris, Mary Dobbing and Amy Hailwood. *Convenient Killing: Armed Drones and the 'Playstation' Mentality*. Oxford: Fellowship of Reconciliation, 2010.

Coleman, Stephen. *Military Ethics: An Introduction with Case Studies*. New York: Oxford University Press, 2013.

Conot, Robert E. *Justice at Nuremburg*. New York: Carroll & Graf, 1993.

Cook, Martin L. *The Moral Warrior: Ethics and Service in the U.S. Military*. Albany, NY: State University of New York Press, 2004.

Cook, Martin L. 'Drone Warfare and Military Ethics', in *Drones and the Future of Armed Conflict*, ed. David Cortright, Rachel Fairhurst and Kirsten Wall. Chicago and London: University of Chicago Press, 2015: 46–62.

Corbett, Andrew. 'Military Virtues', *Journal of Military Ethics*, 18 (3) (2019): 263–5.

Coughlan, Sean. 'A-levels and GCSEs: Boris Johnson blames "mutant algo-rithm" for exam fiasco', *BBC News*, 26 August 2020, <https://www.bbc.co.uk/news/education-53923279>.

Cowan, Jane. 'US launches Predator drones in Libya conflict', *ABC News*, 22 April 2011, <http://www.abc.net.au/news/stories/2011/04/22/3198588.htm>.

Creveld, Martin van. *The Transformation of War*. New York: The Free Press, 1991.

Cronin, Audrey Kurth. 'The Strategic Implications of Targeted Drone Strikes for US Global Counterterrorism', in *Drones and the Future of Armed Conflict*, ed. David Cortright, Rachel Fairhurst and Kirsten Wall. Chicago and London: University of Chicago Press, 2015: 99–120.

Cronin, Bruce. *Bugsplat: The Politics of Collateral Damage in Western Armed Conflicts*. New York: Oxford University Press, 2018.

Crowley, Michael. *Tear Gassing by Remote Control: The Development and Promotion of Remotely Operated Means of Delivering or Dispersing Riot Control Agents*. London: Oxford Research Group, 2015.

Currier, Cora. 'White House finally releases its "playbook" for killing and capturing terror suspects', *The Intercept*, 6 August 2016, <https://theintercept.com/2016/08/06/white-house-finally-releases-its-playbook-for-killing-and-capturing-terror-suspects/>.

Currier, Joseph M., Jason M. Holland, and Jesse Malott. 'Moral Injury, Meaning Making, and Mental Health in Returning Veterans', *Journal of Clinical Psychology*, 71 (3) (2015): 229–40.

Danchev, Alex. 'Bug Splat: The Art of the Drone', *International Affairs*, 92 (3) (2016): 703–13.

Danner, Mark. 'Bosnia: Breaking the Machine', *The New York Review*, 19 February 1998, <https://www.nybooks.com/articles/1998/02/19/bosnia-breaking-the-machine/>.

DARPA. 'AlphaDogfight trials foreshadow future of human–machine symbiosis', *Defense Advanced Research Projects Agency*, 26 August 2020, <https://www.darpa.mil/news-events/2020-08-26>.

Dassault Aviation. 'nEUROn', *Dassault Aviation*, no date, <https://www.dassault-aviation.com/en/defense/neuron/> (accessed 7 February 2022).

Davies, Rob. 'Civil liberty fears as police consider using drones that film from 1,500ft', *The Guardian*, 29 October 2021, <https://www.theguardian.com/uk-news/2021/oct/29/police-england-wales-long-range-drone-footage-tender-filming>.

Davis, Oliver. 'Theorizing the Advent of Weaponized Drones as Techniques of Domestic Paramilitary Policing', *Security Dialogue*, 50 (4) (2019): 344–60.

Defence Ethics Committee. 'Opinion on the Integration of Autonomy into Lethal Weapon Systems', *French Government*, 29 April 2021, <https://www.defense.gouv.fr/salle-de-presse/communiques/communique_le-comite-d-

ethique-de-la-defense-publie-son-rapport-sur-l-integration-de-l-autonomie-des-systemes-d-armes-letaux>.

Delalande, Arnaud. 'How Libya's skies became battleground for UAE-Turkey proxy war', *Middle East Eye*, 27 August 2019, <https://www.middleeasteye.net/news/how-libyas-skies-became-battleground-uae-turkey-proxy-war>.

Della Cava, Marco. 'Police taser drones authorized in N.D.', *USA Today*, 28 August 2015, <https://eu.usatoday.com/story/tech/2015/08/28/police-taser-drones-authorized--north-dakota/71319668/>.

Department of Public Information. 'Security Council approves "no-fly zone" over Libya, authorizing "all necessary measures" to protect civilians, by vote of 10 in favour with 5 abstentions', *United Nations*, 17 March 2011, <http://www.un.org/press/en/2011/sc10200.doc.htm>.

Desert Wolf. 'Skunk Riot Control Copter', *Desert Wolf*, no date, <http://www.desert-wolf.com/dw/products/unmanned-aerial-systems/skunk-riot-control-copter.html> (accessed 7 February 2022).

DeWees, Brad, Chris Umphres and Maddy Tung. 'Machine learning and life-and-death decisions on the battlefield', *War on the Rocks*, 11 January 2021, <https://warontherocks.com/2021/01/machine-learning-and-life-and-death-decisions-on-the-battlefield/>.

Dill, Janina. 'The Informal Regulation of Drones and the Formal Legal Regulation of War', *Ethics and International Affairs*, 29 (1) (2015): 51–8.

Director of National Intelligence. 'Summary of Information Regarding U.S. Counterterrorism Strikes Outside Areas of Active Hostilities', *Office of the Director of National Intelligence*, US Government, 1 July 2016, <https://www.dni.gov/files/documents/Newsroom/Press%20Releases/DNI+Release+on+CT+Strikes+Outside+Areas+of+Active+Hostilities.PDF>.

Dobos, Ned. 'War as a Workplace: Ethical Implications of the Occupational Shift', *Journal of Military Ethics*, 18 (3) (2019): 248–60.

Dowd, Alan. 'Moral hazard: drones & the risks of risk-free war', *Providence*, 15 December 2016, <https://providencemag.com/2016/12/moral-hazard-drones-risks-risk-free-war/>.

Downes, Chris. '"Targeted Killings" in an age of terror: the legality of the Yemen strike', *Journal of Conflict & Security Law*, 9 (2) (2004): 277–94.

Doyle, Michael W. *Empires*. Ithaca, NY: Cornell University Press, 1986.

Drescher, Kent D., David W. Foy, Caroline Kelly, Anna Leshner, Kerrie Schutz and Brett Litz. 'An Exploration of the Viability and Usefulness of the Construct of Moral Injury in War Veterans', *Traumatology*, 17 (1) (2011): 8–13.

Drone pilot (US) interviewed by Daniel Rothenberg. 'It Is War at a Very Intimate Level', in *Drone Wars: Transforming Conflict, Law, and Policy*, ed. Peter L. Bergen and Daniel Rothenberg. New York: Cambridge University Press, 2015: 113–28.

Drone Wars. 'Who has armed drones?', *Drone Wars*, May 2022, <https://drone-wars.net/who-has-armed-drones/> (accessed 25 May 2022).

Dunn, David. 'Drones: Disembodied Aerial Warfare and the Unarticulated Threat', *International Affairs*, 89 (5) (2013): 1237–46.

Dyndal, Gjert Lage, Tor Arne Berntsen and Sigrid Redse-Johansen. 'Autonomous military drones: no longer science fiction', *NATO Review*, 28 July 2017, <https://www.nato.int/docu/review/articles/2017/07/28/autonomous-military-drones-no-longer-science-fiction/index.html>.

Edney-Browne, Alex. 'Embodiment and Affect in a Digital Age: Understanding Mental Illness among Military Drone Personnel', *Krisis: Journal for Contemporary Philosophy*, Issue 1 (2017): 18–32.

Edney-Browne, Alex. 'What it's really like to live with drone warfare', *ABC Radio National*, 22 August 2017, <https://www.abc.net.au/news/2017-08-18/perspectives-from-the-front-line-of-the-drone-war/8793400>.

Edney-Browne, Alex. 'The Psychosocial Effects of Drone Violence: Social Isolation, Self-Objectification, and Depoliticization', *Political Psychology*, 40 (6) (2019): 1341–56.

Elinson, Zusha. 'Taser Explores Concept of Drone Armed with Stun Gun for Police Use', *Wall Street Journal*, 20 October 2016, <https://www.wsj.com/articles/taser-explores-concept-of-drone-armed-with-stun-gun-for-police-use-1476994514>.

Emery, John, and Daniel R. Brunstetter. 'Drones as Aerial Occupation', *Peace Review*, 27 (4) (2015): 424–31.

Emery, John, and Daniel R. Brunstetter. 'Restricting the Preventive Use of Force: Drones, the Struggle against Non-State Actors, and *Jus ad Vim*', in *Preventive Force: Drones, Targeted Killing, and the Transformation of Contemporary Warfare*, ed. Kerstin Fisk and Jennifer M. Ramos. New York: New York University Press, 2016: 257–82.

Enemark, Christian. *Armed Drones and the Ethics of War: Military Virtue in a Post-Heroic Age*. London: Routledge, 2014.

Engberts, Bart, and Edo Gillissen. 'Policing from Above: Drone Use by the Police', in *The Future of Drone Use: Opportunities and Threats from Ethical and Legal Perspectives*, ed. Bart Custers. The Hague: TMC Asser Press, 2016: 93–113.

Engel, Richard. 'Former drone operator says he's haunted by his part in more than 1,600 deaths', *NBC News*, 6 June 2013, <http://investigations.nbc-news.com/_news/2013/06/06/18787450-former-drone-operator-says-hes-haunted-by-his-part-in-more-than-1600-deaths>.

Englund, Scott H. 'A Dangerous Middle-Ground: Terrorists, Counter-terrorists, and Gray-Zone Conflict, *Global Affairs*, 5 (4–5) (2019): 389–404.

Epps, Garrett. 'Why a secret court won't solve the drone-strike Problem', *The Atlantic*, 16 February 2013, <https://www.theatlantic.com/politics/archive/2013/02/why-a-secret-court-wont-solve-the-drone-strike-prob-lem/273246/>.

Epstein, Elizabeth Gingell and Ann Baile Hamric. 'Moral Distress, Moral Residue, and the Crescendo Effect', *Journal of Clinical Ethics*, 20 (4) (2009): 330–42.

Espinoza, Marina, and Afxentis Afxentiou. 'Editors' Introduction: Drones and State Terrorism', *Critical Studies on Terrorism*, 11 (2) (2018): 295–300.

Etzioni, Amitai. 'Unmanned Aircraft Systems: The Moral and Legal Case', *Joint Force Quarterly*, issue 57, 2nd quarter (2010): 66–71.

European Court of Human Rights. 'Convention for the Protection of Human Rights and Fundamental Freedoms', Rome, 4 November 1950, <https://www.echr.coe.int/Pages/home.aspx?p=basictexts&c>.

European Parliament. Resolution of 12 September 2018 on autonomous weapon systems (2018/2752(RSP)).

European Parliament. Resolution of 20 January 2021 on artificial intelligence: questions of interpretation and application of international law in so far as the EU is affected in the areas of civil and military uses and of state authority outside the scope of criminal justice (2020/2013(INI)).

Evans, Jake. 'Australian Defence Force invests $5 million in "killer robots" research', *ABC News*, 28 February 2019, <https://www.abc.net.au/news/2019-03-01/defence-force-invests-in-killer-artificial-intelligence/10859398>.

Evans, Michael. 'Israeli firm develops Smash Dragon, the drone that fires a rifle as it flies', *The Times*, 11 January 2022, <https://www.thetimes.co.uk/article/israeli-firm-develops-smash-dragon-the-drone-that-fires-a-rifle-as-it-flies-5778j52bd>.

Evans, Michael, and Jane Flanagan. 'Ethiopia's war turns into a testing ground for the deadliest drones', *The Times*, 31 December 2021, <https://www.thetimes.co.uk/article/civilians-are-drone-warfare-guinea-pigs-in-ethiopia-r5x50b230>.

Everstine, Brian. 'Inside the Air Force's drone operations', *Air Force Times*, 22 June 2015, <https://www.airforcetimes.com/news/your-air-force/2015/06/22/inside-the-air-force-s-drone-operations/>.

Farooq, Umar. 'The Second Drone Age', *The Intercept*, 14 May 2019, <https://theintercept.com/2019/05/14/turkey-second-drone-age/>.

Ferraro, Tristan. 'Determining the Beginning and End of an Occupation under International Humanitarian Law', *International Review of the Red Cross*, 94 (885) (2012): 133–63.

Fifth Amendment – U.S. Constitution, *FindLaw*, <https://constitution.findlaw.com/amendment5.html>.

Fifth Review Conference of the High Contracting Parties to the Convention on Prohibitions or Restrictions on the Use of Certain Conventional Weapons Which May Be Deemed to Be Excessively Injurious or to Have Indiscriminate Effects. *Final Document of the Fifth Review Conference* (CCW/CONF.V/10), Geneva, 23 December 2016.

Finlay, Christopher J. 'The Concept of Violence in International Theory: A Double-Intent Account', *International Theory*, 9 (1) (2017): 67–100.

Firdaus, Febriana. 'Global protests throw spotlight on alleged police abuses in West Papua', *The Guardian*, 11 June 2020, <https://www.theguardian.com/global-development/2020/jun/11/global-protests-throw-spotlight-on-alleged-police-abuses-in-west-papua>.

Fisher, Lucy. 'Soldiers get lessons in morality of drone killings', *The Times*, 25 September 2018, <https://www.thetimes.co.uk/article/soldiers-get-lessons-in-morality-of-drone-killings-52zqt2ckc>.

Fisher, Lucy. 'Stress of killing from afar creates shortage of MoD drone operators', *The Times*, 13 January 2020, <https://www.thetimes.co.uk/article/stress-of-killing-from-afar-creates-shortage-of-mod-drone-operators-0fnm36r6t>.

Fontenrose, Kirsten, and Andy Dreby. 'Turkish drones won't give Ukraine the edge it needs', *Defense News*, 1 April 2022, <https://www.defensenews.com/opinion/commentary/2022/04/01/turkish-drones-wont-give-ukraine-the-edge-it-needs/>.

Ford, S. Brandt. '*Jus ad Vim* and the Just Use of Lethal Force-Short-of-War', in *Routledge Handbook of Ethics and War: Just War Theory in the Twenty-First Century*, ed. Fritz Allhoff, Nicholas G. Evans and Adam Henschke. New York: Routledge, 2013: 63–75.

Fotion, Nicholas. *War and Ethics: A New Just War Theory*. London: Continuum, 2007.

Fowler, Mike. 'The Strategy of Drone Warfare', *Journal of Strategic Security* 7 (4) (2014): 108–19.

Frankfurt, Sheila, and Patricia Frazier. 'A Review of Research on Moral Injury in Combat Veterans', *Military Psychology*, 28 (5) (2016): 318–30.

French, Shannon E. *The Code of the Warrior*. Lanham, MD: Rowman & Littlefield, 2003.

French, Shannon E., Victoria Sisk and Caroline Bass. 'Drones, Honor, and Fragmented Sovereignty', in *The Ethics of War and Peace Revisited*, ed. Daniel R. Brunstetter and Jean-Vincent Holeindre. Washington, DC: Georgetown University Press, 2018: 201–19.

Friedersdorf, Conor. ' Every person is afraid of the drones": the strikes' effect on life in Pakistan', *The Atlantic*, 25 September 2012, <https://www.theatlantic.com/international/archive/2012/09/every-person-is-afraid-of-the-drones-the-strikes-effect-on-life-in-pakistan/262814/>.

Friedersdorf, Conor. 'Drone attacks at funerals of people killed in drone attacks', *The Atlantic*, 24 October 2013, <https://www.theatlantic.com/international/archive/2013/10/drone-attacks-at-funerals-of-people-killed-in-drone-strikes/280821/>.

Frowe, Helen. 'On the Redundancy of *Jus ad Vim*: A Response to Daniel Brunstetter and Megan Braun', *Ethics & International Affairs*, 30 (1) (2016): 117–29.

Frowe, Helen. *The Ethics of War and Peace: An Introduction*, 2nd edn. London: Routledge, 2016.

Fryer-Biggs, Zachary. 'Coming soon to a battlefield: robots that can kill', *The Atlantic*, 3 September 2019, <https://www.theatlantic.com/technology/archive/2019/09/killer-robots-and-new-era-machine-driven-warfare/597130/>.

Fuller, Christopher J. *See It / Shoot It: The Secret History of the CIA's Lethal Drone Program*. Yale University Press, 2017.

Gade, Emily Kalah. 'Defining the Non-Combatant: How Do We Determine Who is Worthy of Protection in Violent Conflict?', *Journal of Military Ethics*, 9 (3) (2010): 219–42.

Gaggioli, Gloria. 'Lethal Force and Drones: The Human Rights Question', in *Legitimacy and Drones: Investigating the Legality, Morality and Efficacy of UCAVs*, ed. Steven J. Barela. New York: Routledge, 2017: 91–115.

Gaggioli, Gloria. 'Remoteness and Human Rights Law', in *Research Handbook on Remote Warfare*, ed. Jens David Ohlin. Cheltenham: Edward Elgar, 2017: 133–85.

Gaggioli, Gloria, and Pavle Kilibarda. 'Counterterrorism and the Risk of Over-Classification of Situations of Violence', *International Review of the Red Cross*, 103 (916–17) (2021): 203–36.

Galliott, Jai C. *Military Robots: Mapping the Moral Landscape*. Farnham: Ashgate, 2015.

GAO. *Actions Needed to Strengthen Management of Unmanned Aerial System Pilots* (GAO-14-316). Washington, DC: United States Government Accountability Office, 2014.

Gaulkin, Thomas. 'Drone pandemic: will coronavirus invite the world to meet big brother?', *Bulletin of the Atomic Scientists*, 1 April 2020, <https://thebulletin.org/2020/04/drone-pandemic-will-coronavirus-invite-the-world-to-meet-big-brother>.

Gellman, Barton. 'CIA weighs "targeted killing" missions: administration believes restraints do not bar singling out individual terrorists', *Washington Post*, 28 October 2001: A01.

General Atomics. 'Predator C Avenger', *General Atomics*, no date, <https://www.ga-asi.com/remotely-piloted-aircraft/predator-c-avenger> (accessed 7 February 2022).

Gettinger, Dan. 'The Disposition Matrix', *Center for the Study of the Drone*, Bard College, 25 April 2015, <http://dronecenter.bard.edu/the-disposition-matrix/>.

Gibbons, Katie. 'Drones with sausages lure missing dog out of danger', *The Times*, 20 January 2022, <https://www.thetimes.co.uk/article/drones-with-sausages-lure-missing-dog-out-of-danger-xf9fn8xdj>.

Gibbons-Neff, Thomas. 'Killing and the Drone Warrior', *War on the Rocks*, 6 November 2013, <http://warontherocks.com/2013/11/killing-and-the-drone-warrior/>.

Gibbs, Samuel. 'Musk, Wozniak and Hawking urge ban on warfare AI and autonomous weapons', *The Guardian*, 27 July 2015, <https://www.theguardian.com/technology/2015/jul/27/musk-wozniak-hawking-ban-ai-autonomous-weapons>.

Gibson, Jennifer. 'We're quickly moving toward a world where drone executions are the norm', *Los Angeles Times*, 13 November 2019, <https://www.latimes.com/opinion/story/2019-11-13/drone-killings-war-syria-turkey>.

Gillespie, Tony. 'Good Practice for the Development of Autonomous Weapons', *The RUSI Journal*, 165 (5–6) (2020): 58–67.

Gilli, Andrea, and Mauro Gilli, 'The Diffusion of Drone Warfare? Industrial, Organizational, and Infrastructural Constraints', *Security Studies*, 25 (1) (2016): 50–84.

Glinski, Stefanie. 'Afghan families torn apart by drone strikes – picture essay', *The Guardian*, 6 December 2019, <https://www.theguardian.com/news/2019/dec/06/afghan-families-torn-apart-drone-strikes-picture-essay>.

Government Publishing Office. '3 CFR 13732 – Executive Order 13732 of July 1, 2016. United States Policy on Pre- and Post-Strike Measures to Address Civilian Casualties in U.S. Operations Involving the Use of Force', *US Government Publishing Office*, <https://www.govinfo.gov/app/details/CFR-2017-title3-vol1/CFR-2017-title3-vol1-eo13732/summary>.

Graham v. Connor et al., 490 U.S. 386, 388 (1989).

Greenwald, Glenn. 'US drone strikes target rescuers in Pakistan – and the West stays silent', *The Guardian*, 20 August 2012, <https://www.theguardian.com/commentisfree/2012/aug/20/us-drones-strikes-target-rescuers-pakistan>.

Greenwood, Faine. 'Can a police drone recognize your face?', *Slate*, 8 July 2020, <https://slate.com/technology/2020/07/police-drone-facial-recognition.html>.

Greenwood, Faine. 'Drones and distrust in humanitarian aid', *Humanitarian Law & Policy*, 22 July 2021, <https://blogs.icrc.org/law-and-policy/2021/07/22/drones-distrust-humanitarian/>.

Gregory, Derek. 'From a View to a Kill: Drones and Late Modern War', *Theory, Culture & Society*, 28 (7–8) (2011): 188–215.

Gregory, Derek. 'Drone Geographies', *Radical Philosophy*, 183 (2014): 7–19.

Gregory, Derek. 'Dirty Dancing: Drones and Death in the Borderlands', in *Life in the Age of Drone Warfare*, ed. Lisa Parks and Caren Kaplan. Durham, CT, and London: Duke University Press, 2017: 25–58.

Gregory, Thomas. 'Drones, Targeted Killings, and the Limitations of International Law', *International Political Sociology*, 9 (2015): 197–212.

Gross, Michael L. 'Assassination and Targeted Killing: Law Enforcement, Execution or Self-Defence?', *Journal of Applied Philosophy*, 23 (3) (2006): 323–35.

Grossman, Dave. *On Killing: The Psychological Cost of Learning to Kill in War and Society*, revised edition. Boston, MA: Back Bay Books, 2009.

Grossman, Nicholas. *Drones and Terrorism: Asymmetric Warfare and the Threat to Global Security*. London: I. B. Tauris, 2018.

Grylls, George. 'German drone to direct Ukrainian fire from the skies', *The Times*, 18 April 2022, <https://www.thetimes.co.uk/article/german-drone-to-direct-ukrainian-fire-from-the-skies-kmsxvd7tj>.

Guizzo, Erico, and Evan Ackerman. 'Do we want robot warriors to decide who lives or dies?', *IEEE Spectrum*, 31 May 2016, <https://spectrum.ieee.org/robotics/military-robots/do-we-want-robot-warriors-to-decide-who-lives-or-dies>.

Guoira, Amos, and Jeffrey Brand, 'The Establishment of a Drone Court: A Necessary Restraint on Executive Power', in *Legitimacy and Drones: Investigating the Legality, Morality and Efficacy of UCAVs*, ed. Steven J. Barela. Farnham: Ashgate, 2015: 323–58.

Gunneflo, Markus. *Targeted Killing: A Legal and Political History*. Cambridge: Cambridge University Press, 2016.

Gusterson, Hugh. *Drone: Remote Control Warfare*. London: MIT Press, 2016.

Harbour, Frances V. 'Reasonable Probability of Success as a Moral Criterion in the Western Just War Tradition', *Journal of Military Ethics*, 10 (3) (2010): 230–41.

Hardison, Chaitra M., Eyal Aharoni, Christopher Larson, Steven Trochlil and Alexander C. Hou. *Stress and Dissatisfaction in the Air Force's Remotely Piloted Aircraft Community: Focus Group Findings*. Santa Monica, CA: RAND, 2017.

Harnden, Toby. 'Bin Laden is wanted: dead or alive, says Bush', *The Telegraph*, 18 September 2001, <https://www.telegraph.co.uk/news/worldnews/asia/afghanistan/1340895/Bin-Laden-is-wanted-dead-or-alive-says-Bush.html>.

Harpootlian, Allegra, and Emily Manna. 'The new face of American war is a robot', *The Nation*, 29 April 2019, <https://www.thenation.com/article/archive/tom-dispatch-american-warfare-drones-military-tech-robot/>.

Hart, Robert. 'The case for banning autonomous weapons rests on morality, not practicality', *Bulletin of the Atomic Scientists*, 24 April 2017, <http://thebulletin.org/case-banning-autonomous-weaponsrests-morality-not-practicality10707>.

Harvey, David. *The New Imperialism*. Oxford: Oxford University Press, 2003.

Harwell, Drew. 'Amazon extends ban on police use of its facial recognition technology indefinitely', *Washington Post*, 18 May 2021, <https://www.washingtonpost.com/technology/2021/05/18/amazon-facial-recognition-ban/>.

Hazelton, Jacqueline L. 'Drone Strikes and Grand Strategy: Toward a Political Understanding of the Uses of Unmanned Aerial Vehicle Attacks in US Security Policy', *Journal of Strategic Studies*, 40 (1–2) (2017): 68–91.

Heaven, Douglas. 'Expression of Doubt', *Nature*, 578 (27 February 2020): 502–04.

Heller, Kevin Jon. 'One Hell of a Killing Machine: Signature Strikes and International Law', *Journal of International Criminal Justice*, 11 (2013): 89–119.

Heng, Yee-Kuang. 'The "Transformation of War" Debate: Through the Looking Glass of Ulrich Beck's *World Risk Society*', *International Relations*, 20 (1) (2006): 69–91.

Hennigan, W. J. 'A fast-growing club: countries that use drones for killing by remote control', *Los Angeles Times*, 22 February 2016, <https://www.latimes.com/world/africa/la-fg-drone-proliferation-2-20160222-story.html>.

Hennigan, W. J. 'The U.S. is now routinely launching "danger-close" drone strikes so risky they require Syrian militia approval', *Los Angeles Times*, 15 August 2017, <https://www.latimes.com/world/la-fg-raqqah-drones-20170808-story.html>.

Heyns, Christof. 'Report of the Special Rapporteur on Extrajudicial, Summary or Arbitrary Executions' (A/HRC/17/28), 23 May 2011. New York: Human Rights Council, United Nations General Assembly, 2011.

Heyns, Christof. 'Report of the Special Rapporteur on Extrajudicial, Summary or Arbitrary Executions' (A/HRC/23/47). New York: Human Rights Council, United Nations General Assembly, 9 April 2013.

Heyns, Christof. 'Report of the Special Rapporteur on Extrajudicial, Summary or Arbitrary Executions' (A/HRC/26/36), 1 April 2014. New York: Human Rights Council, United Nations General Assembly, 2014.

Heyns, Christof. 'Preface: Coming to Terms with Drones', in *Drones and the Future of Armed Conflict*, ed. David Cortright, Rachel Fairhurst and Kirsten Wall. Chicago and London: University of Chicago Press, 2015: vii–xi.

Heyns, Christof. 'Human Rights and the Use of Autonomous Weapons Systems (AWS) During Domestic Law Enforcement', *Human Rights Quarterly*, 38 (2016): 350–78.

Heyns, Christof, Dapo Akande, Lawrence Hill-Cawthorne and Thompson Chengeta. 'The International Law Framework Regulating the Use of Armed Drones', *International and Comparative Law Quarterly*, 65 (2016): 791–827.

Hijazi, Alaa, Christopher J. Ferguson, F. Richard Ferraro, Harold Hall, Mark Hovee and Sherrie Wilcox. 'Psychological Dimensions of Drone Warfare', *Current Psychology*, 38 (2019): 1285–96.

Hippler, Thomas. *Governing from the Skies: A Global History of Aerial Bombing*, trans. David Fernbach. London: Verso, 2017.

Hitchens, Theresa. 'Skyborg AI flies second drone; demos "portability"', *Breaking Defense*, 30 June 2021, <https://breakingdefense.com/2021/06/skyborg-ai-flies-second-drone-demos-portability/>.

Holder, Eric. 'Attorney General Eric Holder speaks at Northwestern University School of Law', *US Department of Justice*, 5 March 2012, <https://www.justice.gov/opa/speech/attorney-general-eric-holder-speaks-northwestern-university-school-law>.

Holewinski, Sarah. 'Just Trust Us: The Need to Know More about the Civilian Impact of US Drone Strikes', in *Drone Wars: Transforming Conflict, Law, and Policy*, ed. Peter L. Bergen and Daniel Rothenberg. New York: Cambridge University Press, 2015: 42–70.

Holmqvist, Caroline. *Policing Wars: On Military Intervention in the Twenty-First Century*. Basingstoke: Palgrave Macmillan, 2014.

Holmqvist-Jonsäter, Caroline. 'War as Perpetual Policing', in *The Character of War in the 21st Century*, ed. Caroline Holmqvist-Jonsäter and Christopher Coker. London: Routledge, 2010: 103–18.

Holz, Jacob. 'Victimhood and Trauma within Drone Warfare', *Critical Military Studies* (2021): 1–16, <DOI: 10.1080/23337486.2021.1953738>.

Hookham, Mark. '"Killing jihadist fathers is hard": RAF drone pilots reveal stress of taking out targets', *The Sunday Times*, 18 June 2017, <https://www.thetimes.co.uk/article/killing-jihadist-fathers-is-hard-british-drone-operators-reveal-stress-they-face-in-taking-out-targets-s7pnvfbt2>.

Horowitz, Michael C. 'Drones aren't missiles, so don't regulate them like they are', *Bulletin of the Atomic Scientists*, 26 June 2017, <https://thebulletin.org/2017/06/drones-arent-missiles-so-dont-regulate-them-like-they-are/>.

Hughes, Zach. 'Fog, friction, and thinking machines', *War on the Rocks*, 11 March 2020, <https://warontherocks.com/2020/03/fog-friction-and-thinking-machines/>.

Human Rights Clinic at Columbia Law School and the Center for Civilians in Conflict. *The Civilian Impact of Drones: Unexamined Costs, Unanswered Questions*, 11 September 2012, <https://civiliansinconflict.org/publications/research/civilian-impact-drones-unexamined-costs-unanswered-questions/>.

Human Rights Watch. 'Precisely wrong: Gaza civilians killed by Israeli drone-launched missiles', *Human Rights Watch*, June 2009, <https://www.hrw.org/report/2009/06/30/precisely-wrong/gaza-civilians-killed-israeli-drone-launched-missiles>.

Human Rights Watch. 'Losing humanity: the case against killer robots', *Human Rights Watch*, 19 November 2012, <https://www.hrw.org/report/2012/11/19/losing-humanity/case-against-killer-robots>.

Human Rights Watch. 'The need for new law to ban fully autonomous weapons: memorandum to convention on conventional weapons delegates', *Human Rights Watch*, 13 November 2013, <https://www.hrw.org/news/2013/11/13/need-new-law-ban-fully-autonomous-weapons>.

Human Rights Watch and Harvard Law School International Human Rights Clinic. *Losing Humanity: The Case against Killer Robots*. Human Rights Watch, 2012, <https://www.hrw.org/report/2012/11/19/losing-humanity/case-against-killer-robots>.

Hurka, Thomas. 'Proportionality in the Morality of War', *Philosophy and Public Affairs*, 33 (1) (2005): 34–66.

Hurst, Luke. 'Indian police buy pepper spraying drones to control "unruly mobs"', *Newsweek*, 7 April 2015, <https://www.newsweek.com/pepper-spraying-drones-control-unruly-mobs-say-police-india-320189>.

ICRC. 'Protocol Additional to the Geneva Conventions of 12 August 1949, and relating to the Protection of Victims of International Armed Conflicts (Protocol I)', Geneva, 8 June 1977. *International Committee of the Red Cross*, <https://ihl-databases.icrc.org/ihl/INTRO/470>.

ICRC. 'ICRC position on autonomous weapon systems', *International Committee of the Red Cross*, 12 May 2021, <https://www.icrc.org/en/document/icrc-position-autonomous-weapon-systems>.

Ignatieff, Michael. *Empire Lite*. London: Vintage, 2003.

IMEG. 'The Independent Medical Expert Group (IMEG) 5th Report: Report and recommendations on medical and scientific aspects of the Armed Forces Compensation Scheme', *UK Government*, February 2020, <https://assets.publishing.service.gov.uk/government/uploads/system/uploads/attachment_data/file/865824/20200213_IMEG_FIFTH_REPORT___FINAL_VERSION.pdf>.

Insinna, Valerie. 'Under Skyborg program, F-35 and F-15EX jets could control drone sidekicks', *Defense News*, 22 May 2019, <https://www.defensenews.com/air/2019/05/22/under-skyborg-program-f-35-and-f-15ex-jets-could-control-drone-sidekicks/>.

Insinna, Valerie. 'Could a commercial drone replace the MQ-9 Reaper? The Air Force is considering it', *Defense News*, 12 March 2020, <https://www.defensenews.com/air/2020/03/12/could-a-commercial-drone-replace-the-mq-9-reaper-the-air-force-is-considering-it/>.

International Association of Chiefs of Police. 'Unmanned Aircraft', April 2019, <https://www.theiacp.org/resources/policy-center-resource/unmanned-aircraft>.

International Association of Chiefs of Police. 'Recommended Guidelines for the Use of Unmanned Aircraft', August 2012, <https://www.theiacp.org/sites/default/files/all/i-j/IACP_UAGuidelines.pdf>.

International Covenant on Civil and Political Rights. Adopted and opened for signature, ratification and accession by General Assembly resolution 2200A (XXI) of 16 December 1966, entry into force 23 March 1976, Office of the High Commissioner for Human Rights, United Nations, <https://www.ohchr.org/en/professionalinterest/pages/ccpr.aspx>.

International Human Rights and Conflict Resolution Clinic at Stanford Law School and Global Justice Clinic at NYU School of Law. *Living Under Drones: Death, Injury, and Trauma to Civilians From US Drone Practices in Pakistan*, September 2012, <http://www.livingunderdrones.org/>.

Issacharoff, Samuel, and Richard Pildes. 'Drones and the Dilemma of Modern Warfare', in *Drone Wars: Transforming Conflict, Law, and Policy*, ed.

Peter L. Bergen and Daniel Rothenberg. New York: Cambridge University Press, 2015: 388–420.

Jaffe, Greg. 'The watchers: airmen who surveil the Islamic State never get to look away', *Washington Post*, 6 July 2017, <https://www.washingtonpost.com/world/national-security/the-watchers-airmen-who-surveil-the-islamic-state-never-get-to-look-away/2017/07/06/d80c37de-585f-11e7-ba90-f5875b7d1876_story.html>.

Jaffer, Jameel. 'The Justice Department's White Paper on targeted killing', *American Civil Liberties Union*, 4 February 2013, <https://www.aclu.org/blog/national-security/targeted-killing/justice-departments-white-paper-targeted-killing>.

Jaffer, Jameel. *The Drone Memos: Targeted Killing, Secrecy and the Law*. New York: The New Press, 2016.

Jajal, Tannya D. 'Distinguishing between Narrow AI, General AI and Super AI', *Medium*, 21 May 2018, <https://medium.com/mapping-out-2050/distinguishing-between-narrow-ai-general-ai-and-super-ai-a4bc44172e22>.

Jameton, Andrew. *Nursing Practice: The Ethical Issues*. Englewood Cliffs, NJ: Prentice Hall, 1984.

Jinkerson, Jeremy. 'Moral injury as a new normal in the modern wars', *The Military Psychologist*, October 2014, <http://www.apadivisions.org/division-19/publications/newsletters/military/2014/10/moral-injury.aspx>.

Joh, Elizabeth E. 'Policing Police Robots', *UCLA Law Review*, 2 November 2016, <https://www.uclalawreview.org/policing-police-robots/>.

Johnson, Aaron. 'The Morality of Autonomous Robots', *Journal of Military Ethics* 12 (2) (2013): 129–41.

Johnson, Boris. 'Why we should chuck Chequers', *The Spectator*, 28 July 2018, <https://www.spectator.co.uk/2018/07/boris-johnson-why-we-should-chuck-chequers/>.

Johnson, Chalmers. *Blowback: The Costs and Consequences of American Empire*. New York: Time Warner, 2002.

Johnson, James Turner. *Ethics and the Use of Force: Just War in Historical Perspective*. Farnham: Ashgate, 2011.

Johnson, James Turner. 'The Ethics of Insurgency', *Ethics & International Affairs*, 31 (3) (2017): 367–82.

Johnson, Zeke. 'Why drone death courts are a terrible idea', *Amnesty International*, 25 February 2012, <http://blog.amnestyusa.org/us/why-drone-death-courts-are-a-terrible-idea/>.

Johnston, Patrick B., and Anoop K. Sarbahi. 'The Impact of US Drone Strikes on Terrorism in Pakistan', *International Studies Quarterly*, 60 (2) (2016): 203–19.

Jones, Ben, and John M. Parrish. 'Drones and Dirty Hands', in *Preventive Force: Drones, Targeted Killing, and the Transformation of Contemporary*

Warfare, ed. Kerstin Fisk and Jennifer M. Ramos, New York: New York University Press, 2016: 283–312.

Jones, Christopher. 'Risky Business: How Remote Operations Shift the Risks of Combat', *Global Affairs*, 3 (4–5) (2017): 431–40.

Jones, Edgar. 'Moral Injury in Time of War', *The Lancet*, 391 (2018): 1766–7.

Jones, Nigel. *Countdown to Valkyrie: The July Plot to Assassinate Hitler*. Barnsley: Frontline Books, 2009.

Joshi, Shashank, and Aaron Stein. 'Emerging Drone Nations', *Survival*, 55 (5) (2013): 53–78.

Jünger, Ernst. *Storm of Steel*, trans. Michael Hoffman. New York: Penguin, 2004.

Kaag, John, and Whitley Kaufman. 'Military Frameworks: Technological Know-How and the Legitimization of Warfare', *Cambridge Review of International Affairs*, 22 (4) (2009): 585–606.

Kaempf, Sebastian. *Saving Soldiers or Civilians? Casualty-Aversion versus Civilian Protection in Asymmetric Conflicts*. Cambridge: Cambridge University Press, 2018: 244.

Kahn, Paul. 'The Paradox of Riskless Warfare', *Philosophy and Public Policy Quarterly*, 22 (3) (2002): 2–8.

Kahn, Paul. 'Imagining Warfare', *European Journal of International Law*, 24 (1) (2013): 199–226.

Kania, Elsa B. 'The critical human element in the machine age of warfare', *Bulletin of the Atomic Scientists*, 15 November 2017, <https://thebulletin.org/2017/11/the-critical-human-element-in-the-machine-age-of-warfare/>.

Kania, Elsa B. 'Chinese Military Innovation in the AI Revolution', *RUSI Journal*, 164 (5–6) (2019): 26–34.

Kaplan, Jerry. 'Artificial Intelligence: Think Again', *Communications of the ACM*, 60 (1) (2017): 36–8.

Katyal, Neal K. 'Who will mind the drones?', *New York Times*, 21 February 2013: A27.

Kearns, Oliver. 'Secrecy and Absence in the Residue of Covert Drone Strikes', *Political Geography*, 57 (1) (2017): 13–23.

Kelion, Leo. 'African Firm is selling pepper-spray bullet firing drones', *BBC News*, 18 June 2014, <https://www.bbc.co.uk/news/technology-27902634>.

Kelley, Michael B. 'more evidence that drones are targeting civilian rescuers in Afghanistan', *Business Insider*, 25 September 2012, <https://www.businessinsider.com/drone-double-tap-first-responders-2012-9>.

Kiai, Maina, and Christof Heyns. 'Joint Report of the Special Rapporteur on the Rights to Freedom of Peaceful Assembly and of Association and the Special Rapporteur on Extrajudicial, Summary or Arbitrary Executions on the Proper Management of Assemblies' (A/HRC/31/66), 4 February 2016. New York: Human Rights Council, United Nations General Assembly, 2016.

Killingray, David. '"A swift agent of government": Air Power in British Colonial Africa, 1916–1939, *Journal of African History*, 25 (4) (1984): 429–44.

King, Desmond. 'When an Empire is Not an Empire: The US Case', *Government and Opposition*, 41 (2) (2006): 163–96.

King, Laura, Nabih Bulos and Sarah Parvini. 'Defense secretary "didn't see" intelligence backing Trump's claim of Iran plot against U.S. embassies', *Los Angeles Times*, 12 January 2020, <https://www.latimes.com/world-nation/story/2020-01-12/iran-leaders-protests-ukrainian-plane>.

Kinghorn, Warren. 'Combat Trauma and Moral Fragmentation: A Theological Account of Moral Injury', *Journal of the Society of Christian Ethics*, 32 (2) (2012): 57–74.

Kirkpatrick, Jesse. 'Drones and the Martial Virtue Courage', *Journal of Military Ethics*, 14 (3–4) (2015): 202–19.

Kirkpatrick, Jesse. 'State Responsibility and Drone Operators', in *Drones and Responsibility: Legal, Philosophical, and Sociotechnical Perspectives on Remotely Controlled Weapons*, ed. Ezio Di Nucci and Filippo Santoni de Sio. London: Routledge, 2016: 101–16.

Klaidman, Daniel. *Kill or Capture: The War on Terror and the Soul of the Obama Presidency*. Boston, MA: Houghton Mifflin Harcourt, 2012.

Knight, Will. 'A dogfight renews concerns about AI's lethal potential', *Wired*, 25 August 2020, <https://www.wired.com/story/dogfight-renews-concerns-ai-lethal-potential/>.

Knight, Will. 'Russia's killer drone in Ukraine raises fears about AI in warfare', *Wired*, 17 March 2022, <https://www.wired.com/story/ai-drones-russia-ukraine/>.

Koch, Bernhard. 'Moral Integrity and Remote-Controlled Killing: A Missing Perspective', in *Drones and Responsibility: Legal, Philosophical, and Sociotechnical Perspectives on Remotely Controlled Weapons*, ed. Ezio Di Nucci and Filippo Santoni de Sio. London: Routledge, 2016: 83–100.

Koh, Harold Hongju. 'The Obama Administration and International Law', *US Department of State*, 25 March 2010, <https://2009-2017.state.gov/s/l/releases/remarks/139119.htm>.

Kudo, Timothy. 'How we learned to kill', *New York Times*, 1 March 2015: SR1.

Lacher, Wolfram. 'Drones, deniability, and disinformation: warfare in Libya and the new international disorder', *War on the Rocks*, 3 March 2020, <https://warontherocks.com/2020/03/drones-deniability-and-disinformation-warfare-in-libya-and-the-new-international-disorder/>.

Langford, Eleanor. 'Home office plans to use military-grade drones to pursue suspects and monitor protests are raising privacy concerns', *PoliticsHome*, 17 September 2020, <https://www.politicshome.com/news/article/military-grade-drones-home-office>.

Lee, Peter. 'Remoteness, Risk and Aircrew Ethos', *Air Power Review*, 15 (1) (2012): 1–19.

Lee, Peter. 'Rights, Wrongs and Drones: Remote Warfare, Ethics and the Challenge of Just War Reasoning', *Air Power Review*, 16 (3) (2013): 30–49,

Lee, Peter. 'Drone crews and moral engagement', *The Psychologist*, June 2017, <https://thepsychologist.bps.org.uk/volume-30/june-2017/drone-crews-and-moral-engagement>.

Lee, Peter. 'The Distance Paradox: Reaper, the Human Dimension of Remote Warfare, and Future Challenges for the RAF', *Air Power Review*, 21 (3) (2018): 106–30.

Lee, Peter. *Reaper Force: The Inside Story of Britain's Drone Wars*. London: John Blake, 2019.

Lee, Steven P. 'Human Rights and Drone "Warfare"', *Peace Review*, 27 (2015): 432–9.

Lee, Steven P. 'The Ethics of Current Drone Policy', *International Journal of Applied Philosophy*, 30 (1) (2016): 115–32.

Leveringhaus, Alex. 'Drones, Automated Targeting, and Moral Responsibility', in *Drones and Responsibility: Legal, Philosophical, and Sociotechnical Perspectives on Remotely Controlled Weapons*, ed. Ezio Di Nucci and Filippo Santoni de Sio. London: Routledge, 2016: 169–81.

Levick, Ewan. 'Boeing's autonomous fighter jet will fly over the Australian Outback', *IEEE Spectrum*, 2 January 2020, <https://spectrum.ieee.org/aerospace/military/boeings-autonomous-fighter-jet-will-fly-over-the-australian-outback>.

Levine, Shira. 'Why navigation apps have a gender issue', *BBC*, 3 March 2016, <http://www.bbc.com/autos/story/20160303-are-you-gps-gender-biased>.

Lewis, Michael W. 'Drones: actually the most humane form of warfare ever', *The Atlantic*, 21 August 2013, <https://www.theatlantic.com/international/archive/2013/08/drones-actually-the-most-humane-form-of-warfare-ever/278746/>.

Lieb, Peter. 'Suppressing Insurgencies in Comparison: The Germans in the Ukraine, 1918, and the British in Mesopotamia, 1920', *Small Wars & Insurgencies*, 23 (4) (2012): 627–47.

Lieblich, Eliav. 'Beyond Life and Limb: Exploring Incidental Mental Harm under International Humanitarian Law', in *Applying International Law in Judicial and Quasi-Judicial Bodies*, ed. Derek Jinks, Jackson Nyamuya Maogoto and Solon Solomon. The Hague: Asser Press, 2014: 185–218.

Lifton, Robert Jay. *Home from the War: Learning from Vietnam Veterans*. New York: Other Press, 2005.

Lifton, Robert Jay. 'The Dimensions of Contemporary War and Violence: How to Reclaim Humanity from a Continuing Revolution in the Technology of Killing', *Bulletin of the Atomic Scientists*, 69 (4) (2013): 9–17.

Lin-Greenberg, Erik. 'Game of drones: what experimental wargames reveal about drones and escalation', *War on the Rocks*, 10 January 2019, <https://warontherocks.com/2019/01/game-of-drones-what-experimental-wargames-reveal-about-drones-and-escalation/>.

Lindberg, Kari Soo, and Colum Murphy. 'Drones take to China's skies to fight coronavirus outbreak', *Bloomberg*, 4 February 2020, <https://www.bloomberg.com/news/articles/2020-02-04/drones-take-to-china-s-skies-to-fight-coronavirus-outbreak>.

Linden, Harry van der. 'Drone Warfare and Just War Theory', in *Drones and Targeted Killing: Legal, Moral, and Geopolitical Issues*, 2nd edn, ed. Marjorie Cohn. Northampton, MA: Olive Branch Press, 2018: 179–204.

Linebaugh, Heather. 'I worked on the US drone program. The public should know what really goes on', *The Guardian*, 29 December 2013: <http://www.theguardian.com/commentisfree/2013/dec/29/drones-us-military>.

Lipsett, Anthea. 'Drones and big data: the next frontier in the fight against wildlife extinction', *The Guardian*, 18 February 2019, <https://www.theguardian.com/education/2019/feb/18/drones-and-big-data-the-next-frontier-in-the-fight-against-wildlife-extinction>.

Litz, Brett T., Nathan Stein, Eileen Delaney, Leslie Lebowitz, William P. Nash, Caroline Silva and Shira Maguen. 'Moral Injury and Moral Repair in War Veterans: A Preliminary Model and Intervention Strategy', *Clinical Psychology Review*, 29 (8) (2009): 695–706.

Loveluck, Louisa. 'Iran vows revenge after U.S. drone strike kills elite force commander', *Washington Post*, 3 January 2020, <https://www.washingtonpost.com/world/middle_east/iran-vows-revenge-after-us-drone-strike-kills-elite-force-commander/2020/01/03/345127d6-2df4-11ea-bffe-020c88b3f120_story.html>.

Lubell, Noam, and Nathan Derejko. 'A Global Battlefield: Drones and the Geographical Scope of Armed Conflict', *Journal of International Criminal Justice*, 11 (2013): 65–88.

Lubold, Gordon, and Warren P. Strobel. 'Secret U.S. missile aims to kill only terrorists, not nearby civilians', *Wall Street Journal*, 9 May 2019, <https://www.wsj.com/articles/secret-u-s-missile-aims-to-kill-only-terrorists-not-nearby-civilians-11557403411>.

Lucas Jr., George R. 'Industrial Challenges of Military Robotics', *Journal of Military Ethics*, 10 (4) (2011): 274–95.

Luscombe, Richard. 'US drone strike mistakenly targeted Afghan aid worker, investigation finds', *The Guardian*, 11 September 2021, <https://www.theguardian.com/us-news/2021/sep/11/us-drone-strike-mistakenly-targeted-afghan-aid-worker-investigation-finds>.

Macdonald, Sarah. 'An interview with an executioner', *Daily Life*, 27 March 2012, <http://www.dailylife.com.au/news-and-views/news-features/an-interview-with-an-executioner-20120326-1vu0a.html>.

Macfarlane, Leslie. *Violence and the State*. London: Nelson, 1974.

MacNair, Rachel M. *Perpetration-Induced Traumatic Stress: The Psychological Consequences of Killing*. Westport, CT: Praeger, 2002.

Majumdar, Dave. 'U.S. drone fleet at "breaking point," Air Force Says', *The Daily Beast*, 5 January 2015, <http://www.thedailybeast.com/articles/2015/01/04/exclusive-u-s-drone-fleet-at-breaking-point-air-force-says.html>.

Marcus, Jonathan. 'Combat drones: we are in a new era of warfare – here's why', *BBC News*, 4 February 2022, <https://www.bbc.co.uk/news/world-60047328>.

Marino, Dante, and Guglielmo Tamburrini. 'Learning Robots and Human Responsibility', *International Review of Information Ethics* 6 (2006): 46–51.

Marks, Paula Mitchell. *And Die in the West: The Story of the O.K. Corral Gunfight*. New York: Morrow, 1989.

Marlantes, Karl. *What It Is Like to Go to War*. New York: Grove Press, 2011.

Marouf, Hasain. *Drone Warfare and Lawfare in a Post-Heroic Age*. Tuscaloosa, AL: University of Alabama Press, 2016.

Marshall, S. L. A. *Men against Fire: The Problem of Battle Command in Future War*. New York: William Morrow, 1961.

Masood, Azhar. 'Pakistani tribesmen settle scores through US drones', *Arab News*, 23 May 2011, <www.arabnews.com/node/378426>.

Mayer, Michael. 'The New Killer Drones: Understanding the Strategic Implications of Next-Generation Unmanned Combat Aerial Vehicles', *International Affairs*, 91 (4) (2015): 765–80.

Maynard, Katherine, Jarod Kearney and James Guimond. *Revenge versus Legality: Wild Justice from Balzac to Clint Eastwood and Abu Ghraib*. Abingdon and New York: Birkbeck Law Press, 2010.

Mazzetti, Mark, Eric Schmitt and Robert F. Worth. 'C.I.A. Strike kills U.S.-born militant in a car in Yemen', *New York Times*, 1 October 2011: A1.

McCaleb, Ian Christopher. 'Bush vows justice will be done', *CNN*, 21 September 2001, <http://edition.cnn.com/2001/US/09/21/gen.president.speech/>.

McCoy, Alfred W. *Policing America's Empire: The United States, the Philippines, and the Rise of the Surveillance State*. Madison, WI: University of Wisconsin Press, 2009.

McCurley, T. Mark. 'I was a drone warrior for 11 years. I regret nothing', *Politico Magazine*, 18 October 2015, <https://www.politico.com/magazine/story/2015/10/drone-pilot-book-213263/>.

McDonald, Henry. 'AI expert calls for end to UK use of "racially biased": algorithms', *The Guardian*, 12 December 2019, <https://www.theguardian.com/technology/2019/dec/12/ai-end-uk-use-racially-biased-algorithms-noel-sharkey>.

McGuire, M. R. 'The Laughing Policebot: Automation and the End of Policing', *Policing & Society*, 31 (1) (2021): 20–36.

McKelvey, Tara. 'Interview with Harold Koh, Obama's defender of drone strikes, *Daily Beast*, 8 April 2012, <https://www.thedailybeast.com/interview-with-harold-koh-obamas-defender-of-drone-strikes>.

McKernan, Bethan. 'Trench warfare, drones and cowering civilians: on the ground in Nagorno-Karabakh', *The Guardian*, 13 October 2020, <https://www.theguardian.com/artanddesign/2020/oct/13/trench-warfare-drones-and-cowering-civilians-on-the-ground-in-nagorno-karabakh>.

McLeary, Paul. 'Iranian drones now hitting rebel targets in Syria', *Foreign Policy*, 29 February 2016, <https://foreignpolicy.com/2016/02/29/iranian-drones-now-hitting-rebel-targets-in-syria/>.

McMahan, Jeff. *Killing in War*. Oxford: Oxford University Press, 2009.

McMaster, H. R. 'Remaining True to Our Values – Reflections on Military Ethics in Trying Times', *Journal of Military Ethics*, 9 (3) (2010): 183–94.

McNeal, Gregory S. 'Just call it a drone'. *Forbes*, 2 March 2013, <http://www.forbes.com/sites/gregorymcneal/2013/03/02/just-call-it-a-drone/>.

McNeal, Gregory. 'Targeted Killing and Accountability', *Georgetown Law Journal*, 102 (2014): 681–794.

Meloni, Chantal. 'State and Individual Responsibility for Targeted Killings by Drones', in *Drones and Responsibility: Legal, Philosophical, and Sociotechnical Perspectives on Remotely Controlled Weapons*, ed. Ezio Di Nucci and Filippo Santoni de Sio. London: Routledge, 2016: 47–64.

Melzer, Nils. *Interpretive Guidance on the Notion of Direct Participation in Hostilities under International Humanitarian Law*. Geneva: International Committee of the Red Cross, 2009.

Metz, Cade. 'Police drones are starting to think for themselves', *New York Times*, 7 December 2020: B1.

Mewett, Christopher. 'Understanding war's enduring nature alongside its changing character', *War on the Rocks*, 21 January 2014, <https://warontherocks.com/2014/01/understanding-wars-enduring-nature-alongside-its-changing-character/>.

Michel, Arthur Holland. 'Some cautionary notes on the new "knife missile"', *Defense One*, 10 May 2019, <https://www.defenseone.com/ideas/2019/05/some-cautionary-notes-new-knife-missile/156943/>.

Michel, Arthur Holland. 'The killer algorithms nobody's talking about', *Foreign Policy*, 20 January 2020, <https://foreignpolicy.com/2020/01/20/ai-autonomous-weapons-artificial-intelligence-the-killer-algorithms-nobodys-talking-about/>.

Michel, Arthur Holland. *Unarmed and Dangerous: The Lethal Applications of Non-Weaponized Drones*. Annandale-on-Hudson, NY: Center for the Study of the Drone at Bard College, 2020.

Miller, Greg. 'Plan for hunting terrorists signals U.S. intends to keep adding names to kill lists', *Washington Post*, 23 October 2012, <http://articles.

washingtonpost.com/2012-10-23/world/35500278_1_drone-campaign-obama-administration-matrix>.

Miller, Greg. 'CIA didn't know strike would hit Al-Qaeda leader', *Washington Post*, 17 June 2015, <https://www.washingtonpost.com/world/national-security/al-qaedas-leader-in-yemen-killed-in-signature-strike-us-officials-say/2015/06/17/9fe6673c-151b-11e5-89f3-61410da94eb1story.html>.

Miller, Seumas. *Shooting to Kill: The Ethics of Police and Military Use of Lethal Force*. New York: Oxford University Press, 2016.

Ministry of Defence. *Future Operating Environment 2035*, 1st edn. UK Government, 14 December 2015, <https://www.gov.uk/government/publications/future-operating-environment-2035>.

Ministry of Defence. *Unmanned Aircraft Systems* (Joint Doctrine Publication 030.2), 12 September 2017, <https://www.gov.uk/government/uploads/system/uploads/attachment_data/file/673940/doctrine_uk_uas_jdp_0_30_2.pdf>:

Ministry of Defence. 'Joint Concept Note 1/18: Human-Machine Teaming', *UK Government*, 21 May 2018, <https://www.gov.uk/government/publications/human-machine-teaming-jcn-118>.

Mitib, Ali. 'Drones fly to the rescue of patients in remote areas of Scotland', *The Times*, 27 December 2021, <https://www.thetimes.co.uk/article/drones-fly-to-the-rescue-of-patients-in-remote-areas-of-scotland-dmkv0p5bl>.

Mogherini, Federica. 'Speech by High Representative/Vice-President Federica Mogherini at the Annual Conference of the European Defence Agency', *European Union External Action Service*, 29 November 2018, <https://eeas.europa.eu/headquarters/headquarters-homepage/54646/speech-high-representativevice-president-federica-mogherini-annual-conference-european-defence_en>.

Molendijk, Tine, Eric-Hans Kramer and Désirée Verweij. 'Moral Aspects of "Moral Injury": Analyzing Conceptualizations on the Role of Morality in Military Trauma', *Journal of Military Ethics*, 17 (1) (2018): 36–53.

Moorhead, Caroline. *Dunant's Dream: War, Switzerland and the History of the Red Cross*. London: HarperCollins, 1998.

Morkevičius, Valerie. 'Looking Inward Together: Just War Thinking and Our Shared Moral Emotions', *Ethics and International Affairs*, 31 (4) (2017): 441–51.

Moskos, Charles C., and Frank R. Wood (eds). *The Military: More Than Just a Job?* Oxford: Pergamon-Brassey's, 1988.

Motlagh, Jason. 'U.S. takes terror fight to Africa's "Wild West"', *SFGate*, 27 December 2005, <https://www.sfgate.com/politics/article/U-S-takes-terror-fight-to-Africa-s-Wild-West-2555454.php>.

Moyes, Richard. 'Key elements of Meaningful Human Control', *Article 36*, April 2016, <http://www.article36.org/wp-content/uploads/2016/04/MHC-2016-FINAL.pdf>.

Moyn, Samuel. 'Drones and Imagination: A Response to Paul Kahn', *European Journal of International Law*, 24 (1) (2013): 227–33.

Mukerji, Nikil. 'Autonomous Killer Drones', in *Drones and Responsibility: Legal, Philosophical, and Sociotechnical Perspectives on Remotely Controlled Weapons*, ed. Ezio Di Nucci and Filippo Santoni de Sio. London: Routledge, 2016: 197–214.

Munro, Campbell A. O. 'Mapping the Vertical Battlespace: Towards a Legal Cartography of Aerial Sovereignty', *London Review of International Law*, 2 (2) (2014): 233–61.

Munro, Campbell. 'The Entangled Sovereignties of Air Police: Mapping the Boundary of the International and the Imperial', *Global Jurist*, 15 (2) (2015): 117–38.

Murphy, Jeffrie G. 'People We Hire as Executioners: Who are They? Who are We?, *Criminal Justice Ethics*, 35 (2) (2016): 87–99.

Nash, William P., Jennifer Vasterling, Linda Ewing-Cobbs, Sarah Horn, Thomas Gaskin, John Golden and Patricia Lester. 'Consensus Recommendations for Common Data Elements for Operational Stress Research and Surveillance: Report of a Federal Interagency Working Group', *Archive of Physical Medicine and Rehabilitation*, 91 (11) (2010): 1673–83.

Neocleous, Mark. 'Air Power as Police Power', *Environment and Planning D: Society and Space*, 31 (2013): 578–93.

Noack, Rick. 'In victory for privacy activists, France is banned from using drones to enforce coronavirus rules', *Washington Post*, 14 January 2021, <https://www.washingtonpost.com/world/in-victory-for-privacy-activists-france-is-banned-from-using-drones-to-enforce-covid-rules/2021/01/14/b384eb40-5658-11eb-acc5-92d2819a1ccb_story.html>.

Northrop Grumman. 'X-47B UCAS', Northrop Grumman, no date, <https://www.northropgrumman.com/what-we-do/air/x-47b-ucas/> (accessed 8 February 2022).

Norton-Taylor, Richard, and Alice Ross. 'RAF base may be legitimate target for Isis, says ex-Nato commander', *The Guardian*, 25 November 2015, <https://www.theguardian.com/uk-news/2015/nov/25/raf-base-may-be-legitimate-target-isis-ex-nato-commander>.

Obama, Barack. 'Letter from the President on the War Powers Resolution', *The White House*, 15 June 2011, <https://obamawhitehouse.archives.gov/the-press-office/2011/06/15/letter-president-war-powers-resolution>.

Obama, Barack. 'Remarks by the President at the National Defense University', *The White House*, 23 May 2013, <https://obamawhitehouse.archives.gov/the-press-office/2013/05/23/remarks-president-national-defense-university>.

Obama, Barack. 'Remarks by the President at the United States Military Academy Commencement Ceremony', *The White House*, 28 May 2014, <https://obamawhitehouse.archives.gov/the-press-office/2014/05/28/remarks-president-united-states-military-academy-commencement-ceremony>.

Obama, Barack. 'Remarks by the President in a Conversation on the Supreme Court Nomination', *The White House*, 8 April 2016, <https://obama-whitehouse.archives.gov/the-press-office/2016/04/08/remarks-president-conversation-supreme-court-nomination>.

O'Connell, Mary Ellen. 'The Law on Lethal Force Begins with the Right to Life', *Journal on the Use of Force and International Law*, 3 (2) (2016): 205–9.

Ofek, Hillel. 'The Tortured Logic of Obama's Drone War', *The New Atlantis*, Spring (2010): 35–44.

Okiror, Samuel. '"Gamechanger": Uganda launches drone delivering HIV drugs to remote islands', *The Guardian*, 4 May 2021, <https://www.theguardian.com/global-development/2021/may/04/gamechanger-uganda-launches-drone-delivering-hiv-drugs-to-remote-islands>.

Olsthoorn, Peter. *Military Ethics and Virtues: An Interdisciplinary Approach for the 21st Century*. London: Routledge, 2010.

Olsthoorn, Peter. 'Ethics for Drone Operators: Rules versus Virtues', in *Ethics of Drone Strikes: Restraining Remote-Control Killing*, ed. Christian Enemark. Edinburgh: Edinburgh University Press, 2021: 115–29.

Omissi, David E. *Air Power and Colonial Control: The Royal Air Force, 1919–1939*. Manchester: Manchester University Press, 1990.

Osofsky, Michael J., Albert Bandura and Philip G. Zimbardot. 'The Role of Moral Disengagement in the Execution Process', *Law and Human Behavior*, 29 (4) (2005): 371–93.

Otto, Jean L., and Bryant J. Webber. 'Mental Health Diagnoses and Counselling among Pilots of Remotely Piloted Aircraft in the United States Air Force', *Medical Surveillance Monthly Reports* (US Armed Forces Health Surveillance Branch), 20 (3) (2013): 3–8.

Ovalle, David. 'From above, Miami-Dade police drone recorded crack cocaine sale live. It's a first, cops say', *Miami Herald*, 16 January 2020, <https://www.miamiherald.com/news/local/crime/article239246988.html>.

Owen, Taylor. 'Drones don't just kill. Their psychological effects are creating enemies', *The Globe and Mail*, 13 March 2013, <https://www.theglobeandmail.com/opinion/drones-dont-just-kill-their-psychological-effects-are-creating-enemies/article9707992/>.

Parasuraman, Raja, and Victor Riley. 'Humans and Automation: Use, Misuse, Disuse, Abuse', *Human Factors*, 39 (2) (1997): 230–53.

Paris, Michael. 'Air Power and Imperial Defence, 1880–1919', *Journal of Contemporary History*, 24 (2) (1989): 209–25.

Parliamentary Assembly of the Council of Europe. 'Drones and targeted killings: the need to uphold human rights and international law' (Resolution 2051(2015)), 23 April 2015.

Pashakhanlou, Arash Heydarian. 'Air Power in Humanitarian Intervention: Kosovo and Libya in Comparative Perspective', *Defence Studies*, 18 (1) (2018): 39–57.

Pashakhanlou, Arash Heydarian. 'AI, Autonomy, and Airpower: The End of Pilots?', *Defence Studies*, 19 (4) (2019): 337–52.

Pavia, Will. 'Diary of a drone pilot', *The Times*, 23 April 2016, <https://www.thetimes.co.uk/article/diary-of-a-drone-pilot-wfg50mkb7>.

Pearl, Mike. 'What it's like to be a death row executioner in America', *Vice*, 27 May 2015, <https://www.vice.com/en/article/bnpxp5/how-do-you-get-a-job-as-an-executioner-in-america-526>.

Pejic, Jelena. 'Extraterritorial Targeting by Means of Armed Drones: Some Legal Implications', *International Review of the Red Cross*, 96 (893) (2014): 67–106.

Pfaff, C. Anthony. 'Military Ethics below the Threshold of War', *Parameters*, 50 (2) (2020): 69–77.

Phelps, Wayne. *On Killing Remotely: The Psychology of Killing with Drones*. New York: Little, Brown and Company, 2021.

Phillips, Macon. 'Osama Bin Laden dead', *The White House*, 2 May 2011, <https://obamawhitehouse.archives.gov/blog/2011/05/02/osama-bin-laden-dead>.

Phillips, Tom. 'Heavily armed police launch bid to reclaim control of Rio de Janeiro favela', *The Guardian*, 20 January 2022, <https://www.theguardian.com/world/2022/jan/19/hundreds-of-armed-police-storm-rio-de-janeiro-favela>.

Pincus, Walter. 'Are drones a technological tipping point in warfare?', *Washington Post*, 24 April 2011, <http://www.washingtonpost.com/world/are-predator-drones-a-technological-tipping-point-in-warfare/2011/04/19/AFmC6PdE_story.html>.

Pitzke, Marc. 'How drone pilots wage war', *Spiegel International*, 12 March 2010, <https://www.spiegel.de/international/world/remote-warriors-how-drone-pilots-wage-war-a-682420.html>.

Pollard, Ruth. 'The Second Drone Age is here and it's a free-for-all', *Bloomberg*, 2 January 2022, <https://www.bloomberg.com/opinion/articles/2022-01-02/the-second-drone-age-is-a-weaponized-free-for-all-energized-by-global-commerce>.

Porter, Amanda A. 'Law Enforcement's Use of Weaponized Drones: Today and Tomorrow', *Saint Louis University Law Journal=*, 61 (2) (2017): 351–70.

Powell, H. Jefferson. *Targeting Americans: The Constitutionality of the U.S. Drone War*. New York: Oxford University Press, 2016.

Power, Matthew. 'Confessions of a drone warrior', *GQ*, 23 October 2013, <http://www.gq.com/story/drone-uav-pilot-assassination>.

Prenzler, Tim. *Ethics and Accountability in Criminal Justice: Towards a Universal Standard*, 1st edn. Brisbane: Australian Academic Press, 2009.

Press, Eyal. 'The wounds of the drone warrior', *New York Times*, 13 June 2018, <https://www.nytimes.com/2018/06/13/magazine/veterans-ptsd-drone-warrior-wounds.html>.

Prieve, Judith. 'East Bay police department adds drones to crime-fighting arsenal', *The Mercury News*, 20 July 2019, <https://www.mercurynews.com/2019/07/20/east-bay-police-department-adds-drones-to-its-crime-fighting-arsenal/>.

Prinz, Janosch, and Conrad Schetter. 'Conditioned Sovereignty: The Creation and Legitimation of Spaces of Violence in Counterterrorism Operations of the "War on Terror"', *Alternatives: Global, Local, Political*, 41 (3) (2016): 119–36.

Pryer, Douglas A. 'Moral injury: what leaders don't mention when they talk of war', *Army*, 14 August 2014, <http://www.armymagazine.org/2014/08/14/moral-injury-what-leaders-dont-mention-when-they-talk-of-war/>.

Pubby, Many. 'India all set to get missile armed drones from Israel', *Economic Times*, 14 July 2018, <https://economictimes.indiatimes.com/news/defence/india-all-set-to-get-missile-armed-drones-from-israel/articleshow/57980098.cms>.

Punch, Maurice. *Shoot to Kill: Police Accountability, Firearms and Fatal Force*. Bristol: Policy Press, 2011.

Puniewska, Maggie. 'Healing a wounded sense of morality', *The Atlantic*, 3 July 2015, <http://www.theatlantic.com/health/archive/2015/07/healing-a-wounded-sense-of-morality/396770/>.

Purkiss, Jessica, and Jack Serle. 'US drones appear to have returned to Pakistan', *Bureau of Investigative Journalism*, 6 March 2017, <https://www.thebureau-investigates.com/stories/2017-03-06/us-drones-return-to-pakistan>.

Purves, Duncan, Ryan Jenkins, and Bradley J. Strawser. 'Autonomous Machines, Moral Judgment, and Acting for the Right Reasons', *Ethical Theory and Moral Practice*, 18 (2015): 851–72.

Rabkin, Jeremy, and John Yoo. '"Killer robots" can make war less awful', *Wall Street Journal*, 1 September 2017, <https://www.wsj.com/articles/killer-robots-can-make-war-less-awful-1504284282>.

Rae, James DeShaw. 'Drones and a Culture of Death', *Peace Review*, 27 (4) (2015): 477–83.

Ramsden, Michael. 'Targeted Killings and International Human Rights Law: The Case of Anwar Al-Awlaki', *Journal of Conflict & Security Law*, 16 (2) (2011): 385–406.

Rao, Rahul. 'The Empire Writes Back (to Michael Ignatieff)', *Millennium: Journal of International Studies*, 33 (1) (2004): 145–66.

Rasmussen, Sune Engel. 'Suspected US drone strike targeting Isis killed civilians in Afghanistan, UN says', *The Guardian*, 29 September 2016, <https://www.theguardian.com/world/2016/sep/29/us-drone-strike-kills-civilians-isis-afghanistan>.

Ratcliffe, Rebecca. 'Police in Malaysia use drones to detect high temperatures amid Covid surge', *The Guardian*, 7 June 2021, <https://www.theguardian.com/world/2021/jun/07/police-in-malaysia-use-drones-to-detect-high-temperatures-amid-covid-surge>.

Ray, Vin. 'The US Air Force's commuter drone warriors', *BBC News*, 8 January 2017, <https://www.bbc.co.uk/news/magazine-38506932>.

Reardon, Sara. 'I spy, with my faraway eye', *New Scientist*, (26 January 2013): 46–9.

Renic, Neil C. 'A Gardener's Vision: UAVs and the Dehumanisation of Violence', *Survival*, 60 (6) (2018): 57–72.

Renic, Neil C. 'Battlefield Mercy: Unpacking the Nature and Significance of Supererogation in War', *Ethics and International Affairs*, 33 (3) (2019): 343–62.

Retica, Aaron. 'Drone-pilot burnout', *New York Times*, 14 December 2008: MM55.

Reuters. 'A wild frontier', *The Economist*, 18 September 2008, <https://www.economist.com/asia/2008/09/18/a-wild-frontier>.

Reuters. 'Obama: We took out Pakistani Taliban chief', *ABC News*, 22 August 2009, <https://www.abc.net.au/news/2009-08-21/obama-we-took-out-pakistani-taliban-chief/1399370>.

Reuters. 'US drone strike intended for Isis hideout kills 30 pine nut workers in Afghanistan', *The Guardian*, 19 September 2019, <https://www.theguardian.com/world/2019/sep/19/us-drone-strike-deaths-afghanistan-pine-nut-workers>.

Reuters. 'Killing Iran general delivered "American justice", Trump tells rally', *The Guardian*, 10 January 2020, <https://www.theguardian.com/us-news/2020/jan/10/killing-iran-general-suleimani-american-justice-donald-trump-ohio-rally>.

Richardson, Michael. '"Pandemic drones": useful for enforcing social distancing, or for creating a police state?', *The Conversation*, 31 March 2020, <https://theconversation.com/pandemic-drones-useful-for-enforcing-social-distancing-or-for-creating-a-police-state-134667>.

Ridge, Michael. 'Moral Non-Naturalism', *Stanford Encyclopedia of Philosophy*, ed. Edward N. Zalta (Fall 2019 Edition), <https://plato.stanford.edu/archives/fall2019/entries/moral-non-naturalism/>.

Ritter, Joe. 'Hellfires wanted: it's time to start tasking armed drones as combat aircraft', *War on the Rocks*, 24 June 2021, <https://warontherocks.com/2021/06/hellfires-wanted-its-time-to-start-tasking-armed-drones-as-combat-aircraft/>.

Riza, M. Shane. *Killing without Heart: Limits on Robotic Warfare in an Age of Persistent Conflict*. Washington, DC: Potomac Books, 2013.

Riza, M. Shane. 'Two-Dimensional Warfare: Combatants, Warriors, and Our Post-Predator Collective Experience', *Journal of Military Ethics*, 13 (3) (2014): 257–73.

Robin, Gerald D. 'The Executioner: His Place in English Society', *The British Journal of Sociology*, 15 (3) (1964): 234–53.

Robin, Paul, Nigel De Lee and Don Carrick. *Ethics Education in the Military*. Aldershot: Ashgate, 2008.

Robinson, Jennifer. '"Bugsplat": the ugly US drone war in Pakistan', *Al Jazeera*, 29 November 2011, <https://www.aljazeera.com/opinions/2011/11/29/bugsplat-the-ugly-us-drone-war-in-pakistan/>.

Rodin, David. 'Terrorism without Intention', *Ethics*, 114 (July 2004): 752–71.

Rodin, David, and Henry Shue. 'Introduction', in *Just and Unjust Warriors: The Moral and Legal Status of Soldiers*, ed. David Rodin and Henry Shue. Oxford: Oxford University Press, 2008: 1–18.

Roff, Heather M. 'Killing in War: Responsibility, Liability, and Lethal Autonomous Robots', in *Routledge Handbook of Ethics and War: Just War Theory in the Twenty-First Century*, ed. Fritz Allhoff, Nicholas G. Evans and Adam Henschke. New York: Routledge, 2013: 352–64.

Rosen, Brianna. 'To end the forever wars, rein in the drones', *Just Security*, 16 February 2021, <https://www.justsecurity.org/74690/to-end-the-forever-wars-rein-in-the-drones/>.

Royakkers, Lambèr, and Rinie van Est. 'The Cubicle Warrior: The Marionette of Digitalized Warfare', *Ethics and Information Technology*, 12 (2010): 289–96.

Rucker, Philip, John Hudson, Shane Harris and Josh Dawsey. '"Four embassies": the anatomy of Trump's unfounded claim about Iran', *Washington Post*, 13 January 2020, <https://www.washingtonpost.com/politics/four-embassies-the-anatomy-of-trumps-unfounded-claim-about-iran/2020/01/13/2dcd6df0-3620-11ea-bf30-ad313e4ec754_story.html>.

Russon, Mary-Ann. 'US firm reveals gun-toting drone that can fire in mid-air', *BBC News*, 11 August 2017, <https://www.bbc.co.uk/news/technology-40901393>.

Ryan, Klem. 'What's Wrong with Drones? The Battlefield in International Humanitarian Law', in *The American Way of Bombing: Changing Ethical Norms from Flying Fortresses to Drones*, ed. Matthew Evangelista and Henry Shue. Ithaca, NY: Cornell University Press, 2014: 207–23.

Sabbagh, Dan. 'Killer drones: how many are there and who do they target?', *The Guardian*, 18 November 2019, <https://www.theguardian.com/news/2019/nov/18/killer-drones-how-many-uav-predator-reaper>.

Sabbagh, Dan. 'UK accused of "targeted killing" after drone strike on arms dealer to IS', *The Guardian*, 6 January 2022, <https://www.theguardian.com/world/2022/jan/06/uk-accused-of-targeted-killing-after-drone-strike-on-arms-dealer-to-is>.

Sabbagh, Dan, Jason Burke and Bethan McKernan. '"Libya is ground zero": drones on frontline in bloody civil war', *The Guardian*, 27 November 2019, <https://www.theguardian.com/news/2019/nov/27/libya-is-ground-zero-drones-on-frontline-in-bloody-civil-war>.

Sackur, Stephen. 'Electric chair haunts US former executions chief', *BBC News*, 23 February 2014, <https://www.bbc.co.uk/news/magazine-26273051>.

Salter, Michael. 'Toys for the Boys? Drones, Pleasure and Popular Culture in the Militarisation of Policing', *Critical Criminology*, 22 (2) (2014): 163–77.

Sanders, Rebecca. 'Legal Frontiers: Targeted Killing at the Borders of War', *Journal of Human Rights*, 13 (4) (2014): 512–36.

Sandvik, Kristin Bergtora. 'The Public Order Drone: Promises, Proliferation and Disorder in Civil Airspace', in *The Good Drone*, ed. Kristin Bergtora Sandvik and Maria Gabrielsen Jumbert. London: Ashgate, 2016: 109–28.

Sardoč, Mitja. 'Re-thinking Violence: An Interview with C. A. J. Coady', *Critical Studies on Terrorism*, 12 (4) (2019): 735–47.

Satariano, Adam. 'Will there be a ban on killer robots?', *New York Times*, 19 October 2018: F8.

Satia, Priya. *Spies in Arabia: The Great War and the Cultural Foundation of Britain's Covert Empire in the Middle East*. Oxford: Oxford University Press, 2008.

Satia, Priya. 'Drones: A History from the British Middle East', *Humanity*, 5 (1) (2014): 1–31.

Sauer, Frank, and Niklas Schörnig. 'Killer Drones: "The Silver Bullet" of Democratic Warfare?', *Security Dialogue*, 43 (4) (2012): 363–80.

Savage, Charlie. 'Relatives sue officials over U.S. citizens killed by drone strikes in Yemen', *New York Times*, 19 July 2012: A7.

Savage, Charlie, and Eric Schmitt. 'Biden quietly limits drone strikes away from war zones', *New York Times*, 4 March 2021: A12.

Schaller, Christian. 'Using Force Against Terrorists "Outside Areas of Active Hostilities": The Obama Approach and the Bin Laden Raid Revisited', *Journal of Conflict & Security Law*, 20 (2) (2015): 195–227.

Scheffler, Samuel. 'Is Terrorism Morally Distinctive?' *The Journal of Political Philosophy*, 14 (1) (2006): 1–17.

Schillings, Sonja. *Enemies of All Humankind: Fictions of Legitimate Violence*. Hanover, NH: Dartmouth College Press, 2017.

Schmidt, Dennis R., and Luca Trenta. 'Changes in the Law of Self-Defence? Drones, Imminence, and International Norm Dynamics', *Journal on the Use of Force and International Law*, 5 (2) (2018): 201–45.

Schmitt, Carl. *The Nomos of the Earth: In the International Law of the Jus Publicum Europaeum*, trans. G. L. Ulmen, New York: Telos Press, 2003.

Schmitt, Eric. 'Embassies open, but Yemen stays on terror watch', *New York Times*, 12 August 2013: A1.

Schmitt, Eric. 'U.S. kills Qaeda leader with secretive missile', *New York Times*, 25 September 2020: A10.

Schmitt, Michael N. '21st Century Conflict: Can the Law Survive?', *Melbourne Journal of International Law*, 8 (2007): 443–76.

Schogol, Jeff. 'Air Force losing more drone pilots than it trains', *Military Times*, 9 January 2015, <http://www.militarytimes.com/story/military/careers/2015/01/09/air-force-losing-drone-pilots/21503301/>.

Schuller, Alan. 'Autonomous weapon systems and the decision to kill', *Just Security*, 21 September 2017, <https://www.justsecurity.org/45164/autonomous-weapon-systems-decision-kill/>.

Schulzke, Marcus. 'Rethinking Military Virtue Ethics in an Age of Unmanned Weapons, *Journal of Military Ethics*, 15 (3) (2016): 187–204.

Schulzke, Marcus. 'The Morality of Remote Warfare: Against the Asymmetry Objection to Remote Weaponry', *Political Studies*, 64 (1) (2016): 90–105.

Schulzke, Marcus. *The Morality of Drone Warfare and the Politics of Regulation*. Palgrave Macmillan, 2017.

Schwarz, Elke. *Death Machines: The Ethics of Violent Technologies*. Manchester: Manchester University Press, 2018.

Sehrawat, Vivek. 'Legal Status of Drones under LOAC and International Law', *Penn State Journal of Law and International Affairs*, 5 (1) (2017): 165–206.

Shane, Scott. 'Judging a long, deadly reach', *New York Times*, 1 October 2011: A1.

Shane, Scott. 'The moral case for drones', *New York Times*, 15 July 2012: SR4.

Shanker, Thom, and Matt Richtel. 'In new military, data overload can be deadly', *New York Times*, 17 January 2011: A1.

Sharkey, Amanda. 'Autonomous Weapons Systems, Killer Robots and Human Dignity', *Ethics and Information Technology*, 21 (2019): 75–87.

Sharkey, Noel. 'Are we prepared for more killer police robots?', *The Guardian*, 12 July 2016, <https://www.theguardian.com/commentisfree/2016/jul/12/killer-police-robots-legal-consequences-dallas>.

Shaw, Ian G. R. *Predator Empire: Drone Warfare and Full Spectrum Dominance*. Minneapolis: University of Minnesota Press, 2016.

Shaw, Ian, and Majed Akhter. 'The Unbearable Humanness of Drone Warfare in FATA, Pakistan', *Antipode*, 44 (4) (2012): 1490–509.

Shaw, Martin. 'Post-Imperial and Quasi-Imperial: State and Empire in the Global Era', *Millennium: Journal of International Studies*, 31 (2) (2002): 327–36.

Shay, Jonathan. *Achilles in Vietnam: Combat Trauma and the Undoing of Character*. New York: Atheneum, 1994.

Shay, Jonathan. 'Moral Injury', *Intertexts*, 16 (1) (2012): 57–66.

Sherman, Nancy. *Stoic Warriors: The Ancient Philosophy behind the Military Mind*. Oxford: Oxford University Press, 2007.

Sherman, Nancy. *The Untold War: Inside the Hearts, Minds, and Souls of Our Soldiers*. New York: Norton, 2010.

Shevardnadze, Sophie, and Bruce Black. 'Former drone pilot, Lieutenant-Colonel: Obama personally orders drone killings', *RT*, 29 November 2013, <https://www.rt.com/shows/sophieco/weapon-drones-industry-demand-465/>.

Shinkman, Paul D. 'Military stalls on efforts to repair drone troubles depicted in "Good Kill"', *U.S. News and World Report*, 13 May 2015, <http://www.usnews.com/news/articles/2015/05/13/military-stalls-on-efforts-to-repair-drone-pilots-troubles>.

Shlaim, Avi. 'Ten years after the first war on Gaza, Israel still plans endless brute force', *The Guardian*, 7 January 2019, <https://www.theguardian.com/commentisfree/2019/jan/07/ten-years-first-war-gaza-operation-cast-lead-israel-brute-force>.

Shue, Henry. 'Do We Need a "Morality of War"?', in *Just and Unjust Warriors: The Moral and Legal Status of Soldiers*, ed. David Rodin and Henry Shue. Oxford: Oxford University Press, 2008: 87–111.

Shurtleff, D. Keith. 'The Effects of Technology on Our Humanity', *Parameters* (Summer 2002): 100–12.

Singer, Peter W. 'Do drones undermine democracy?', *New York Times*, 22 January 2012: SR5.

Skerker, Michael, Duncan Purves and Ryan Jenkins. 'Autonomous Weapons Systems and the Moral Equality of Combatants', *Ethics and Information Technology*, 22 (2020): 197–209.

Smith, David. 'Pepper-spray drone offered to South African mines for strike control', *The Guardian*, 20 June 2014, <https://www.theguardian.com/world/2014/jun/20/pepper-spray-drone-offered-south-african-mines-strike-control>.

Smith, Helena. 'Greece to use drones to stop crowds gathering for Orthodox Easter', *The Guardian*, 17 April 2020, <https://www.theguardian.com/world/2020/apr/17/greece-to-use-drones-to-stop-crowds-gathering-for-orthodox-easter-covid-19>.

Sonnenberg, Stephan. 'Why Drones Are Different', in *Preventive Force: Drones, Targeted Killing, and the Transformation of Contemporary Warfare*, ed. Kerstin Fisk and Jennifer M. Ramos. New York: New York University Press, 2016: 115–41.

Sparrow, Robert. 'Killer Robots', *Journal of Applied Philosophy*, 24 (1) (2007): 62–77.

Sparrow, Robert. 'Robotic Weapons and the Future of War', in *New Wars and New Soldiers: Military Ethics in the Contemporary World*, ed. Jessica Wolfendale and Paolo Tripodi. Farnham: Ashgate, 2011: 117–36.

Sparrow, Robert. 'Robots as "Evil Means"? A Rejoinder to Jenkins and Purves', *Ethics and International Affairs*, 30 (3) (2016): 401–3.

Stanley, Jay. 'Five reasons armed domestic drones are a terrible idea', *American Civil Liberties Union*, 27 August 2015, <https://www.aclu.org/blog/privacy-technology/surveillance-technologies/five-reasons-armed-domestic-drones-are-terrible>.

Stein, Aaron. 'From Ankara with implications: Turkish drones and alliance entrapment', *War on the Rocks*, 15 December 2021, <https://warontherocks.

com/2021/12/from-ankara-with-implications-turkish-drones-and-alliance-entrapment/>.

Stelmack, Kyle. 'Weaponized Police Drones and Their Effect on Police Use of Force', *Pittsburg Journal of Technology Law & Policy*, 15 (2) (2015): 276–92."

Stevenson, Beth. '"Loyal Wingman" part of the future of air combat', *AIN online*, 13 June 2019, <https://www.ainonline.com/aviation-news/defense/2019-06-13/loyal-wingman-part-future-air-combat>.

Stewart, Heather. 'Britain "on same page" as US over Suleimani killing, says Raab', *The Guardian*, 5 January 2020, <https://www.theguardian.com/politics/2020/jan/05/britain-sympathetic-to-us-over-killing-of-qassem-suleimani>.

Stohl, Rachel. *An Action Plan on U.S. Drone Policy: Recommendations for the Trump Administration*. Washington, DC: Stimson Center, 2018.

Strawser, Bradley Jay. 'Moral Predators: The Duty to Employ Uninhabited Aerial Vehicles', *Journal of Military Ethics*, 9 (4) (2010): 342–68.

Sullins, John P. 'When is a Robot a Moral Agent?', *International Review of Information Ethics*, 6 (2006): 23–30.

Swift, Hilary. '"Terminator Conundrum": robots that could kill on their own', *New York Times*, 25 October 2016, <https://www.nytimes.com/2016/10/26/us/pentagon-artificial-intelligence-terminator.html>.

Tahir, Madiha. 'The Containment Zone', in *Life in the Age of Drone Warfare*, ed. Lisa Parks and Caren Kaplan. Durham, CT, and London: Duke University Press, 2017: 220–40.

Talai, Andrew B. 'Drones and *Jones*: The Fourth Amendment and Police Discretion in the Digital Age', *California Law Review*, 102 (3) (2014): 729–80.

Thielman, Sam. 'Use of police robot to kill Dallas shooting suspect believed to be first in US history', *The Guardian*, 8 July 2016, <https://www.theguardian.com/technology/2016/jul/08/police-bomb-robot-explosive-killed-suspect-dallas>.

Thomas, Claire. 'Why Don't We Talk about "Violence" in International Relations?', *Review of International Studies*, 37 (4) (2011): 1815–36.

Thompson, Semon Frank. 'What I learned from executing two men', *New York Times*, 18 September 2016: SR3.

Tibori-Szabó, Kinga. 'Self-Defence and the United States Policy on Drone Strikes', *Journal of Conflict & Security Law*, 20 (3) (2015): 381–413.

Tirpak, John A. 'Air Force to upgrade MQ-9's mission and capabilities for near-peer fight', *Air Force Magazine*, 21 April 2021, <https://www.airforcemag.com/air-force-to-upgrade-mq-9s-mission-and-capabilities-for-near-peer-fight/>.

Toner, Christopher. 'Military Service as a Practice: Integrating the Sword and Shield Approaches to Military Ethics', *Journal of Military Ethics*, 5 (3) (2006): 183–200.

Toner, Christopher. 'The Logical Structure of Just War Theory', *The Journal of Ethics*, 14 (2) (2010): 81–102.

Tonkens, Ryan. 'The Case against Robotic Warfare: A Response to Arkin', *Journal of Military Ethics*, 11 (2) (2012): 149–68.

Trump, Donald. 'Remarks by President Trump on the Strategy in Afghanistan and South Asia', *The White House*, 21 August 2017, <https://www.whitehouse.gov/briefings-statements/remarks-president-trump-strategy-afghanistan-south-asia/>.

Tucker, Patrick. 'America's drone pilot shrink says they need a vacation from war', *Defense One*, 18 June 2015, <http://www.defenseone.com/management/2015/06/americas-drone-pilot-shrink-says-they-need-vacation-war/115498/>.

UK Parliament. 'UK Lethal Drone Strikes in Syria' (HC 1152), Intelligence and Security Committee of Parliament. London: House of Commons, 2017.

UN General Assembly. 'Protection of human rights and fundamental freedoms while countering terrorism' (A/RES/68/178), New York, United Nations, 18 December 2013; European Parliament resolution of 27 February 2014 on the use of armed drones (2014/2567(RSP)).

UN Human Rights Council. 'Ensuring use of remotely piloted aircraft or armed drones in counterterrorism and military operations in accordance with international law, including international human rights and humanitarian law' (A/HRC/RES/25/22). New York: UN General Assembly, 15 April 2014.

UNIDIR. *Increasing Transparency, Oversight and Accountability of Armed Unmanned Aerial Vehicles*, United Nations Institute for Disarmament Research, 2017.

United Nations. 'Code of Conduct for Law Enforcement Officials'. Adopted by General Assembly Resolution 34/169. 17 December 1979. *Office of the High Commissioner for Human Rights*. <https://www.ohchr.org/EN/ProfessionalInterest/Pages/LawEnforcementOfficials.aspx>.

United Nations. 'Basic Principles on the Use of Force and Firearms by Law Enforcement Officials'. Adopted by the Eighth United Nations Congress on the Prevention of Crime and the Treatment of Offenders, Havana, Cuba, 27 August to 7 September 1990. *Office of the High Commissioner for Human Rights*. <https://www.ohchr.org/en/professionalinterest/pages/useofforceandfirearms.aspx>.

United Nations. *Moving Away from the Death Penalty: Arguments, Trends and Perspectives*, 2nd edn. New York: United Nations, Office of the High Commissioner for Human Rights, 2015.

United Nations. *Resource Book on the Use of Force and Firearms in Law Enforcement*. New York: United Nations Office on Drugs and Crime and Office of the United Nations High Commissioner for Human Rights, 2017.

United Nations. *United Nations Human Rights Guidance on Less-Lethal Weapons in Law Enforcement*. New York and Geneva: Office of the High Commissioner for Human Rights, United Nations, 2020.

United Nations High Commissioner for Human Rights. 'Impact of new technologies on the promotion and protection of human rights in the context of
assemblies, including peaceful protests' (A/HRC/44/24), New York, Human
Rights Council, United Nations General Assembly, 24 June 2020.

US Department of Defense. 'Autonomy in Weapon Systems', Directive no.
3000.09 (21 November 2012), *Washington Headquarters Services*, <http://
www.esd.whs.mil/Portals/54/Documents/DD/issuances/dodd/300009p.pdf>.

US Department of Defense. *Unmanned Systems Integrated Roadmap 2017–
2042* (issued 28 August 2018): 20. Available at: US Naval Institute, 'Pentagon Unmanned Systems Integrated Roadmap 2017–2042', *USNI News*,
30 August 2018, <https://news.usni.org/2018/08/30/pentagon-unmanned-
systems-integrated-roadmap-2017-2042>.

US Department of Defense. 'Statement by the Department of Defense',
US Department of Defense, 2 January 2020, <https://www.defense.
gov/Newsroom/Releases/Release/Article/2049534/statement-by-the-
department-of-defense/>.

USAF. 'MQ-1B Predator', *US Air Force*, September 2015, <https://www.af.mil/
About-Us/Fact-Sheets/Display/Article/104469/mq-1b-predator/> (accessed 4
February 2022).

USAF. 'MQ-9 Reaper', *US Air Force*, March 2021, <https://www.af.mil/About-
Us/Fact-Sheets/Display/Article/104470/mq-9-reaper/> (accessed 5 February
2022).

USAF. 'Annex 3-60 – Targeting', *U.S. Airforce Doctrine*, updated 12 November
2021, <https://www.doctrine.af.mil/Portals/61/documents/AFDP_3-60/3-60-
AFDP-TARGETING.pdf>.

Valdovinos, Maria, James Specht and Jennifer Zeunik. *Law Enforcement &
Unmanned Aircraft Systems (UAS): Guidelines to Enhance Community
Trust*. Washington, DC: Office of Community Oriented Policing Services,
US Department of Justice, 2016.

Vasko, Timothy. 'Solemn Geographies of Human Limits: Drones and the Neocolonial Administration of Life and Death', *Affinities: A Journal of Radical
Theory, Culture, and Action*, 6 (1) (2013): 83–107.

Vilmer, Jean-Baptiste Jeangène. 'France and the American Drone Precedent',
in *The Ethics of War and Peace Revisited*, ed. Daniel R. Brunstetter and
Jean-Vincent Holeindre. Washington, DC: Georgetown University Press,
2018: 97–116.

Vilmer, Jean-Baptiste Jeangène. 'A French opinion on the ethics of autonomous weapons', *War on the Rocks*, 2 June 2021, <https://warontherocks.
com/2021/06/the-french-defense-ethics-committees-opinion-on-autonomous-
weapons/>.

Vladeck, Steve. 'Drone courts: the wrong solution to the wrong problem', *Just
Security*, 2 December 2014, <https://www.justsecurity.org/17914/drone-
courts-wrong-solution-wrong-problem/>.

Vogel, Ryan J. 'Drone Warfare and the Law of Armed Conflict', *Denver Journal of International Law and Policy*, 39 (1) (2010): 101–38.

Vogel, Ryan J. 'Droning On: Controversy Surrounding Drone Warfare is Not Really about Drones', *The Brown Journal of World Affairs*, 19 (2) (2013): 111–21.

Vries, Peer de. 'Virtue Ethics in the Military: An Attempt at Completeness', *Journal of Military Ethics*, 19 (3) (2020): 170–85.

Wakefield, Jane. 'AI emotion-detection software tested on Uyghurs', *BBC News*, 26 May 2021, <https://www.bbc.co.uk/news/technology-57101248>.

Waldron, Greg. 'GA-ASI to conduct AI, machine learning work with MQ-9', *Flight Global*, 18 September 2019, <https://www.flightglobal.com/military-uavs/ga-asi-to-conduct-ai-machine-learning-work-with-mq-9/134362.article>.

Walker, Lauren. 'Death from above: confessions of a killer drone operator', *Newsweek*, 19 November 2015, <http://europe.newsweek.com/confessions-lethal-drone-operator-396541>.

Wallach, Wendell, and Colin Allen. *Moral Machines: Teaching Robots Right from Wrong*. New York: Oxford University Press, 2009.

Walsh, James Igoe. *The Effectiveness of Drone Strikes in Counterinsurgency and Counterterrorism Campaigns*. Carlisle, PA: Strategic Studies Institute, 2013.

Walzer, Michael. *Just and Unjust Wars: A Moral Argument with Historical Illustrations*, 4th edn. New York: Basic Books, 2006.

Walzer, Michael. 'Response to McMahan's Paper, *Philosophia*, 34 (2006): 43–5.

Walzer, Michael. 'Just and Unjust Targeted Killing and Drone Warfare', *Daedalus*, 145 (4) (2016): 12–24.

Warren, Aiden, and Ingvild Bode. 'Altering the Playing Field: The U.S. Redefinition of the Use-of-Force', *Contemporary Security Policy*, 36 (2) (2015): 174–99.

Warrick, Joby, and Peter Finn. 'CIA Director says secret attacks in Pakistan have hobbled al-Qaeda', *Washington Post*, 18 March 2010: A01.

Watling, Jack, and Nicholas Waters. 'Achieving Lethal Effects by Small Unmanned Aerial Vehicles', *The RUSI Journal*, 164 (1) (2019): 40–51.

Wedgwood, Ralph. 'The Price of Non-reductive Moral Realism', *Ethical Theory and Moral Practice*, 2 (3) (1999): 199–215.

West, Jonathan P., and James S. Bowman. 'The Domestic Use of Drones: An Ethical Analysis of Surveillance Issues', *Public Administration Review*, 76 (4) (2016): 649–59.

Westcott, Kathryn. 'How and why Gardner was shot', *BBC News*, 18 June 2010, <http://www.bbc.co.uk/news/10254279>.

Whetham, David. 'Killer Drones: The Moral Ups and Downs', *RUSI Journal*, 158 (3) (2013): 22–32.

White House. 'The Vice President appears on *Meet the Press* with Tim Russert', *The White House, President George W. Bush*, 16 September 2001,

<https://georgewbush-whitehouse.archives.gov/vicepresident/news-speeches/speeches/vp20010916.html>.

Williams, Alison J. 'Enabling Persistent Presence? Performing the Embodied Geopolitics of the Unmanned Aerial Vehicle Assemblage', *Political Geography*, 30 (2011): 381–90.

Williams, John. 'Distant Intimacy: Space, Drones, and Just War', *Ethics and International Affairs*, 29 (1) (2015): 93–110.

Wintour, Patrick. 'Donald Trump "cancelled Iran strikes with planes in the air"', *The Guardian*, 21 June 2019, <https://www.theguardian.com/world/2019/jun/21/united-airlines-halts-some-flights-mumbai-to-avoid-iran-after-drone-attack>.

Wintour, Patrick. 'European leaders call for de-escalation of crisis after Suleimani killing', *The Guardian*, 3 January 2020, <https://www.theguardian.com/world/2020/jan/03/qassem-suleimani-killing-may-spell-end-iran-nuclear-deal-europe-fears>.

Wintour, Patrick. 'Iran to execute "CIA agent" over Gen Suleimani intelligence', *The Guardian*, 9 June 2020, <https://www.theguardian.com/world/2020/jun/09/iran-to-execute-cia-agent-over-gen-suleimanis-death>.

Wintour, Patrick, and Julian Borger. 'Trump says he stopped airstrike on Iran because 150 would have died', *The Guardian*, 21 June 2019, <https://www.theguardian.com/world/2019/jun/21/donald-trump-retaliatory-iran-airstrike-cancelled-10-minutes-before>.

Wirtz, James J. 'The "Terminator Conundrum" and the Future of Drone Warfare', *Intelligence and National Security*, 32 (4) (2017): 433–5.

Wolf, Zachary B., and Veronica Stracqualursi. 'The evolving US justification for killing Iran's top general', *CNN*, 8 January 2020, <https://edition.cnn.com/2020/01/07/politics/qasem-soleimani-reasons-justifications/index.html>.

Wolfendale, Jessica. 'Military sexual assault is a moral injury', *War on the Rocks*, 21 May 2021, <https://warontherocks.com/2021/05/the-military-justice-improvement-act-and-the-moral-duty-owed-to-sexual-assault-victims/>.

Woods, Chris. *Sudden Justice: America's Secret Drone Wars*. London: Hurst & Co., 2015.

Work, Robert O. 'Establishment of an Algorithmic Warfare Cross-Functional Team (Project Maven)'. Memorandum from the Deputy Secretary of Defense. *US Department of Defense*, 26 April 2017, <https://www.govexec.com/media/gbc/docs/pdfs_edit/establishment_of_the_awcft_project_maven.pdf>.

Wuschka, Sebastian. 'The Use of Combat Drones in Current Conflicts: A Legal Issue or a Political Problem?', *Goettingen Journal of International Law*, 3 (2011): 891–905.

Zenko, Micah. 'The Coming Future of Autonomous Drones', *Council on Foreign Relations*, 4 September 2012, <https://www.cfr.org/blog/coming-future-autonomous-drones>.

INDEX

Abney, Keith, 168
Aero Surveillance, 68
Afghanistan, 7, 35, 104, 107
Afxentiou, Afxentis, 102
Akhter, Majed, 97
Al Qaeda, 59–61
Amnesty International, 94
Amoroso, Daniele, 179
armed drones
  definition, 4
  small-sized armed drones, 5,
    29–30
  users of, 6–8
  uses for, 4–6
artificial general intelligence (AGI),
  163, 164
artificial intelligence (AI)
  in air-to-air scenarios, 163–4
  as an artificial moral agent,
    169–72, 189
  in bello discrimination principle,
    170
  in bello proportionality principle,
    170–1
  data analysis, 166
  devolved (to AI) violence, 161–6
  drone control functions, 6, 9, 148,
    161, 164–5, 188–9
  ethics of non-human controlled
    aircraft, 161–2

for fighter aircraft, 161
  intelligence capabilities, 164,
    165, 166
  within the kill chain concept, 165
  operational response speed, 165–6,
    175, 177
  partial control over drone-based
    weapon system, 162, 163–4
  Project Maven, 166
  use of force capabilities, 164–5
  within weapons systems, 164, 202
  see also human-machine
    interaction (HMI); lethal
    autonomous weapon systems
    (LAWS)
autonomous, term, 173
al-Awlaki, Anwar, 61, 65, 123
Azerbaijan, 8

al-Badawi, Jamal, 55–6
BAE, 6
Baggaley, Katherine, 135
Baggiarini, Bianca, 127
Bandura, Albert, 132
Baudrillard, Jean, 10
Biden, Joe, 93
Bin Laden, Osama, 60–1
Blair, Dave, 127
Blair, Dennis, 124
Boulanin, Vincent, 167

Boyle, Michael, 33, 54
Brennan, John, 61, 62, 109
Brooks, Rosa, 109
Brown, Nicholas, 127
Bush, George W., 60
Byman, Daniel, 124
Byrnes, Michael, 161, 186

Calhoun, Laurie, 102
Callamard, Agnès, 2
Cerberus GL, 5
Chapa, Joseph, 136, 137
Cheney, Dick, 60
China, 5, 7
civilians
    civilian harm conceptual
        parameters, 40, 41–2
    combatant/civilian distinctions,
        36–8, 39
    deaths during signature strikes, 96,
        98, 102–3, 111
    double-tap strikes and, 37,
        102–3
    emotional threat from grey drone
        violence, 101–2, 111
    jus in vi requirements, 99
    killed by drone strikes, 35
    as non-combatants (term), 96
    non-physical harm, 41–2
    proportionality principle and,
        38–9, 41–2
    rapid-response capacities to
        protect, 32
    right authority to protect, 32
Clark, Ian, 10
Clausewitz, Carl von, 28
Coady, Tony, 41, 112
Cole, USS, 55, 56
colonialism
    colonial air policing, 104–5
    internal colonialism concept, 107
    quasi-imperialism, 106–7

Convention on Certain Convention
    Weapons (CCW), 167, 173
Cook, Martin, 141–2

Daley, William, 62
Dassault Aviation, 6
Davis, Oliver, 69
Desert Wolf, 68
devolved violence
    to artificial intelligence, 161–6
    concept of meaningful human
        control (MHC), 174–8
    human decision-making
        capabilities, 167–8, 172
    operational factors for, 165–6
    see also artificial intelligence (AI);
        lethal autonomous weapon
        systems (LAWS)
Dill, Janina, 40, 147
Doyle, Michael, 105
Drescher, Kent, 130
drone operators
    adherence to jus in bello principles,
        137, 138, 142
    dehumanisation of targets, 135,
        137, 148
    discretion and moral courage
        strategies, 123, 147, 148
    drone killing as 'too easy', 124
    exposure to physical risk, 29–30,
        124, 141–2, 144, 145
    geographical factors, 30, 124
    individual moral agency, 39–40,
        123, 125, 129–30
    judgements of, 123, 124,
        125
    mental health, 136, 145–6
    military/civilian identity tensions,
        140–1
    moral injury, 124, 125, 130,
        136–43, 146, 148
    moral self-harm, 123, 124–5

physical risk and moral
permission, 141–3
post-strike surveillance, 128
regard for the humanity of targets,
42, 124, 125, 127–8, 139
of small, short-range drones,
29–30
state responsibilities of care
towards, 143–7, 148
term, 127
training and retention, 165
as victims of state-sanctioned
violence, 123–4, 144, 148
video imagery and intimacy with
the target, 126–8, 137–9
see also tele-intimate violence
drone strikes
double-tap strikes, 37, 102–3
dynamic targeting, 37
government secrecy and public
scrutiny, 32–3
the kill chain concept, 165
moral uncertainties over, 2–3
strategic overreach (mission creep),
33
timings for, 36–7
see also personality strikes;
signature strikes
drone violence
conceptualisations, 12, 27–31,
95, 200–3
during conditions of war, 27–8,
200
multiple moralities of, 12–13
term, 9
see also grey drone violence
drone warfare, term, 8–9
drones
association with military
violence, 70
non-violent uses, 3
privacy and surveillance issues, 65

public order drones, 55
term, 3
see also armed drones

Eastwood, Clint, 58, 59
ethics
contestability of, 171
legality and, 12
military ethics, 10, 14, 70–1,
96–7, 99, 129, 146, 148, 167,
171–2
thin concepts of, 169–70,
171
uses of drone technologies, 2–3
value judgements, 9
virtue ethics, 129
see also morality
Ethiopia, 8
European Convention on Human
Rights, 53–4

Ford, Shannon, 99
FQ-X hypothetical aircraft, 161
France, 7, 68
Fuller, Christopher, 54

Gade, Emily Kalah, 10
General Atomics, 5, 162
Geneva Conventions, 26
Germany, 8
Göring, Hermann, 59
Gregory, Derek, 104
grey drone violence
conceptual uncertainties, 94, 95,
96–7, 100–1, 201–2
continuity with colonial violence,
104
imminence concept and, 109
impact on civilian populations,
101–2, 111
as imperialistic violence, 94,
104–6, 113

grey drone violence (*cont.*)
  legal innovations around, 97–8
  moralities of quasi-imperialistic
    violence, 109–12, 113
  non-war drone violence
    conceptualisations, 96–9,
    112–13
  outside areas of active hostilities,
    93–4, 96–7
  as quasi-imperialistic violence,
    94–5, 106–8
  and the right to life, 94–5,
    101, 108
  as risk-management
    counterterrorism, 108
  as self-defence targeting, 98–9
  as terroristic violence, 94, 101–4,
    113
  US drone strikes outside war
    zones, 93–4
  as *vim* ('force short of war'), 94,
    99–101, 113
  see also signature strikes
Gross, Michael, 10
Grossman, Dave, 138–9

Haas, Michael, 137
Hellfire air-to-ground missile, 4, 5, 8,
  38, 69
Heyns, Christof, 40, 72
Hippler, Thomas, 105
Holder, Eric, 62, 109
House, Karen, 127
human rights
  European Convention on Human
    Rights, 53–4
  human right to life, 27, 53–4
  non-war drone violence and, 94–5,
    98, 101, 108
  quasi-imperialistic violence
    and the right to life, 94–5,
    108, 109

  the right to life and police violence,
    57, 66, 71–3
human-machine interaction (HMI)
  clutter in the operating
    environment, 181–2, 183, 184,
    185, 186
  in different operational
    circumstances, 182–4
  green-light systems, 179, 183,
    185–8, 189
  in law enforcement settings, 182,
    183, 184, 187
  offensive and defensive
    purposes, 180–1, 183, 184,
    185, 186–7
  red-light systems, 179, 183,
    184–5, 189
  in relation to meaningful
    human control principles,
    178–87
  target identification and selection,
    179, 180, 183, 188

Ignatieff, Michael, 107
India, 8, 68
International Committee of the
  Red Cross, 40
international human rights law
  (IHRL), 2
international humanitarian law
  (IHL), 2, 126, 167–8
Iran, 1–2, 7, 8, 33
Iraq, 1–2, 6, 7, 33, 95, 104, 142
Israel, 7, 177–8
Italy, 8

Jameton, Andrew, 130
Johnson, Boris, 64
jus ad bellum (justice of resorting
  to war)
  division of *jus in bello* and *jus ad
    bellum*, 35, 43

drone warfare and, 31–4
drone warfare as 'too easy', 31,
    43, 124
just cause principle, 31–2
principles, 26, 31
proportionality principle, 31,
    33
reasonable prospect of success
    principle, 31, 33–4
right authority principle, 31,
    32–3
Security Council Resolution
    1973, 32
war as a last resort principle, 31,
    34
jus ad vim ('force short of war'), 94,
    99–101, 113
jus in bello (just conduct of war)
armed drones harm-avoidance
    capacity, 36–7
combatant/civilian distinctions,
    36–8, 39
discrimination principle, 35–8, 39,
    40–1, 43, 170
division of *jus in bello* and *jus ad
    bellum*, 35, 43
for drone operators, 137, 138,
    142
enemy targetability concepts,
    40–1
mala in se weapons, 36
principles, 26, 34–5, 135
proportionality principle, 35, 36,
    38–9, 41–2, 43, 170–1
signature strikes, 37–8
Just War morality
conceptualisations of war, 26,
    42–4
principles, 26–7, 135
revisionist approaches, 35

Kahn, Paul, 28–9

Koch, Bernard, 54
Koh, Harold, 61–2, 98
Kudo, Timothy, 135
Kuwait, 33, 142

law enforcement
in absentia trials, 64–6
definition, 53
ethical superiority of lethal
    autonomous weapon systems,
    168
human-machine interaction
    (HMI), 182, 183, 184, 187
moral disengagement of
    executioners, 132–4
moralities of violence for, 10–12,
    27, 53, 54, 201–2
to prevent criminal wrongdoing,
    53, 54, 55
prohibition on arbitrary killings,
    57
as punitive, 53, 54–5, 56–7, 63–6,
    79–80, 201
reasonable seizure under
    the Fourth Amendment
    (US), 76
in relation to terrorist occupied
    spaces, 97
and the right to life of a targeted
    person, 55
see also personality strikes;
    policing
laws
human right to life, 53–4
for Just War principles, 26
legal justice contrasted with wild
    justice, 57–8
non-war drone violence and, 97
principle of legalism, 57, 58–9,
    62
prohibition on arbitrary
    killings, 57

lethal autonomous weapon systems
    (LAWS)
  AI decision-making functions,
    167–8, 169, 171–2
  artificial moral agency, 169–72, 189
  autonomous as a contested term,
    173–4
  control within temporal
    constraints, 185
  dignity-based argument against,
    169
  diplomatic debate over, 166–7,
    173
  the Harpy, 177–8
  meaningful human control (MHC)
    principle, 174–8
  moral responsibility, 172–3
  potential for violence escalation,
    168
  see also human-machine
    interaction (HMI)
Leveringhaus, Alex, 172
Libya, 7, 32, 95, 104
Lieb, Peter, 105
Litz, Brett, 130

McMahan, Jeff, 11
MacNair, Rachel, 131
Marlantes, Karl, 131
Marshall, Samuel, 131
Maynard, Katherine, 57–8
meaningful human control (MHC)
  avoidance of anthropomorphism
    of AI, 176
  concept, 174, 189
  contexts of human-machine
    interactions, 178–87
  control of the system's 'critical'
    functions, 174–5, 188
  control within temporal
    constraints, 175, 177
  human accountability, 176–7

  non-excessive trust in the AI, 175–6
  temporal elements, 185–6
  weapon system design, 177–8, 188
  see also human-machine
    interaction (HMI)
Mehsud, Baitullah, 60
military
  dehumanisation of targets, 135
  killer warriors and moral injury,
    134–6
  military ethics, 10, 14, 70–1, 96–7,
    99, 129, 146, 148, 167, 171–2
  moral agency and rule-breaking,
    123, 139, 147, 148, 172
  obedience conditioning, 146–7
  protection of serving personnel,
    144–5
  virtue ethics, 129
  warriors' exposure to physical risk,
    141–2, 144
  warriors' moral dilemmas, 131
Miller, Seamus, 97, 128
morality
  individualist morality, 11–12
  moral dilemmas, 171–2
  moral injury, 124, 125, 130–1,
    136–43, 146, 148
  moral judgements, 9–12
  moral properties as physical
    properties, 170
  moral self-harm, 123, 124–5
  moral uncertainties over drone
    strikes, 2–3
  multiple moralities, 12–13
  physical risk and moral permission
    for violence, 141–3
  see also ethics; Just War morality
Morkevičius, Valerie, 12
MQ-1 Predator, 4–5, 161
MQ-9 Reaper, 1, 5, 161
MQ-20 Avenger, 5–6, 162
Munro, Campbell, 104

Nash, William, 130
Nazi Germany, 59
Nigeria, 7
9/11 terrorist attacks, 59, 60
Northrop Grumman, 6, 162

Obama, Barack
  on armed drones over US soil, 65
  authorisation of drone strikes in
    Libya, 32
  killing of Bin Laden, 60–1
  non-war drone violence and, 97–8
  personality strikes under, 56–7, 61–3
  rules on drone strikes, 62–3, 93
  signature strikes, 96
Ortega, Hernando, 139

Pakistan
  drone use, 7
  Federally Administered Tribal
    Areas (FATA), 59, 94, 107
  US drone strikes in, 60, 113
  US drone strikes in the FATA
    region, 94, 96, 97, 101, 103
personality strikes
  in absentia trials, 64–6
  as administrative executions, 61–3
  administrative practices of, 62–3
  and the existence of a condition of
    war, 56–7
  killing of al-Awlaki, 61, 65, 123
  killing of al-Badawi, 55–6
  killing of Mehsud, 60
  killing of Soleimani, 1–2
  non-judicial authorisation of
    lethal punishments, 54–5,
    56–7, 62–3, 123
  under the Obama administration,
    56–7, 61–3
  in Pakistan, 60
  as punitive law enforcement, 56–7,
    63–6, 79–80

under the Trump administration,
  56, 64
Trump's redemptive use of drone
  violence, 63–4
as wild justice, 54, 57–61, 62, 80
Phelps, Wayne, 123
policing
  adherence to meaningful human
    control principles, 182
  application of bodily force, 75–6
  *Basic Principles on the Use of
    Force and Firearms by Law
    Enforcement Officials*, 71, 74
  *Code of Conduct for Law
    Enforcement Officials*, 71
  colonial air policing, 104–5
  ethical principles for the use of
    violence, 65, 67, 70–3, 80
  militarisation of, 69–70
  necessity for use of force principle,
    72, 73, 76–8, 79, 109
  perception of circumstances, 76–8
  police ethics as distinct from
    military ethics, 70–1
  precaution principle, 73, 75, 79
  proportionality principle, 72–3,
    77, 78, 79
  of public assemblies, 78–9, 80
  public order drones, 55
  the right to life, 57, 66, 71–3
  risk reduction to police officers,
    74–6
  state violence by institutional
    actors, 128
  tele-present police officers, 55, 74–9
  use of armed drones, 55, 65–6, 78,
    80, 95, 187, 201
  use of camera-equipped drones,
    55, 66, 67–8
  use of non-lethal armed drones,
    68–9, 78–9
  see also law enforcement

postcolonial studies, 104
Pryer, Douglas, 136

Riza, Shane, 140–1
Rodin, David, 103, 112

Salter, Michael, 69
Satia, Priya, 104, 105
Schmitt, Carl, 28, 43
Schmitt, Michael, 35
Schulzke, Marcus, 39–40
Schwarz, Elke, 12
Shaw, Ian, 69
Shaw, Martin, 106–7
Shay, Jonathan, 130
Sherman, Nancy, 134, 135
Shue, Henry, 29
signature strikes
  civilian deaths during, 96, 98,
    102–3, 111
  counterterrorism strikes outside
    areas of active hostilities, 96–8
  drone operators' intimate
    knowledge of the target, 127–8
  moral uncertainties, 37–8
  under the Obama administration, 96
  in Pakistan's FATA region, 94, 96,
    97, 101, 103
  pattern-of-life analysis, 95–6
  security benefits of, 110
  in Somalia, 96
  as terrorist disruption strikes, 95
  in Yemen, 96
Smash Dragon, 5
Soleimani, Qasem, 1–2
Somalia, 7, 96, 97, 104, 105, 107,
    108, 113
South Africa, 68
Stanley, Jay, 76
state violence
  decision-making, 167
  by institutional actors, 128–9

moral disengagement from, 131–2
moral injury of institutional actors,
    128–36
by natural (noninstitutional)
    actors, 128
permissibility judgements, 111–12
responsibility of care to personnel,
    144
self-defence targeting, 98–9
as *vim* ('force short of war'),
    99–101
Stelmack, Kyle, 75
Strawser, Bradley, 39, 145
Syria, 6, 7, 64, 95, 104

Tahir, Madiha, 107
Tamburrini, Guglielmo, 179
tele-intimate violence
  conceptualisations, 126–8, 148, 202
  lack of physical risk, 124
  moral injury, 124, 125
  post-strike surveillance, 128
  tele-present police officers, 55, 74–9
  video imagery and intimacy with
    the target, 126–8, 137–9
  see also drone operators; video
    imagery
terrorism
  definitions, 102
  grey drone violence as terroristic
    violence, 94, 101–4, 113
  myth of redemptive violence, 59, 60
  9/11 terrorist attacks, 59, 60
  risk-management counterterrorism,
    108
  Trump's redemptive violence
    approach, 63–4
  US War on Terror, 59–61
  see also grey drone violence;
    signature strikes
Tikad, 5
Trump, Donald

drone strike against Qasem
Soleimani, 1, 2
on the killing of Jamal al-Badawi, 55
personality strikes under, 56, 64
potential retaliatory strikes against
Iran, 33
redemptive use of drone violence,
63–4
Turkey, 7
Tuttle, Steve, 68–9

Ukraine, 8
United Kingdom (UK), 7, 104–5
United Nations (UN), 2, 26
United States of America (US)
drone use, 6, 7
myth of redemptive violence, 58–60
police use of armed drones, 68–9, 70
support for the principle of
legalism, 59
use of armed drones, 4
see also Obama, Barack; Trump,
Donald
US Central Command, 55

video imagery
for harm-avoidance to civilians,
36–7
intimacy with the target and, 126–8,
137–9
real-time tactical observation, 39
of a target's family, 42
violence
conceptualisations, 9–11, 26, 202–3
individualist morality, 11–12
as law enforcement, 10–12, 53
moral judgements, 9–12, 26
myth of redemptive violence, 58–60
as war, 10–12, 95

Walzer, Michael, 11, 101, 124,
135
War on Terror, 59–61
warfare
civilian harm conceptual
parameters, 35, 40, 41–2
combatant/civilian distinctions,
36–8, 39
conceptualisations of, 28–9,
42–4, 95
conceptualisations of
drone violence as, 27–31,
200
endangerment of national
personnel, 34
enemy targetability concepts,
40–1
higher standards of moral conduct
for drone warfare, 39–40
mischaracterisation of drones
strikes as, 56–7
moralities of violence for, 10–12,
26–7
mutual exposure to physical risk,
28, 29, 30–1, 42–3, 142
raising moral standards, 39–42
secrecy and deniability risks, 32
thresholds of, 1
violence conceptualised as, 10–12,
95
war-as-contest concept, 28–9, 30
see also jus ad bellum (justice of
resorting to war); *jus in bello*
(just conduct of war); Just War
morality
Work, Bob, 166

Yemen, 7, 55, 56, 61, 96, 97, 104,
105, 107, 108, 113, 123

EU representative:
Easy Access System Europe
Mustamäe tee 50, 10621 Tallinn, Estonia
Gpsr.requests@easproject.com

www.ingramcontent.com/pod-product-compliance
Lightning Source LLC
Chambersburg PA
CBHW050347270326
41926CB00016B/3633